Effective
INSTRUCTIONAL STRATEGIES

Effective
INSTRUCTIONAL
STRATEGIES
From Theory to Practice

KENNETH D. MOORE
Henderson State University

SAGE Publications
Thousand Oaks ▪ London ▪ New Delhi

For information:

 Sage Publications, Inc.
2455 Teller Road
Thousand Oaks, California 91320
E-mail: order@sagepub.com

Sage Publications Ltd.
1 Oliver's Yard
55 City Road
London EC1Y 1SP
United Kingdom

Sage Publications India Pvt. Ltd.
B-42, Panchsheel Enclave
Post Box 4109
New Delhi 110 017 India

Printed in the United States of America

Library of Congress Cataloging-in-Publication Data

Moore, Kenneth D.
Effective instructional strategies : from theory to practice / Kenneth D. Moore.
    p. cm.
Includes bibliographical references and index.
ISBN 1-4129-0661-X (pbk.)
  1. Effective teaching. 2. Teacher effectiveness. 3. Teachers—Training of. I. Title.
LB1025.3.M662 2005
371.102—dc22

                                            2004024567

This book is printed on acid-free paper.

05 06 07 08 09 10 9 8 7 6 5 4 3 2 1

Acquiring Editor:	Diane McDaniel
Editorial Assistant:	Marta Peimer
Production Editor:	Sanford Robinson
Typesetter:	C&M Digitals (P) Ltd.
Copy Editor:	Taryn Bigelow
Indexer:	Molly Hall
Cover Designer:	Michelle Kenny

Brief Contents

Detailed Contents

PREFACE

Effective Teaching Strategies: From Theory to Practice is designed to better prepare students for the complex world of the school classroom. The aim is to prepare prospective teachers to meet the challenges of today's changing classrooms. Becoming an effective teacher requires extensive knowledge and skills, as well as hard work, commitment, an inquiring mind, and the ability to learn from experiences. The quest for excellence will be difficult, but the satisfaction is worth the effort. This book, therefore, is designed to provide you with the tools for facilitating the quest and the means for achieving excellence. It was further designed to expand the pedagogical teaching knowledge of teachers and their instructional repertoires.

I have described in detail proven instructional methods, coupled with the best in planning and instructional theory, to prepare preservice teachers for entry into the classroom. The textbook will not only help prospective teachers analyze their own teaching but also will provide the means for translating this thinking into effective practice, which will lead to the accomplishment of our society's educational goals. In short, it is my hope that future teachers will find this book valuable as a guide to sound educational practices. This text is intended for use in undergraduate general methods courses, but it could be a useful reference for a variety of courses and for inservice teachers.

Theory to Practice Approach to Instruction

This text embraces a theory to practice theme which runs throughout the book. It takes the latest research on teaching and applies it to the classroom. The book emphasizes the intelligent use of teaching theory and research to improve classroom instruction. Whenever possible, specific examples and teacher viewpoints are presented, not just suggestions for things to try.

No one can deny that teachers matter or that their skills will have a profound impact on student achievement. To make that impact positive, teachers must have both a deep understanding of the powerful principles of teaching as they apply to effective teaching and a clear sense of how these principles can be applied to the classroom. The effective teacher is one who constantly reflects on his or her practices and makes instructional decisions based on a clear conception of how theories and practices affect students. Effective teaching is neither a bag of tricks nor a set of abstract principles; rather, it is intelligent application of research-based teaching principles to address the reality of the classroom. This text will provide the theoretical knowledge and help you develop the practical skills needed to do the most important job you will ever do—teach.

Features of the Text

Several special features make *Effective Teaching Strategies: From Theory to Practice* more accessible to you. Each chapter begins with an overview, objectives, and a reflective classroom case related to the key aspects of the chapter. Scattered throughout each chapter are innovative focal points. The view from the classroom, the public view of education, summary, discussion questions and activities, connection with the field, and Praxis II connections at the end of each chapter provide materials that address your present and future professional needs.

Overview

The overview provides an outline of what is covered in the chapter. It provides you with a cognitive set for the chapter content. The overview gives you the major concepts covered in the chapter and the organization of the chapter. As such, it represents a quick reference to the chapter content.

Objectives

The objectives inform you of the instructional intent of the chapter. It gives you an idea of the main information to be learned. It tells you exactly what to expect and what you should be able to do upon completion of the chapter.

Reflections on Teacher Practice

Another opening feature of each chapter gives you the opportunity to hear directly from teachers in the field about topics to be explored. These cases show the major principles in the chapter in action. Each case is an experience taken from a real-life situation. The case describes how principles were applied in classroom settings and the results of each application. They represent brief words of wisdom, strategies, and philosophy from teachers in our elementary, middle, and high schools.

Apply and Reflect

This feature encourages you to stop at key points within the chapter narrative and think carefully and reflect about the issues being presented. They are designed to help you begin to identify and analyze your beliefs about learning and teaching. They deal with important or controversial information or provide thought-provoking exercises pertinent to the subject under discussion. These apply and reflect features reinforce the content, examine contentious topics, and challenge you to explore how your own ideas and beliefs inform your teaching practice.

Web Link

This feature is designed to encourage you to explore links to websites where you can learn more about the teaching profession by researching issues, learning more about research application, and looking at the practical application of the material being presented in the text. These links will help you think more deeply about the issues and questions posed.

Expansion Activity

This feature gives you the opportunity to spend additional time investigating current issues and topics that affect teaching and learning. Each issue or topic highlighted has been chosen because of its direct impact on schooling and its potential for impacting teaching and learning.

Review, Extension, and Reflective Exercise

These exercises present the most important ideas of the chapter for review and study. They relate the ideas and content to INTASC standards and the NBPTS and reintroduce section content in a meaningful and personalized manner. Major focus questions provide the framework around which the sections were built. Each exercise uses a series of thought-provoking review questions embedded directly in the text material and reflective questions to help you develop deeper insights into the issues and concepts being discussed.

View from the Classroom

Poll results from classroom teachers relative to school issues and topics are shared. The results represent the attitudes and feelings of teachers in the field.

The Public View of Education

The poll results of the public feelings regarding school issues and topics are presented. The results represent the general attitudes and feelings of the general public toward the problems with education and the job that is presently being done by our schools.

Summary

This feature provides a complete summary review of each chapter's main points. This summary is an excellent resource for study and review. The information is presented in bulleted form under each major chapter heading to make it easier to access the information in the chapter.

Discussion Questions and Activities

The discussion questions and activities that follow each chapter will help you pursue further topics introduced in the chapter. This section provides critical- and creative-thinking activities that allow you to work with the issues brought up in the chapter and to think about the ideas the chapter has explored. It gives you a chance to take what you have learned in the chapter and apply it to real-world teaching issues or problems in the classroom.

Connection With the Field

These connections are suggested field experiences to introduce you to the profession from many perspectives, providing suggestions for classroom observation of teaching and learning, interviews with teachers and administrators, and interactions within the schools. Questions provide opportunities for reflection and allow you to gain additional insights into the classroom.

Praxis II Connection

These Praxis II connections are short-answer questions formatted to connect chapter content with relevant sections of the Praxis II: Principles of Learning and Teaching and other state pedagogical exams. These questions provide additional insight and practice in exam areas. They also direct you to material that will be very important in passing licensure examinations.

Organization of the Text

Part One, **Setting the Stage for Successful Learning**, provides an orientation to teaching. In Chapter 1, we will get ready for the classroom. The chapter focuses on the art and science of teaching, effective teaching skills, constructivism, expectations and standards, accountability, and the licensing of teachers. The second chapter deals with the school curriculum. A comprehensive model of teaching is presented and discussed. Chapter 2 provides coverage of planning instruction, with a focus on identifying content, student needs, and technology in the classroom.

Part Two, **Sequencing and Organizing Instruction**, deals with establishing instructional intent and planning instruction. Chapter 3 provides comprehensive coverage of setting goals, writing objectives, and the backward design approach to identifying instructional intent. Chapter 4 focuses on developing unit and daily lesson plans. Course, unit, weekly, and daily lesson planning are presented and discussed. Team teaching and teaching special education and gifted and talented students are also covered. Several practical lesson plan formats are illustrated.

Part Three, **Monitoring and Evaluating Student Learning,** addresses student evaluation, test construction, and grading, and presents various techniques and procedures. Chapter 5 focuses on evaluation types, systems of evaluation, and information sources. Chapter 6 covers types of assessment, grading systems, and assigning grades.

Part Four, **Designing Instruction to Maximize Student Learning,** relates to selecting instructional strategies. These chapters focus on using the direct, integrated, and indirect teaching methods for instructional delivery. This part also includes a pertinent chapter on skills instruction, which stresses the importance of critical thinking and the development of creative thinking as part of the school curriculum.

Part Five, **Leading the Dynamic Classroom,** covers the implementation of instruction. The focus is on communication, motivation, and classroom management. The importance of classroom management cannot be overemphasized. Indeed, a classroom must be well managed if learning is to take place. Several management models are covered.

CD-Based Ancillary Materials for the Instructor

An instructor's manual is available on CD to help instructors plan and teach their courses, designed to make the classes as interesting as possible for students. For each chapter, this supplement includes:

A **Restatement of Chapter Objectives** to use as a laptop projection, transparency, or handout in classes.

Major Text Terms, also usable as a study aid in classes (the text terms are available to students on their study site as electronic flashcards).

Chapter Outlines to assist you in planning your lecture materials.

Support Materials from the text itself to use during classes (text figures, tables, and exercises).

Recommended Supplementary Readings to enhance your lecture materials, discussion prompters, and assignments.

A **Test Bank** of exam questions (both objective and essay questions) to either use as tests or adapt to your own test formats.

Web-Based Student Study Site

A web-based student study site can be found at http://www.sagepub.com/eis These resources can also be used by the instructor to supplement instruction. For each chapter, the site offers the following:

Vignette study questions to prompt students to think about the vignettes accompanying each chapter.

Supplementary student activities, web exercises, and discussion questions to help students feel more engaged with the materials presented.

Electronic flash cards of major terms to help students memorize new terminology.

A review quiz and reading extension to help students prepare for tests and conduct further research for assigned papers.

The website also features an extended list of educational websites as well as content-related journal articles with focus questions to prompt further discussion and motivate students to research issues in more depth.

Acknowledgments

I am, indeed, grateful to hundreds of students and teachers who provided critical feedback and served as invaluable sources in the preparation of this text. Moreover,

I would like to thank the many educators who helped identify the major ideas presented in this textbook. Special gratitude also goes to the school districts that opened their doors to me and offered their support.

Many colleagues contributed to this textbook. I am especially indebted to Dr. Sally Beisser at Drake University, who developed three of the lesson plan formats presented in Chapter 4 and wrote the Chapter 4 section on Teaching the Gifted and Talented Student, and to Dr. Chris Merrill at Illinois State University, who wrote the Chapter 9 section on Systemic Problem Solving. Finally, I would like to thank my wife, Susan, for all the support and for acting as a sounding board for many of the ideas presented in the text. The textbook is much stronger, due to the innovative ideas and efforts of these talented colleagues.

I wish to thank the following prospectus reviewers for their assistance and constructive suggestions:

Holly L. Anderson, Boise State University

Paulette Patterson Dilworth, Indiana University at Bloomington

W. Scott Hopkins, University of South Alabama

Cynthia J. Hutchinson, University of Central Florida

Andrew C. Kemp, University of Louisville

Susie Oliphant, Bowie State University

David B. Peterson, Morehead State University

I also wish to extend special thanks to and acknowledge these reviewers for their assistance with the preliminary drafts of this textbook:

Holly L. Anderson, Boise State University

Sally Beisser, Drake University

W. Scott Hopkins, University of South Alabama

John Kiraly, Western Kentucky University

Chris P. Merrill, Illinois State University

I would also like to thank the staff at Sage who helped bring this textbook to life. Diane McDaniel, who got the project started and kept it on track, deserves special thanks. Her leadership will always be remembered and appreciated. Special thanks also go to Marta Peimer, Editorial Assistant, who provided much technical and research assistance.

K.D.M.

Part I

SETTING THE STAGE FOR SUCCESSFUL LEARNING

What is the purpose of education? Careful consideration of this question should be one of the first concerns of a prospective teacher. Historically, education has undergone constant change. Changes in society are often reflected in more demands being placed on our educational system.

Teaching is a challenge that requires long hours of work and preparation. Part 1 addresses the constantly changing field of education. The purpose of this first section is to help you gain insight into the process of teaching and to put that process into a framework that will assist you in preparing to teach.

Prospective teachers need to understand teaching as a profession. Thus, Chapter 1 presents some background information on where education is coming from and how it is constantly changing. On the other hand, because schools function to bring about learning, prospective teachers need a basic understanding of effective teaching, effective teaching skills, expectations and standards, accountability, professional standards, and licensure requirements. Chapter 1 covers these essential topics.

Chapter 2 deals with the school curriculum. The key to success as a teacher is a well-designed curriculum based on student needs and societal needs. The program design must be based on sound research and state and national standards. It is the teacher, however, who has the final say in what will be taught. As such, a comprehensive model of teaching is presented and discussed. Chapter 2 also provides comprehensive coverage of planning a course of instruction.

1

GETTING READY FOR THE CLASSROOM

The human contribution is the essential ingredient.
It is only in the giving of oneself to others that we truly live.

ETHEL PERCY ANDRUS

OVERVIEW

Teachers must be mentors, effective subject matter experts, counselors, and social psychologists. Teachers must learn to use time effectively to maximize learning. Moreover, effective teachers must (1) engage in quality planning and preparation, (2) prepare a positive classroom environment, (3) use proven instructional techniques, and (4) exhibit professional behavior.

Teachers teach students. The intent is to bring about learning. Therefore, to maximize learning, one must take into account student needs, differences, and abilities. Many factors will influence development, teaching, and learning; I will focus my attention, however, on those that are relevant to the classroom.

Becoming a teacher requires that you meet state and national standards. Most states require that you demonstrate that you are a highly qualified teacher by passing a state or national exam.

OBJECTIVES

After completing your study of Chapter 1, you should be able to do the following:

1. Define teaching and explain the concept of teaching as an art and as a science.
2. Describe the characteristics and skills associated with effective teaching and reflective teaching as well as the constructivist approach to learning.
3. Differentiate among the five categories of time found in schools.
4. Describe the expectations and standards associated with teaching and learning.
5. Explain why teachers need an understanding of students.
6. Explain the provisions of Public Law 94-142, IDEA, and No Child Left Behind.
7. Discuss the importance of and techniques for teaching students how to learn.

8. Explain the role of parents and the community in the learning process.
9. Explain the purposes of accreditation agencies and analyze the benefits of accreditation for various constituencies.
10. Explain the state licensure/certification process.

What makes a "good" teacher, an "effective" teacher, a "successful" teacher? Are there certain identifiable skills that make one an effective teacher? Let's set the stage for our study of effective methods by focusing on what it means to teach and on standards for preparing effective teachers.

Teaching

What does it mean to teach? Moore (2001) defines teaching as "the actions of someone who is trying to assist others to reach their fullest potential in all aspects of development" (p. 5). The personal characteristics and skills needed to accomplish this noble task have been debated for years. Generally, the argument centers on the questions: (1) Is teaching an art or a science and (2) exactly what is effective teaching?

Teaching as an Art and a Science

Do some teachers have better instincts for teaching than others? If so, can these instincts be identified and taught? Some educators argue that teachers are born and not made and the ability to be an effective teacher cannot be taught. Conversely, other educators argue that teaching is a science with specific laws and principles, which can be taught.

Those who think *teaching is an art* may argue that good teaching is primarily a creative act. That is, teachers create learning in a spontaneous manner by combining individual pieces of education and experience into a new whole that is specially made for the circumstances they see in their situation. These individuals may recognize the need for a strong educational background, but believe that once you are in the classroom you operate from a gut-level feeling that leads you to know how to put theory into practice. This theory of teaching suggests that there are some who possess a special sense of knowing what to do and when to do it that cannot be taught. And although this idea doesn't leave the prospective teacher with a list of tangible options for putting together the pieces of education, it does explain a mysterious aspect of teaching that many spend a lifetime seeking. Indeed, this may be the mystery that has motivated so much research in the hope that perfect formulas will be discovered to direct us in our search for best practices and methods in education.

Those holding that *teaching is a science* believe that good teaching is the result of having a deep knowledge of the subject matter and a solid understanding of the principles of teaching and learning. They believe it is possible to learn and master the skills and strategies needed to be a successful teacher. Decades of research have provided specific information about how learning occurs, what influences motivation, and which particular teacher skills produce learning. Promoters of the teaching as a science theory offer specific methods and skills that are attainable for the prospective teacher. It is believed that persons who learn to use these skills will be successful.

Today, most educators are in agreement with Gagne (1985), who argues that there is a scientific basis for the art of teaching. Experienced teachers know it is not simply a matter of sharing what they know with their students. Teaching is a complex and challenging profession. A good teacher must be able to transform knowledge into learning activities that motivate students to learn. Thus, teaching can be viewed as having both artistic and scientific elements. Essentially, educators are accepting the viewpoint that individuals who have an interest in teaching fall somewhere along a continuum like that shown in Figure 1.1. Further, many agree that specific artistic and scientific elements can be transmitted effectively.

Figure 1.1

Teaching as an Art and a Science

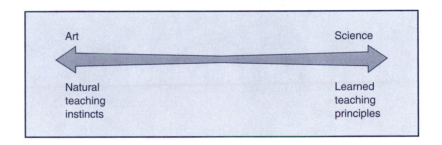

"I can't tell you what a relief it is to relax after a whole year of teaching!"

Teaching is both an
art and a science.

Effective Teaching

The search for the elements of effective teaching is not a new one. Teaching requires a large repertoire of skills and the ability to put these skills to use in different situations. Good teachers improvise: No one approach works equally well all the time and in all situations. In short, effectiveness depends on the subject, students, and environmental conditions.

Effective teaching is complicated. The better teachers, however, are proactive; that is, they are active information processors and decision makers. They are strongly committed to the importance of content delivery and tend to be task-oriented. They understand the demands of teaching their content, the characteristics of their students, and the importance of decision making in keeping students on task. Research suggests that teacher knowledge of subject matter, student learning, and teaching methods are important elements of effective teaching. Indeed, according to *What Matters Most: Teaching for America's Future* (National Commission on Teaching & America's Future, 1996), teacher knowledge and what teachers do are the most important influences on what students learn.

Contrasting ideas about effective teaching have recently emerged. No matter what view of effective teaching is held, however, the dynamic and complex nature of teaching warrants that teachers be prepared to be self-monitoring individuals. Self-monitoring requires that teachers have skills that enable self-analysis of teaching episodes; they reflect and focus on events rather than on personalities, and on systematic observations for patterns and trends in teaching and learning behavior. These contrasting ideas suggest that to be effective, teachers must inquire into students' experiences and build an understanding of learners and a capacity to analyze what occurs in classrooms and in the lives of their students. In effect, you change your orientation from a view of teaching as static, with simple formulas and cookbook rules, to teaching as dynamic and ever changing. This change requires that you become a reflective teacher.

Reflective teachers learn all they can about teaching from both theory and practice. They teach and reflect on the teaching. They think deeply about the theory and practice of teaching. Such teaching requires that you be sensitive to the diversity of students' needs and family background. Reflective teaching requires that you ask basic, but often difficult, questions about the appropriateness and success of your teaching. If a lesson is unsuccessful, you should be asking how you could change your teaching to make it successful. If students aren't motivated, what can you do to motivate them? If grades are poor, how can you improve achievement? Reflective teaching, then, is the continued self-monitoring of satisfaction with effectiveness. Valuable insight into your reflective and self-monitoring efforts can be provided by websites such as that established by ProTeacher (www.proteacher.com) and MiddleWeb (www.middleweb.com) and by resources such as *Best Practices for High School Classrooms* (Stone, 2002). The Through the Eyes of Teachers interlude gives an overview of the ProTeacher site.

Through the Eyes of Teachers

ProTeacher Community (www.proteacher.net)

A popular and carefully moderated discussion site for elementary schoolteachers, ProTeacher, is host to hundreds of active and changing discussions, and tens of thousands of teaching ideas contributed by teachers nationwide.

Professional classroom teachers, specialists, substitute teachers, student teachers, and administrators working in early childhood, elementary, and middle school are invited to participate—and many do. Although ProTeacher has been designed primarily for elementary schoolteachers, the discussions and ideas are often applicable to all grade levels.

Participation is free of charge and no registration is required. All newcomers, however, should first read their "tips and guidelines" page, which contains helpful advice for first-time visitors, as well as established rules and policies. Special rules apply to student teachers.

The ProTeacher motto is "By sharing ideas and being helpful, we're encouraging others to do the same!" With experienced teachers from across the country doing just that, ProTeacher is definitely worth a visit!

Effective teachers know that good teaching is more than simply explaining, lecturing, and discussing. To be effective, teachers must be well organized.

APPLY AND REFLECT: The debate continues as to whether teaching is a profession similar to law and medicine. Or is teaching a semi-profession? Or is teaching a calling? What is your view of the professionalism of teaching? Discuss your views with your class.

Effective Organization

Classrooms can be organized or disorganized. Better-quality instruction is structured around appropriate content, materials and methods, and interaction patterns. The thoughtfully structured classroom is one in which students engage in meaningful tasks. Matching of instructional tasks with all the interacting variables in a classroom, however, is not easy because of the differences in student ability and potential for learning.

Well-organized classrooms are businesslike. Classes get started on time, and students know what they are to do with class time. Moreover, students know when it is time to get back to work, and they understand the reasons behind and importance of assignments.

Finally, when a lecture is presented or a group activity is conducted, it should be well organized, with clear, well-illustrated explanations. Lesson content should be constructed and presented in logical order, with ideas that are interrelated and interwoven. In effect, thoughtful lessons are designed so students have meaningful and coherent material to learn. Outlines, schematic diagrams, and hierarchies are effective techniques for organizing and presenting lesson content. Complete Web Link: The World Wide Web to explore some websites that you may find useful.

W E B   L I N K   The World Wide Web
The World Wide Web offers educators unlimited resources for increasing their effectiveness in the classroom. Examine a couple of websites for educators. How could the available resources contribute to your effectiveness as a teacher?

Skills of Effective Teachers

Effective teaching is a complex occupation requiring the development of knowledge and essential teaching skills, as well as continuous professional growth. After a thorough analysis of current research, Danielson (1996) suggested four main skill areas for effective teaching. Effective teachers (1) engage in quality planning and preparation, (2) prepare a positive classroom environment, (3) use proven instructional techniques, and (4) exhibit professional behavior. These skill areas are derived from the work of the Educational Testing Service (ETS) in the development of Praxis III. Praxis III: Classroom Performance Assessments is used to assess actual teaching skills and classroom performance. The Danielson skill areas are grounded in the constructivist approach to learning and are based on formal analyses of important tasks required of beginning teachers: reviews of research, analyses of state regulations for teacher licensing, and extensive fieldwork. Further information on constructivism will be presented later in this chapter.

Quality Planning and Preparation

Many people assume all you really need to be an effective teacher is an understanding of content. They assume that once you know your content, it is simply a matter of telling others what you know. In reality, knowing your subject is only part of the instructional process. Effective teachers must spend considerable time and energy planning the activities, materials, and evaluation elements associated with teaching the content. Danielson (1996) found that effective teachers need

- a knowledge of content and pedagogy (Know their subject and how to teach it),
- a knowledge of students (Know how students learn and develop),
- the ability to select instructional goals (Set appropriate expectations),
- a knowledge of resources (Can locate materials and people that will enhance instruction),
- the ability to design instruction (Can plan effective lesson plans), and
- the ability to design student evaluation (Can design fair and meaningful evaluation).

Effective teachers must carefully orchestrate these elements into a coherent teaching plan of instruction.

The Classroom Environment

Effective teachers must create and maintain an environment in which learning can take place. Danielson (1996) found planning classroom environments that allow for positive student learning experiences requires skill at

- creating an environment of respect and rapport (Create caring teacher-student and peer relationships),
- establishing a culture for learning (Create an environment in which learning is valued and meaningful experiences occur),
- managing the classroom (Success at management of the business of the classroom),
- managing student behavior (Effectively responding to appropriate and inappropriate student behavior), and
- organizing physical space (Positive use of classroom space).

Instructional Techniques

Instructional techniques must be planned that will captivate the interest of students and motivate them to learn. Techniques would include such skills as questioning, using student ideas and contributions, and reinforcing. Danielson (1996) found that effective teachers plan and use instructional techniques that

- communicate clearly and accurately (Use strong verbal and written communication skills),
- use effective questioning and discussion techniques (Use different types of questions and responses),
- engage students in learning (Actively involve students in learning),
- provide feedback to students (Provide information on progress), and
- are flexible and responsive (Spontaneously modify lessons based on feedback).

Professional Behavior

Teaching often goes beyond traditional classroom instruction. Effective teachers embrace these extra tasks and strive to improve their knowledge and skills in instruction while working to make significant contributions to their school and community. They work to become true professionals. Danielson (1996) found that true professional teachers

- reflect on their teaching (Thoughtfully consider what was taught and how well it was taught),
- maintain accurate records (Keep written records to document student learning),
- communicate with families (Stay in written and verbal contact with families to support student progress),
- contribute to the school and district (Support functions of the school and district),
- grow as professionals (Take courses and workshops and consult with others), and
- show professionalism (Serve as advocates for students and families).

A relatively new theory of learning and teaching has recently emerged—constructivism. Constructivism constitutes a paradigm shift in how teaching is viewed.

APPLY AND REFLECT: Are effective teachers "born" or can an individual be taught to be an effective teacher?

Constructivism

The essence of the constructivist approach to learning is the idea that learners individually discover and build their own knowledge (Anderson, Greeno, Reder, & Simon, 2000; Brooks & Brooks, 1999; Waxman, Padron, & Arnold, 2001). Learners construct a unique mental image by combining information in their heads with the information they receive from their sense organs. With the constructivist approach, students control some of the learning focus and activities; teacher-centered strategies, such as lectures, are minimized; multiple ways of knowing (through arts, for example) are honored; learning activities and assessments are often rooted in authentic situations; and much learning occurs in groups. The constructivist theory views learners as active participants in their own learning, not passive recipients of information. Learners construct their own meaning by negotiating that meaning with others, making connections with and modifying prior conceptions, and addressing content in a variety of contexts. This approach calls for a more active role for students in their own learning than is typical in many classrooms. Learning is a search for meaning. This constructivism perspective can be conveyed through the ancient Chinese proverb: "I hear and I forget; I see and I remember; I do and I understand."

Constructivism is basically a theory about how people learn. It says that students will construct their own understanding and knowledge of the world, through experiencing things and reflecting on those experiences. When students encounter something new, they have to reconcile it with their previous ideas and experiences, maybe changing what they believe, or maybe discarding the new information as irrelevant. Meaning requires understanding wholes as well as parts. And parts must be understood in the context of wholes. The learning process focuses on primary concepts, not isolated facts. In any case, students will be active creators of their own knowledge. To do this, they must be allowed to ask questions, explore, and assess what they know. The purpose of learning is for an individual to construct his or her own meaning, not just memorize the "right" answers and regurgitate someone else's meaning.

Teachers must focus on making connections between facts and fostering new understanding in students. They must tailor their teaching strategies to student responses and encourage students to analyze, interpret, and predict information. Teachers must rely heavily on open-ended questions and promote extensive dialogue among students. Students cannot be treated as though their brains are *blank slates* to be written upon or *empty vessels* to be filled up. Learners are not, in other words, passive. Rather, they often are quite active in learning. Students need to use and test ideas, skills, and so on through relevant activities. Often, this involves concrete experiences that combine with abstract ideas that have just been presented to learners.

The constructivist view of learning requires a reconceptualization of teaching. Teachers must focus on helping students construct understanding of concepts themselves. Instead of spending time memorizing material, filling in the blanks on worksheets, and repeating large numbers of similar problems, students need to learn to solve novel problems, integrate information, and create knowledge for themselves. The teacher's role is to foster and direct this work on the part of students. The teacher encourages students to use active techniques (experiments, real-world problem solving) to create more knowledge and then to reflect on and talk about what they are doing and how their understandings are changing. The teacher makes sure he or she understands the students' preexisting conceptions, and guides the learning to address them and then build on them. Constructivist teachers encourage students to constantly assess how the learning activity is helping them gain understanding. By questioning themselves and their strategies, students in the constructivist classroom ideally become "expert learners." This gives them ever-broadening tools to keep learning. With a well-planned classroom environment, the students learn HOW TO LEARN. Teaching is getting students to see things in new ways. One of the biggest jobs becomes *asking good questions.*

To be effective, teachers must be well organized, but they must also make effective use of time. You must learn to use classroom time to maximize learning.

Figure 1.2
School and Classroom Time

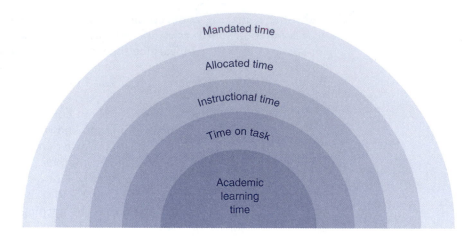

Time in Schools and Classrooms

Time is a valuable and limited classroom resource that must be used wisely. It is often divided into five distinct categories: mandated time, allocated time, instructional time, engaged time, and academic learning time. Figure 1.2 illustrates how the five time categories relate to each other.

The total time available for all activities carried out in a school is established by the state. Typically, schools are in session approximately 7 hours a day for 180 to 190 days. This **mandated time** must be used for academic, as well as for nonacademic activities.

State-mandated time must be divided among a variety of subjects that must be taught, with time allotted for other school activities, such as lunch, announcements, recess, transitions between classes, and so on. The time appropriated for each of these activities is often called **allocated time**. For example, 45 minutes of each day may be used for lunch, and 50 minutes may be needed for changing classes. An important school goal is to expand the amount of allocated time available for learning.

Teachers must translate the available allocated time into learning through **instructional time**. Despite your best efforts, however, not all students will stay on task or pay attention all the time. For example, some students may be daydreaming when you are explaining, some may be goofing off, and others may simply be thinking about other things they would rather be doing. As a result, educators refer to another area within instructional time called time on task.

Time on task, or **engaged time**, differs from mandated, allocated, and instructional times in that it is the actual time individual students engage in learning. In effect, students are actively (physically or mentally) participating in the learning process during time on task. This active participation may simply involve listening to you explain something, reading, writing, or solving problems. If students are not actually on task in the learning process, they do not learn; so another important goal of the instructional process is to improve the quality of time use by keeping students on task. Time on task depends on routine classroom practices, student motivation, and the quality of instruction. Typically, time on task varies from lows of 50 percent in some classrooms to as high as 90 percent in others (Berliner, 1987).

Time on task isn't always productive. Indeed, students often engage in class activities at a superficial level, with little understanding or retention taking place. For example, they could be watching a film while actually concentrating very little on what is being shown. Thus, you must plan your instruction to make the time on task more productive. In other words, you must maximize **academic learning time**. For some educators (Block, Efthim, & Burns, 1989), academic learning time ideally should reflect student performance on assigned tasks at an 80 percent level or better.

A lot of instructional time is lost in today's classrooms. In fact, some educators contend that as many as 50 to 60 days are wasted each year. Some common time wasters are listed below:

1. *Starting classes.* Many teachers take 5 to 10 minutes per class to record attendance and make announcements. Systems should be devised for speeding up these housekeeping chores. The use of assigned seats or seating diagrams, for instance, will speed up this duty.
2. *Excessive use of films.* Films are often shown that have little instructional value or are simply used as time fillers—especially on Fridays. Instructional tools, such as films and computer activities, should be justified in terms of their classroom value.
3. *Discipline time.* Disciplinary actions take time and often interrupt instruction. The use of nonverbal actions in curbing misbehavior allows a lesson to proceed without interruption. The use of nonverbal methods will be discussed at length in Chapter 13.
4. *Early finishes.* Much instructional time is lost when lessons are finished early. This tendency can be avoided by planning more instruction than you'll need.
5. *Extracurricular activities.* Students are often dismissed early for athletic events, plays and rehearsals, music and band activities, and other such activities. Schools should schedule special events on activity days or after school hours.

How can you tell when students are off task? This is not easy. Sharpen your observation skills. Watch students' eyes: Are they watching you during your presentations, or do their eye movements suggest that they are engaged in other interests? Finally, do they ask or answer questions? Be sensitive to the signal indicators that indicate that students are engaged and on task.

Keeping students engaged and on task isn't always easy. Your orientation, dispositions, and attitudes toward students and learning will often impact student engagement.

Dispositions and Attitudes

The National Council for Accreditation of Teacher Education (NCATE) defines dispositions as the values, commitments, and professional ethics that influence behaviors toward students, families, colleagues, and communities and affect student learning, motivation, and development, as well as the educator's own professional growth. Dispositions are guided by beliefs and **attitudes** related to values such as caring, fairness, honesty, responsibility, and social justice.

Although every teacher holds his or her own dispositions and attitudes, there are several common dispositions and attitudes that effective teachers hold. First of all,

Making Education Meaningful

1. What roles do teachers assume in the school environment? Are teachers adequately prepared for these roles?
2. Should parents and community leaders have a voice in school academic decisions? Other school decisions?

Education should be painless. I believe the education of students should be a partnership between teacher and student and it is the greatest gift we can give a student.

Students approach education in different ways. Some are easily stimulated and are easily taught. Others are harder to reach. The trick is to balance the teaching approach to benefit each student as an individual. Education should encompass a variety of experiences that add up to a complete entity, the educated person.

Students need encouragement, a stable classroom/school environment, and a chance to succeed. In our modern world of fast-moving images and strong media influence, a student's ability is often taken for granted. Since we are inundated with information, it is easy to assume students are being educated when they are out of the classroom. In most cases, however, this is not the case. Students need a stable classroom environment in which to be the students they are and learn what they need to know.

Students deserve the chance to succeed. By manipulating some situations, it is possible to give each student the satisfaction of being a success.

Effective teachers should be flexible and should be able to wear a lot of different hats. Sometimes these different hats have to be worn at once, so flexibility is paramount. Flexibility allows for trial and error. If one teaching method or strategy isn't working, something new should be tried. A teacher isn't just a teacher anymore, which accounts for the many hats. A teacher has to assume the role of parent, counselor, and disciplinarian. An effective teacher should be able to assimilate these roles into one package. In addition to flexibility and juggling hats, an effective teacher has to be both receptive and perceptive. A receptive teacher is open to new ideas, which is important when trying to teach a variety of different students. A perceptive teacher is able to see the student. By keeping a close watch on students and student performances, you open up opportunities to reach them.

Teachers should involve families and the community in the school. Parents should be seen as partners in the education of students. Parents should be kept informed of progress both good and bad. The old adage, "No news is good news" is outdated. Parents need to be made a part of the education of students. When possible, parents should be used as a classroom resource. Many parents have skills or experiences that can be tapped for classroom use as a speaker or helper.

The community should be welcome in the school. The community supports public schools financially through taxes and fund-raising and should feel a part of the school. In most cases, the school is a central focus in the community. This focus should be a good thing, not a bad one. The community has vast resources for schools both financial and academic. Through programs like "adopt a classroom" and others, the community can be brought into the school for a purpose and both school and community benefit. The education of students should not occur behind closed schoolhouse doors. The community and parents should feel a connection to the school and feel they are part of the education of our children.

—RACHEL, *elementary school teacher*

SOURCE: Reprinted with permission from ProTeacher, a professional community for elementary school teachers (http://www.proteacher.net)

effective teachers are real. Within reason, they share their true selves with students. Second, effective teachers have positive expectations for *all* students. They have realistic, yet challenging, expectations for *all* of their students. Third, effective teachers are caring about their students. They have an attitude of acceptance and trust. Fourth, effective teachers are excited about teaching and learning. They demonstrate love of teaching and learning. Fifth, effective teachers value diversity. They treat *all* students equally and fairly. Finally, effective teachers are willing to collaborate. They see themselves as part of an educational team and community. Great teachers do not just love kids. They facilitate a love of learning in the students they teach.

APPLY AND REFLECT: What are the dispositions of your teacher education program? Do you agree they are dispositions that effective teachers should possess?

Expectations and Standards

The intent of teaching is learning. **Learning** can be defined as a change in an individual's capacity for performance as a result of experience. Changes that come about through development (such as sexual maturity or growing taller) are not considered to be learning. People are constantly absorbing information, both intentionally and unintentionally. For example, students may intentionally learn to read but may unintentionally learn to fear the dentist. Of course, your main concern will be with intentional learning. Don't totally discount unintentional learning, however, because as you teach students are determining that the subject is interesting or dull, useful or useless. This learning, although unintentional, is important to the learning process.

Standards for student performance have changed as expectations about what exactly education should *do* has changed. One unresolved problem of schools is how to provide equal educational opportunity to learn while assuring the public that a high-quality education is being provided.

Despite the increased focus on the diversity among K–12 students, studies suggest that many schools and teachers still often treat girls, racial- and language-minority students, and working-class students differently from boys, nonminority, and middle- and upper-class students and have lower expectations for them (Kaufman, Westland, & Engvall, 1997; McCall, 1995; Padron, 1994). Factor into this equation the 1970s legislation that mandated equal opportunities for children with handicapping conditions (to take place in an integrated setting), and you can begin to appreciate the competing expectations and demands with which schools and teachers must contend.

Most schools are organized around a set of expectations or benchmarks regarding the purposes of education. The public has sought, even demanded, that schools focus on the needs of more and more groups of young people. In addition, the public has demanded that schools include coursework that addresses health, economic, and societal issues as well as the "basics." Funding for these needs has been sporadic and inadequate; yet the public has also demanded **accountability** for student performance, particularly in the area of basic skill acquisition.

Physical development is
an important aspect
of schooling.

The attempt to control quality in the public schools and ensure some form of standardization has resulted in an **accreditation** process that mandates review at the state level and rewards approval at the regional level. All states require periodic review of programs for accreditation. A few states have used this process to declare some schools "educationally bankrupt" and have assumed control of such schools. Often, students who wish to attend more prestigious institutions of higher education must attend regional accredited schools. Moreover, school choice plans (students choose the school they attend) and No Child Left Behind legislation are likely to increase the demand for careful scrutiny of school programs as parents "shop" for schools for their children.

APPLY AND REFLECT: Many states have established benchmark standards for the different

subject content areas and grade levels. Do you support this policy? Why or why not?

Schools must focus
on state and national
standards.

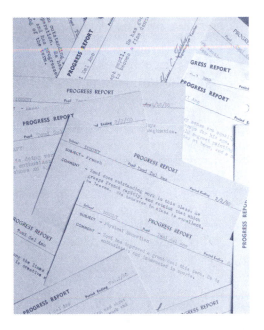

Students

Students are the intended audience for the curriculum. Therefore, you must have some general information about the nature of the students in the schools in which you will be teaching.

Children do not look and act like they did 20 or 30 years ago, and the differences are not only the result of changes in dress and hairstyles. Today, schools are showing major increases in non-White student populations. Moreover, the need to acculturate newly arrived immigrants is still an important part of the schooling process. But the faces of immigrant youth are no longer predominantly European faces. They are increasingly the faces of Asians, Hispanics, and others. A large percentage of the Asians are from Southeast Asia and a large percentage of the Hispanics are from Latin America. As a result of this new influx of immigrants, more foreign languages are being spoken in our schools than ever before and many of these languages have yet to become a part of the formal curriculum.

As a teacher, you will be required to plan very carefully to meet the needs of such a diverse student population. Failure to recognize and address the needs of these students could result in a large portion of the future adult population of this country that cannot participate successfully in the marketplace or as citizens.

APPLY AND REFLECT: How are students and families different than they were a decade ago? Have you seen many changes in your state? If so, what kinds?

Needs of Students

The more you know about your students, the easier will be your task of bringing about the desired learning. In short, to be an effective educator, you must identify your students' needs—their strengths, weaknesses, aspirations, limitations, and deficiencies. These student needs can be academic or social. Some students may be lacking in reading or in mathematics, whereas others may be gifted, academically talented, or creative. An awareness of these differences is needed, so you can devise ways to provide adequate instruction. In addition, you must take into account differences in social and cultural background, as well as different student abilities.

Some of your students will be academically able or even bright, whereas others will be slower, **disabled**, or **handicapped**. Student differences often require that you adapt the classroom's physical environment and your instructional strategies to better accommodate the unique needs of mainstreamed or special students. In other words, you must learn to modify your instruction to fit the unique needs of special students.

Public Law 94-142 (PL 94-142), the Education for All Handicapped Children Act, was enacted to require that every school system in the nation provide a free, appropriate public education for every child between the ages of 3 and 21. In 1990, PL 94-142 was recast as the Individuals With Disabilities Education Act (IDEA). IDEA spells out broad mandates for services to all children with disabilities. These include evaluation and eligibility determination, appropriate education and an individualized education plan (IEP), and education in the least restrictive environment (LRE). The IEP must state present levels of functioning, long- and short-term educational goals, services to be provided, and plans for initiating and evaluating the services. Carrying out IEP goals and objectives may require lesson modifications, such as adapting assigned work, developing special reproduced materials for teaching difficult concepts, planning and writing special study guides, and obtaining and using special equipment. In 1997, the Individuals with Disabilities Education Act Amendments of 1997, or IDEA '97 was passed to reauthorize and strengthen the original act. Among the goals of this law are raising educational expectations for children with disabilities, increasing the role of parents in the education of their children with disabilities, assuring that regular classroom teachers are involved in planning for and assessment of these children, including students with disabilities in local and state assessments, and supporting professional development for all who educate children with disabilities. Complete Web Link: Individual Education Plan (IEP) to review some sample IEPs.

W E B   L I N K   Individualized Education Plan (IEP)

Teachers who work with children with special needs are generally involved in the development of an individualized education plan (IEP) for each child. Review sample IEPs on-line, and discuss how all students could benefit from receiving the type of feedback present in an IEP.

The use of differentiated assignments is a must when working with mainstreamed special needs students. This is accomplished by varying the length and the difficulty of assignments, and by individualizing the curriculum as much as possible. For example, you might require only half as much writing for a student with motor difficulties, or you might allow students to write a paper instead of giving a speech when a student has speech difficulties.

Under the IDEA, children with disabilities must be educated in the least restrictive environment (LRE). This means an environment as similar as possible to the one in which children who do not have a disability are educated. The education of children with a disability in the regular classroom was referred to as *mainstreaming*. This term, however, has been replaced by the term *inclusion*, which means educating a child with special educational needs full-time in the regular classroom with other children (Idol, 1997). One recent study found that the achievement of students with learning disabilities benefited from inclusion (Rea, McLaughlin, & Walther-Thomas, 2002).

APPLY AND REFLECT: As a classroom teacher, you will have students with special needs mainstreamed into your classes. Do you support or not support the inclusion concept?

Student Performance

There exists a learning gap in this country. As early as fifth grade, U.S. students lag far behind their counterparts in other countries. Reformers are increasingly aware of this learning gap and are seeking ways to address it. The challenge is to find a way to improve classroom teaching so that our educational goals can be realized. Virtually every state is working to develop high student standards, along with means for assessing students' progress. Educators must now find ways of providing students with the learning opportunities they need to reach the new standards.

Forty-nine states in the United States have adopted state-mandated testing that aims to raise standards of performance for children in our schools in a manner that assigns accountability to schools and teachers. No longer does policy permit students to be promoted solely on the basis of completing a particular grade with acceptable grades—even though some teachers continue to do so. An increasing number of states have instituted programs that call for testing at certain grades to determine if students continue to the next grade. One issue that has received considerable attention is the increased use of **minimum competency tests** to award graduation diplomas. At issue is whether or not such tests are accurate measures of the scope of knowledge and ideas learned in school. For those who fail to pass the tests, a certificate of attendance is usually awarded. Many believe this practice will have a chilling effect on minority students and students with special needs.

In January 2002, a piece of federal legislation called the No Child Left Behind Act was signed into law. This act has been designed and enacted to help low-income and minority students perform at the same achievement level as their peers. The law requires states and school districts to test at least 95 percent of students annually to assess their academic skills in reading and mathematics in grades 3 through 8 and at least once in grades 10 through 12. Schools also must have 95 percent participation from all major subgroups of students, such as minority or disabled youngsters. Schools in which 95 percent or more of eligible test-takers don't take the required exams may be identified as needing academic improvement—just like schools in which students do not meet minimum test score requirements. Schools identified as academically troubled and in need of improvement face consequences. These consequences range from having to permit students to transfer to other, higher achieving schools to replacing the faculty at a school. By school year 2007–2008, assessments (or testing) in science will be underway. The legislation also couples testing requirements with a push for qualified teachers in all classrooms by 2005–2006 and strict sanctions when schools fail to improve test scores for *all* students. No Child Left Behind also targets resources to support learning in the early years, requires that more information be provided to parents about their child's progress, and gives parents the option to transfer their child out of low-performing schools.

APPLY AND REFLECT: Student assessment and testing has become a national issue. Are we emphasizing testing too much in our schools?

Teaching Students to Learn

Children often need help in learning how to learn. Basically, you will have three types of students in your classes: students who can learn on their own, students who need some help in learning, and students who need a lot of help in learning. Your job will be to provide training to those students who need help with the skills needed in building concepts. You must learn to make information meaningful, to help students develop learning and study skills, and to teach so knowledge can be applied or transferred to other areas. Too much classroom learning is rote; that is, it is the memorization of facts or associations, such as math facts, rules of grammar, words in foreign languages, or presidents and vice presidents of the United States. Optimal learning takes place when information is made meaningful. Essentially, information must be well organized and tied into an existing cognitive structure. For example, the study of mammals could be tied into an organizational hierarchy of the animal kingdom. The use of **advance organizers** (an orientation statement about the material to be learned) can also be quite effective in making subject matter meaningful to students. Moreover, advance organizers can help structure new information and relate it to knowledge students already possess. Advance organizers will be discussed further in Chapter 7.

Learning for understanding requires that students possess elaboration skills, note-taking skills, summarizing skills, and the ability to form questions related to studied information. Elaboration encourages students to think about new material in ways that connect it to information or ideas already in the students' minds. One strategy for accomplishing this goal is to question students about the material as it is taught (see Chapter 7). Other commonly used strategies for increasing student understanding of reading material or lecture material are to have students take notes over the main ideas as they are presented or read, to have them write brief summary statements about what they have heard or read, and to have them generate their own questions about the material.

The ultimate goal of teaching and learning is to develop students' ability to apply classroom-acquired information outside the classroom or in different subjects. For

"Have you had any experience working with children?"

example, students should be able to write a letter outside the classroom, and they should be able to use mathematical skills in their science class. This ability is referred to as **transfer**. With transfer, you are trying to develop the ability to apply knowledge acquired in one situation to new situations. Presumably, students in a Spanish class will be able to communicate with people who speak Spanish. The likelihood of transfer can be enhanced by making the original learning situation as similar as possible to the situation to which information or skills will be applied. For instance, science should be taught through the use of realistic problems from your students' daily lives. Of course, another means for accomplishing transfer is thorough learning: Students cannot use information they do not thoroughly understand. Finally, similarity and thoroughness make it more likely that students will be able to apply newly acquired information in real-life problem situations.

Parent and Community Involvement

Parent and community involvement is an important factor in improving the academic learning of students. Parent and community involvement is a process wherein parents and educators are encouraged to cooperate in and support the education of students. This involvement can come in four different forms and levels: instruction at school, instruction at home, school governance, and community service.

Getting parents involved in the educational process is not always easy. Parents and teachers live in different worlds that are often separated by psychosocial barriers. Indeed, parents frequently have preconceived and sometimes biased views of schools and teachers. Even with these constraints, however, parent and community involvement will generally positively impact the educational process.

Ultimately, educators must find ways to open and support culturally responsive communication between parents and schools. Too often, low-income and minority families face sustained isolation from the school culture. Such isolation can result in an "us" versus "them" mentality. Teachers then often blame parents for student academic failures. Keep in mind, however, that because of changes in modern families (e.g., non-English-speaking, single-parent families, decreasing family size, both parents working, and increased poverty), it often takes a whole community to educate our young people. To further explore parent involvement in the schools, complete Expansion Activity: Parent Involvement.

EXPANSION ACTIVITY

Parent Involvement

Research shows that parent involvement greatly influences students' school attitudes, interest, attendance, and academic achievement. Develop an action plan for involving parents in your classroom in a variety of ways. What are some barriers you must overcome to involve parents? How are you going to overcome those barriers? Should parents, families, and community members be recognized and encouraged to participate in the elementary school program? Secondary school programs?

This completes my introduction to teaching. Table 1.1 summarizes the concepts addressed in this section. Review the summary and complete Review, Extension, and Reflective Exercise 1.1.

Professional Teaching Standards

Research shows that what teachers know, do, and value has a significant influence on the nature, extent, and rate of student learning. Recognition of the critical teacher impact and relationship between teacher and learner highlights the need to better define and build on what constitutes effective teaching. Professional teaching standards provide a powerful mechanism for achieving this aim.

Challenges in Preparing to Teach

There are many new regulations from local, state, and federal agencies that have brought new challenges to teaching. As you prepare for a career in teaching, you will become familiar with rules that govern such things as length of time spent on subjects taught, textbooks used for instruction, guidelines for teacher conduct and interactions with students, as well as requirements for student promotion. Regulating agencies also require institutions, like the university or college you are attending, to meet rigid standards within teacher education programs that are preparing teachers for the classroom. There are standards and benchmarks used

TABLE 1.1 Teaching Concepts

Concept	Description
Teaching as Art	Effective teachers have natural instincts for teaching.
Teaching as Science	Effective teaching comes from learned laws and principles of teaching.
Organized Classroom	Classroom is structured around businesslike atmosphere and well-planned appropriate lessons.
School and Classroom Time	Total time is established by the state for schooling.
Public Law 94-142	The Education for All Handicapped Children Act requires that all students with disabilities be given a free, appropriate public education and provides the funding to help implement this education.
Individuals With Disabilities Education Act (IDEA)	The act spells out broad mandates for services to all children with disabilities, including evaluation and determination of eligibility, appropriate education and an individualized education plan (IEP), and education in the least restrictive environment (LRE).
Individualized Education Plan (IEP)	A written statement that outlines a program specifically tailored for the student with a disability
Least Restrictive Environment (LRE)	A setting that is as similar as possible to the one in which children who do not have a disability are educated.
Transfer	The ability to use information acquired in one situation in new situations.

to measure instruction and student learning that will affect you as you prepare to learn the necessary skills of a beginning teacher. Although there are a growing number of new requirements guiding the profession, many teachers express satisfaction with the amount of control they have in presenting instruction within their classrooms. On the other hand, some teachers may feel somewhat isolated and miss adult interaction.

Several national groups and professional associations have invested considerable time, energy, and resources in establishing a rationale for teaching standards, in working with classroom practitioners to design and test various models and approaches to professionalize teaching. These efforts resulted in the recommendation and establishment of standards and teacher testing. Playing a central role in these efforts were the National Council for Accreditation of Teacher Education (NCATE), the National Board for Professional Teaching Standards (NBPTS), the Interstate New Teacher Assessment and Support Consortium (INTASC), and the Educational Testing Service (ETS).

APPLY AND REFLECT: No Child Left Behind legislation requires that every classroom have a highly qualified teacher. States define highly qualified teacher differently. How would you define highly qualified teacher?

Review, Extension, and Reflective Exercise 1.1

Define teaching and describe the skills associated with effective teaching.

Connections to INTASC Standards:
- Standard 1: Subject Matter. The teacher must understand the central concepts, tools of inquiry, and structures of the discipline(s) he or she teaches and be able to create learning experiences that make these aspects of subject matter meaningful for students.
- Standard 4: Instructional Strategies. The teacher must understand and use a variety of instructional strategies to encourage students' development of critical thinking, problem solving, and performance skills.
- Standard 5: Learning Environment. The teacher must be able to use an understanding of individual and group motivation and behavior to create a learning environment that encourages positive social interaction, active engagement in learning, and self-motivation.
- Standard 9: Reflection and Professional Development. The teacher must be a reflective practitioner who continually evaluates the effects of his or her choices and actions on others (students, parents, and other professionals in the learning community) and who actively seeks out opportunities to grow professionally.

Connections to the NBPTS:
- Proposition 2: Teachers must know the subjects they teach and how to teach those subjects to students.

- Proposition 4: Teachers must think systematically about their practice and learn from experience.
- Proposition 5: Teachers must be members of learning communities.

Review
- Is teaching an art or a science?
- Are there specific skills that effective teachers should develop? What standards should we have for teachers? Students?
- How is time used in the classroom?

Reflection
- Teachers have many different responsibilities in today's schools. Do you think teachers are asked to do too many things? If so, what can be done to improve the working conditions of teachers? Do you feel qualified to carry out the diverse roles of a teacher? Do you have strong areas? Weak areas? Understanding and willingness to adapt (to be responsive) are often suggested as attributes of the successful teacher. Do you possess these attributes? What other attributes do you feel are important to teachers?
- Write a short essay explaining what effective teachers must know and be able to do. Explain how the following terms are related to effective teaching: (1) knowledge of subject, (2) time, (3) teaching skills, and (4) standards.

National Council for Accreditation of Teacher Education (NCATE)

The National Council for Accreditation of Teacher Education (NCATE) is one of two national agencies that accredit colleges, schools, or departments of education in the United States. The second agency, the Teacher Education Accreditation Council (TEAC), was recognized by the Council on Higher Education Accreditation (CHEA) in fall 2003. The agencies differ in that NCATE applies external criteria for accreditation, whereas TEAC applies internal criteria.

NCATE is an alliance of 33 national professional education and public organizations (see www.ncate.org). NCATE currently accredits more than 550 colleges of education with more than 100 in candidacy. NCATE accreditation is a mark of distinction, and provides recognition that the college or school of education has met national professional standards for the preparation of teachers and other educators. These standards include a conceptual framework that provides structure and direction for programs, courses, teaching, candidate performance, faculty scholarship and service, and accountability.

Standard 1: Candidate knowledge, skills, and dispositions

Standard 2: Assessment system and evaluation

Standard 3: Field experiences and clinical practice

Standard 4: Diversity

Standard 5: Faculty qualifications, performance, and evaluation

Standard 6: Governance and resources

The performance-based NCATE standards require that institutions provide evidence of competent teacher candidate performance. Candidates must know the subject matter they plan to teach and how to teach it effectively.

The Teacher Education Accreditation Council (TEAC) was founded in 1997 by a nonprofit organization dedicated to improving academic degree programs for professional educators. TEAC's accreditation process examines and verifies evidence teacher education programs have to support their claims that they prepare competent, caring, and qualified professional educators. To be accredited, an institution submits a research monograph, called an *Inquiry Brief,* in which the institution documents the following:

- Evidence of their students' learning
- Evidence that their assessment of student learning is valid
- Evidence that the program's continuous improvement and quality control is based on information about its students' learning

TEAC accredits the institution's programs based on an audit of the *Inquiry Brief.*

National Board for Professional Teaching Standards (NBPTS)

The National Board for Professional Teaching Standards (NBPTS) is an independent, nonpartisan organization governed by a board of directors, the majority of whom are classroom teachers. The mission of the National Board is to advance the quality of teaching and learning by

- establishing high and rigorous standards for what effective teachers should know and be able to do,
- developing a national voluntary system to certify teachers who meet National Board standards, and
- advocating related education reforms to integrate National Board Standards in American education for the purpose of improving student learning.

The National Board formed five core propositions relative to what teachers should know and be able to do to bring about student learning. The five propositions essential to effective teaching are as follows:

Proposition 1: Teachers are committed to students and their learning.

Proposition 2: Teachers know the subjects they teach and how to teach those subjects to students.

Proposition 3: Teachers are responsible for managing and monitoring student learning.

Proposition 4: Teachers think systematically about their practice and learn from experience.

Proposition 5: Teachers are members of learning communities.

The propositions with detailed discussions can be accessed on-line at the NBPTS website (www.nbpts.org/about/coreprops.cfm). The NBPTS further details what constitutes effective teaching in every subject and for students at all stages of development. The standards provide career-long learning curriculum for accomplished teaching.

The Interstate New Teacher Assessment and Support Consortium (INTASC)

The Interstate New Teacher Assessment and Support Consortium (INTASC) was formed in 1987 to create broad standards that could be reviewed by professional organizations, state agencies, and teacher preparation institutions as a basis for licensing and preparing beginning teachers. The 10 broad INTASC standards (see Figure 1.3) are further explicated in terms of teacher knowledge, dispositions, and performances that all beginning teachers should have regardless of their specialty area. These standards present a wide range of content knowledge, pedagogical methodologies and strategies, and personal beliefs and personal behaviors that promote student learning. The 10 INTASC standards along with supporting discussion can be accessed on-line (http://education.wlsc.edu/intasc.html). Most teacher preparation programs are specifically aligned with these standards.

Assessment of Standards

To ensure that the INTASC standards are being met, many states are requiring all teacher candidates to successfully pass a standardized test that assesses their understanding of the subject they will teach and knowledge of teaching and learning. One exam that is commonly used for the purpose is the Praxis II, which was developed by the Educational Testing Service (ETS). Some states, however, have developed state tests to assess whether candidates meet INTASC standards. Forty states now use the Praxis Series to assess the national standards.

Figure 1.3

The 10 INTASC Standards

Standard 1: Subject Pedagogy. The teacher must understand the central concepts, tools of inquiry, and structures of the discipline(s) he or she teaches and be able to create learning experiences that make these aspects of subject matter meaningful for students.

Standard 2: Student Development. The teacher understands how children learn and develop and can provide learning opportunities that support their intellectual, social, and personal development.

Standard 3: Diverse Learners. The teacher understands how students differ in their approaches to learning and creates instructional opportunities that are adapted to diverse learners.

Standard 4: Instructional Strategies. The teacher must understand and use a variety of instructional strategies to encourage students' development of critical thinking, problem solving, and performance skills.

Standard 5: Learning Environment. The teacher must be able to use an understanding of individual and group motivation and behavior to create a learning environment that encourages positive social interaction, active engagement in learning, and self-motivation.

Standard 6: Communication. The teacher uses knowledge of effective verbal, nonverbal, and media communication techniques to foster active inquiry, collaboration, and supportive interaction in the classroom.

Standard 7: Planning Instruction. The teacher plans instruction based upon knowledge of subject matter, students, the community, and curriculum goals.

Standard 8: Assessment. The teacher understands and uses formal and informal assessment strategies to evaluate and ensure the continuous intellectual, social, and physical development of the learner.

Standard 9: Reflection and Professional Development. The teacher must be a reflective practitioner who continually evaluates the effects of his or her choices and actions on others (students, parents, and other professionals in the learning community) and who actively seeks out opportunities to grow professionally.

Standard 10: Collaboration. The teacher fosters relationships with school colleagues, parents, and agencies in the larger community to support students' learning and well-being.

The Educational Testing Service (ETS) developed the Praxis Series to assist state education agencies in making licensing decisions. The Praxis Series: Professional Assessments for Beginning Teachers is a set of rigorous and carefully validated assessments designed to provide accurate, reliable licensing information. An overview of the Praxis Series can be accessed at the ETS website (www.ets.org/praxis). The Praxis Series is used by nearly 80 percent of states that include tests as part of their licensing process. Access www.ets.org/praxis/prxstate.html to check Praxis test requirements for specific states.

The three categories of assessment in the Praxis Series correspond to the three decision points in teacher preparation:

- Entry into a teacher training program: Praxis I: Academic Skills Assessments
- Requirement for initial licensure into profession: Praxis II: Subject and Pedagogy Assessments
- Requirement for permanent licensure: Praxis III: Classroom Performance Assessments

Only the Praxis I and II are used extensively by states in their licensure process. The Praxis I: Academic Skills Assessments (Pre-Professional Skills Tests, or PPST) tests candidates relative to their reading, writing, and mathematics abilities. The Praxis II: Subject and Pedagogy Assessments contains two types of tests: Multiple Subjects Assessments and Principles of Learning and Teaching Assessments.

The Praxis II: Multiple Subjects Assessments tests the subject matter knowledge of teacher candidates. Some of these subject area tests include multiple exams and some include a pedagogy exam. For example, the social studies and English exams consist of two content exams and a pedagogy exam. Most of the exams are one or two hours in duration.

The Praxis II: Principles of Learning and Teaching Assessments is designed to assess pedagogical knowledge in such areas as educational psychology, human growth and development, classroom management, instructional design and delivery techniques, evaluation and assessment, and other preparation. The assessments are divided into early childhood, grades K–6, grades 5–9, and grades 7–12 to reflect the different levels of licensure. Each assessment includes four case histories each followed by three short-answer questions about the case and 24 multiple-choice questions. The multiple-choice questions cover candidate knowledge in the following areas:

Students as Learners
    Student Development and the Learning Process
    Students as Diverse Learners
    Student Motivation and the Learning Environment

Instruction and Assessment
    Instructional Strategies
    Planning Instruction
    Assessment Strategies

Communication Techniques
    Basic, effective verbal and nonverbal communication techniques
    Effect of cultural and gender differences on communications in the classroom
    Types of communications and interactions that can stimulate discussion in different ways for particular purposes

Profession and Community
    The Reflective Practitioner
    The Larger Community

Because you will probably be required to demonstrate competency relative to the INTASC standards during your initial teacher preparatory program and perhaps to the NBPTS in an advanced program, I will focus on these standards throughout this text. I will also indicate how the text content relates to sections of the Praxis II: Principles of Learning and Teaching Assessments. Before turning to the next section, complete Expansion Activity: Becoming a Teacher, which will let you explore your self-concept of teaching.

EXPANSION ACTIVITY

Becoming a
Teacher

After some thinking, write a personal statement about the following. What kind of teacher do you want to become? How will the NCATE standards, INTASC standards, **and the NBPTS help you become that teacher? What strengths do you want to have? What potential weaknesses might you need to overcome?**

APPLY AND REFLECT: Most states now require that prospective teachers pass licensure/certification exams. Is this a good idea? Should individuals with only a degree and no teacher preparation training be allowed to teach by simply passing a test?

Licensure/Certification

Licensure/certification is the process by which teachers receive state permission to teach. The licensure of teachers is as old as the nation. Licensing is generally viewed as absolutely essential to ensure the quality of our teaching force. The goal is to have a fully qualified licensed teacher in every classroom.

Licensure regulations vary a great deal among states. Some states offer relatively few licenses, others offer many. Most states require applicants to pass examinations like the Praxis II or a state-developed exam before applicants can be granted a regular license. Although some states will grant a temporary license to an applicant licensed in another state, the applicant often has to fulfill additional requirements, such as a specific test or additional courses, to obtain a regular license. Due to the growing teacher shortage, however, some state policymakers are mandating that their state accept out-of-state licenses without additional subsequent requirements. Others have mandated that their state accept certificates issued by the National Board for Professional Teaching Standards (NBPTS).

Clearly, many changes can be anticipated in the licensing of teachers in the next few years. Indeed, most states are experimenting with and implementing alternative means of authorizing people to teach. Many mid-career professionals are showing interest in pursuing second careers in education. These older applicants have a college education and life experiences that make them attractive as teachers. Requirements for alternative routes to teacher licensure vary greatly with some preparing excellent teachers, whereas others are preparing weak teachers who leave the profession after a short stay.

Preparing quality teachers is a complex and challenging process. Table 1.2 summarizes the components of the process. Review the summary and complete the Review, Extension, and Reflective Exercise 1.2.

Teachers and school personnel must meet state licensure/certification requirements.

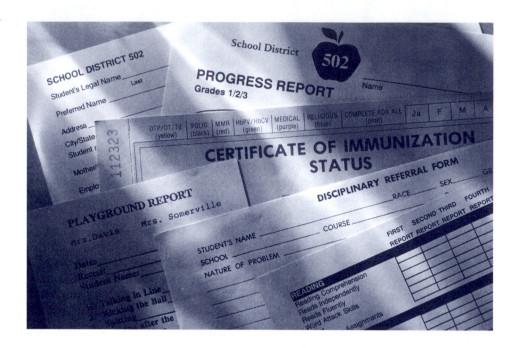

TABLE 1.2 **National Teacher Standards**	
Agency	**Description**
National Council for Accreditation of Teacher Education (NCATE)	National agency that accredits colleges, schools, or departments of education
Teacher Education Accreditation Council (TEAC)	National agency that accredits colleges, schools, or departments of education
National Board for Professional Teaching Standards (NBPTS)	Independent, nonpartisan organization created to advance the quality of teaching and learning
Interstate New Teacher Assessment and Support Consortium (INTASC)	National standards created to form a basis for licensing and preparing beginning teachers
Educational Testing Service (ETS)	Praxis Series tests developed to assist state education agencies in making licensing decisions

A good understanding of teaching will greatly facilitate one of the major missions of education—literacy. To fully realize this mission will be difficult, but along with a greater knowledge of all aspects of education comes success. Now, let's develop a teaching model to complete the picture of effective teaching.

Review, Extension, and Reflective Exercise 1.2

Name and describe the professional standards for preparing teachers.

Connections to INTASC Standards:

• Standard 9: Reflection and Professional Development. The teacher must be a reflective practitioner who continually evaluates the effects of his or her choices and actions on others (students, parents, and other professionals in the learning community) and who actively seeks out opportunities to grow professionally.

Connections to the NBPTS:

• Proposition 5: Teachers must be members of learning communities.

Review

• What is the purpose of NCATE and TEAC?
• What are INTASC standards and the NBPTS?

Reflection

• What are the assessment requirements for teacher candidates to be licensed in your state? Does your state require teacher candidates to pass a test series? Is it a state-developed test or the Praxis Series? Do you think teacher candidates should be held accountable and required to pass a test to be licensed?

VIEW FROM THE CLASSROOM

What do teachers think about teaching? Teacher survey results relative to topics presented in this chapter are expressed below. Review these results and discuss with classmates.

Are you very satisfied with teaching as a career?

Yes	70%
No	30%

Before you began your teaching career, what do you wish you would have known?

More strategies for behavior	33%
The amount of time required for lesson preparation and paperwork	30%
How quickly expectations placed on schools would increase	16%
The nature of school administration	15%
How difficult it is for schools to change	5%

Look back on your own education. Do children today get a better or worse education than you did?

Much better (I wish I was in school now.)	34%
Much worse (I feel concern for today's students.)	25%
Slightly better (They have a slight advantage over what I had.)	23%
Slightly worse (Education needs a change for the better.)	11%
Neutral (Education is of comparable quality.)	7%

How has the "No Child Left Behind Act" affected your teaching duties?

It has made my job more difficult.	80%
It has had no effect on my job.	12%
It has made my job easier.	7%

The most successful method for involving parents/guardians in your classroom has been:

Having them volunteer or visit during the school day	30%
Allowing for an open classroom	20%
Holding family evening events	18%
Creating a periodic print newsletter	14%
Scheduling appointments	11%
Creating a periodic electronic newsletter	7%

How do you think schooling will change in the next decade?

More reliance on technology in all areas	58%
More home schooling	23%
Longer school days with longer school year	16%
No change	2%

SOURCE: Excerpted from *Teach-nology*, available at www.teach-nology.com/poll

THE PUBLIC VIEW OF EDUCATION

What does the public think of our schools? Public trends and attitudes toward education tend to give education a high national importance. Review these results and discuss with classmates.

What do you think are the biggest problems with which the public schools of your community must deal?

Lack of financial support/funding/money	25%
Lack of discipline/more control	16%
Overcrowded schools	14%
Use of drugs/dope	9%
Difficulty getting good teachers/quality teachers	5%
Standards/quality/basics	4%
Fighting/violence/gangs	4%
Low pay for teachers	4%

Do you think your local public school system has a hard time GETTING good teachers?

Yes, has a hard time	61%
No, does not	37%
Don't know	2%

Do you think your local public school system has a hard time KEEPING good teachers?

Yes, has a hard time	66%
No, does not	31%
Don't know	2%

Do you think salaries for teachers in your community are too high, too low, or just about right?

Too high	6%
Too low	59%
Just about right	33%
Don't know	2%

What do you think would be the most important factor in improving public education?

Better pay for teachers	13%
Smaller classes	33%

(Continued)

THE PUBLIC VIEW OF EDUCATION (Continued)

More innovative teaching methods	10%
A return to basic teaching methods	11%
More parental involvement	28%
Other	2%

How often are you in contact with your child's teacher?

Every day	30%
Every week	28%
A couple of times a month	26%
Once every three months	10%
Once every six months or less	3%

SOURCE: Excerpted from *BabyCenter*, available at www.parentcenter.babycenter.com and *The 35th Annual Phi Delta Kappa/Gallup Poll of the Public's Attitudes Toward the Public Schools* (2003) by Lowell C. Rose and Alec M. Gallup, available at www.pdkintl.org/kappan/k0309pol.htm

Summary

It is possible to train someone to be an effective teacher.

Teaching

- Teaching can be defined as the actions of someone who is trying to assist others to reach their fullest potential in all aspects of development.
- Debate continues regarding whether teaching is an art or a science and what is effective teaching.
- Effective teaching is an art as well as a science.
- Teaching requires a repertoire of skills and the ability to put these skills to use.
- Effectiveness depends on the subject, students, and environmental conditions.
- Danielson (1996) suggests four skill areas are needed for effective teaching: (1) quality planning and preparation, (2) preparation of a positive classroom environment, (3) use of proven instructional techniques, and (4) professional behavior.
- Constructivism focuses on actively involving students in their own learning. Students construct their own meanings.
- Time mandated by the state must be allocated both to instructional and noninstructional uses. Instructional time must be organized so that time on task is maximized.
- Time on task must be turned into academic learning time (performance on assigned tasks at 80 percent or better) for teachers to be truly effective.
- Quality instruction requires that teachers structure instruction around appropriate content, materials and methods, and interaction patterns.
- Learning can be defined as a change in an individual's capacity for performance as a result of experience.

- Forty-nine states have adopted state-mandated testing.
- The No Child Left Behind Act was designed and enacted to help low-income and minority students perform at the same achievement level as their peers.
- Parent and community involvement is an important factor in improving the academic learning of students.

Professional Teaching Standards

- Research shows that what teachers know, do, and value has a significant influence on the nature, extent, and rate of student learning.
- Several groups and organizations have been involved in professionalizing teaching.
- The National Council for Accreditation of Teacher Education (NCATE) and the Teacher Education Accreditation Council (TEAC) were organized to accredit teacher education programs.
- The National Board for Professional Teaching Standards (NBPTS) was organized to advance the quality of teaching and learning. The majority of the NBPTS board of directors consists of classroom teachers.
- The Interstate New Teacher Assessment and Support Consortium (INTASC) created broad standards to serve as a basis for licensing and preparing beginning teachers.
- The Educational Testing Service (ETS) developed the Praxis Series to assist state education agencies in making licensing decisions.
- Licensure/certification is the process by which teachers receive state permission to teach.
- Licensure regulations vary a great deal among states.

Discussion Questions and Activities

1. **The challenge.** Think about the grade level you expect to teach. Consider at least two ways that your classroom at that grade level is likely to be challenging. Write about how you will cope with this.
2. **Teaching knowledge.** Some teaching knowledge is gained only through experiences and cannot be found in a textbook or in a college course. Do you agree with this statement? Give some examples.
3. **School and classroom time.** How could you improve academic instructional time? Academic time on task? What procedures and/or rules would you implement for changing activities or starting (and ending) your class to increase instructional time?
4. **Personal traits.** Make a list of personal traits you possess that will assist you in teaching at your planned grade level. If you plan to be an elementary level teacher, compare your list with a future secondary teacher and if you are planning to be a secondary teacher, compare your list with a future elementary teacher. Are there differences? In what areas do differences exist?
5. **Teaching all students.** Remember that a teacher's job is to teach all students and assume an attitude that all students can learn. Research techniques and strategies that can be used to accomplish this task. Sources of information include the library, the Internet, current journals, and recent books.

Connection With the Field

1. **Classroom observation.** Observe a kindergarten, elementary, middle school, and high school classroom and focus on teaching and learning effectiveness, the use of classroom time, and the characteristics of students. Collect and analyze data with regard to your observations.
2. **Teachers' view of effective teaching and learning.** Interview several teachers. How do they define effective teaching and learning? How do they know when it has occurred in their classrooms? How would they measure effective teaching and learning? Are there differences at the elementary and secondary levels?
3. **Principals' view of effective teaching and learning.** Interview two elementary and two secondary school principals. How do they view effective teaching and learning? Is their view the same as that of the teachers? If not, which view do you tend to support?
4. **Evaluation of effective teaching and learning.** Visit at least two local school districts. Do these school districts evaluate their teachers? If so, who does the evaluation? What criteria are used? What do teachers think of the evaluative process? What do you think of the criteria? Would you want to be evaluated using the criteria?
5. **Parent and community involvement.** Interview several teachers from local schools about how they foster parent and community involvement. Try to visit with a kindergarten teacher, an elementary teacher, a middle school teacher, and a high school teacher. Summarize your discoveries.

Praxis II Connection

The following test preparation exercises are intended to help you prepare for the Praxis II: Principles of Learning and Teaching Assessments or the state-developed exam that may be required by your teacher education preparatory program and state certification or licensing. These exercises will give you direct access to pedagogical knowledge that will be expected of you on the Praxis II exam and other pedagogical exams that may be required at the end of your teacher preparation program.

Case Histories Format

The Educational Testing Service (ETS) has developed four Tests at a Glance sites to give teacher education candidates practice with the Praxis II: Principles of Learning and Teaching (PLT) Assessments. These sites have been designed for early childhood (test 0521), grades K–6 (test 0522), grades 5–9 (test 0523), and grades 7–12 (test 0524) candidates. Access the site below that corresponds to the grade levels you expect to teach. Review the site and complete the site sample exercises. This will give you the opportunity to become familiar with the PLT format.

PLT: Early Childhood:
ftp://ftp.ets.org/pub/tandl/0521.pdf

PLT: Grades K–6:
ftp://ftp.ets.org/pub/tandl/0522.pdf

PLT: Grades 5–9:
ftp://ftp.ets.org/pub/tandl/0523.pdf

PLT: Grades 7–12:
ftp://ftp.ets.org/pub/tandl/0524.pdf

Topic Connections

1. Teacher Professionalism (IV. A1)

Practicing teachers can access various professional organizations for professional development and learning resources for their classroom. Take a look at the appropriate websites below for the area you expect to teach. If the appropriate site is not listed, do a Web search to locate the applicable site. Summarize your findings relative to their approach to professionalism and learning.

- National Council of Teachers of English (www.ncte.org)
- International Reading Association (www.reading.org)
- National Science Teachers Association (www.nsta.org)
- National Council for the Social Studies (www.ncss.org)
- National Council of Teachers of Mathematics (www.nctm.org)
- National Association for the Education of Young Children (Early Childhood) (www.naeyc.org)
- Association for Childhood Education International (Elementary Education) (www.udel.edu/bateman/acei/standhp.htm)
- American Council on the Teaching of Foreign Languages (www.actfl.org)
- National Middle School Association (www.nmsa.org/services/teacher_prep/index.htm)
- American Alliance for Health, Physical Education, Recreation, and Dance (www.aahperd.org/naspe/template.cfm?template=programs-ncate.html)
- Council for Exceptional Children (www.cec.sped.org/ps/)

2. Teacher Professionalism (IV. A2)

Review the professional journals applicable to the grade level and/or subject area(s) you expect to teach. How will they help you grow as a professional?

3. Reflective Practices (IV. A3)

Read Joan M. Ferraro's *Reflective Practice and Professional Development,* which can be accessed on-line (www.ed.gov/databases/ERIC_Digests/ed449120.html). Summarize the benefits derived from reflective practices.

4. Individualized Education Plan (IEP) (I. B3)

Explain the purpose of an IEP. Identify the components of an IEP and the information that should be included in the typical IEP.

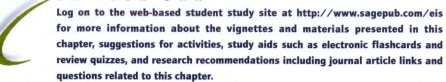

ON YOUR OWN

Log on to the web-based student study site at http://www.sagepub.com/eis for more information about the vignettes and materials presented in this chapter, suggestions for activities, study aids such as electronic flashcards and review quizzes, and research recommendations including journal article links and questions related to this chapter.

2

PLANNING AND
ORGANIZING FOR TEACHING

*The extent to which you are able to transform
your "self-concern" into "other-concern" will determine
your effectiveness in getting others to follow along.*

ANONYMOUS

OVERVIEW

Good teaching requires planning. A six-step cyclic teaching model is presented to assist you in this most important planning process.

The curriculum is one of the most important ingredients in a school program. Indeed, the curriculum often makes or breaks a school. Therefore, a school curriculum must be identified and selected with care.

An effective education is achieved when the learning situation is accurately diagnosed as to the appropriateness of the curriculum to be taught. In other words, content must be selected for the appropriate entry level of students. This selection process cannot occur by chance: it must thoughtfully weigh the needs of both the students and the society, and it must be based on the structure of the subject itself.

Diagnosis of needs requires that information be collected. Such information can be obtained from students' cumulative records, from personal contact, and from other concerned parties. Whatever the sources, it is important to seek such input prior to planning a course.

The final decision as to what will be taught in the classroom will be up to you as the classroom teacher. In some cases, assistance in making curriculum decisions will be available from curriculum committees or from curriculum specialists. In most cases, however, you alone will make the curriculum decisions.

Once students' entry level has been determined, courses must be planned. Specific units must be formed, sequenced, and time allotments made for the units. These plans must remain flexible so adjustments can be made as the year progresses.

American classrooms are changing. Teachers must now plan for a multicultural classroom. The elimination of racism, sexism, and ethnic prejudice has become a challenge for our schools. Moreover, not all students are the same, which calls for differentiation of instruction to some extent.

The use of technology in the classroom offers a viable alternative to traditional classroom instruction. The use of computers in the classroom has proven to enhance student motivation to learn.

OBJECTIVES

After completing your study of Chapter 2, you should be able to do the following:

1. Describe the six steps to teaching excellence.
2. Define *curriculum* and describe the different kinds of curricula.
3. Describe the *backward design model* for curriculum design.
4. Differentiate between the initial and continuous phase of diagnosis, as well as sources for information for each phase.
5. Identify the sources and tools that can be used in supplying diagnostic information for making educational decisions.
6. Outline and explain the influences of students' abilities, society issues, the subject structure, and brain research on the school curriculum.
7. List and explain the areas that must be addressed in planning a course for the year.
8. Discuss the changing nature of American classrooms.
9. Explain how technology can be used in the classroom.

Soon you will have a classroom of students to get to know, lessons to launch, routines to establish, and a host of other activities to get underway. To do all this, you must be organized. You will soon learn that organization is central to effective teaching. Let's begin our look at organizing for teaching with a model for good teaching.

A Model of Teaching

Good teaching requires that you make a constant series of professional decisions that affect the probability that students will learn. Thus, good teaching is a multifaceted quest to help students achieve mastery of a subject. Basically, this quest is a six-step cyclic process. The six sequential steps in a model of effective teaching follow:

1. Diagnosing the learning situation
2. Planning the course
3. Planning the instruction
4. Guiding learning activities
5. Evaluating learning
6. Following up

This sequential teaching process is illustrated in Figure 2.1.

Figure 2.1

A Model of Teaching: The model is both sequential and cyclic in nature.

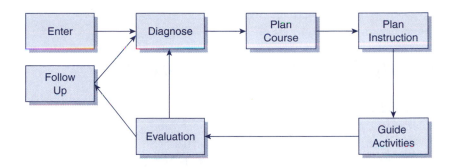

Step 1 involves selecting the curriculum to be taught. This selection process is based upon the needs of students, the society, and the subject. Essentially you must diagnose the situation to find out what students already know. You may want to strengthen some areas and reteach some concepts.

Once the situation has been diagnosed, Step 2 is to plan and outline exactly what will be taught in the course. That is, you identify the curriculum areas to be addressed and the amount of time allotted to the areas outlined.

In Step 3, unit and daily plans are developed. In other words, you decide exactly what students should know and plan the activities that will bring the desired results. Essentially, objectives are written and the instructional strategy is selected.

Step 4 involves teaching the planned activities. You guide the students through the planned sequence of activities, using your knowledge of students, learning theory, and effective teaching techniques.

In Step 5, you determine whether you have accomplished the instructional intent; that is, you must evaluate students' mastery of the specifics taught. The results of the evaluation tell you what to do next. If students show mastery, you start the next planning cycle (Step 1). If mastery is not demonstrated, follow-up will be needed.

The follow-up (Step 6) can be a relatively brief summary of the material covered, while at other times extensive reteaching may be necessary. The extent of your follow-up will depend upon the findings of the evaluation analysis.

As you can see, achieving teaching excellence is a major undertaking. The steps in the model of good teaching will be highlighted in subsequent chapters.

APPLY AND REFLECT: Good teachers plan well and are organized. Does this sound like you? Do you plan well and are you organized? What area(s) do you need to work on?

The Curriculum

What is curriculum? That is, what exactly is the curriculum of a typical elementary or secondary school? Schools are similar in many respects, but they also vary in some important ways. The curriculum, student body, and teaching strategies of a

REFLECTIONS ON TEACHER PRACTICE

Computing in the Classroom

1. Should computer time be used as a reward for academic achievement and/or personal behavior?
2. Is the Internet a viable resource for classroom teachers? How can teachers use the Internet to provide better instruction?

I recommend task computing as an effective way to use computers in your classroom. You will be using your computers to enhance the curriculum and your students' learning. Please do not use the computer as a reward for early finishers and good behavior (the strugglers and behavior problems might be the students who need computer time the most). I just completed my thesis on how this valuable form of technology is being ineffectively used in so many classrooms. Basically, I found that poorer and lower-ability kids get less classroom computer time (and often use it for drill and practice) and richer and higher-ability kids get more classroom computer time (and are doing media presentations and problem solving).

Think of the computer as another area you need to plan for weekly. Plan daily or weekly tasks that every student needs to accomplish. For example, they may have to visit the website of an author whose novel you are reading and find five interesting facts about him or her. The next day, they might take that information and construct a paragraph in Microsoft Word. The next task might be to copy the author's picture onto their document and print it (or e-mail it to the teacher). There are great math sites with problems of the day or week. I especially like Math Maven's Mysteries, where the students read a story and problem solve. The science-related sites are incredible. The possibilities are endless. With task computing, your computers will be in use more time than they are idle. Check out this website: www.framingham.k12.ma.us/k5/task.htm.

—JOAN, *elementary school teacher*

SOURCE: Reprinted with permission from ProTeacher, a professional community for elementary school teachers (http://www.proteacher.net)

school will reflect the values, attitudes, beliefs, and goals of the community in which it exists. If we define the **curriculum** as all the learning, intended and unintended, that takes place under the sponsorship of the school, then we have set the stage for a broad interpretation of curriculum, and of schooling. Specialists have suggested, however, several different definitions for the term *curriculum* (Armstrong, 2002; Oliva, 2000). For our purposes, let us define **curriculum** as all the planned and unplanned learning experiences that students undergo while in a school setting.

The teacher's responsibility involves selecting the curriculum on both a long-term and short-term basis. To accomplish this task, the teacher must consult a variety of sources, including state curriculum frameworks, district curriculum guides, school guidelines, and relevant adopted textbooks. These plans become the blueprint for instruction.

Eisner (1985) suggests that schools teach more than they intend. Some of what is taught is formal (planned), whereas other material conveyed is not. The **formal**

curriculum consists of intentional learning experiences. Instruction has been carefully planned; resources—including money, space, time, and personnel—have been allocated for the accomplishment of curricular goals; curricular plans have been written in documents that are readily available; the curriculum is evidenced in the lessons taught in the classroom; and the learning experience is formally evaluated. The formal curriculum encompasses the sequence of courses and objectives mandated by the state, the curriculum guide developed by the school district, the textbooks used in the classrooms, and the array of classes available for students. Based on the framework established by the state, the formal curriculum generally derives from local curriculum development efforts, with curriculum guides being developed that assist teachers with implementation. Figure 2.2 illustrates the levels of curriculum-planning involvement as it flows from the state to the classroom. As illustrated, the ultimate goal of the curriculum is to bring about learning and growth.

Some of the formal curriculum is determined at the federal level. Laws like the Individuals With Disabilities Education Act (IDEA) dictate the degree and nature of service to be provided for children with special needs. Court cases also have further defined the curriculum. For instance, placement of limited-English-speaking students

Figure 2.2

Levels of Curriculum Planning

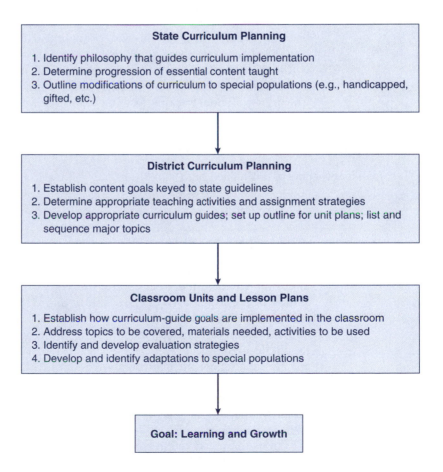

in classes for the mentally retarded on the basis of intelligence tests administered in English has been declared illegal by the Supreme Court.

Local concerns can have a tremendous impact on the formal curriculum. For example, a rash of teenage suicides led one school district to increase the number and type of counselors available to students. A rural area would likely resist eliminating home economics and agricultural courses in the face of financial cutbacks but might be willing to sacrifice a vocal-music program. A high school with a nearby vocational school may choose not to offer industrial arts or business classes.

Whatever the curricular imperatives for a given school, they are formalized in documents available to the school's patrons. It is the formal curriculum that the teachers and administrators spell out when they tell parents exactly what their children are required to know. The **hidden curriculum** is sometimes referred to as the "unintended" curriculum. The hidden curriculum consists of learning experiences—both positive and negative—that produce changes in students' attitudes, beliefs, and values but are not part of the formal curriculum. Some students learn negative behaviors and attitudes, such as how to cheat, how to dislike school, and how to manipulate adults. Still others learn positive behaviors and attitudes, such as how to learn effectively and how to cooperate with others. As you can see, you must guard against communicating and modeling undesirable behaviors and attitudes. Negative behaviors and attitudes are often easily learned by students.

The hidden curriculum often reflects societal values, such as rewarding great success, ignoring average performance, and criticizing or punishing failure. The social "pecking order"—in terms of gender, language, cultural differences, and socioeconomic status—is an inherent part of the hidden curriculum. The control mechanisms within the school and the classroom are part of the hidden curriculum. The distribution of resources that support the school curriculum is part of the hidden curriculum. The decisions about tracking, both for student and teacher assignments, convey messages about relative worth and, as such, are part of the hidden curriculum.

APPLY AND REFLECT: Recognize that there is often a hidden curriculum being taught in schools. Can you identify some of this hidden curriculum?

Curriculum Mapping

There can be a large gap between what is specified in a district curriculum guideline and what is actually taught in classrooms. The gap can represent a challenge to personnel trying to improve the curriculum in a district. Unless they know what is really being taught, they are working in the dark. *Curriculum mapping* can help.

Curriculum mapping is a technique for gathering data on what is actually being taught through the course of a school year (Jacobs, 1997). When operationalized, all teachers at a school enter information about their classroom curricula for the year into a computer database. Teachers enter major activities related to three types of data: content, specific skills, and assessments. The process should be totally nonjudgmental about the teacher's styles, techniques, and materials. By carefully analyzing the maps, schools can detect and fix curriculum gaps, address repetitions in the curriculum, and refine scope and sequence connections. The school can also

Instruction should be based on accurate student information.

identify potential areas for curriculum integration, better align their assessments with state and district standards, and even consider ways to upgrade teaching strategies and materials.

Backward Curriculum Design

Wiggins and McTighe (1998) offer an alternative approach to curriculum design. Unlike many instructional design models, the Wiggins and McTighe *backward design model* is well suited for the academic community. The backward design model centers on the idea that the design process should begin with identifying the desired results and then "work backwards" to develop instruction rather than the traditional approach, which is to define what topics need to be covered. The Wiggins and McTighe framework identifies three main stages (see Figure 2.3):

- Stage 1: Identify desired outcomes and results.
- Stage 2: Determine what constitutes acceptable evidence of competency in the outcomes and results (assessment).
- Stage 3: Plan instructional strategies and learning experiences that bring students to these competency levels.

Stage 1. Identify Desired Results

In traditional design models, Stage 1 would be defining goals and objectives. Wiggins and McTighe (1998), however, ask that teachers identify not only course goals and objective, but also the *enduring understanding. Enduring understanding* is the learning that should endure over the long term. Backward design uses a

Figure 2.3
Backward Design Process

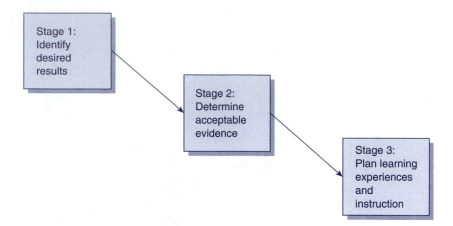

question format rather than measurable objectives. These questions focus on the line of inquiry leading to the desired learning. The desired learning is determined by national standards and state standards or benchmarks. These standards and benchmarks are turned into question form. Possible examples are "Is there enough water to go around?" or "Does art reflect culture or shape it?" Asking such inquiry-based questions facilitates the students finding the answers.

The backward approach to curricular design departs from common school practice. Instead of starting with a textbook to determine the curriculum, the teacher starts with the end—the desired results (goals, standards, or benchmarks). The curriculum is derived from the evidence of learning (performance) called for by the standard or benchmark.

Stage 2. Assessment

The second stage in the design process is to define what forms of assessment will demonstrate that students have acquired the desired knowledge, understanding, and skill. Wiggins and McTighe (1998) define three types of assessment: performance task (an authentic task of understanding), criteria referenced assessment (quiz, test), and unprompted assessment and self-assessment (observations, dialogues, etc.).

Stage 3. Plan Learning Experience and Instruction

In this stage, it is determined what sequence of teaching and learning experiences will equip students to develop and demonstrate the desired understanding. This will include the research-based repertoire of learning teaching strategies. These are the activities students will do during the unit and what resources and materials will be needed.

APPLY AND REFLECT: Many experienced teachers use the backward curriculum model.

Can you see a rationale for this decision?

Curriculum Reform

The curriculum taught in American schools has changed in recent years. In general, reform efforts can be seen as focusing on either a subject-centered approach to curriculum planning or a student-centered one. The pendulum has swung from one extreme to the other in an attempt to create either relevant or rigorous content for students at all levels within the K–12 system. New views of learning and teaching require changes in other components of schooling, namely, curriculum and assessment. The new curriculum and teaching strategies ask that students not only master factual information but also learn to apply that information by reasoning and solving novel problems.

Recent studies of the brain and how it learns have also given educators new insights about teaching and learning. New findings indicate, for example, that the idea of learners being predominantly left- or right-brained is misleading. The brain is much more complex than that. We do not operate in one function for science and mathematics and another for the fine arts.

Brain research indicates that the brain needs six to twelve glasses of water per day. Without enough water, we don't learn as well. Hannaford (1995) identifies dehydration as a common classroom problem that can lead to impaired learning. Researchers further suggest that the school environment should challenge brain development in nonthreatening ways by making use of the arts for teaching thinking and for building emotive expressiveness and memory. Findings indicate that physical activity is also essential in promoting the growth of mental functions. Jensen (1998) suggests that learning is enhanced by daily stretching, walking, and dancing, as well as other physical movement.

Researchers agree that an optimal learning environment requires comfortable temperatures and protection from distracting sounds. Noise and physical discomfort often send distress messages to the brain, which limits the brain's normal operations. Researchers suggest that the significance of the learning environment cannot be underestimated. The brain learns faster in challenging, creative, accommodating, relaxed, and healthy environments. Suggested teaching strategies that enhance brain-based learning include the use of manipulatives, active learning, field trips, guest speakers, and real-life projects that allow students to use many learning styles and multiple intelligences. Integrated and interdisciplinary curriculum also reinforces brain-based learning, because the brain can better make connections when material is presented in an integrated way, rather than as isolated bits of information.

Curriculum Structure

Generally, a school district has the flexibility to pattern its curriculum any way it chooses (Oliva, 2000). Typically, these organizational patterns tend to range between the extremes of being subject-centered on one side to student-centered on the other (see Figure 2.4). The subject-centered curricular organization tends to be content-oriented; conversely, if a curriculum follows a student-centered pattern, it is learner-oriented. In general, most districts organize their curriculum (1) as an eclectic combination of several patterns, (2) with most programs somewhere toward the middle of the continuum, and (3) with a good deal of variety from class to class and teacher to teacher. The organization of the curriculum is influenced strongly by the district's philosophical position on the purpose of education.

Figure 2.4
Curriculum Patterns

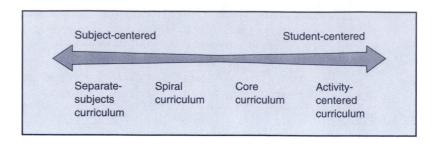

Subject-Centered Curriculum

The **subject-centered curriculum** is still the most widely used curriculum pattern in United States schools. It regards learning primarily as cognitive development and the acquisition of knowledge and information. With this approach, all the subjects for instruction are separated. In general, the content areas are taught in isolation, with no attempt at integration.

The subject-centered curriculum places emphasis on oral discourse and extensive explanations. It expects teachers to plan instruction before teaching begins and to organize it around the content, and it assumes that certain content should be taught to all students. The subject-centered curriculum usually consists of a study of specific facts and ideas. The teaching methods usually include the direct strategies: lectures, discussions, and questions (see Chapter 7).

The most widely used subject-centered curriculum is the separate-subjects curriculum. The separate-subjects curriculum content is divided into fairly discrete areas of study—reading, language arts, algebra, history, composition, chemistry, literature, and so forth. The required subjects (general education) usually make up most of the school program, and students are given little choice in selecting courses. Some districts, however, are giving students more opportunity to select electives.

Some feel that the subject-centered curriculum does not adequately foster critical or creative thinking or develop an understanding of societal issues. This approach often places emphasis on the memorization of facts and ideas, and moreover, tends to focus on the past. For example, social studies instruction often consists of the study of the past and the related facts.

Supporters and defenders of a subject-centered curriculum argue that the approach has stood the test of time and that not all subjects can be studied at once—as other curriculum approaches propose to do. They further argue that study cannot be all-inclusive: There is simply too much information, and it must be ordered as well as segmented.

A second type of subject-centered curriculum is referred to as a spiral curriculum. The spiral curriculum is organized around the material to be taught. It is similar to the separate-subjects pattern but differs in two notable ways. First, the spiral curriculum puts more emphasis on the concepts and generalizations; in other words, it emphasizes the structure of knowledge. Second, it is designed to fit sequentially with students' developmental thinking stages.

Student-Centered Curriculum

A **student-centered curriculum** can be described as an activity curriculum. In effect, a student-centered curriculum focuses on student needs, interests, and activities. In its purest form, a student-centered curriculum operates with students as the center of the learning process. Activities are planned jointly by the teacher and students. The teacher is seen as a stimulator and facilitator of student activity. The student-centered curriculum is the most appropriate curriculum pattern for the elementary school level but has never secured a firm foothold at the secondary level.

One kind of student-centered curriculum is the core curriculum. The core curriculum is a student-centered pattern with several subject-centered characteristics. Typically, it combines subjects into broad fields of study. This pattern of organization is most frequently found in middle and junior high schools. The subjects most often combined in core curricula are social studies and language arts, mathematics and science, and social studies and science.

Still another type of student-centered curriculum is called activity-centered curriculum. Like the core curriculum pattern, the activity-centered curriculum is patterned around the needs and interests of students. The content coverage, however, is more flexible than in the core curriculum. Learning by doing and problem solving are emphasized. As such, detailed lessons often are not planned, because the teacher cannot anticipate what student interests will surface or where their inquiry will take them.

The subject-centered curriculum and the student-centered curriculum patterns represent two opposite ends of a curriculum continuum. Table 2.1 contrasts the two curriculum patterns.

Curriculum Integration

Curriculum integration is one of several reforms designed to enhance the quality of student learning. **Curriculum integration** is a form of teaching and learning that draws upon the knowledge and skills of a variety of discipline areas as they become necessary in problem solving (Beane, 1995). It is argued that such a strategy better reflects real-world problem solving than does single-subject instruction. It is maintained that an integrated curriculum provides holistic, problem-based learning that leads to a greater ability to make connections and to solve problems.

TABLE 2.1 **Contrasting Curriculum Patterns**	
Subject-Centered Curriculum	**Student-Centered Curriculum**
Focus on subject matter	Centered on learner needs
Centered on subjects	Centered on cooperative determination of subject matter
Subject matter organized by teacher before instruction	Emphasis on variability in exposure to learning
Emphasis on facts, knowledge, and information	Emphasis on skills
Generally lower-level learning	Emphasis on immediate meanings of learning
Emphasis on uniformity of exposure	Emphasis on indirect strategies
Emphasis on direct strategies	

Ross and Olsen (1993) offer five models for implementing an integrated curriculum. Each provides foundation for the model that follows.

1. *Single-Subject Integration:* A teacher presents a single subject and requires students to solve real problems.
2. *The Coordinated Model:* Two or more teachers cooperate in teaching integrated single subjects.
3. *The Integrated Core Model:* A single teacher remains with students for two or three periods. A teacher might teach science in the context of math or social studies as the "core" around which the rest of the school day is planned.
4. *The Integrated Double Core Model:* Two teachers teach integrated "cores" to the students. One might teach math in the context of science, while the other teaches language arts within the context of social studies.
5. *The Self-Contained Core Model:* A single teacher with multiple credentials teaches one group of students all day within a single meaningful context.

Each of these five models offers teachers useful, logical, and flexible ways to organize and offer an integrated curriculum and engage students in meaningful and functional learning activities.

Curriculum Selection

Students and, ultimately, society will be the consumers of the school curriculum. As such, both deserve to supply input as to what should be taught. Moreover, the structure of a subject often dictates the content to be taught, as well as the sequence of teaching that content. The well-planned curriculum, then, will take into account student and societal **needs** as well as the subject itself. Keep in mind, however, that students, society, and the subject structure are influenced by other factors, as depicted in Figure 2.5.

Diagnostic information gives curriculum developers valuable data that can be interpreted for a variety of purposes. Most frequently, however, such information is used strictly for establishing and checking standards of achievement. Achievement test scores, for example, are often used for nothing more than making comparisons of district group scores with national norms; renewed instructional emphasis is then placed on those areas found to be below the national norms. Such use of achievement test scores is the narrowest interpretation and use of diagnostic data.

Needs of Students

As noted in Chapter 1, the more you know about students the easier it will be to bring about desired learning. Thus, you must have the ability to identify your students' needs. But, how do you go about diagnosing students' needs, especially when you usually won't meet them until the start of the school year? Diagnosis is a two-phase process, with an initial phase and a continuous phase. The initial phase takes place prior to the arrival of students in your classroom, whereas the continuous phase follows their arrival.

Figure 2.5
Influences on
Curriculum Selection

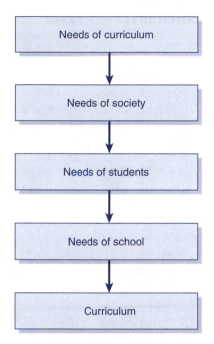

A more enriching
classroom curriculum is
one that supplements
the textbook content
with issues related to
student interests.

Initial Diagnosis Phase

Initial **diagnostic evaluations** are usually administered prior to the beginning of the school year to determine students' entry level (readiness) in curriculum areas. These diagnoses provide the information needed for the correct placement of students in tracks and courses.

Diagnostic information generally comes from two sources: performance in past coursework and performance on achievement tests. Too frequently, students are placed solely on the basis of performance in a completed class or on the basis of grades received in past related courses. Such procedures may lead to incorrect placement if performance information is incorrectly analyzed. For example, a teacher's bias or high expectations may lead to unrealistic placement. Moreover, grades can often give misleading information as to overall ability.

One critical piece of diagnostic information all teachers need is their students' reading levels. If your potential students have reading difficulties, you need to secure materials that will aid them with their comprehension and understanding.

Sometimes, teachers gather diagnostic information with a pretest at the beginning of a unit. The information provided by such tests tells the teacher where to start instruction. At times, it may be necessary to teach or review needed prerequisite skills before the beginning of a new unit.

As a teacher with five or six different classes or preparations per day, you will often not have much time to determine students' entry level. Indeed, sometimes the only way to obtain diagnostic information on students will be to ask fellow teachers. At other times, you may even have to rely on intuition at the beginning of a unit, until you can obtain more accurate information as the unit is being taught.

APPLY AND REFLECT: Teachers should collect as much information as possible on students' entry levels prior to the start of the school year. Do you see a good reason for doing so? How would you go about getting needed information?

Continuous Diagnosis Phase

Diagnosis should be a never-ending process. After you begin a unit of study, the original diagnosis should be revised as you glean more information from students' performance on oral and written work. As you note individual student deficiencies, you should plan remedial work for bringing each student up to the level of his or her peers. Some students may need even more assistance than you can provide. At such a time, you should seek outside assistance from specialists, if available.

APPLY AND REFLECT: You should seek professional assistance when students have needs that are beyond your abilities to handle. Can you think of situations that you might encounter in the classroom that might result in your need for outside assistance?

No matter what form of diagnostic evaluation takes place during instruction, an evaluation should be administered at the end of each unit. The data obtained from these evaluations should be carefully analyzed when determining the need for follow-up. Follow-up is essential in keeping all students at the same level of mastery.

Diagnostic Tools

Accurate diagnosis requires an ample supply of information about students. Therefore, you need to be familiar with the different sources of diagnostic information. Because diagnostic tools will be addressed in detail in Chapter 5, only a brief overview will be presented at this time. Four particularly useful diagnostic tools follow:

1. **Cumulative record folder.** The **cumulative record** usually comprises a record of all the student's test scores (aptitude, intelligence, achievement, etc.), as well as the student's health records. In addition, this file contains various anecdotal comments made by the student's teachers over the years.
2. **Personal contact.** Working with students on an individual basis will give you the opportunity to gather considerable information. In other words, your direct observations, analysis of students' work, and conversations with students provide valuable diagnostic information.
3. **Conferences.** Many times, parents, counselors, and other teachers can serve as viable sources of diagnostic information. When problems develop, individual conferences with others who are in a position to supply pertinent information should be planned.
4. **Open-ended themes and diaries.** Giving students opportunities to write about their feelings and their in-school and out-of-school lives can lead to some valuable diagnostic data. Frequently, such information provides insight into the reasons for student problems and inadequacies.

Caution should be exercised when referring to cumulative records and conferences, so that expectations are not unduly influenced by information gleaned from these sources. In other words, take care in making sure your decisions are objective and fair. Your attitudes and expectations may serve as **self-fulfilling prophecy**—that is, students may behave in the manner consistent with your expectations, rather than in response to other factors.

Needs of Society

A curriculum must be planned not only in terms of student needs but also in terms of the needs of society in relation to students. In a complex society in which vast and rapid changes are occurring, however, establishing what demands society should make on education is a difficult task. Some curriculum planners take a more simplistic view of what skills are needed to be a fully functioning member of society: some educators feel that mastery of basic skills, preparation for a vocation or college, the ability to drive, consumer knowledge and skills, and a broad and general knowledge represent the essential curriculum for students.

Other curriculum planners, impressed with the multitude of concerns faced by society, are not sure of the role education will play in a future that is increasingly unpredictable and technological. Certainly, education for national citizenship is, to a great extent, the function of the school. Thus, education needs to embrace not only intellect but also the whole person—with the ability to think, reason, and apply.

Indeed, many curriculum planners feel that education must vitalize and address world political freedom, basic humanity, and social and economic problems. What will be required, then, are curricula that foster basic skills and include programs that provide citizenship, consumer, global, health, career, and sex education.

Issues for curricula are constantly changing in step with societal changes and new expectations. Some educators claim, however, that today's education has failed to probe deeply into the realities of society and, therefore, has essentially failed to address rapidly shifting societal forces (Boyer, 1983; Goodlad, 1984; and Sizer, 1984). These educators further argue that, too often, schools are loaded with coursework that is irrelevant to the needs of students and society.

The decline in achievement test scores has received widespread attention from the press, lawmakers, educators, and the public. Some observers have argued, based on these declining scores and other assessment efforts, that schools are failing in their primary function of educating students. Some have gone so far as to suggest that the school curriculum has ceased to be relevant and viable for our present societal needs.

Many curriculum reformers of the 1980s and 1990s now realize that schools have been asked to do too much and have attempted to define some unifying major purposes for schools. Some of these reformers have suggested that schools concentrate on students' academic competencies.

Decisions regarding the curriculum to be included in today's schools will not be easily made. Teachers and curriculum specialists must work together in developing and implementing a truly viable curriculum for a modern society. We must not be satisfied with only a good education, but we must require a great one—one that addresses the realities of our age.

Needs Derived From the Subject

Because the curriculum is also defined by the structure of a subject that students should learn and teachers should teach, a school curriculum must be in vital contact with two areas of reality: the growing body of knowledge in the field itself and the extent of understanding of the subject needed by the ordinary person. Therefore, current curricula for schools must focus on these two areas.

First and foremost, the school curriculum must be valid. But, a field of study is never static; it continues to grow. The mainstay of current curriculum—specific facts—is educationally the least valuable. Yet, specific facts should form the core of the curriculum. It is the basic ideas, concepts, and modes of thought that form the true essence of the curriculum. As Jerome Bruner (1977) suggests, it is the "structure of the subject," the "basic ideas," and the "fundamental principles" that permit understanding and make a subject meaningful. Therefore, the school curriculum should focus on carefully selected principles, which constitute the basic core of a subject. To learn the structure of a subject, in short, is to learn a body of knowledge.

Too often, a textbook is the sole source of content for a course, with discipline scholars determining what is included in the textbook. From the subject-matter perspective, it is believed that discipline scholars know best how subjects should be structured and organized in a text, as well as the relative emphasis that various topics should be given in the curriculum area. Most students, however, do not share the scholars' aspirations for becoming scientists, mathematicians, musicians, or historians. This fact should be kept in mind as a relevant curriculum is developed for implementation in the classroom. In selecting the content, you must watch out for the discipline scholars' tendency to "protect their turf" by extolling its importance.

Recently, the structure of a subject has been dictated in terms of competencies to be demonstrated by learners. For example, the state of Oklahoma has established learning outcomes for students completing all grades and subjects, whereas Arkansas has established benchmarks for all subjects and grades. These standards relate to the basic principles that undergird the different curriculum areas. Basically, the competencies and benchmarks represent the minimum knowledge and skills individual students need at their respective grade levels.

Schools must pay particular attention to their curricula, and curriculum developers need to direct their attention to three major areas of need: the learner, the society, and the subject. Keep in mind that curricula, student needs, and societies change over time—and no curriculum has reached a state of perfection. Therefore, you need to decide the appropriate content to be taught in your classroom. Complete Expansion Activity: The Curriculum, which will let you further your understanding of the content you will be teaching.

EXPANSION ACTIVITY

The Curriculum

With four or five other students in your class, decide how much of the curriculum should include group activities and how much should involve individual activities at each of these grades.

Kindergarten
Elementary school
Middle school
High school

Also, discuss whether some subject areas might lend themselves better than others to group activities. Evaluate whether some children might benefit more than others from group work.

"Yes, your findings are correct. No, I don't believe you should publish your findings."

TABLE 2.2 The Classroom Curriculum

Concept	Description
Curriculum	Planned and unplanned experiences that students undergo in school settings
Formal Curriculum	Information, skills, and attitudes that a school intends to teach
Hidden Curriculum	Behaviors, attitudes, and knowledge that a school unintentionally teaches
Subject-Centered Curriculum	Curriculum pattern wherein subjects are separated into separate courses of study
Student-Centered Curriculum	A curriculum that focuses on student needs, interests, and activities
Needs	Academic and social areas in which students have weaknesses, limitations, or deficiencies

Most school districts offer at most only limited curriculum assistance to teachers. As such, teachers are often obliged to undertake course planning on their own. We will look at procedures for accomplishing this task in the next section.

Table 2.2 summarizes the concepts related to school curriculum and areas of curriculum need. Before you continue with the next section, review Table 2.2 and complete Review, Extension, and Reflective Exercise 2.1.

Planning the Course

All teachers are responsible for the instructional emphasis within their classrooms. They are responsible for organizing instruction in such a way that students receive instruction in, and achieve mastery of, the state-mandated curricula. But state-mandated curricula do not complete the picture of those things deemed important for students to learn. There are "generic" lessons that take place in the classroom that are rarely found in the curriculum documents of the state or the district. There also are worthy "enrichment" activities that the teacher and students deem important. Decisions must be made about the time, personnel, energy, and resources allocated to each of these important components of the curriculum.

APPLY AND REFLECT: It is suggested that you learn as much as possible about the

school and community in which you teach. How will this make you a better teacher?

Planning Instruction

Glatthorn (1987) suggests that 60 to 75 percent of instructional time should be allocated to the state-mandated curriculum. Glatthorn calls this the **mastery curriculum** and defines it as the learning considered essential for all students to know. He further states that the teaching of the mastery curriculum requires highly structured, well-planned, sequenced units and lessons that produce measurable results. The generic curriculum comprises the interpersonal and intrapersonal attitudes,

Review, Extension, and Reflective Exercise 2.1

Define curriculum and how it impacts the classroom.

Connections to INTASC Standards:

- Standard 1: Subject Pedagogy. The teacher must understand the central concepts, tools of inquiry, and structures of the discipline(s) he or she teaches and be able to create learning experiences that make these aspects of subject matter meaningful for students.
- Standard 2: Student Development. The teacher understands how children learn and develop and can provide learning opportunities that support their intellectual, social, and personal development.
- Standard 3: Diverse Learners. The teacher understands how students differ in their approaches to learning and creates instructional opportunities that are adapted to diverse learners.
- Standard 7: Planning Instruction. The teacher plans instruction based upon knowledge of subject matter, students, the community, and curriculum goals.

Connections to the NBPTS:

- Proposition 1: Teachers are committed to students and their learning.
- Proposition 2: Teachers must know the subjects they teach and how to teach those subjects to students.
- Proposition 3: Teachers are responsible for managing and monitoring student learning.
- Proposition 4: Teachers must think systematically about their practice and learn from experience.

Review

- What factors influence curriculum decisions?
- How important are the formal curriculum and hidden curriculum?
- What is the difference between subject-centered and student-centered curricula?
- In what ways do textbooks influence curricula in schools?
- How has increased emphasis on diversity issues impacted school curricula?

Reflection

- Many factors impact curriculum decisions in a school district, school, and classroom. Think about how you will make curriculum decisions for your classroom. Will you alone make the decisions? Will you ask for assistance in making the decisions? Will you consult district, state, and national guidelines in making your decisions?
- Think back on your own K–12 learning experiences and recall the curriculum (formal curriculum and hidden curriculum) that had the greatest impact on your life.

beliefs, skills, and knowledge that do not tend to lend themselves to a highly structured plan of instruction. Enrichment includes the things that are nice to know but are not essential for all students. A graphic model of curricular allocation as suggested by Glatthorn is shown in Figure 2.6.

Figure 2.6
Allocating Curricular Time

Mastery Curriculum	
60–75% of time Highly structured	
Generic Curriculum	**Enrichment**
Unstructured	

Figure 2.6
Allocating Curricular Time

The procedures for identifying the content for a complete school program (K–12) can be quite sophisticated. Essentially, such procedures should be left to textbook writers in deciding what to include in a textbook series or to developers of curriculum programs for a school district. Only rarely will the classroom teacher be expected to develop the scope and sequence of a program. As noted earlier, however, teachers should plan their courses in terms of student needs, district goals, and the needs of society.

Frequently, your first task as a teacher will be to plan your course(s) for the school year (Posner & Rudnitsky, 2000). Basically, you must lay out your instruction for the year for each subject you teach. To do so, you must address the following questions:

1. What major topics (chapters) will be covered? Can you justify your selections?
2. Should the class textbook content (chapters) be supplemented?
3. How should the topics (chapters) be grouped to form units of study? Why?
4. In what sequence should the planned units be taught? Why?
5. How much emphasis should each unit receive? In a 35-week course, how much time should each unit receive (in weeks and fractions of weeks)?

Your answers to such questions should result in a systematic layout of your course for the year. You will need to consult the curriculum guidelines of your state and school district and any standardized tests your students are required to take. Most teachers use an adopted course textbook as the core for planning. Such a procedure could, for example, yield a unit sequence of study and time allotments for a course as follows:

Unit 1 The Universe (3 weeks)

    Chapter 1   Stars

    Chapter 2   Galaxies

Unit 2 The Solar System (4 weeks)

    Chapter 4   The Earth

    Chapter 5   The Moon

Unit 3 The Earth's Atmosphere (4 1/2 weeks)

    Chapter 6   Atmosphere

    Chapter 8   Sun, Water, and Wind

    Chapter 9   Weather

Unit 4 The Earth's Crust (5 weeks)

    Chapter 11   Rocks

    Chapter 12   Volcanoes

    Chapter 13   Earthquakes

Unit 5 The Changing Crust (4 weeks)

    Chapter 14   Weathering

    Chapter 15   Erosion

    Chapter 10   Mountain Building

Unit 6 The Earth's History (4 weeks)

    Chapter 16   Geologic Time

    Chapter 17   Stories in Stone

Unit 7 Animal Life (4 weeks)

    Chapter 3   Place and Time

    Chapter 18   Development of Life

Unit 8 Human Life (4 1/2 weeks)

    Chapter 20   Human Life Begins

    Chapter 19   The Human Environment

Your course plan should be flexible, so changes can be made during the year. As you analyze the textbook and select chapters to be covered, recognize that not all chapters need to be covered, that the textbook chapters may not include all the content areas you want to teach, that the text sequence is not always the best sequence for every class, and that not all chapters are equally important. Also, make time allotments based on your intended methods and procedures and on the importance you place on the topic.

Finally, leave open a couple of weeks at the end of the year, in case more time is required than originally planned to finish some of your units. The extra time can always be used for review or enrichment if it is not needed for unit instruction.

One of the chief values of course planning is that it permits you to better anticipate desirable media and instructional materials (e.g., films, special equipment, computer programs, and special books). In fact, some school districts even require that all special materials be requested at the beginning of the year. In such districts, course planning will be essential.

Course planning is essential to effective teaching.

Multicultural Classroom

The face of many American classrooms is changing. The United States has always been a multicultural society and the growth of minority populations is projected to increase rapidly in the next few decades. It is projected that, by the year 2040, children of color will compose more than half the children in classrooms. Along with ethnic and racial diversity, we will have linguistic diversity. Increasing numbers of children are entering school from minority language backgrounds and have little or no competence in English. Also, as a result of Public Law 94-142 and its successors, students with a variety of disabilities now spend increasing amounts of time in traditional classrooms while still receiving the services they need.

Multicultural education is being implemented widely in our schools. Indeed, more classroom teachers have studied the concepts of multicultural education than in past years. Textbook publishers are now also integrating ethnic and cultural content into their books. Despite the growing successes, however, multicultural education faces serious challenges.

Banks (2002) suggests there are two broad goals for multicultural education. First, to improve educational equality for students from various ethnic and cultural groups and for students with special needs. Second, multicultural education should help all (including those who are Caucasian) build the knowledge, skills, and attitudes they need to be successful in a diverse society.

A variety of strategies should be planned for the classroom to meet these goals. Campbell (2000) identifies four major components to multicultural education:

1. **Making the curriculum more inclusive of different cultural perspectives and contributions.** For example, a course in science should include information and discussion of the contributions of African American, Native American, and Hispanic peoples.
2. **Raising the academic achievement of minority groups.** Teachers must be committed to helping all students academically, regardless of race and ethnicity.
3. **Improving intergroup relations.** Teachers need to break down thinking and actions that are prejudicial, stereotypic, and discriminatory.
4. **Helping students understand and deal with social and structural inequities in society.** Discuss racism, sexism, and class prejudice.

The goal of creating a multicultural classroom is to eliminate racism, sexism, and ethnic prejudice while providing equal educational opportunities for all students. To reach this goal and to meet the challenge of teaching in a multicultural classroom you should let three general principles guide your teaching. First, know your students, students' families, and communities. Try to spend time outside of school with students and parents. Ask parents to help in class or to speak to your students about their hobbies, jobs, or history and heritage of their ethnic group. Second, respect your students. Know the struggles they face and the obstacles they must overcome. Show genuine acceptance. Help your students maintain a sense of pride in their cultural group and who they are. Finally, teach all students to read, write, speak, compute, think, and create. Don't limit the goals for low-SES (social economic status) or minority students. Hold high standards for all students. Now complete Expansion Activity: Multicultural Education to explore your thoughts on multicultural education.

EXPANSION ACTIVITY

Multicultural
Education

In the context of education, are racial and ethnic differences negative? Come up with some differences that might be positive in your classroom. In terms of multicultural education, what do you hope to do differently as a teacher than what your former teachers did?

Differentiated Instruction

Not all students are alike. As such, teachers need to be flexible in their approach to teaching and adjust the curriculum and presentation of content to learners rather than expecting students to modify themselves for the curriculum. **Differentiated instruction** is a teaching theory based on the premise that instructional approaches should vary and be adapted in relation to individual and diverse students in the classroom. Differentiated instruction means that classroom teachers make vigorous attempts to meet students where they are in the learning process and move them along as quickly and as far as possible in the context of a mixed-ability classroom (Tomlinson, 1995).

To differentiate instruction is to recognize students' varying background knowledge, readiness, language, preferences in learning, and interests, and to react responsively. Differentiated instruction is a way to approach teaching and learning for students of differing abilities in the same class. The intent of differentiating instruction is to maximize each student's growth and individual success by meeting each student where he or she is, and assisting in the learning process.

In differentiated classrooms, teachers are able to reach students by appealing to differing interests and by using varied rates of instruction along with varied degrees of complexity. Teachers in differentiated classes use time flexibly and use a range of instructional strategies. Teachers can differentiate at least four classroom elements based on students' readiness, interest, or learning profile.

1. **Content.** What the student needs to learn or how the student will get access to the information. Teachers can use reading materials at varying readability levels, put text on tape, present ideas through both auditory or visual means, and reteach an idea or skill in small groups to struggling learners, or to extend the thinking or skills of advanced learners.
2. **Process.** Activities in which the students engage to make sense of or master the content. Teachers can provide interest centers; offer different activities with different levels of support, challenge, or complexity; offer manipulatives or other hands-on supports; and vary the length of time a student may take to complete an activity.
3. **Products.** Culminating projects that ask the students to rehearse, apply, and extend what they have learned in a unit. Teachers can give students options on how to express required learning (e.g., write a letter or use a computer), use rubrics that match and extend students' varied skill levels, allow students to work alone or in small groups on projects, and encourage students to create their own product assignments.
4. **Learning Environment.** The way the classroom works and feels. Teachers can make sure there are quiet places in the room to work, provide materials that reflect a variety of cultures and home settings, set clear guidelines for independent work, and help students understand that some students have to be active to learn.

There is ample evidence that students are more successful in school, and find it more satisfying, if they are taught in ways that are responsive to their readiness levels, interests, and learning profiles.

Students who are gifted and talented also need an appropriately differentiated curriculum designed to address their individual characteristics, needs, abilities, and interests. An effective curriculum for students who are gifted is essentially a basic curriculum that has been modified to meet their needs. Developing curriculum that is sufficiently rigorous, challenging, and coherent for students who are gifted can be a challenging task. A class is not differentiated when assignments are the same for all learners and the adjustments consist of varying the level of difficulty of questions for certain students, grading some students harder than others, or letting students who finish early play games for enrichment. It is not appropriate to have more advanced learners do extra math problems, extra book reports, or after completing their "regular" work be given extension assignments. Karnes and Bean (2000) suggest several ways in which the learning environment should be modified for gifted students in order to facilitate effective teaching and learning:

- Create a learner-centered environment that allows for student choice, flexibility, and independence.
- Focus on complexity rather than simplicity.
- Provide for high mobility within the classroom and various grouping arrangements.
- Express openness to innovation and exploration.

There is no recipe for differentiation. Rather, it is a way of thinking about teaching and learning that values the individual and can be translated into classroom practice in many ways.

This concludes our discussion of planning a course. But before I leave the topic of organizing for teaching, let's take a brief look at an area that has been receiving attention by educators—technology in the classroom.

APPLY AND REFLECT: It is suggested that you learn as much as possible about students' home lives (without exceeding a reasonable right to privacy). How will this information affect your ability to better work with students and parents?

Technology in the Classroom

Technology is evolving at an astonishing rate. There is growing consensus that today's technologies possess incredible potential to improve and even revolutionize our schools. As such, technology literacy must be integrated into the school curriculum.

Most students now have access to computers and the Internet in their classrooms, nearly all students have access somewhere in their schools, and a majority of teachers report using computers or the Internet for instructional purposes. Technology is changing the way teachers teach and students learn. It is also offering new ways for all involved in education to be openly accountable to parents, communities, and students. Children have grown up with technology. They have been raised in a world of instant access to information, a world where vivid images embody and supplement information formerly presented solely through text. They are used to an environment where they control information flow and access, whether through toys, or a video game controller, remote control, mouse, or touch-tone phone.

The most dramatic area of technology growth has occurred in the use of computers. The decreasing cost and increasing availability of microcomputers and other technologies in schools have led educators to become more interested in technology, particularly as a means of meeting students' diverse needs. Technology, and computers in particular, are being viewed as essential parts of instruction to help students develop basic and critical thinking skills.

Instructional use of computers varies from helping students learn basic facts to teaching them complex thinking strategies. Their value to students along the learning continuum from disabled to gifted and talented comes from their ability to adapt instruction to meet the diverse needs of students.

The idea behind computer-based instruction (CBI) is to use the computer as a tutor to present information, give students practice, and assess their level of understanding. CBI programs generally share the following characteristics: (1) using a structured curriculum; (2) letting students work at their own pace; (3) giving students controlled, frequent feedback and reinforcement; and (4) measuring performance quickly and giving students information on their performance.

Most teachers also use computers to enhance instruction. Word processing is the most common instructional use of computers by teachers. Teachers can create handouts for students, write letters to parents, and respond to administrators' requests for information. Computers are also commonly used for record keeping, creating grade books, and storing standardized test results and lesson plans. Most teachers also use computer technology for communicating via e-mail, generating exams for students, and using the Internet as a resource for lesson planning.

Although computers are one of the most important technological advances, technology actually includes much more that this. Technology in the classroom makes possible the instant exchange of information between classrooms as well as individual students; it allows instant access to databases and on-line information services, and provides multimedia technical resources such as interactive audio and video. Technology also allows for the repurposing of preexisting educational materials across media formats: print, static illustrations, still and digital photographs, digital audio, still and motion video, still and motion film, animations, computer graphics, and hypermedia can all be accessed and combined in novel ways.

To incorporate technology more fully into the classroom, teachers must be provided with the time and support to explore technology on their own. Administrators must provide the time for teachers, who now suffer from larger classes and more responsibility than ever, to take a break from teaching to start learning.

Whatever the format, technology has a motivating quality for students. They often work longer and harder than they would with comparable paper-and-pencil tasks. Complete the Computers in the Classroom Web Link. It should generate an array of potential computer activities for your classroom.

APPLY AND REFLECT: Are you technology literate? What are your strengths and weaknesses relative to technology?

W E B   L I N K   Computers in the Classroom
Browse the World Wide Web to locate examples of K–12 uses of computers in the
classroom. What types of activities are the most common? Discuss the benefits
gained from your findings. Include benefits to students and teachers.

This completes our study of planning courses and the use of technology in the classroom. Review the planning and technology topics in Table 2.3 and complete Review, Extension, and Reflective Exercise 2.2 to explore related concepts.

TABLE 2.3 Classroom Planning

Concept	Description
Course Planning	Establishing the curriculum and instructional emphasis of a course for a year
Multicultural Classroom	Valuing the ethnic, racial, and linguistic diversity of cultural groups
Differentiated Instruction	Modifying instruction in the classroom to reflect the different abilities of students
Technology	Using multimedia in the classroom to enhance instruction

Review, Extension, and Reflective Exercise 2.2

Outline the process you would follow and the issues you would address in designing a course.

Connections to INTASC Standards:

- Standard 1: Subject Pedagogy. The teacher must understand the central concepts, tools of inquiry, and structures of the discipline(s) he or she teaches and be able to create learning experiences that make these aspects of subject matter meaningful for students.
- Standard 2: Student Development. The teacher understands how children learn and develop and can provide learning opportunities that support their intellectual, social, and personal development.
- Standard 3: Diverse Learners. The teacher understands how students differ in their approaches to learning and creates instructional opportunities that are adapted to diverse learners.
- Standard 5: Learning Environment. The teacher must be able to use an understanding of individual and group motivation and behavior to create a learning environment that encourages positive social interaction, active engagement in learning, and self-motivation.
- Standard 7: Planning Instruction. The teacher plans instruction based upon knowledge of subject matter, students, the community, and curriculum goals.

Connections to the NBPTS:

- Proposition 1: Teachers are committed to students and their learning.
- Proposition 3: Teachers are responsible for managing and monitoring student learning.
- Proposition 4: Teachers must think systematically about their practice and learn from experience.

Review

- What is involved in planning a course for a year?
- How do cultural differences affect teaching and learning?
- How has the increased emphasis on diversity issues affected school curricula?
- What is the impact of technology on teaching and learning?

Reflection

- How important is it to plan a course for the year? Can't you just adopt and follow a good textbook for your course plan? What problems could develop if you covered only the content in the adopted textbook?
- There has been much debate in the media over possible bias in the school curriculum. What can you as a teacher do to reduce or eliminate school curriculum bias and its effects?
- What are the strengths and limitations of technology in individual classrooms? Should classroom computers be connected to the Internet?

VIEW FROM THE CLASSROOM

What do teachers think about organizing for teaching? Teacher survey results relative to topics presented in this chapter are expressed below. Review these results and discuss with classmates.

How well prepared are you for this school year's curriculum?

I'm planned a week ahead of delivery time.	30%
I'm planned a few days ahead of delivery time.	23%
I'm planned for tomorrow, I think.	21%
I'm planned a month or more ahead of delivery time.	14%
I'm planned two to three weeks ahead of delivery time.	12%

When do you start planning for the new school year?

Planned before the school year ends	46%
Close to month before the first day of school	34%
About two weeks before school starts	12%
Use plans from previous years	4%
Close to one week before the start	4%

Who should control schooling and determine the curriculum?

Local school communities	53%
Local or state government	27%
Private sector	11%
Federal government	10%

Does the curriculum that you use to teach meet the interests of today's youth?

In some ways, but needs to be revised in some areas.	57%
Yes, it meets the interests.	25%
No, the curriculum is way out of date.	13%
It doesn't need to meet their interests.	5%

What role does computer technology play in today's classrooms?

Improve student performance	85%
Improve students' attention in class	74%
Posting homework assignments on-line increased completion rates	58%
Increase communications with parents	63%
Students with computers at home have major advantage over those that do not	72%

Why do you think teachers are sometimes reluctant to use technology in teaching?

All of these reasons	45%
Not enough time to plan with technology	26%
No training in technology use	15%
Lack of technology resources	11%
Belief that technology is not effective in teaching	2%

SOURCE: Excerpted from *Teach-nology*, available at www.teach-nology.com/poll and *How Teachers View Technology*, available at www.educationworld.com/a_tech/tech/tech180.shtml

THE PUBLIC VIEW OF EDUCATION

What does the public think of issues related to organizing for teaching?
Review these results and discuss with classmates.

Who should have the greatest influence in deciding what is taught in the public schools?

Federal government	15%
State government	22%
Local school board	61%
Don't know	2%

Should students enrolled in special education be required to meet the same standards as all other students in the school?

Yes, should	31%
No, should not	67%
Don't know	2%

How important do you think *interest on the part of the student* is on the difference in achievement between White children and Black and Hispanic children?

Very important	80%
Somewhat important	15%
Not very important	3%
Not at all important	1%
Don't know	1%

How important do you think *home life and upbringing* is on the achievement gap between White children and Black and Hispanic children?

Very important	87%
Somewhat important	10%
Not very important	2%
Not at all important	1%
Don't know	0%

How important do you think *community environment* is on the achievement gap between White children and Black and Hispanic children?

Very important	66%
Somewhat important	28%
Not very important	4%
Not at all important	1%
Don't know	1%

(Continued)

THE PUBLIC VIEW OF EDUCATION (Continued)

What percentage of the students in your state would you say are not performing at an acceptable level?

50 to 60%	31%
40 to 50%	19%
30 to 40%	21%
20 to 30%	12%
Below 20%	10%
Don't know	7%

SOURCE: Adapted from *The 35th Annual Phi Delta Kappa/Gallup Poll of the Public's Attitudes Toward the Public Schools* (2003) by Lowell C. Ross and Alec M. Gallup. Available at www.pdkintl.org/kappan/k0309pol.htm

Summary

A Model of Teaching

- Good teaching requires both a sequential and cyclic planning process.
- Effective teachers must diagnose, plan the course, plan instruction, guide planned activities, evaluate, and, when necessary, follow up.

The Curriculum

- The curriculum of a school consists of all the planned and unplanned experiences students undergo in the school setting.
- The two categories of school curriculum are the formal curriculum and the hidden curriculum.
- Curriculum mapping can be used to identify gaps in the curriculum being taught.
- The backward design model offers an alternative approach to curriculum design.
- Brain research gives educators new insights about teaching and learning.

Curriculum Structure

- The curriculum pattern can be subject-centered, student-centered, or an integrated combination of both forms.

Curriculum Selection

- Content selection should be planned so that instruction fulfills the needs of students, society, and the structure of the subject.

- Devices available for diagnosing learning situations include students' cumulative record, personal contact with students, conferences with parents and other school personnel, and students' written comments.

Planning the Course

- Teachers must often plan their course for the year with little assistance.
- Teachers often use an adopted textbook as a source for the selection of course topics.
- Chapter topics are often combined into units and a sequence for the units along with unit time allotments are then established.
- A course plan should remain flexible so needed modifications can be made during the year.
- Teachers must plan for a multicultural classroom.
- A major school goal is to eliminate racism, sexism, and ethnic prejudice.
- Not all students are alike, which calls for differentiated instruction in the classroom.
- Technology is changing the way teachers teach and students learn.
- Computer-based instruction (CBI) can be used as a tutor to present information, give students practice, and assess students' level of understanding.

Discussion Questions and Activities

1. **The curriculum.** Obtain a state and district curriculum guide for elementary or secondary education. How would you improve the curriculum at the level you plan to teach? Should teachers be free to determine what they will teach? What forces commonly influence the school curriculum? The formal curriculum? The hidden curriculum?
2. **The hidden curriculum.** How important is the hidden curriculum when compared with the formal curriculum of the school?
3. **Planning a course.** Select a basic textbook from your area of specialization. Using the selected textbook, plan a 35-week course. Select the topics (chapters) to be covered, supplement the textbook where needed, combine the topics (chapters) into appropriate units of study, and make unit time allotments.
4. **Textbook examination.** Examine some elementary and secondary textbooks and other materials for the classroom. Do you see any racial, gender, or ethnic biases?

Connection With the Field

1. **The teaching model.** Visit several schoolteachers. Discuss their planning. Do they follow the six-step planning model presented in this chapter or a modification of the model? Describe the models used by the teachers.
2. **The school curriculum.** Examine the documents that outline the curriculum at a nearby school. Interview several students about the school curriculum. Ask them what they are learning. What attitudes do the students have about their school experiences? Determine if there is a parallel relationship between what the school teaches and the career aspirations of students.
3. **Classroom observation.** Complete several classroom interaction observational activities in different classrooms. Focus the collection of information on
   a. Actions that help you better understand students and their behaviors;
   b. Information gained from conversations within the classroom environment that help you understand students' needs, likes, and dislikes; and
   c. Student weaknesses and strengths gained from verbal examination of students' class work and homework.
4. **Diagnostic devices.** Visit with several schoolteachers. Make a list of diagnostic tools that are commonly use to diagnose students' strengths, needs, and weaknesses. Do the teachers make effective use of achievement test results in planning instruction? Do they provide follow-up instruction based on evaluation results?

Praxis II Connection

The following test preparation exercises are intended to help you prepare for the Praxis II: Principles of Learning and Teaching exam that may be required by your teacher education preparatory program and for state certification or licensing. These exercises will give you direct access to pedagogical knowledge from Chapter 2 that will be expected of you on the Praxis II and other pedagogical exams that may be required at the end of your teacher education program.

Topic Connections

1. Curriculum (II. B1)

Most states have curriculum guidelines or benchmarks. For the state in which you plan to teach, locate and study the state curriculum guidelines that have been developed for all students. In many instances, this information is available on state department of education websites. Summarize your findings.

2. Student-Centered Models (II. A3)

Teacher and student roles in student-centered instruction are significantly different from those in subject- or teacher-centered instruction. Describe and contrast practices that are typically student-centered with those of subject- or teacher-centered instruction.

3. Differentiated Instruction (I. B4)

Students are different. As such, you need to know how to adapt instruction to students of differing abilities. What elements and components of these elements can you adjust to meet individual student ability levels?

4. Multicultural Education (I. B)

What are the major dimensions of multicultural education? Describe these dimensions and their influences upon each other.

5. Technology (II. A4)

Technology and the Internet are relatively new additions to America's schools. What are some of the most important teacher and student uses of technology and the Internet in today's schools?

ON YOUR OWN

Log on to the web-based student study site at http://www.sagepub.com/eis for more information about the vignettes and materials presented in this chapter, suggestions for activities, study aids such as electronic flashcards and review quizzes, and research recommendations including journal article links and questions related to this chapter.

SEQUENCING AND ORGANIZING INSTRUCTION

The central focus of Part 2 is preparing for teaching. Effective teachers must plan and plan well. They identify lesson learning intent, select appropriate media, and select and implement appropriate teaching strategies and methods. A major purpose of this section is to assist you in becoming a better planner. To do so you must decide where you want to go and the best method of getting there. The backward design approach to identifying instructional intent is also presented and discussed.

Chapter 3 covers the process of determining and organizing the intended goals of a course. This chapter relates to determining where you want to go in terms of developing your skill at writing well-stated objectives.

Chapter 4 centers on how to design and carry out course, unit, weekly, and daily planning. It shows you how to plan presentations that achieve the stated objectives and focuses on teaching content and thinking skills. Chapter 4 also explores how to plan for students with different abilities. Teaching special education students and gifted and talented students is covered. Finally, several practical lesson plan formats are illustrated and discussed.

3
SETTING GOALS AND OBJECTIVES

The aim [of education] should be to teach us
rather how to think, than what to think.

JAMES BEATTIE

OVERVIEW

Selecting the curriculum is only the beginning in planning for instruction. You must now clarify your purpose and your instructional intent: You must decide exactly what you want students to learn, how they will learn it, and how you will know they have learned it. Generally these three steps occur simultaneously with the setting of priorities regarding time, objectives, materials, and methods of instruction.

This chapter will address the establishment of goals and objectives whereas Chapters 4, 5, and 6 will be devoted to lesson planning, evaluation of student learning, and testing and grading, respectively.

OBJECTIVES

After completing your study of Chapter 3, you should be able to do the following:

1. Give valid rationales for stating instructional goals and objectives.
2. Contrast the terms *educational goals*, *informational objectives*, and *instructional objectives*.
3. Prepare (write) educational goals.
4. Describe the four components that make up a properly written instructional objective.
5. Describe the three domains of learning.
6. Classify objectives into cognitive, affective, and psychomotor domains and rate them as higher- or lower-level within each domain.
7. Prepare (write) informational objectives and instructional objectives at different levels of cognitive, affective, and psychomotor sophistication.
8. Describe the *backward design* approach to stating instructional intent.

Almost anything you try in the classroom will result in some type of learning, but it is not always desirable learning. To be effective, learning must have direction; it must have purpose. For example, your school might want to focus on reading and writing skills. Your task would then be to decide on the specific learning that will lead to the attainment of this goal. Thus, even though they are broad and basic skills, reading and writing would be integrated into course content and related specific objectives. Viewed in this context, your objective can be defined as a clear and unambiguous description of instructional intent. It is finite and measurable. Its accomplishment can be verified.

An **objective** is not a statement of what you plan to do; instead, it is a statement of what your students should be able to do after instruction. For example, if the purpose of instruction is to foster student understanding of the conditions that led to our focus on the exploration of space, the objective would *not* be "The *teacher will present* information about our ventures into space." It does not matter at all what the teacher does if students do not learn. Remember the purpose of instruction is to get students to learn. Therefore, the objective should be "The *student will discuss* world conditions that led to our focus on the exploration of space." Objectives, then, should place the emphasis on student outcome or performance.

There are a number of approaches to writing objectives. The behavioral objectives approach proposed by Robert Mager (1997) and the general/specific objectives approach proposed by Norman Gronlund (1999) are the most common. Mager proposes writing specific statements about observable outcomes that can be built up to become a curriculum (an inductive approach). An example of a behavioral objective would be

> Given 3 minutes of class time, the student will solve 9 out of 10 addition problems of the type: $5 + 4 =$ _____.

Gronlund, on the other hand, proposes starting with a general statement and providing specific examples of topics to be covered or behaviors to be observed (a deductive approach). An example of a general/specific objective would be

> The student can perform simple addition:
>
>   a.   can define what addition means, in his or her own words.
>   b.   can define relevant terms such as "addend" and "sum."
>   c.   can solve problems of the type $5 + 4 =$ _____.

While there are advantages and disadvantages to each approach, this text will focus on Mager's approach, because it is the most widely used and perhaps the most inclusive.

Rationale for Objectives

Teaching, as noted in Chapter 2, can be envisioned as a six-phase process (review Figure 2.1). Once the content to be taught has been selected, objectives must be written related to the selected content. The written objectives will then set the framework for the instructional approach and the student evaluation.

Establishing Objectives

1. Should students be involved in determining educational intent? Do students really know what they need?
2. What impact will student attitudes have on the desire to learn?

My fifth-grade class goes to a physical education teacher once a week. The physical education teacher was complaining about the performance of my students during their once-a-week physical education class. My first response was, "What do you expect me to do?" Yet, I began noticing student attitudes toward their physical education class were very negative and getting progressively worse. Some were bringing notes from home asking that they be excused from physical education for various reasons. The physical education teacher indicated he would give students an unacceptable grade if they had any further notes from home.

I decided to schedule additional physical education time into our daily schedule in an effort to find out what was going on. I perceived that my students needed to somehow develop a deeper appreciation for physical activity so I decided to take them out to play kick ball and see for myself what was going on. I selected kick ball because it is the simplest, physical game I know. It has simple rules, requires little or no setup time, and the only materials I needed was a ball for them to kick and bases. I required everyone to participate while I observed.

On our first day of kick ball, there was much arguing, intentional cheating by some, disgruntled players, reluctant/discouraged players, and a few (two or three) eager students. The attitudes were awful! Even the eager students had no sense of fair play or team spirit. Some of the students were unable to kick the ball without falling down. Several couldn't run. I mean they really didn't know how to run or even where to run. Some didn't know the correct base order to tag bases. Two students didn't speak English. Furthermore, name calling and negative remarks were the general basis for communication. Indeed, the frustration level for the group was extremely high. Obviously, they were finding very little satisfaction from their learning time. Of course the big question was, "Are they learning anything?" I certainly learned a

lot from them. First, I learned that when students do not have explicit objectives for their activities, they tend to devise their own. I asked my group what our objectives should be to justify our time outside each day. Each of them had different ideas about the goals and objectives of physical education time. No wonder they seemed to be going in 20 different directions.

With the help of my class, we made a list of objectives that would address our immediate needs in an effort to focus the group. We made a list of skills needed to be successful at kick ball. The list of objectives gave the group a focus and gave me a tool for evaluation of each student's progress. Students began to focus less on winning and losing and more on skills needed for the game to run smoothly. Certainly, there is nothing wrong with focusing on winning as long as prerequisite skills are not neglected.

The result of having specific objectives focused everyone and the assessment was built into the accomplishment of the objectives. The results were astounding! I've never been more pleased with my work. First, I learned that many of my students honestly didn't know how to run. I guess I thought that was something that just came naturally to children. I learned many of my students rarely played outside. As a result of this, I began communicating more with parents to find out more about my students. My teaching became more personable and I began to realize the connection between what my students could learn and what was going on in their personal lives. I watched each student become more and more proficient with the physical skills needed for their physical education class. Their attitudes about themselves and each other improved dramatically. Many students expressed pride in their accomplishments and began to talk about how they now liked physical education. Getting to know my students on a personal level along with the use of specific, obtainable objectives made a huge difference.

—SUSAN MOORE, *5th grade,*
Pike Elementary School, Fort Smith, AR

SOURCE: Courtesy of Susan Moore, Van Buren, AR. Used with permission.

Objectives establish the framework for instruction: they compel you to provide the environment and sequence of activities that will allow students to reach the stated intent. For example, if your objective is the instant recall of specific information (such as the elements in the periodic table), your activities must include practice in the recall of the information. If, on the other hand, the objective is related to the use of information in problem solving, practice in problem solving procedures must be provided. Thus, objectives spell out general strategies and specific activities for their attainment.

Objectives also prescribe exactly what skills and knowledge students must manifest as a result of instruction. In other words, your objectives will set the framework for the evaluation process.

Communication of Intent

Objectives also serve an important communication function. Clear and measurable objectives need to be stated for the benefit of students, parents, and program accountability. Through the use of properly written objectives, educators can show where students are, as a group or as individuals, with respect to the stated objectives.

An essential part of planning is writing the objectives that set the framework for the total instructional process.

Administrators can communicate similar information to school boards or the community at large.

Objectives make clear to students your expectations prior to instruction. This communication eliminates guesswork related to students' learning (e.g., "Will this be on the test?"). Thus, when you communicate your objectives, students know exactly what is expected of them, and they no longer have to guess what is important. They know whether it will be on the test.

Objectives are being widely used in education today. Public Law 94-142 (**PL 94-142**) and its successors, for example, require that an Individual Education Plan (IEP) be written for every handicapped student in your class. And, for each of these plans, specific objectives must be written for the students. Furthermore, individualized program and mastery learning techniques, as well as some state and district regulations, require the specification of objectives. Thus, you, as a prospective teacher, must understand and develop the skills for prescribing and writing your instructional intent (objectives).

Teacher Accountability

Finally, the movement for teacher accountability has become a simple extension of objectives, testing, and evaluation. Teacher accountability means that teachers are

"What did I learn today? My mother will want to know."

A. Figure 3.1
A Three-Stage
Accountability Model

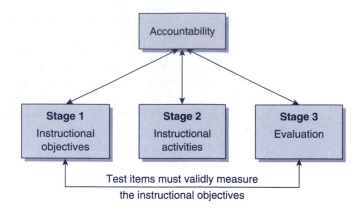

responsible for the quality of their instruction and the progress of their students. Generally, teacher performance related to planning and instruction is measured through classroom-based observation and evaluation by administrators. Typically, student progress is measured by performance on nationally normed standardized tests.

A three-stage accountability model is depicted in Figure 3.1. The first stage in the model is the establishment of objectives—that is, learning intent. In stage 2, instructional activities designed to develop student mastery are implemented. The final stage is a determination of whether the intent was accomplished. In other words, did you do the intended job? You must show that the intended learning outcome has taken place. You are being held accountable for students' acquisition of the desired learning as stated in the objectives.

APPLY AND REFLECT: Do you think teachers should be held accountable for the

progress of their students? Why or why not? Should teacher salary increases or merit

pay be related to student test scores?

As shown in Figure 3.1, objectives drive the entire instructional process. Therefore, it is essential that objectives be clear and measurable, because the evaluation will be determined by the objectives. That is, the evaluation must measure the outcome that is specified in the objective. The following examples illustrate incorrect and correct evaluation of intended learning outcomes.

Objective:	The student will use geometric formulas.
Wrong Evaluation:	Derive geometric formulas.
Better Evaluation:	Please find the area and volume.
Objective:	The student will swim 100 yards in boiling oil.
Wrong Evaluation:	Explain the theory and philosophy of oil swimming.
Better Evaluation:	Please swim.

Note that the first objective calls not for being able to derive geometric formulas but for using them. Likewise, the second objective does not require that students explain the theory and philosophy of oil swimming but, rather, that they actually swim. Obviously, your evaluation must assess what was specifically stated in your objectives. These specifics were the learning intent.

Instructional intent can be stated at varying levels of specificity. At the general level, statements of instructional intent are presentations of the broad goals of instruction. At the more specific level, instructional intent tells what students will be able to do following instruction. When writing instructional intent, you begin by identifying your goals at a broad level and follow these with the more specific objectives. Thus, movement is from a general frame of reference to a more specific frame. Let's now look at this deductive process in greater detail.

Objective Specificity

There is a difference in the level of specificity at which instructional intent should be written. Whereas **goals** are usually broad statements used to describe the purposes of schooling or the purposes of a course, objectives are narrower statements of the intended learning of a unit or specific lesson. A nomenclature that makes a distinction between goals and objectives has been developed; however, there is little agreement about terminology. The terms *educational aims, educational goals,* and *general objectives* are often used to denote broad instructional intent, whereas the terms *performance objectives, informational objectives, behavioral objectives,* and *instructional objectives* are often used to denote the more specific instructional intent.

This text will address three levels of specificity: educational goals, informational objectives, and instructional objectives. Educational goals and the more specific instructional objectives can be thought of as forming a continuum from general to specific, with goals being written for a school course or unit, followed by (in descending order) informational and instructional objectives written for specific lessons and exercises. Examples of these three levels of specificity are shown in Table 3.1. Note that the level of specificity increases as you move down through the examples, with the informational objective being subordinate to the educational goal and instructional objective being subordinate to the informational objective.

Educational goals are broad and may take an extended period of time to be accomplished. Note how the goal in Table 3.1 is the actual intent of the course: It is what the teacher wishes to accomplish in the broadest sense—in this case, computer literacy. The informational and instructional objectives, then, support the educational goal. They tell what the student will do to show that they are computer literate. Following are other examples of educational goals:

1. The students will develop a command of standard English.
2. The students will expand their leisure activities.
3. The students will develop good ethical character.
4. The students will formulate an appreciation for all people.
5. The students will develop good health habits.

TABLE 3.1 Examples of Educational Goal and Objective Specificity

Type	Example
Educational Goal	The student will develop computer literacy.
Informational Objectives	The student will be able to use a word processing software program.
Instructional Objective	Given a set of specific requirements, the student will be able to use a word processing program to write a one-page paper with no errors.

Note that these statements are so general that they appear to give us little help in instruction. Yet, on closer examination, they do give us general direction and, therefore, represent the first step in deciding what to teach. They set the general direction we wish to go with our instruction. To this end, educational goals are usually concerned with covert (nonobservable), internal changes, which are less clearly measurable than are the behaviors associated with the more specific objectives. Some handy verbs that should prove helpful in writing educational goals are listed in Table 3.2. Notice that many of the verbs used in writing educational goals are rather vague and open to interpretation. They lack the specification of exactly what, in observable terms, the student is to do to show that the intended learning has taken place. Complete Expansion Activity: Educational Goals, which will let you explore goals for your expected grade level or content area.

EXPANSION ACTIVITY

Educational Goals

Educational goals give direction to our instructional intent. Research the national, state, and district goals of the grade level or content area you expect to teach. What are some of the broad goals for instruction for the grade or content subject you expect to teach? List them.

TABLE 3.2 Some Illustrative Verbs for Writing Goals

A	E	L
apply	enjoy	like
appreciate	F	R
B	familiarize	realize
believe	fully appreciate	recognize
C	G	T
comprehend	grasp	think
cope	I	U
D	imagine	understand
demonstrate	K	V
develop	know	value

Our next step in the planning process is to decide the specifics related to our goals. That is, we must now decide more precisely what students should know and, consequently, do to demonstrate that they have accomplished these goals. These decisions are stated in our more specific objectives: informational and instructional.

APPLY AND REFLECT: Educational goals should be written to set the framework for writing the more specific instructional intent. What sources and guides should be used to establish your goals?

Stating Objectives

The primary purpose of school is to cause students to learn. Thus, as a result of your instruction, there should be a change in state within your students. This change in state must be overt (observable), with students acting differently than they did before being involved in the learning process.

Objectives must lay out everything you intend but must not imply things you do not want to say. Consequently, informational and instructional objectives must be unambiguous as well as being testable and measurable. Table 3.3 suggests some verbs that are appropriate for informational and instructional objectives. Note the difference in clarity of language between the verbs listed in Tables 3.2 and 3.3.

TABLE 3.3 Illustrative Verbs for Writing Informational and Instructional Objectives

A	draw	P
add	**E**	pick
adjust	explain	point
analyze	**G**	pronounce
arrange	graph	**R**
B	**I**	read
build	identify	recite
C	**L**	run
calculate	label	**S**
choose	list	select
circle	locate	sing
classify	**M**	sort
compare	measure	state
construct	**N**	**U**
contrast	name	underline
D	**O**	**W**
define	operate	write
describe	order	

A well-written objective clearly defines the mastery level. How well students achieve this level tells the teacher whether the instructional plan has been successful.

Elements of Instructional Objectives

Instructional objectives precisely communicate learning intent. Mager (1997) outlines three components to instructional intent: behavior, conditions, and criterion. This book, however, recommends that an expression of instructional intent comprise these four elements:

1. Spell out the terminal behavior, or *performance,* that details the actions that will be accepted as evidence that the intent has been achieved.
2. Specify the *product* or what is to be produced by the student actions.
3. Describe the *conditions* under which the student action is to be expected.
4. State the *criteria* of acceptable performance; you are describing how well you want the students to perform.

At times, not all of these elements are necessary. The object is to clearly communicate your intent. Thus, sometimes informational objectives (addressed later in this chapter) will suffice, and sometimes not.

Element One: The Performance

The first element of an instructional objective is the specification of what students are expected to do after they receive instruction. This action is clarified in your selection of a word, usually a verb, that indicates what students are to do or produce. Because the purpose of instruction is to elicit a predetermined action, instructional objectives should always be written in terms of observable student performance. Special care must be taken in selecting the proper verb, so that you achieve clarity of language with no ambiguity in meaning. You, your interested colleagues, and your principal must interpret the same meaning from each verb used in your objectives. Subjective terms, such as *know, realize,* and *understand,* should not be used as performance verbs in writing your objectives. These terms are open to interpretation and have different meanings to different individuals. In a word, you should use terms that denote observable (overt) actions or behaviors. Verbs, for example— such as *list, name, state, bisect,* and *graph*—prompt observable behaviors that, in turn, will help you evaluate your instructional intent. Review Table 3.3 for further examples of appropriate verbs for writing instructional objectives.

Element Two: The Product

The second element of an instructional objective is to specify what is to be the result of the students' performance. It is this product of students' actions that you will evaluate in determining whether the objective has been mastered. This product can be a written sentence, a written sum, listed names, a demonstrated skill, or a constructed object. Students, for example, could be asked to produce a 300-word essay, a list of nouns, an analysis of the characters in a play, or the solutions to a set of basic addition facts.

The product is the outcome that you've planned to result from the instructional process. In other words, it is what you want students to be able to do after your instruction that they (supposedly) couldn't do prior to instruction.

Element Three: The Conditions

The third element in the statement of an instructional objective is to establish the conditions under which the learner is to perform the prescribed action. Conditional elements can refer to the materials, information, or special equipment that will or will not be available to students; any special restrictions as to time and space; and any other applicable requirements. Consider this example: "Given the formula, the student will be able to calculate the attractive force between two masses." This objective tells students that they need not memorize the formula—that they will be given the formula and they should simply know how to use it. Note the use of "Given the formula" for the conditional statement. Terms and phrases such as "Given" or "With (Without) the aid of" are commonly used in conditional statements.

Conditions must be realistic and clearly communicate expectations to students. They should make your desires more explicit. Following are other examples of conditions that might be included in an instructional objective:

Given a list of verbs . . .

After reading Chapter 10 . . .

Using class notes . . .

With a ruler, protractor, and compass . . .

Within a 10-minute time interval and from memory . . .

On an essay test . . .

Given the necessary materials . . .

During a 5-minute interval . . .

From a list of compound sentences . . .

Without the aid of references . . .

These are a few examples of how conditions can be included as elements in instructional objectives. Essentially, you should attempt to visualize under what conditions you want students to show mastery and prescribe these conditions in your objectives. As shown in the examples, conditions are usually written as the first component in the objective, but their placement can be anywhere in the objective. For example, the objective "The student will identify, on a multiple-choice test, Newton's laws of motion with 100 percent accuracy" has the conditional component (on a multiple-choice test) toward the middle of the objective.

Element Four: The Criterion

The fourth, and last, element of an instructional objective is the level of acceptable student performance. This is where you state the lowest level of performance that you will accept as showing mastery. This component can be established in terms of time limits, percentage of correct answers, minimum number of correct answers, ratios of correct to incorrect responses permitted, an acceptable tolerance, and other observable operations. This standard, or criterion, should be stated clearly so that students know in advance exactly what the standards are by which their performance will be judged. In other words, criterion levels should be stated as in the following specific examples:

. . . at least three reasons . . .

. . . 9 of the 10 cases . . .

. . . with no spelling errors.

. . . with 80 percent accuracy.

. . . 90 percent of the 20 problems.

. . . within plus or minus 10 percent.

. . . to the nearest hundredth.

. . . correct to the nearest percent.

. . . within 10 minutes.

. . . in less than 5 minutes.

. . . at least two problems within a 5-minute period.

. . . within 20 minutes with 80 percent accuracy.

Each of these criterion levels represents well-defined standards toward which students can strive. Usually such standards are selected rather arbitrarily on the basis of past experiences and class expectations.

Carefully defined levels of desired performance are essential for effective instruction. You should take care, however, not to set standards that are too high. You should also guard against watering down your expectations. You should know your students so you can set reasonable levels of performance.

Now that you know the four elements of an instructional objective, you are ready to differentiate between informational and instructional objectives.

Informational Objectives

Frequently, you will want 100 percent of the class to attain 100 percent of the objective—that is, 100 percent mastery. Furthermore, objectives often have no special conditions. In these cases, informational objectives usually meet your instructional needs.

Informational objectives are abbreviated instructional objectives. Whereas instructional objectives contain the four elements noted earlier, informational objectives specify only the student performance and the product. Consider, for example, the following instructional and informational objectives written for the same instructional intent.

Instructional Objective: Given the voltage and resistance, the student will be able to calculate the current in a series and parallel circuit with 100 percent accuracy.

Informational Objective: The student will be able to compute the current in a series or parallel circuit.

Notice that the informational objective is an abbreviation of the instructional objective in that it omits the conditions ("given the voltage and resistance") and the criterion for judging minimum mastery ("100 percent accuracy"). The informational objective contains only the performance ("to calculate") and the product ("the current in a series or parallel circuit"). Frequently, the conditions are such that they are understood. In the cited example of an informational objective, it is understood that the necessary information must be provided to calculate the current. Moreover, it should be understood that only 100 percent accuracy would be desired.

Informational objectives are often adequate when you share your instructional intent with students. If you feel more information is needed to communicate the exact intent, however, you should write instructional objectives, or perhaps informational objectives with the conditions or the criterion added. Let's now look at the communication of objectives.

APPLY AND REFLECT: Objectives are generally used as an aid in designing evaluation procedures. Some teachers, however, feel this process should be reversed. Which order do you think is the most educationally sound? Why? Which order do you prefer? Why?

Communication of Objectives

As noted earlier in the chapter, you should spell out objectives for students if you are to get maximum value from the objectives. This communication is usually presented at the beginning of a unit of study in written form. One useful format that is recommended for stating multiple objectives is to use an introductory statement to communicate common needed conditions and/or a criterion level. The remainder of each individual objective is then listed with the performance verb, the product, and additional desired conditions—for example, upon completion of "The Earth in the Universe" unit, you should be able, on an end-of-unit exam, to perform the following with 70 percent proficiency:

1. Identify the various stars discussed in class.
2. Use constellations to locate stars.
3. Identify three current ideas about how the universe originated and developed.
4. Describe nebulas, where they occur, and how they may form.
5. Find latitude and longitude of places from globes or maps, and locate places on globes or maps from latitude and longitude.
6. Name the planets in their order from the sun.
7. Identify some of the physical characteristics of each of the planets.
8. Describe the actual and relative sizes of the Earth and its moon, as well as the paths they follow around the sun.

The exact format used in communicating objectives is not critical, but they should be spelled out in precise terms. You should tailor your communication of objectives to the specific needs of your students. With younger children, you usually want to communicate your intent orally.

This concludes our formal discussion of goals and objectives. Table 3.4 summarizes the key concepts covered to this point. Review the summary and complete Review, Extension, and Reflective Exercise 3.1, which will check your understanding of goals and objectives.

TABLE 3.4 Instructional Intent

Concept	Description
Educational Goal	Broad statement of instructional intent used to describe general purpose of instruction.
Instructional Objective	A narrow four-component statement of learning intent. The components include: the performance, a product, the conditions, and the criterion.
Informational Objective	Abbreviation of the instructional objective with only the performance product specified.

Review, Extension, and Reflective Exercise 3.1

Define an instructional objective and write different kinds of objectives.

Connections to INTASC Standards:

- Standard 1: Subject Matter. The teacher must understand the central concepts, tools of inquiry, and structures of the discipline(s) he or she teaches and be able to create learning experiences that make these aspects of subject matter meaningful for students.
- Standard 7: Planning Instruction. The teacher plans instruction based upon knowledge of subject matter, students, the community, and curriculum goals.

Connections to the NBPTS:

- Proposition 2: Teachers must know the subjects they teach and how to teach those subjects to students.
- Proposition 3: Teachers are responsible for managing and monitoring student learning.

Review

- What is an objective?
- Differentiate between an educational goal and an instructional objective.
- What are the components (elements) of a well-written instructional objective?

Reflection

- What goals should be generic to all schools? Should goals be different for elementary and secondary schools?
- How important are instructional objectives? Should teachers be required to submit weekly objectives?
- When writing objectives do you really need all four elements? Which would you eliminate?
- How will you communicate your objectives to students?

"Recess is my most important subject. I'm going to be a congressman.

Taxonomies of Objectives

Objectives can be classified into three primary categories on the basis of their instructional focus: thinking, attitudes, and physical skills. These areas of focus represent the three domains of learning: cognitive, affective, and psychomotor. In reality, however, the domains do not occur in isolation. Whereas some behaviors are easily classifiable into one of the three domains, others will overlap a great deal. This overlap is diagrammed in Figure 3.2. A good example of this overlap is seen when students are required to complete an assignment that involves a written response. In so doing, they must recall information and think (cognitive); they will have some emotional response to the task (affective); and they must use fine motor skills to make the necessary writing movements (psychomotor).

The three domains for objectives were designed to form hierarchical taxonomies of student learning—from simple to complex—with each level making use of and building on the behaviors addressed in the preceding level. The levels do not imply, however, that behaviors must be mastered sequentially from the lowest level to the highest level. Indeed, instruction can be directed toward any level of complexity.

Don't write objectives at specific taxonomy levels just to have objectives at all levels. Although it is possible to write objectives at any of the taxonomy levels of the three domains of learning, Mager (1997) suggests that, once you have made a suitable analysis of your instructional intent, you will know what you want your students to learn and you will automatically write your objectives at the intended levels. Furthermore, you must guard against falling into the habit of writing objectives only for the lower levels of learning within a particular domain because writing higher-level learning objectives is more difficult. A working knowledge of the taxonomy of the domains can prevent this pitfall to some extent. In other words, you can use your knowledge of the taxonomies to formulate the best possible objectives for your teaching intent, to not write objectives at a particular level, and to ensure that your teaching is not focused totally on the lower levels.

Although an overview of the three domains of learning and the associated major categories of each taxonomy follows, a more detailed description of the domains can be found by referring to one of the objective references. The information presented

Figure 3.2

The Three Domains

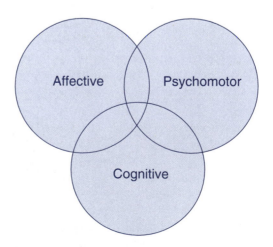

about cognitive taxonomy levels is adapted from the work of Bloom, Engelhart, Furst, Hill, and Krathwohl (1956); the material on affective taxonomy levels, from the work of Krathwohl, Bloom, and Masia (1964); and the coverage of the psychomotor taxonomy, from the works of Harrow (1972) and Jewett and Mullan (1977).

Cognitive Domain

Objectives in the **cognitive domain** are concerned with the thinking and reasoning ability of students. Because the ability to think can range from simple recall of information to more complex thinking behaviors, Benjamin Bloom (1956) and his associates developed a hierarchical classification system, or taxonomy, to help teachers gain a better perspective on the behaviors to be emphasized in instructional planning.

Bloom's Taxonomy classifies cognitive ability into six categories, ranging from the fairly simple recall of information to the complex assimilation of information and evaluation. These categories, along with verbs commonly used to express the required behaviors, are listed in Table 3.5. Let's now briefly examine the six levels of Bloom's Taxonomy.

Level One: Knowledge

The term *knowledge* learning refers to the simple recall or recognition of previously learned materials. This may involve the recall of terminology, basic principles, generalizations, and specific facts such as dates, events, persons, and places. For the most part, no manipulation or interpretation of the learned material is required of students. The information is usually retrieved in the same form that it was stored. Students, for example, could be required to remember the names of major scientists, to memorize a poem, to recognize chemical symbols, or to recall basic mathematics facts.

TABLE 3.5 Bloom's Taxonomy and Illustrative Action Verbs

Level	Student Action
Knowledge	Identify, define, list, match, state, name, label, describe, select
Comprehension	Translate, convert, generalize, paraphrase, rewrite, summarize, distinguish, infer, alter, explain
Application	Use, operate, produce change, solve, show, compute, prepare, determine
Analysis	Discriminate, select, distinguish, separate, subdivide, identify, break down, analyze, compare
Synthesis	Design, plan, compile, compose, organize, conclude, arrange, construct, devise
Evaluation	Appraise, compare, justify, criticize, explain, interpret, conclude, summarize, evaluate

Knowledge-level objectives usually focus on the storage and retrieval of information in memory. In other words, the thinking ability required is in tapping the appropriate signals, cues, and clues to find and retrieve knowledge from memory. In a sense, the knowledge-level category lays a foundation for the higher-thinking ability categories in that it provides the basic information needed for thinking at the higher levels. At times, however, teachers overuse the knowledge category. An example of an informational knowledge-level objective follows:

The student will be able to identify the major characters in an assigned short story.

Level Two: Comprehension

Comprehension represents the first level of understanding. The handling of information extends beyond the memorization of previously learned material to changing its form or making simple interpretations. Comprehension activities could require that students translate material to new forms, explain and summarize material, or estimate future trends. For example, you could ask students to interpret given information, translate information from one medium to another, or simply describe something in their own words. An example of an informational comprehension-level objective follows:

Given a graph of economic data, the student will be able to interpret the information in his or her own words.

Level Three: Application

Application entails putting learned information to use in reaching a solution or accomplishing a task. Students are asked to use remembered principles or generalizations to solve concrete problems. The process may require the application of rules, general ideas, concepts, laws, principles, or theories. For example, students apply the rules of grammar when writing a term paper, or they apply geometrical theorems when solving geometry problems. To be categorized as an application activity, a problem must be unique—that is, it must not be one that was addressed in class or in the textbook. An example of an instructional application-level objective follows:

Given a simple sentence, the student will be able to determine its noun and verb.

Level Four: Analysis

Analysis can be defined as breaking down complex material into its component parts so it can be better explained. This may involve subdividing something to explain how it works, analyzing the relationships between parts, or the recognizing of motives or organizational structures. A science teacher, for example, might ask how the circulatory system works, a second-grade teacher might ask for ideas on how to use a word in a sentence, or a social studies teacher might ask for a description of the national attitude toward the environment. An example of an informational analysis-level objective follows:

Given a chemical compound, the student will be able to correctly break it down into its simplest elements.

Level Five: Synthesis

Synthesis occurs when components are combined to form a new whole. With synthesis, a new and unique form must be produced from available elements. This may involve the creation of a unique composition, communication, plan, proposal, or scheme for classifying information. The unique creation may be in verbal or physical form. Students, for example, could be asked to use the British and American forms of government to create a completely unique governmental system. The key to synthesis-level activities is the incorporation of known ideas to form unique patterns or to create new ideas. A possible instructional synthesis-level objective follows:

> Given a societal problem, the student will be able to propose at least two possible solutions to the problem.

Level Six: Evaluation

Evaluation means that a judgment is required as to the value of materials or ideas. Students are required to make quantitative and qualitative judgments on the extent to which an internal or external criterion is satisfied. To accomplish this end, students must (1) set up or be given appropriate criteria or standards, and (2) determine to what extent an idea or object meets the standards. For example, students could be asked to decide who was the greatest president, or they could be asked to determine the best source of energy for the United States. Indeed, most questions that ask students to decide the best/worst or identify the least/most important require thinking and reasoning at the evaluation level. An example of an informational evaluation-level objective follows:

> Given a video of a tennis match, the students will rate the match in terms of the tennis tactics and skill outlined in class.

The advantage of the Bloom Taxonomy is its utility in different subjects. The body of work by Orlich et al. (1990), Arons (1988), Haller, Child, and Walberg (1988), Wittrock (1986), Nickerson (1985), and Beyer (1984), however, has led to a novel interpretation of how the cognitive taxonomy may operate. Instead of the six major categories viewed as a ladder (Figure 3.3) that must be climbed one level at a time, a three-dimensional model (Figure 3.4) can be offered. This model is analogous to an apple. The outward peel represents knowledge, the first level. The meat of the apple is analogous to the comprehension (understanding) level, and the higher levels of thinking represent the core of all understanding. This model views the cognitive categories as interactive, with the comprehension level being the key to unlocking the other levels. That is, once you truly understand the knowledge, then you can branch into any of the remaining four categories—application, analysis, synthesis, or evaluation. There is no need for one to move through the categories one step at a time. Students can move from comprehension to evaluation, from comprehension to analysis thinking, from comprehension to synthesis, or from comprehension to application.

Figure 3.3
Traditional Model of
Cognitive Taxonomy as a
Ladder

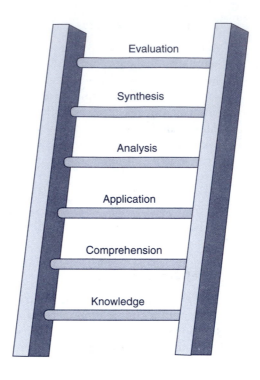

Figure 3.4
Three-Dimensional
Model of the Cognitive
Taxonomy

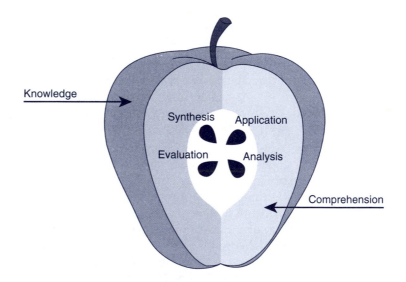

Affective Domain

Objectives in the **affective domain** are concerned with the development of students'
attitudes, feelings, and emotions. They can vary according to the degree of internalization of the attitude, feeling, or emotion.

Clearly, because teachers must be concerned with the total development of students, not just development in the cognitive domain—the writing of objectives for the affective domain should be an integral part of the planning process. Yet, because of the difficulty of writing objectives for the affective domain, this has not been the case. Affective-domain objectives are difficult to write because attitudes, feelings, and emotions are hard to translate into overt, observable behaviors. For example, the affective objective "The student will value the need for rules" is not properly written. The behavior "value" is not observable or measurable. The verb *value* must be replaced with an action that shows observable behavior: "The student will support the school rules during class discussions on class rules." This objective would be one, and only one, of many possible indicators that the student "values" the need for rules.

Behaviors related to the affective domain must take place in a "free choice" situation if they are to give a true indication of student attitudes, likes and dislikes, and feelings. If not out of free choice, students may exhibit the desired behaviors for a reward, or because they want to please you. For example, students who attend class every day may not be doing so because they like coming to your class or because they like the subject but because of the grade. But the objective "The student will eagerly participate in class discussions" would specify one possible indicator that the student likes the class.

Another free-choice technique sometimes used to reveal attitudes, feelings, emotions, and interests is the administration of various affective-domain inventories. These instruments will be discussed at length in Chapter 5.

David Krathwohl and associates (1964) developed a classification system for categorizing affective responses into five levels, according to the degree of internalization. That is, it is organized as to the degree to which an attitude, feeling, value, or emotion has become part of the individual. The taxonomy levels and some illustrative verbs commonly used for revealing the extent of internalization are given in Table 3.6. In a sense, the taxonomy forms a hierarchical continuum of internalization—ranging from a person's merely passive awareness to an individual's being characterized by certain values and attitudes. Let's now take a brief look at the taxonomy levels.

TABLE 3.6 Affective Domain Taxonomy and Illustrative Action Verbs

Level	Student Action
Receiving	Follow, select, rely, choose, point to, ask, hold, give, locate, attend
Responding	Read, conform, help, answer, practice, present, report, greet, tell, perform, assist, recite
Valuing	Initiate, ask, invite, share, join, follow, propose, read, study, work, accept, do, argue
Organization	Defend, alter, integrate, synthesize, listen, influence, adhere, modify, relate, combine
Characterization by a Value or Value Complex	Adhere, relate, act, serve, use, verify, question, confirm, propose, solve, influence, display

Level One: Receiving

Receiving can be defined as being aware of and willing to attend freely to stimuli and messages in the environment (listen and look). All teachers want their students to listen to and be aware of classroom stimuli. At this level, students are attending to what the teacher is presenting, but the attention is not active involvement. An example of an informational receiving-level objective follows:

> The student will follow given directions, without their needing to be repeated because of student inattentativeness.

Note that the student must be attentive and make a conscious effort to pay attention to the classroom environment rather than to other stimuli. The attention, however, can be rather passive.

Level Two: Responding

Responding requires active participation: A person is not only freely attending to stimuli but also voluntarily reacting to those stimuli. This involves physical, active behavior, where students make choices about issues. An example of an informational responding-level objective follows:

> The student will willingly assist other students with their homework when they encounter problems.

At this level, students have developed an interest and make a choice to participate. Further, they are satisfied with this participation.

Level Three: Valuing

Valuing refers to voluntarily giving worth to an idea, a phenomenon, or a stimulus. Behaviors at this level are selected even when there are alternatives. Students not only accept the worth of a value, but they also internalize that worth. An example of an instructional value-level objective follows:

> When given alternatives, the student will share concerns about the need for clean air and water on at least two occasions.

Note that students are given alternatives and the opportunity to repeat the choice. Also notice that the choice must be made freely.

Level Four: Organization

The term *organization* refers to building an internally consistent value system. At this level, a set of criteria is established and applied in choice making. The individual takes on value positions and is willing to defend them. An example of an informational organization-level objective follows:

> The student will voluntarily seek information related to career opportunities and will prepare for selected career goals.

Organization means one has made a commitment. In a sense, a "philosophy of life" has been internalized.

Level Five: Characterization by a Value or Value Complex

If behaviors reveal that an individual has developed a value system and acts consistently with the internalized values, then *characterization by a value* or *value complex* has been established. At this level, the person displays individuality and self-reliance. An example of an informational objective at the level of characterization by a value or value complex follows:

> In a class discussion, the student will defend the rights of *all* individuals to express their ideas and opinions.

Demonstration of this behavior would reveal that an individual is acting consistently with an established value system.

Psychomotor Domain

Objectives in the **psychomotor domain** relate to the development of muscular abilities that range from simple reflex movement to precision and creativity in performing a skill. The psychomotor domain is especially relevant in physical education, music, drama, art, and vocational courses, but all subjects will relate to this domain to some degree.

Although the psychomotor domain was the last to have a taxonomy developed for it, several systems have now been developed. The four-level system presented here is based on and adapted from the work of Harrow (1972) and Jewett and Mullan (1977). As you read through the levels and illustrative verbs presented in Table 3.7, notice how the processes can be applied to such areas as physical education, music, art, and vocational education.

Level One: Fundamental Movement

Fundamental movements are those that form the basic building blocks for the higher-level movements—for example, the ability to track objects, grasp objects, or crawl and walk. A sample informational objective for the fundamental-movement level follows:

> The student will be able to hold a tennis racket properly for the backhand.

Notice that this objective deals with the fundamental movement of the proper grasp of a tennis racket. Indeed, it is basic to the higher-level tennis movements.

Level Two: Generic Movement

Generic movement refers to the ability to carry out the basic rudiments of a skill when given directions and under supervision. At this level, effective motor patterns, timing, and coordination are being developed and refined. Awareness of the body in motion and of the arrangement and use of the body parts is learned. The total act, however, is

The development of motor skills is an essential part of the learning intent in many classrooms.

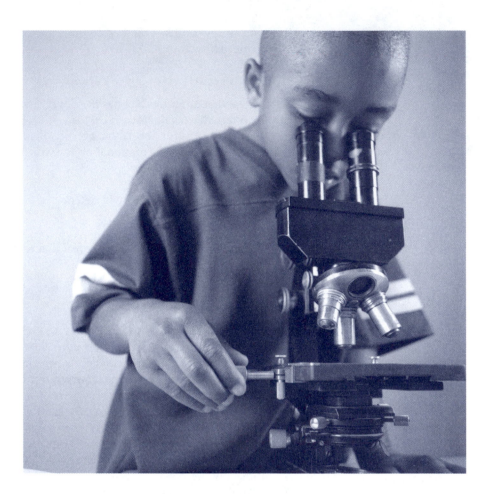

TABLE 3.7 Psychomotor Domain Taxonomy and Illustrative Action Verbs	
Level	**Student Action**
Fundamental Movement	Track, crawl, hear, react, move, grasp, walk, climb, jump, grip, stand, run
Generic Movement	Drill, construct, dismantle, change, hop, clean, manipulate, follow, use, march
Ordinative Movement	Play, connect, fasten, make, sketch, weigh, wrap, manipulate, play, swim, repair, write
Creative Movement	Create, invent, construct, manipulate, play, build, pantomime, perform, make, compose

not performed with skill. An example of an instructional generic-movement level objective follows:

> Under supervision, the student will be able to perform a required musical score with no more than five errors.

This level of motor skill requires supervision in that it represents the initial learning of a series of movements.

Level Three: Ordinative Movement

Ordinative movement marks the competence in performing a skill ably and independently. The entire skill has been organized and can be performed in sequence. Conscious effort is no longer needed: the skill has been mastered, and there is precision of performance. At this level, the skill can be carried out by habit under complex conditions. An example of an informational ordinative-movement level objective follows:

> Given a dive to perform, the student will be able to carry out the step-by-step technique without pausing to think.

Level Four: Creative Movement

Creative movement, which calls for the ability to produce and compose, serves the personal purposes of the performer. That is, the individual should be able to invent unique motor options, improvise originality into a movement, combine several movements into a personal unique motor design, or invent a new movement pattern. An example of an informational creative-movement level objective might be as follows:

> Given a dance routine, the student will be able to make appropriate changes to incorporate personal dance strengths.

Instruction and learning in the classroom frequently contain elements of all three domains. Nevertheless, your objectives usually will place primary emphasis on either the cognitive, affective, or psychomotor domain. Furthermore, remember that the three domain taxonomies can be valuable tools for upgrading your writing of objectives. But don't become a slave to the taxonomies; instead, base your objectives on the needs of your class and use the taxonomies as a guide. Finally, strive to incorporate the higher levels of each taxonomy in your learning experiences. Before finishing this chapter, complete Web Link: Examples of Objectives to further refine your understanding of objectives.

W E B   L I N K   Examples of Objectives

Access the examples of instructional objectives and student activities on Internet URL sites www.adprima.com/examples.htm and http://adprima.com/user-menu.htm. Analyze the objectives. Are objectives written for all three domains? Are they clear? How could they be improved?

APPLY AND REFLECT: You should analyze your instructional intent prior to writing your objectives; then focus your objectives on the appropriate domain and taxonomy level. What domain and taxonomy levels will be emphasized in the area you expect to teach?

This concludes our discussion of the three learning domains and their respective taxonomies. Before leaving this chapter, however, let's look at the new backward design concept for identifying instructional intent. Many of the best teachers use this approach.

Backward Design Approach

The *backward design* approach to instruction offers an alternative view to the traditional way of determining intent (see Figure 2.3). The backward design begins with the end in mind, the enduring understandings that you want students to learn and apply. In other words, what knowledge is *worth* understanding? Examples of enduring understandings might include an understanding of community helpers by kindergarteners, an understanding of the digestive system by 5th graders, an understanding of the role of technology in peoples' lives by 7th graders, and an understanding of proper writing techniques by 10th graders. District, state, and national standards are often used in establishing enduring understandings.

After establishing the enduring understandings, related essential questions are developed that cover the full range of the understandings. These questions should be geared to help students take an inquiry approach toward the various learning experiences that will be designed. Good essential questions should

- Be open-ended with no simple or single right answer.
- Be deliberately thought provoking, counterintuitive, and/or controversial.
- Require students to draw upon content knowledge and personal experience.
- Be framed to provoke and sustain student interest.
- Engage students in evolving dialogue and debate.
- Lead to other essential questions posed by students.

The essential questions should focus on the key knowledge and skills students should acquire.

Take a few minutes to complete Review, Extension, and Reflective Exercise 3.2, which will check your understanding of the concepts presented in this section. Before doing so, however, review the concepts presented in Table 3.8.

TABLE 3.8 Objective Domains

Domain	Description
Cognitive	Category of learning that focuses on the ability to think and reason, consisting of six cognitive taxonomy levels: knowledge, comprehension, application, analysis, synthesis, and evaluation
Affective	Category of learning concerned with emotional development, encompassing five affective domain taxonomy levels: receiving, responding, valuing, organization, and characterization by a value or value complex
Psychomotor	Category of learning related to muscular and motor skill development, consisting of four psychomotor domain taxonomy levels: fundamental movement, generic movement, ordinative movement, and creative movement

Review, Extension, and Reflective Exercise 3.2

Define a taxonomy and the three domains of learning.

Connections to INTASC Standards:

- Standard 1: Subject Matter. The teacher must understand the central concepts, tools of inquiry, and structures of the discipline(s) he or she teaches and be able to create learning experiences that make these aspects of subject matter meaningful for students.
- Standard 7: Planning Instruction. The teacher plans instruction based upon knowledge of subject matter, students, the community, and curriculum goals.

Connections to the NBPTS:

- Proposition 2: Teachers must know the subjects they teach and how to teach those subjects to students.
- Proposition 3: Teachers are responsible for managing and monitoring student learning.

Review

- Name the three learning domains of objectives and the levels within each.

Reflection

- What learning domain will be the focus of most of your instruction?
- Do you think it is important to know the domains of learning and write objectives for each?

VIEW FROM THE CLASSROOM

What do teachers think about establishing instructional intent? Teacher survey results relative to topics presented in this chapter are expressed below. Review these results and discuss with classmates.

What single item, within your classroom, can you not live without:

Computer	52%
Lesson-planning book	23%
Attendance/grade book	13%
Class textbook	12%

What teaching program do you feel most benefits special education students?

Resource	46%
Self-contained	27%
Inclusion	26%

SOURCE: Excerpted from *Teach-nology*, available at www.teach-nology.com/poll

THE PUBLIC VIEW OF EDUCATION

What does the public think of our instructional intent? Review these results and discuss with classmates.

From your knowledge of the No Child Left Behind Act, what is your opinion of the act?

Very favorable	5%
Somewhat favorable	13%
Somewhat unfavorable	7%
Very unfavorable	6%
Don't know enough to say	69%

Under the No Child Left Behind Act, a school's performance is evaluated annually based on the performance of students. Is there a better way to judge the job a public school is doing?

Whether students meet a fixed standard	14%
Whether students show reasonable improvement from where they started	84%
Don't know	2%

Would vouchers that allow parents to choose private schools improve student achievement in our community?

Improve	48%
Would not improve	48%
Don't know	4%

Do today's public schools provide their students with adequate science, math, reading, and writing skills?

Yes	22%
No	72%
Other	3%
Don't know	4%

Social promotion means moving children from grade to grade in order to keep them with others in their own age group. Would you favor stricter standards for social promotion in school even if it meant that significantly more students would be held back?

Favor	72%
Oppose	26%
Don't know	2%

SOURCE: Adapted from *The 35th Annual Phi Delta Kappa/Gallup Poll of the Public's Attitudes Toward the Public Schools* (2003) by Lowell C. Rose and Alec M. Gallup, available at www.pdkintl.org/kappan/k0309pol.htm; *The Internet Party*, available at www.theinternetparty.org/polls/index.php?section_type=pol&cat_name=Education; and *PollingReport.com*, available at www.pollingreport.com/educ2.htm

Summary

- Objectives specify your instructional intent to students. They specify what your students should be able to do following instruction.
- Objectives are finite and measurable.

Rationale for Objectives

- Objectives set the framework for your instructional approach and the evaluation of student learning.
- Objectives serve an important communication function.
- Objectives serve an accountability function.

Objective Specificity

- The specificity of instructional intent varies from broad educational goals to very narrow specific objectives.
- The three levels of learning intent, in order of specificity, are educational goals, informational objectives, and instructional objectives.
- Specific objectives are subordinate to educational goals.

Stating Objectives

- The actions called for by educational goals are overt, nonmeasurable behaviors.
- The actions called for by informational and instructional objectives are overt and measurable.
- Instructional objectives consist of four components: (1) the performance, (2) the product, (3) the conditions, and (4) the criterion.
- Informational objectives specify only the performance and the product; the conditions and criterion are usually not specified.

Communication of Objectives

- Objectives should always be communicated to students. This communication is usually in written form at the beginning of a unit of study.
- Informational objectives will usually suffice for communicating your learning intent.

Taxonomies of Objectives

- Objectives can be written at any of the levels within the three domains of learning: cognitive, affective, and psychomotor.
- The three domains of learning are interrelated.
- Each of the three domains is arranged in hierarchical order from simple to complex.
- Objectives can be written at any of the levels within the three domains of learning. Teachers tend, however, to write objectives at only the lower levels.

Backward Design Approach

- The backward design approach to instructional planning offers an alternative view to the traditional way of determining intent.
- The backward design begins with the establishment of enduring understandings.
- Essential questions are developed to cover the full range of planned enduring understandings.

Discussion Questions and Activities

1. **Analysis of textbook objectives.** Review the teacher's edition of a school textbook from the grade level and/or subject you expect to teach that lists the unit and/or chapter objectives. Address the following questions in your review.

   a. Are informational objectives given for the chapters? Are instructional objectives?
   b. Are objectives written for all three domains of learning?
   c. Are the objectives written at the different taxonomy levels within each of the learning domains?

2. **Writing goals and objectives.** Consider your planned teaching grade level and/or subject and write a broad educational goal that you feel should be addressed at the identified level. Now write at least three different informational and instructional objectives that tell what students should do to show you that the goal has been accomplished.

3. **Writing cognitive, affective, and psychomotor domain objectives.** Write ten cognitive and psychomotor domain objectives for a topic from your area. Make the objectives at various taxonomy levels of sophistication. Now write five affective domain objectives at various taxonomy levels for the same class. Let your classmates review and critique your objectives.

4. **Backward design.** Write an enduring understanding for an area you expect to teach. Write guiding essential questions that cover the enduring understanding.

Connection With the Field

1. **Teacher interviews.** Interview several teachers. Are they required to write objectives? Do they write objectives for all three learning domains? Do they write objectives at different levels within each domain? Do they use the backward design?

2. **Principals' view of objectives.** Interview two elementary and two secondary principals. What is their view of objectives? Are their views similar to that of the teachers? Are objectives a district requirement?

Praxis II Connection

The following test preparation exercises are intended to help you prepare for the Praxis II: Principles of Learning and Teaching. The Praxis II may be required by your teacher education preparatory program and for state certification or licensing. These exercises will give you direct access to pedagogical knowledge from Chapter 3 that may be expected of you on the Praxis II and other pedagogical exams that may be required at the end of your teacher education program.

Topic Connections

1. Instructional Objectives (II. B1)

Describe the key components of instructional (behavioral) objectives. Write an objective for the cognitive, affective, and psychomotor domain for the grade level and/or content area that you expect to teach.

2. Taxonomies of Educational Objectives (II. B1)

List the levels within each of the three domains of learning and describe the focus of each level. Be able to incorporate these objective levels into instructional objectives that you design.

ON YOUR OWN

Log on to the web-based student study site at http://www.sagepub.com/eis for more information about the vignettes and materials presented in this chapter, suggestions for activities, study aids such as electronic flashcards and review quizzes, and research recommendations including journal article links and questions related to this chapter.

4

DEVELOPING UNIT AND DAILY LESSON PLANS

The object of education is to prepare the
young to educate themselves throughout their lives.

ROBERT MAYNARD HUTCHINS

OVERVIEW

Why do teachers plan? This chapter will focus on this question and on techniques for effective planning. I will explore some of what is known about the processes of planning and decision making.

Because planning is essential to achieving excellence in instruction, the planning processes that result in the successful delivery of knowledge, attitudes, values, and skills will be explored. I will consider the different levels of planning, as well as personnel associated with the planning processes. Finally, this chapter will focus attention on the basic components of unit and daily lesson planning. This examination will include a rather detailed explanation of specific planning procedures and several different formats.

OBJECTIVES

After completing your study of Chapter 4, you should be able to do the following:

1. Describe the four levels of planning.
2. Identify and describe the key components of a unit and daily lesson plan.
3. Differentiate between teacher-centered and student-centered instruction and name various methods associated with each.
4. Explain the importance of daily lesson planning in the learning process.
5. Operationally define *set induction* and *lesson closure* and explain their importance to effective teaching.
6. Operationally define *instructional strategy* and name its two components.
7. Describe the four variables that should be considered in the selection of an appropriate instructional method.
8. Develop a unit plan for a given area within your area of specialization.
9. Develop daily lesson plans for a unit or series of units.

No two teachers teach in the same way; similarly, no two teachers plan in exactly the same way. Planning serves two practical functions: It allows you to anticipate instructional needs in advance so materials can be gathered and organized, and it provides a plan that directs classroom interactions. The excellent lesson delivery of effective teachers often appears spontaneous. These teachers, however, have planned—formally or informally—each daily lesson with care. They have the lesson content and the related teaching skills mastered to the extent that their delivery is poised and automatic.

Planning for instruction is one of the most important things a teacher or group of teachers can do. Even experienced teachers spend time planning. They replan the presentation of lessons they have taught many times to avoid becoming stale and routine.

Planning Instruction

As shown in Figure 4.1, teachers should engage in four levels of planning. Course and unit planning are broader in scope than weekly and daily planning. Course and unit plans determine the direction you will take and what the general impact of the entire curriculum will be.

No matter what the level of planning, decisions must be made with respect to the coordination of course content, instructional materials, and the special needs of students. Therefore, before I look at the levels of planning in greater detail, I will focus on teacher-student planning and the selection of instructional materials.

Teacher-Student Planning

Students as well as teachers can be engaged in the planning process. The extent to which students participate in the planning of their own learning activities varies greatly from classroom to classroom. In many classrooms, the only involvement students have is the selection of class projects, reports, and outside readings. By engaging students, however, the teacher gains insights into student interests and areas of weakness and strength. A **teacher-student planning** process promotes "ownership" of the curriculum. If students communicate that they already understand intended instructional material, they could be tested on the material. If, in fact, they do have a good understanding of the material in question, then valuable time and resources could be reallocated to other areas. How many times has each of us studied the colonial period of American history but failed to spend any time on the period following World War II?

Figure 4.1

Levels of Planning

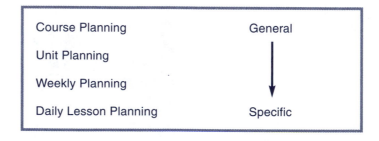

"What homework? These are hall passes, insurance forms, attendance reports, competency updates, and my grocery list."

APPLY AND REFLECT: Do you support teacher-student planning? How much student involvement in the planning process do you feel is feasible at the grade level you expect to teach?

Instructional Materials

Essential to effective planning are the survey and preparation of available media and materials for instruction. Textbooks, audiovisual materials, supplementary reading materials, and supplies and equipment for group and individual projects should be examined and coordinated with your lesson. Time spent on reviewing what is available in the district will be time well spent. You should preview films and computer software, review printed materials, and learn to use the latest instructional technology.

The incorporation of a wide variety of instructional materials will improve your lessons and heighten students' attention and interest. The use of videotapes, the Internet, and computer software in presenting examples and nonexamples of concepts, for instance, will serve as a lesson stimulus. I will address the effective use of various motivational techniques in Chapter 12.

Having looked at some of the general planning of instruction, it is time to look at the four planning levels in greater detail.

Rethinking Unit Planning

1. Does unit planning result in more effective teaching?
2. Should students be given long-term class projects to complete or shorter projects?

I teach middle school and have been rethinking the whole way I do units.

In the past few years, I have been writing units that span nearly a full quarter. Each unit included many learning objectives, smaller assignments that helped students learn content along the way, and a large, final assessment at the end of the quarter. I have been pretty proud of my units because of the time and practice allotted to my students to master concepts before formal assessment. If you had asked me a month ago, I would have told you I would never teach another way. But the thing about teaching I have found is to never say never. Faced with only 5 weeks to complete my fairy tale unit, I had to revamp the unit to fit into the smaller space of time.

In 5 weeks, my students completed two projects. One was to work with a partner to identify five characteristics of fairy tales, develop a definition of a fairy tale, and present using PowerPoint.

While the results for some were poor (largely because of off task behavior), the overall motivation, attitude, and thoughtfulness of my students increased dramatically. No one was asking me "What PowerPoint presentation?" like other students had asked me "What magazine article?" in the previous unit. It seemed this project was more important to them.

The second project was to rewrite a fairy tale of the students' choice from the evil character's point of view. We read several examples, including *The True Story of the Three Little Pigs* by Jon Scieza and *Interview*, a poem by Sara Henderson Hay that presents Cinderella's stepmother's point of view. Students had 2 weeks to write, revise, and type their stories. As a bonus, we sent each student's story in to Barry Lane's writing contest for recycled fairy tales.

With this project, I had very little problem with students being off task at any point, and all but maybe five students turned their stories in on time. I have not

begun to assess them, but after reading through several of the stories during the past week, I am encouraged. I witnessed once again a positive attitude about the task, and students seemed very mindful of the scoring guide and task deadline.

With the results I have been getting, I have to pause to reflect upon why. Why are my students more focused? Why are they more likely to turn in their work? Why are they more interested and excited?

I think the shorter project time has a lot to do with the results I am getting. Middle school students seem to be in a time vacuum; without the immediacy of a task deadline to guide them, I think they are more apt to procrastinate. Students live in the here and now, not in the hazy, distant end of the quarter.

I have decided this realization does not mean I have to give up my longer projects; to the contrary, I think as long as I create intermediate deadlines with tangible products that will be assessed along the way to the larger assessments at the end of the unit, I can create the same sense of urgency and importance as with these smaller units. It is a matter of breaking down the task into manageable parts.

A second reason I think the past two projects have been so successful is that I have made a conscious effort to start first with what my students need to know in a backward design sort of approach. I have tried to do this with my larger units, but using Grant Wiggins's process on a smaller task helped me understand the process a little better, producing better results in task design.

The recycled fairy tale task was designed in response to my students' struggle with point of view, both in class and on a variety of district and state assessments. It felt good to be responsive to my kids, to remember I am teaching kids, not curriculum.

Just when I think I have task design mastered, I find I have much left to learn.

—ELLEN BERG, *sixth grade teacher, English/ language arts, St. Louis, MO*

SOURCE: www.middleweb.com. Reprinted with permission.

Students can be directly involved in planning academic and nonacademic activities.

Course Planning

The most general type of planning you will perform as a classroom teacher is **course planning** (Posner & Rudnitsky, 2000). Although in most cases, the textbook forms the basic structure for course plans, it should not be the main premise of instruction. Beginning teachers should use their textbooks and state-curriculum suggestions as instructional guides and should integrate supplementary material into the basic text structure. Experienced teachers, however, often structure their courses on the basis of experience and use the textbook and state-curriculum suggestions to supplement their experience base.

Unit Planning

Courses are usually divided into a sequence of manageable units of study that represent discrete segments of the year's work. Each unit is organized around a specific theme or a cluster of related concepts. For example, a unit in earth science might be titled "Plants" or a unit in kindergarten might be titled "Community Helpers." Units provide a framework for the design of a course. In effect, a unit is a series of many intended learning activities and experiences, unified around the theme or a cluster of related concepts.

Unit planning can be deemed more critical than other levels of planning. The **unit plan** links the goals, objectives, content, activities, and evaluation you have in mind. These plans should be shared with students to provide the overall road map that explains where you are going. Such communication expresses to students what they are expected to learn.

The unit plan has several components. The plan is titled by the topic that represents the unifying theme for the unit. These topics may follow the chapter headings in your textbook or the areas within your subject that the various curriculum guides direct you to cover. These topics could be derived through teacher planning or through teacher-student planning. As discussed in Chapter 2, unit topics generally are taken from the headings of course plans. The plan should spell out your goals and specific instructional objectives. A somewhat detailed outline of the content should be included, as should learning activities appropriate to the content and to the learners. A list of needed instructional materials and resources should be provided. Finally, the methods you intend to use for evaluating student learning need to be specified. More specifically, a well-constructed unit should include the following components:

1. *A topic:* presumably the subject suggested by a course outline, a textbook, or a state-curriculum guide
2. *Goals and objectives:* a list of your learning intentions in broad and specific terms
3. *Content outline:* an outline of the material to be covered—with as much detail as you feel is needed—which should help clarify the subject and help you with the sequence and organization
4. *Learning activities:* teacher and students activities—comprising introductory, developmental, and culminating activities—that, when arranged into a series of daily lessons, will lead to the desired learning outcomes
5. *Resources and materials:* a list of materials to be selected and prepared for the unit
6. *Evaluation:* an outline of your evaluation procedure—including homework, tests, and special projects—which should be planned and prepared prior to instruction

Units vary greatly in scope and duration, depending on the grade level and subject. Generally, they range in duration from a few days to a few weeks. Other examples of typical units are the court system in government, astronomy in the 10th grade, and geometry in the 5th grade.

A unit structure now being emphasized in many schools is the **thematic unit** (Roberts & Kellough, 2003), the organizational structure of interdisciplinary/curriculum-integrated teaching. Thematic units offer teaching teams a useful, logical, and flexible way to organize for interdisciplinary/cross-curricular teaching over a block of time. It is a curriculum plan that provides opportunities for more relevant, less fragmented, and more stimulating experiences for students. Thematic units may focus on a specific content area or they may be global in nature. For example, in language arts, the focus of a theme may be on realistic fiction, or it may center on a global topic such as conflict. The team plans so that insights and understandings from one discipline, such as science, relate to other disciplines, such as literature and social studies. The planning of thematic units requires the identification of a team of teachers and students and the model to be implemented (see Chapter 2); the identification of a unit theme, including objectives, activities, and evaluative methods; and sufficient planning time made available for team teachers.

There are several sources available for assisting teachers with their unit plans. In some states, the curriculum is quite explicit, and the goals and topics that must be covered are mandated. When this is the case, the prescribed goals and topics are usually presented in terms of minimum requirements, so there is still plenty of justification for the careful planning of additional learning units. Even when a good deal of the course content has been predetermined, it is still necessary to plan the sequence, present the content, and test the outcomes. Many school districts also have a mandated curriculum that must be included in any course plan. These demands for covering specific content do not preclude the need for planning.

The course textbook offers clues for unit planning. Content must be selected and organized, however, with regard to your goals and learners. You must recognize that a particular author's view of sequence, for instance, may not serve your needs or the needs of your students. Textbooks are written for a wide audience and should be viewed as one of the tools for teaching a course, not as the course itself.

The information to be presented forms the bulk of a unit. This material should generally extend beyond the concept contained in the textbook and should be correlated with the unit objectives. Once you have determined the topics, sequence, and time for each topic, you must develop unit objectives that relate to the selected content. The goals should be your guide in determining unit objectives. You must then designate the specific student outcomes desired, as well as the level of behavioral complexity. Of course, keep in mind that the level of complexity sets the framework for your lesson activities and the evaluative process. Since Chapter 3 was devoted to the writing of goals and objectives, I will not discuss them further here.

Learning activities must then be identified that will support the unit. You need to choose the learning activities carefully to ensure that the objectives can be met. In addition, you should group your unit objectives and activities into daily lessons for implementation. Selecting of activities and groupings of your unit objectives and activities require you to decide how best to accomplish your planned goals. If you intend to illuminate the court system at work, you might plan a variety of activities, such as having students read about the court system in their textbooks, holding a mock trial, showing a film about a court case, or taking a trip to a nearby courtroom to observe a trial in session. Indeed, you might decide that a visit from a district attorney or a judge may be in order. These are all decisions you need to make early in the planning process to allow time for arranging these activities.

Always keep in mind that a unit consists of a series of daily lessons. The unit can be viewed as the whole, with the individual lessons as its parts. Thus, the individual lessons must be selected so they are interrelated and address the learner outcomes that are specified in the objectives of the unit as a whole.

Planning for instructional materials is an important part of the entire planning process. You need to familiarize yourself with the materials available in your school building and school district. You also need to investigate your community for possible sources of learning materials. A field trip to a courtroom may be problematic if the nearest court is several miles away and you have failed to contact the court or to arrange for permissions and transportation. Beginning teachers need to establish contact with experienced teachers in their building who are willing to share information with them about how to accomplish these kinds of tasks. As you plan for instructional materials, it is a good idea to keep a notebook or journal of available materials and resources.

Finally, how will you know if the students have learned what you intended in your carefully planned unit? The answer lies in carefully planning for evaluation. Will you give paper-and-pencil tests? If so, how often? Will student participation enter into the evaluation process, and how will you determine the value of each student's participation? These questions and others must be answered in the planning phase. The evaluation process will be addressed in detail in Chapters 5 and 6. Now complete Expansion Activity: Unit Planning, which will further develop your unit planning skills.

EXPANSION ACTIVITY	
Unit Planning	Obtain the teacher's edition of a textbook for a grade level and subject that you expect to teach. Using the textbook as a guide, outline	two units you would teach and the unit time allotment for each unit. Write a rationale for each unit.

Weekly Plans

Most school districts ask that teachers submit a short-form weekly lesson plan so that, in the event the teacher is absent, the substitute teacher has some idea of what was to be

" . . . and the reason we have summer
vacation is so you can go home to help with the crops."

Figure 4.2

Abridged Daily Lesson Format

	Monday	Tuesday	Wednesday	Thursday	Friday
Period 1	Pages 126–134	Activities 1 and 2 Pages 135-136	Activity 3 Page 156	Pages 141–155	Exercises 1–4 Pages 157–160
Period 2	Pages 126–134	Activities 1 and 2 Pages 135–136	Activity 4 Page 157	Pages 135–140	Exercises 2 and 5 Pages 161/164
Period 3	Planning	Planning	Planning	Planning	Planning
Period 4	Pages 126–134	Activities 1 and 2 Pages 135–136	Activity 3 Page 156	Pages 141–155	Exercises 1–4 Pages 157–160
Period 5	Experiment 10 Page 35	Field Trip	Pages 203–210	Activity 11 Page 180	Pages 211–225
Period 6	Pages 126–134	Activities 1 and 2 Pages 135–136	Activity 4 Page 147	Pages 135–140	Exercises 2 and 5 Pages 161/164
Period 7	Experiment 10 Page 35	Field Trip	Pages 203–210	Activity 11 Page 180	Pages 211–225

covered that day. A typical short-form **weekly plan**, as shown in Figure 4.2, outlines each day's lesson for one week on a single sheet of paper. These weekly lesson plans vary greatly in detail from school to school. They essentially are short, watered-down copies of the week's daily lesson plans, written on special forms provided by the school.

Daily Lesson Plans

The most detailed and specific type of plan is a **daily lesson plan**, which simply defines the objectives and class activities for a single day. Thus, unit planning does not eliminate daily planning; rather, because the objectives, activities, experiences, and necessary materials have been specified in the unit plan, the daily lesson plan flows naturally out of the unit plan. The exact structure of the daily lesson plan, however, depends on the type of lesson being designed. Lesson plans should reflect the individual needs, strengths, and interests of the teacher and the students. Lesson planning should never be dictated by rigid standards that prevent and stifle creativity. Indeed, you will rarely carry out a lesson entirely as planned. You must anticipate what is likely to happen as you teach your planned lessons, and you must make modifications as needed. Good teachers expect to adjust their plans as they move along, and they have alternatives in mind in case they are needed. The fact that most plans must be modified as they are taught does not justify the avoidance of thorough initial planning. Few teachers can "wing it." Planning, however, does not ensure success. The delivery counts for a great deal.

Postlesson Evaluation

Student evaluation should be an integral part of every lesson taught. As described here, evaluation entails postinstructional assessment of student performance. During evaluation, you determine the degree to which learners have attained the anticipated outcomes of the lesson.

Once a lesson has ended, a clear picture of how well students have mastered the stated objectives must be in your grasp. If there is a discrepancy between the intent and what was achieved, then you must decide whether reteaching is necessary.

The postlesson assessment that emerges from a lesson can vary widely in specificity and level of formality. Sometimes it will come from information gained during question-and-answer sequences. Sometimes it consists of information gleaned from student-group work, individual seatwork, or completion of class activities. At other times, the assessment is formal (quiz or test).

Postlesson assessments help ensure that students are not pushed on to new content before they have mastered prerequisite skills. In effect, they help you identify learning problems at the end of a unit, when a unit evaluation is usually administered. You can often avoid many classroom problems if you will conduct and use information obtained in postlesson assessments. It is generally wiser to plan reteaching for students who are having difficulty with lesson concepts and to design enrichment activities for those having no difficulty rather than having them proceed to the next lesson.

Planning establishes a proposed course of action that serves as your guide, from which appropriate deviations can be made. Following are some sample daily lesson plans. These formats differ somewhat in style, but each focuses on the type of learning desired.

Lesson Formats

Lesson Plan Format 1. A lesson plan should provide needed structure to a lesson but should be general enough to allow for flexibility. Writers in the area of planning (Jacobson, Eggen, & Kauchak, 1989; Orlich et al., 1990) suggest the following basic lesson plan format:

1. *Objectives:* the specific learning intent for the day, selected from the unit plan
2. *Introduction (set induction):* an activity used at the beginning of the lesson to attract student attention and interest
3. *Content:* a brief outline of the content to be covered in the lesson
4. *Methods and procedure:* a sequential listing of developmental activities for the day, selected from the unit plan
5. *Closure:* the lesson wrap-up activity
6. *Resources and materials:* a list of instructional materials needed for the lesson
7. *Evaluation procedure:* an activity or technique that determines how well students have mastered the intended learning outcomes of the lesson
8. *Assignment:* the in-class or homework assignment to be completed for the next class period

Lesson Plan Format 2. The second format has been suggested by advocates of the Madeline Hunter instructional design. It is a detailed and prescriptive seven-component plan with a highly structured format that emphasizes student involvement and success (Hunter, 1980). It is appropriate for skill learning and many forms of teacher-centered instruction, such as lecturing, lecture recitation, and Socratic questioning. The more student-centered lessons, such as discussions and problem solving, would not fit into this format (Shulman, 1987). The seven components of this format follow:

1. *Anticipatory set:* a teacher activity designed to prompt students to focus on the lesson before the lesson begins
2. *Objective and purpose:* teacher statements that explicitly inform students as to what will be learned in the coming lesson and how it will be useful
3. *Input:* the new knowledge, processes, or skills students are to learn
4. *Modeling:* the examples used in developing an understanding of the knowledge, processes, or skills being taught—including the techniques used to illustrate the new knowledge, processes, or skills
5. *Checking for understanding:* a method for determining whether students understand the learning intent that may occur before or during the teacher-directed activity (modeling) or during the student-guided activity
6. *Guided practice:* student practice of new knowledge, processes, or skills under teacher supervision (in-class)
7. *Independent practice:* unsupervised practice of new knowledge, process, or skill (assigned seatwork or homework)

Lesson Plan Format 3. This format is suggested for use with the small-group learning strategy. Small-group strategies generally require that students be prepared for their task and be debriefed once the assigned task has been addressed. Therefore, the planning process is a student-centered format with the following components:

1. *Objectives:* statements of the specific learning intents or what student should be able to do upon completion of the lesson
2. *Initial focus (set induction):* teacher-directed activity to get student attention and interest focused on the required assigned task
3. *Major task:* teacher-directed presentation of assigned group task, directions for group work, and options available to students
4. *Group activity:* students' task assigned by teacher who can offer strategy options or require that students develop their own
5. *Debriefing:* students' analysis and presentation of the product of the assigned task, as well as of the strategies that were and were not effective
6. *Resources and materials:* listing of the materials needed for groups to work on and complete assigned task
7. *Evaluation:* formal and informal techniques to be used to check whether students have achieved task and objectives

Lesson Plan Format 4. This format is suggested for the backward design approach to instruction. It is based on the concept that a firmer and clearer grasp of where learning is going will be presented when goals or assessments are clearly articulated right from the beginning.

1. *Enduring understanding(s):* knowledge and skills worth being familiar with and important to know and do

2. *Essential questions:* related questions that fully cover the enduring under-standing(s) that will guide and focus teaching/learning
3. *Assessment/Acceptable evidence:* how students will demonstrate understand-ings, knowledge, and skills
4. *Strategies/Best practices used to explicitly teach understandings:* sequence of teaching/learning experience that will equip students and demonstrate the desired understandings designed to hook students and hold their interest
5. *Resources and material:* listing of materials needed to accomplish tasks

The plans presented are intended to be illustrative, not all-inclusive. Some alter-nate lesson plan formats are shown in Figures 4.3 through 4.7. Each alternate format has been logically structured for a specific type of lesson. Note the adaptation and extension planning section in the formats presented in Figures 4.5 through 4.7. You should select the format that will lend direction to your lesson but not be a manu-script from which to read statements verbatim. *(Text continues on page 126).*

Figure 4.3
Outline of Key
Questions/Discussion
Lesson Plan Format

1. **Unit Topic:** _____

2. **Objectives:** _____

_____

3. **Set Induction:** _____

_____

4. **Procedures for Discussion:** _____

_____

5. **Key Questions** _____

    A. _____

    Possible Answers: _____

    _____

    Summary: _____

    _____

    B. _____

    Possible Answers: _____

    _____

    Summary: _____

Figure 4.3
(Continued)

_____

C. _____

Possible Answers: _____

_____

Summary: _____

_____

6. Conclusions: _____

_____

_____

_____

_____

7. Closure: _____

_____

_____

_____

_____

8. Evaluation: _____

_____

_____

_____

_____

9. Assignment: _____

_____

_____

_____

_____

Figure 4.4
Outline of Inquiry and
Problem-Solving
Lesson Plan Format

1. Lesson Topic: _____

2. Objectives: _____

_____

3. Set Induction: _____

_____

4. Procedures or Steps

   A. Problem Identification: _____

   _____

   B. Data Collection: _____

   _____

   C. Formulation of Hypotheses or Assumptions: _____

   _____

   D. Analysis of Data or Materials: _____

   _____

   E. Testing Hypotheses or Assumptions: _____

   _____

   F. Conclusion or Judgment: _____

   _____

5. Closure: _____

_____

6. Evaluation: _____

_____

7. Assignment: _____

_____

Figure 4.5
Concept Attainment
Lesson Plan

Your Name: Grade Level: (circle one) K 1 2 3 4 5 6

Subject: (circle one)   Language Arts   Social Studies   Mathematics   Science

Lesson Title:

Materials Needed:

Prerequisite Skills:

Lesson Objective(s):

Concept Label:

Critical Attributes: [yes]   Non-Critical Attributes: [no]

A feature of a certain concept that   Features found in some but not all
distinguishes it from other concepts   members of a category

Definition of Concept

1. Present objectives: (What are students going to learn?)   *Time:*

2. Provide examples and nonexamples to the class: (Input/modeling)   *Time:*

3. Test for attainment: (Do the students understand the concept?)   *Time:*

4. Analyze student thinking processes and integration of learning: (Are they able to provide additional examples and nonexamples?)   *Time:*

5. Assessment/closure: (How do you evaluate student progress or provide closure for this lesson?)   *Time:*

6. Adaptation for students who need extra help, time, or attention? AND
Extension for students of high ability?   *Time:*

TOTAL LESSON TIME: _____

References Consulted (Curriculum books, teacher resources, websites, etc):

SOURCE: Developed by Dr. Sally Beisser, School of Education, Drake University. ©Beisser, 2000. Used with permission

Figure 4.6
Cooperative Learning
Lesson Plan

Your Name: Grade Level: (circle one) K 1 2 3 4 5 6

Subject: (circle one)   Language Arts   Social Studies   Mathematics   Science

Lesson Title:

Materials Needed:

Prerequisite Skills:

Lesson Objective(s):
   a. Academic
   b. Social

Cooperative Learning Grouping Structure

1. Present objectives: (What are students going to learn?)   *Time:*

2. Present information for the academic goal: *Time:*

3. Organize students into learning teams: *Time:*
      (What is the social goal?)
      (How will you organize the groups?)
      (What group roles will you have?)

4. Assist team work and study: *Time:*
      (How will you monitor progress of the academic and the social goals?)

5. Provide recognition: *Time:*
      (How will students know they have met both academic and social goals?)

6. Assessment/closure: *Time:*
      (How do you evaluate student progress or end this lesson?)

7. Adaptation for students who need extra help, time, or attention?
   AND
   Extension for students of high ability?   *Time:*

TOTAL LESSON TIME: _____

References Consulted (Curriculum books, teacher resources, websites, etc):

SOURCE: Developed by Dr. Sally Beisser, School of Education, Drake University. ©Beisser, 2000. Used with permission

Figure 4.7
Direct Instruction
Lesson Plan

Your Name: _____   Grade Level: (circle one) K 1 2 3 4 5 6

Subject: (circle one)   Language Arts   Social Studies   Mathematics   Science

Lesson Title:

Materials Needed:

Prerequisite Skills:

Lesson Objective:

1. **Provide objectives:** (What are students going to learn?)   *Time:*

2. **Demonstrate knowledge or skill:** (Input/modeling by the teacher)   *Time:*

3. **Provide guided practice:** (Guided practice with the teacher)   *Time:*

4. **Check for understanding and provide student feedback:** (How will you know students understand the skill or concept? How will they know they "get it"?)   *Time:*

5. **Provide extended practice and transfer:** (Independent practice of the skill)   *Time:*

6. **Assessment/closure:** (How do you evaluate student progress or provide closure to this lesson?)   *Time:*

7. **Adaptation for students who need extra help, time, or attention?**
   AND
   Extension for students of high ability?   *Time:*

TOTAL LESSON TIME: _____

References Consulted (Curriculum books, teacher resources, websites, etc):

SOURCE: Developed by Dr. Sally Beisser, School of Education, Drake University. ©Beisser, 2000. Used with permission

As the lesson formats presented in this section suggest, teachers vary widely in their approaches to daily planning. Some develop detailed daily plans, whereas others merely write out a few notes as reminders. The sample lesson plans presented in Figures 4.8 through 4.11 illustrate how the various components are constructed.

(Text continues on page 130).

Figure 4.8
Creativity Lesson Plan

Topic: Creating a School

Objectives:

The students will be able to:

1. Give examples of the special features of different secondary schools.

2. Apply terms associated with secondary schools to an original student project.

Introduction (Set Induction):

Spend 10 minutes using pictures to review various secondary school terms. Students create a glossary of important secondary school terms in the form of a three-column chart giving terms (e.g., curriculum, hidden curriculum, extracurricular activities, administration, scheduling, minicourses, flexible scheduling, modules, learning centers, staff, discipline, and school district), definitions, and examples (e.g., the principal is an administrator).

Content: None

Procedure:

1. Divide class into groups of four or five. Group members are to work cooperatively on planning and drawing an imaginary secondary school.

2. Students are to give their school a name and decide on its main function (prepare students for the workforce, college, or vocational school).

3. Each school should feature a curriculum, disciplinary process, class time scheduling, administration setup, and so forth.

4. Students are to decide on other special features of their school (music programs, sports, busing of students, clubs, etc.).

Closure:

Each group presents its proposed secondary school. The class will discuss the drawbacks and advantages of each group's presented proposal.

Materials:

School pictures, textbooks, glossary, large pieces of drawing paper or poster paper, felt pens or markers

Evaluation:

Observe student participation as they work on assigned project. Check each group's imaginary secondary school and its main function.

Assignment:

Outline problems that must be overcome to implement the secondary school that your group created. Be prepared to discuss the identified problems in class.

Figure 4.9

A Sample Language
Arts Lesson

Topic: The Elements of Story Writing

Objectives:

Given a picture stimulus, students will be able to write a short fiction story that contains the needed elements for a short story.

Introduction (Set Induction):

Read aloud a short fiction story that will be of interest to the class. (*Jumping Mouse*, a short myth, demonstrates the elements in an interesting but condensed form.)

Content:

The Elements of a Short Story

I.   Short Story Beginnings
   A. Describe the setting
   B. Introduce the main character
   C. Introduce the plot (problem or goal the main character attempts to solve or achieve)

II. Middle Story Elements
   A. First Roadblock (character's attempt to reach goal)
   B. Second Roadblock
   C. Climax of Story (character reaches goal)

III. Story Endings
   A. Make conclusions
   B. Wrap up any loose ends

Procedure:

1. After the oral reading, ask students to explain when and how the author introduced the main character.

2. Discuss the promptness that authors use to introduce the main character, setting, and plot in short stories. Record responses on the chalkboard using the bell-shaped curve to portray the elements of short stories. (Bell curve not shown here.)

3. At this point, ask students to summarize the elements needed in a short story's beginning. (They should be able to identify introduction of the main character, description of the story setting, and introduction of the story's plot.) It is important to convey to students that the order in which the elements are introduced is not important; but rather, that the inclusion of these elements is a crucial feature of the short story.

4. Next, ask students to recall the first roadblock (or difficulty the main character had in attempting to reach the intended goal). Record response on bell curve and stress that the middle of a story includes the majority of the story—including the story's climax.

5. As students recall the roadblocks presented in the short book, continue to record these on the bell-shaped curve to demonstrate the rising tension presented in the story.

6. Ask students to describe how the main character finally confronted and solved the problem presented in the introduction of the story. Explain that this element is called the climax of the story. The climax should be placed at the top of the bell-shaped curve to demonstrate it as the peak of the story.

7. Ask students to summarize the elements that constitute the middle parts of a short story. (The bell-shaped curve on the chalkboard should reveal that the middle story elements are composed of roadblocks in the main character's attempt to reach a goal, and the climax or the reaching of that goal is at the peak of the bell curve.)

8. Finally, ask students to talk about the brevity the author uses to end the story once the main character has reached his or her goal. (Again, this is demonstrated by the falling line of the bell curve drawing on the board.)

Closure:

Ask students to make an outline of the elements of a short story using the information presented on the bell-shaped curve.

Evaluation:

Answers to questions during class discussions. Check students' outline of short story as work is being completed.

Assignment:

Let each student choose a picture from a magazine and instruct them to use the outline for short stories as a guide to write a short story about the picture selected.

Topic: Classifying Information

Objective:

At the completion of this lesson, the student will be able to classify information into groups on the basis of similar or common attributes.

Initial Focus:

Why should we learn to classify information into categories or groups? Discuss at least three reasons for classifying information.

Major Task:

Skim text (pages 107–121) for important ideas or items that might be classified. Agree on categories (groups or labels) that could be used to classify text information. Choose three unused practice items in the text and have individual students label the items accordingly. Ask individual students to share their label with the class to ensure understanding. Form groups of three. Instruct the groups to classify the items listed below, in at least two ways.

Items: Wichita, chair, Dallas, Denver, mule, Boston, horse, New York, house, Chicago, deer, bed, picture, Lincoln, elephant, and Oklahoma City

Group:

Students work on classification activity. Each group will produce two schemes. Schemes are to be recorded on transparency film.

Debriefing:

Each group will present their two classification schemes to the class. Class will react and make recommendations.

Resources and Materials:

Textbook, transparency film (two sheets per group), transparency pen (one per group), and classification item list

Evaluation:

Check for students' ability to classify practice items during major task phase of lesson, participation in group activity, and appropriateness of the two classification schemes by each group.

Figure 4.11

Sample Key
Question/Discussion
Lesson Plan

Topic: A Cashless Society

Objectives:

The students will:

1. Explain their feelings about the effects of Electronic Funds Transfer systems (EFT) on society.
2. Participate in group discussion and decision making.

Set Induction:

Money isn't going to be needed in the future. You will have no use for cash in everyday life.

Procedure for Discussion:

Question will be presented to the class for discussion. Responses will be recorded on board. A summary of the responses will be made.

Key question 1: What effect will a cashless society have on daily life?

Possible answers: Computers will deal with money. Everyone will use checks and/or credit cards. Vending machines will change. Some types of crime will decrease while other types will increase.

Summary: We will have to change surprisingly little to become a cashless society.

Key question 2: How do you think Electronic Funds Transfer systems (EFT) will change consumer behavior?

Possible answers: Problems with budgeting money may result. Buying by television, the Internet, catalog, and telephone will increase. People will be less concerned about prices and money.

Summary: Electronic Funds Transfer systems (EFT) will create many problems in society.

Key question 3: Where do you think Electronic Funds Transfer systems (EFT) will have the greatest impact?

Possible answers: More checking accounts will be opened. Banks will issue more credit cards. All stores will take checks and credit cards. Prices will increase because of bad checks and fraud.

Summary: Bank and consumer interaction will increase, as will the incidence of some types of crime.

Conclusions:

A cashless society would have positive and negative effects on society. An Electronic Funds Transfer system (EFT) likely would lead to less individual privacy and more control over people and their daily lives.

Closure:

Review responses recorded on board. Ask pertinent questions regarding recorded responses.

Evaluation:

Consider students' participation in discussion and decision making. Also evaluate question-and-answer sequences.

Assignment:

Keep track of the number of times and the type of transaction in which cash is needed in a 24-hour period. What effect would an Electronic Funds Transfer system (EFT) have on your life?

APPLY AND REFLECT: Which of the planning formats best fits your educational philosophy? Why?

Teachers can also plan as a team and should also make provisions for students who have special needs. Here is a brief look at these two areas.

Team Planning

Team planning can have tremendous value. For example, if all the social studies teachers were to coordinate their course plans, then the possibility of duplicating efforts or of leaving out important lessons would be reduced. Careful planning as a team can increase the time for enrichment activities. Team planning also facilitates coordination efforts among disciplines. The American literature teacher and the American history teacher, for example, could design their courses so that they were covering the same time frames simultaneously. Students would have the opportunity to see the connectedness of the two disciplines. Moreover, reading and writing assignments could be planned to enhance student understanding of how the milieu influenced the writers of a particular era.

Many middle schools are organized around interdisciplinary teams that plan as a group. These planning teams usually consist of a mathematics teacher, a science teacher, a language arts teacher, and a social studies teacher. In some middle schools, a reading teacher, a gifted education teacher, and a special education teacher may also be part of the team. These teachers plan for a common group of students.

Elementary teachers in some schools will work together as grade level teams. These teams work together in developing lessons and designing activities and materials for their lessons. The joint team work of the group of teachers will generally lead to better and more effective teaching.

Opportunities for teachers to engage in critical thinking and analysis are greatly enhanced through team planning. A team approach calls upon teachers to critically analyze the content of their respective courses so the concepts can be merged into a unified, workable whole. Teaming demands careful attention to details so that each team member knows what to do, how to do it, and when to do it. In addition, it requires that evaluation be carefully thought out, to ensure that plans are executed properly and are accomplishing their intended function.

Some of your students will have limited academic abilities, whereas others will be advanced; some will be skilled socially, whereas others will be less poised. You must, however, plan your instruction to fit the individual needs and interests of all students. Let's take a brief look at two special groups.

Teaching Special Education Students

Teachers with special students or mainstreamed students (handicapped students placed in regular classes) must learn to modify their plans and give differentiated assignments. You can do this by modifying or varying the length or difficulty of assignments. For example, in a science class, you might assign two experiments to your slow students, three experiments to the average students, and four—or perhaps more demanding—experiments to high achieving and exceptional students.

Similarly, you might require only half as much writing from English students who experience motor difficulties. Other examples of lesson modifications might include developing special worksheets to help teach difficult concepts, modifying assigned work, developing special study guides, giving oral exams, and obtaining and using special equipment with the physically handicapped.

Another approach to differentiated assignments is to vary the type of work students do. For example, some students can be allowed to complete and submit their written assignments on a word processor. Students occasionally might be allowed to assist each other or work together in groups.

Some planning guidelines for working with students who have special needs follow:

1. Gather information about the nature of the exceptional student's difference and how that difference might affect the learning process.
2. Get help from district special-education or resource experts.
3. Gather the equipment needs (typewriters, computers, VCR, print enlarger, Braille material, etc.) of exceptional students to allow them to function at an optimum level.
4. Adapt the curriculum and your teaching strategies to better serve the needs of the exceptional students.
5. Individualize the curriculum as much as possible in your classroom.
6. Provide for the removal of barriers, both physical and psychological, that limit the full functioning of exceptional students in your classroom.

Teaching the Gifted and Talented Student

In addition to students who need time and attention in order to meet regular curricular expectations, teachers will have gifted learners in their classrooms with exceptional general intellect, specific academic ability, creative productive thinking, leadership ability, or visual and performing art talents (Tomlinson, 1999). Gifted and talented (G/T) students often progress through their education with insufficient levels of challenge due to myths and controversy surrounding gifted education. Table 4.1 presents some of these myths.

Characteristics of Gifted and Talented Students

How will you know when you have an exceptionally gifted or talented learner in your class? Look for characteristics that distinguish students in your class, such as

1. *Advanced Intellect.* Curious; asks intriguing questions; reads avidly; understands abstract concepts and ideas; learns rapidly; memorizes easily; reads rapidly; follows and completes multiple and complex instructions; focuses on problem solving, processes, and explanations; retains information; has interests, knowledge, or hobbies different than peers of similar age; has advanced understanding of mathematical reasoning
2. *High Verbal Skills.* Has a keen sense of humor; uses advanced vocabulary; explains complex ideas in unique and creative ways; fluently exchanges ideas and information; easily completes word games and puzzles; influences thinking of others

TABLE 4.1 Gifted and Talented Student Myths and Facts

Myth	Fact
Gifted learners can "make it on their own" because they are bright. Other students need teacher attention more than G/T students.	Gifted students need specific interventions and educational programs designed to meet their complex learning needs. Without special considerations, gifted students are unlikely to reach their full potential.
All kids are gifted.	Each student is a special person. Some are, however, distinguishably different in talent, ability, or motivation. Some kids are measurably higher (gifted) in one or more areas in comparison to their age peers.
It is undemocratic or "elitist" to give special attention to the gifted learner.	All students need appropriate levels of challenge and should receive educational programming suitable for their needs and abilities. To provide G/T students with inadequate curriculum or low levels of support from teachers or administration is unjust.
Gifted students are unaware of their differences unless they are identified in special programs.	On the contrary, gifted students are often keenly aware of their differences from others. They may hide their talents to escape peer ridicule. Many seek older friends with advanced vocabulary and similar intellectual interests.
All gifted students want to participate in special gifted programs with high levels of challenge for which they have been identified.	Unfortunately, some gifted students do not participate because they go unnoticed or unidentified in school. Others avoid extra work that comes with challenge. Some have never experienced demanding work and may confront such opportunities negatively. Teachers, administrators, and parents can encourage success in programs commensurate with student needs.
Gifted students placed in special programs will have adjustment or social-emotional problems.	The opposite of this myth is more often accurate. If gifted students do not receive essential enrichment and/or accelerated learning opportunities, then poor study habits, social-emotional discontent, or behavioral problems often result.
It is too much work for regular classroom teachers to plan instruction for gifted learners.	Initially, it is time-consuming for teachers to differentiate instruction or plan specifically for gifted learners. Ultimately, many teachers find results worth the effort for both the G/T learners and their peers (Renzulli & Reis, 1997).
Gifted students take pleasure in being good examples for other students.	On the contrary, most G/T students thrive with goals of their own, rather than setting examples for others. Gifted students may be "introverts" who prefer an environment with internal, not public thinking and reasoning (Silverman, 1986). Many G/T students find cooperative learning tasks, with high-medium-low ability groupings, exasperating (Kulik & Kulik, 1992). They need opportunities to share ideas with intellectual peers, not necessarily in the role as tutor or teacher.
Gifted students should strive to fit in conventional classrooms since they will join a majority workforce in their futures.	Mediocre education is inappropriate whenever excellence is necessary to compete in an ever-changing world, where bright minds contribute ideas and solve problems.

3. *Keen Power of Concentration.* Engages in activities for long periods of time; pays attention to novelty and complexity; becomes totally absorbed in an activity; is quickly observant and responsive; maintains interests and activities different from peers

4. *Atypical Response Behaviors.* May be more sensitive or creative than their peers regarding issues or concerns; may take high-level risks; comes up with original ideas and relationships often missed by others; may exhibit perfectionism or procrastination behaviors (or both); displays a strong sense of self; influences behavior of others; identifies with adults or older peers; can display advanced inter- and intrapersonal skills along with leadership and motivational ability

5. *Performance Ability.* Some gifted students display high-level mastery in visual, physical, and performing arts. They master physical and artistic skills beyond their peers

Not all gifted students possess each one of these characteristics. They vary widely in characteristics and potential, just as special education students are different. Some G/T students are well-balanced, personable school leaders, whereas others are socially awkward or have serious emotional problems. Not all G/T students enjoy learning at school. Finally, many students from diverse backgrounds have been historically underrepresented in gifted education programs. Therefore, regular classroom strategies are critical for G/T learners.

Strategies for Teaching Gifted Students

What can you do with gifted and talented learners who exhibit one or more of these characteristics? Numerous strategies (Beisser, 1998) can be employed in the regular classroom where students spend the majority of school time.

1. *Differentiated Instruction.* As noted earlier, differentiation refers to instruction or curriculum that has been modified from a standard approach to meet the needs of particular students (Tomlinson, 1999). Although often used to accommodate special needs students, this approach also works well for gifted students. This means the teacher modifies the lesson or unit to address the needs of G/T students by variation of the process, content, or product required.

2. *Vary Instructional and Grouping Strategies.* An effective whole-class strategy is to use problem-solving, inquiry-based lessons, or group investigation where G/T learners can thrive in their ability to think, reason, and do research independently. Use flexible grouping such as small cluster groups (Renzulli, Gentry, & Reis, 2003) to provide bright students with opportunities to learn and work together within the structure of whole-class or cooperative-learning group assignments. Advanced use of technology (e.g., multimedia and website design) for instruction and communication is another technique that motivates and challenges gifted learners.

3. *Varied Questioning.* Utilize higher levels of questioning at various times for gifted students so they can provide fluent or elaborate explanations, learn to think abstractly, and are not able to get by with quick answers.

4. *Compact the Curriculum.* Why make the G/T students review material or complete tasks they have already accomplished? If they have a sound grasp of skills and content, provide opportunities to demonstrate proficiency (e.g., assign the most difficult problems first or allow completion of the end-of-chapter test in advance) and then move on to more complex concepts and skills (Winebrenner, 2002).

5. *Acceleration.* Gifted students require faster-paced instruction for content, skills, and processes so they can move rapidly through the curriculum. Perhaps they can read above-grade level materials (e.g., supplying chapter books for a kindergarten child); leave the class to work with an upper grade level (e.g., a second grader going to fourth grade math); or take classes earlier than their peers (e.g., taking college algebra while in high school). Many high school students take college level courses through local institutions or on-line offerings.

6. *Independent Study.* Challenge gifted students to explore individual topics of interest. Let them investigate a central question, gather multiple and varied resources, make inferences, provide a hypothesis, explain findings, and cite the sources. An important step in independent study is to share results with an appropriate audience that will appreciate the work they have completed (e.g., a research project on the extinction of the Siberian tiger should be shared with a naturalist or environmentalist).

7. *Tiered Activities.* Tomlinson (1999) suggests that teachers can focus on the same understanding and skills, but at different levels of abstraction and complexity. For example, all students may be reading books with "chocolate" as a central theme, but will use texts with a variety of reading levels and engage in tasks differing in complexity associated with each book level.

8. *Interest Centers.* Renzulli and Reis (1997) suggest that students don't know what interests them until they explore various topics. Establish classroom interest centers with frequently changing themes that may focus on timely events, such as presidential elections or the Olympics, as well as diverse themes derived from students, such as exploring Stonehenge, techniques of playing chess, or serving people in poverty.

9. *Apprenticeships.* Because gifted learners may have interest and skill areas outside of your classroom curriculum, you may find community resource personnel a valuable asset. For example, arrange for a stockbroker to work with a small group of students interested in investing in the stock market or encourage students to be mentored by field area specialists at a local university after school hours.

10. *Teacher Advocacy.* If nothing else, provide educational and emotional support for the gifted student within a rich classroom environment with advanced activities resources, technology, and choices (Beisser, 1998). Hold high standards that help bright students reach their potential. Accept gifted learners in your class, as they have individual needs for challenge and support. The power of a positive, supportive teacher is immense. Learn through the parents of gifted students. They have lived many years with the gifted child who has been placed in your classroom. Speak out on behalf of gifted and talented students at educational meetings and programs. Become informed of local and state curriculum planning decisions or budget allotments for gifted learners. It is easier to have an impact on key decisions before they are made, rather than trying to undo unfavorable determinations. Seek professional information from your state and national gifted education organizations such as the National Association for Gifted Children (NAGC). They have numerous materials and professional growth opportunities such as conferences and workshops. NAGC has a Curriculum Studies Division that focuses on issues, models, and practices related to the development, implementation, and evaluation of curricula for the gifted (see www.nagc.org).

Gifted learners are entitled to be served by teachers with expertise in appropriate differentiated content and instructional methods, involvement in ongoing professional development, and who possess personal and professional traits that promote successful learning for gifted students in their classroom.

APPLY AND REFLECT: Since you will have low-ability, average-ability, and high-ability students in your classes, how will you design your units and lessons to meet the needs of these different ability levels?

Having looked at the general planning of instruction, let us look next at the four planning levels in greater detail.

Table 4.2 offers a summary of the planning concepts covered in this section. Before you move on to the next section, review Table 4.2 and complete Review, Extension, and Reflective Exercise 4.1.

Teachers must often plan for special students.

TABLE 4.2 Planning Concepts

Type	Description
Team Planning	Group or team of teachers organizing instruction so that each supplements the other
Teacher-Student Planning	Involvement of students in planning process. Learning activities are based on students' interests and their involvement promotes ownership
Course Planning	Broad planning of instruction for year or term
Unit Planning	Discrete segment of a year's work organized around a specific theme or cluster of related concepts
Weekly Planning	Short-form outline of instruction for one week on a single sheet of paper
Daily Lesson Planning	Detailed description of objectives and activities for one instructional period. Daily plans should flow naturally out of the unit plan

Review, Extension, and Reflective Exercise 4.1

Explain what is involved in unit and daily planning.

Connections to INTASC Standards:
- Standard 4: Instructional Strategies. The teacher must understand and use a variety of instructional strategies to encourage students' development of critical thinking, problem solving, and performance skills.
- Standard 7: Planning Instruction. The teacher plans instruction based upon knowledge of subject matter, students, the community, and curriculum goals.
- Standard 8: Assessment. The teacher understands and uses formal and informal assessment strategies to evaluate and ensure the continuous intellectual, social, and physical development of the learner.

Connections to the NBPTS:
- Proposition 2: Teachers must know the subjects they teach and how to teach those subjects to students.
- Proposition 3: Teachers are responsible for managing and monitoring student learning.
- Proposition 4: Teachers must think systematically about their practice and learn from experience.

Review
- Why do unit, weekly, and daily plans need to be planned and developed?

Reflection
- In your own experiences, did you ever have a teacher who did not plan well? What was it like for students?

Lesson Plan Structure

As a teacher, you will probably imitate a favorite teacher in your initial planning. Later, you will modify the initial structure to fit your individual style. Regardless of the amount of detail in or the general format of lesson plans, an examination of the various lesson plan formats reveals that each contains three common elements: the set induction (cognitive set), the lesson itself (instructional strategies), and the lesson closure.

Set Induction

The **set induction** is what you do at the outset of a lesson to get students' undivided attention, to arouse their interest, and to establish a conceptual framework for the information that follows.

Until your students are attentive and prepared to listen (until they have a **cognitive set**), it is usually unwise to begin a lesson. Your opening activity—frequently related to the homework assignment or some recent lesson—will have to be repeated if you have not gained their attention.

You must plan some strategies for getting the students' undivided attention. Keep in mind that you will be competing with a host of other attention getters: student-body elections, an assembly, the "big game," a change in weather, and a recent or pending holiday. Whatever the distractions, it is pointless to proceed without the students' attention.

One way to get attention is to do nothing. Stand quietly. Students will soon focus their attention on you. Students are accustomed to teachers' frequent talk. Absence of teacher talk will attract their attention. This is particularly useful if only a few students are inattentive. Another technique is to begin talking in a very low tone, gradually increasing volume. Most of us want to hear what we cannot hear. The low tone of the teacher's voice will attract attention. Some teachers turn the lights on and off. This is generally done in elementary schools but can sometimes be effective at the middle and secondary level. If you use one of these techniques on a regular basis to cue the students to attention, chances are they will begin to look for your cue even before you start. The lesson is guaranteed to be more successful if everyone is ready to learn.

Although getting student attention is important for cognitive set, it is also instrumental in sparking student interest and involvement in the lesson. Provide a tickler. Pose a perplexing problem. Share a story. These are all possibilities for setting the stage to teach.

Motivating student interest is not always an easy task. Be ready and willing to be creative. Let your topic and known student interests provide clues for creating lesson motivators. If the hottest rap group around is doing a concert nearby, use that news to spark a discussion of freedom of expression as you study the Bill of Rights. A recent oil spill could serve as a catalyst for a lesson on pollution problems. A plastic sack filled with a Styrofoam cup, a disposable diaper, a lipstick in three layers of packaging, a can of motor oil, a can of aerosol hairspray, and a bottle of toxic weed killer could serve as an introduction to a lesson on environmental pollution. Several magazine advertisements could provide a springboard for a persuasive-writing lesson.

Suspense can generate excitement, interest, and involvement. Begin the class with a discrepant event or an interesting demonstration. For example, build a working model of a volcano in earth science, show pictures of the Old West in social studies, or mix paints to create various paint colors in art. Make the discrepant events or demonstration as surprising or novel as possible. Even better, involve the students directly in showing the discrepant events or in conducting demonstrations.

Models, diagrams, or pictures situated in visible spots will capture attention and interest. You might begin the lesson by soliciting student comments. For example, you might ask the class to guess what a diagram or picture represents or how a model functions.

Posing a provocative question and presenting a hypothetical problem are also effective lesson starters. Be careful to use truly thought-provoking questions and hypothetical situations that present interesting dilemmas. Superficial use of these techniques provides little motivation for students to become engaged in the learning process. Questions such as "What would happen if . . . ?" and "How do you account for . . . ?" have the potential to spark student interest and participation, whereas questions like "What was the date of . . . ?" or "Who was the author of . . . ?" are likely to bring any interest to a halt after the one "right" answer is given. A hypothetical situation is best used when it can provide a dilemma: "Given the power and the money, how would you solve the problem of . . . ?" is such an example. Used strategically, both of these techniques are promising in their potential for promoting student interest and involvement.

Colorful models can often get a lesson started.

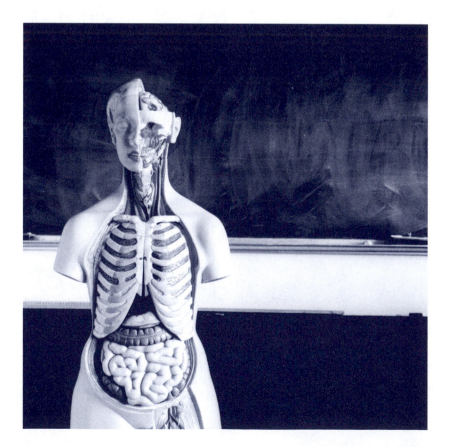

Students generally learn more from a lesson when they know what is expected of them. Thus, to maximize learning, you should plan introductory remarks that provide students with what Ausubel (1963) calls an **advance organizer**: Plan remarks that give students a "what to look for" frame of reference. Basically, the concept of the advance organizer is related closely to the establishment of student interest, but is usually more specific. Advance organizers can be generalizations, definitions, or analogies (Orlich et al., 1990). For example, a science teacher might start a lesson about light with a generalization about the major characteristics of light. A social studies teacher might start a lesson on war by relating it to a football game. No matter what form it takes, an advance organizer serves the purpose of giving students needed background information for the upcoming lesson or of helping them remember and apply old information to the lesson. Thus, the advance organizer acts as a kind of conceptual bridge between the new and old information.

Some teachers use a verbal statement of lesson objectives as the advance organizer. You must take care, however, to translate the written objectives into a form that is both understandable and interesting to students—for example,

Objective: The students will be able to correctly describe the effect of gravity on different objects.

Translation: [*Teacher holds a light and heavy object overhead.*] When I drop these objects, watch them closely. [*Teacher drops objects.*] There was a continuous increase in their speed as they fell, which requires that some force be acting upon them. What is this force and how strong is it? Why do both objects hit the ground at the same time? [*Silence.*] Today, we are going to answer these questions.

You must set the stage for the learning process. If you fail to arouse student attention and interest and to establish a framework for your lesson, the remainder of the lesson may be wasted. Listen to your students' conversations for topics that you can use to start your lessons. A simple remark related to the topic is all that is needed to get the discussion started. Complete Web Link: Sets, which will let you develop some set inductions for your future classes.

W E B   L I N K   Sets

Access the lesson plans at URL websites www.lessonplanspage.com and www.teach-nology.com/teachers/lesson_plans. Locate five lesson plans relative to the grade level and subjects you expect to teach. Analyze and modify the sets to make them more effective for your future students. Do all the lessons include a set? If the selected lesson does not have a set, design one.

APPLY AND REFLECT: Teachers must plan interesting ways of introducing their lessons. What interesting ways of introducing lessons do you foresee using? What techniques have you seen other teachers use?

Strategies and Procedures

How will you teach the objectives you have targeted? What will the students read? Is a short lecture the best method for presenting the information, or would an inquiry lesson better suit your purposes? Should the students work individually or in groups? Would a guest speaker be beneficial, or would a field trip serve your objectives better? These are the kinds of questions you must ask as you prepare daily lessons. Once again, the unit plan and the nature of the material, as well as the resources available, will guide these decisions.

A well-planned lesson consists of the content to be taught, as well as the **instructional strategy** to be employed in teaching it. The instructional strategy consists of two components: the methodology and the lesson procedure. The instructional strategy is the global plan for teaching a particular lesson. It can be viewed as analogous to the overall plan for winning a tennis match or basketball game.

The **methodology** acts as the student motivator and sets the tone for the lesson. It consists of planned patterned behaviors that are definite steps by which the teacher influences learning. The methodology should be designed and organized so that it captures and holds students' attention and involves them as much as possible in the learning situation.

The **lesson procedure** is the sequence of steps that has been designed for leading students to the acquisition of the learning objectives. For example, you may decide on the following sequence for a lesson on atomic energy.

1. Present a short introductory lecture on atomic energy.
2. Show a film on splitting the atom.
3. Conduct a summary discussion on the content of the film.
4. Conduct a question-and-answer session on major points covered in the lecture and in the film.

As you see, the procedure consists of the sequenced teacher and student activities used for achieving the lesson objectives.

When you plan, don't overlook student practice. Students must have the opportunity to test themselves on the content. Providing these opportunities must be a regular part of the daily lesson plan. Two types of practice are important and should take place during the course of each lesson: (1) *guided practice,* or practice with the help and encouragement of the teacher, and (2) *independent practice,* or practice without the help and encouragement of the teacher.

Practice opportunities need not be meaningless worksheets. Guided practice can be oral. Guided practice can be geared for group participation or for group creation of a product or set of ideas. The important thing is to furnish a "safety net." It is through guided practice that the teacher can observe whether or not the students understand the concepts to be learned. Concepts that students have not fully understood can be retaught immediately. Reteaching could be accomplished by allowing the peer group to restate the concepts in the students' language. Immediate reteaching is more effective than trying to return to a previous topic several days later. If the unit requires that learning be cumulative, one misunderstood lesson can have serious consequences for later learning. Once the teacher is confident that students can proceed without the safety net, it is time to provide for independent practice.

Independent practice generally is homework. But homework need not be meaningless worksheets, either. The exploration of one concept in depth; the interview of one appropriate expert; the building of one model, one drawing, one map, one idea—all these avenues for discovery can be more valuable than copying definitions from the textbook.

Finally, you may want to evaluate your daily lesson objectives. You have set the stage, identified the objectives, developed the strategies, and planned for practice. Now you may want to include in your plan a daily evaluation of student learning. There are several techniques for assessing student learning. These will be discussed in detail in Chapters 5 and 6. Always refer to the lesson objectives when determining how you will evaluate student progress. If the objectives are well written, the methods for evaluation are more easily determined.

Your instructional strategy is the actual presentation of the lesson content. It consists of your techniques for giving students the information. Deciding on a methodology requires that you choose from a wide variety of methods, activities, and learning experiences—the techniques you feel will best lead to the desired learning outcomes.

Methodology Selection

Instructional methods can influence students directly through focused, teacher-directed instruction or influence them indirectly by actively involving them in their own learning. Most instruction can be categorized into two basic types: teacher-centered and student-centered. Comparisons of these two methods of instruction are given in Table 4.3. The teacher-centered instructional approaches are more "traditional" or didactic, with students acquiring knowledge by listening to the teacher, by reading a textbook, or both. In the teacher-centered instructional approach, students are passive recipients of information. In contrast, student-centered approaches to instruction invite students to participate actively in their own learning experiences. The two instructional approaches are equally effective in bringing about learning. Concepts in math, for example, can be taught through a teacher-centered approach, such as the lecture method, or through a student-centered approach, such as cooperative learning.

With all these possible methods, which method should be selected for a particular lesson? Suffice it to say that the best choice is often based upon experience. The lesson procedure, as well as other factors, however, must be considered in your selection of methods. Indeed, some writers (Orlich et al., 1990) suggest there are four factors that affect the selection of the appropriate instructional method for a particular lesson: content and objectives of the lesson, teacher characteristics, learner characteristics, and the learning environment.

Your lesson must have a purpose. Are you trying to teach in the cognitive, affective, or psychomotor domain? The selection of a methodology and related experiences depend on the teaching domain. In addition, your selection should be related to such factors as goals, specific learning objectives, and content. For example, if you are trying to teach a psychomotor skill or develop an attitude, the lecture method is not a desirable approach.

Like all teachers, you have a unique set of personal experiences, background knowledge, teaching skills, and personality traits that make you more comfortable

TABLE 4.3 Comparison of Teacher-Centered and Student-Centered Methodologies

Method	Amount of Teacher Control	Intent and Unique Features
Teacher-Centered Instructional Approaches		
Lecture	High	Telling technique: Teacher presents information without student interaction
Lecture-Recitation	High to Moderate	Telling technique: Teacher presents information and follows up with question-and-answer sessions
Socratic	Moderate	Interaction technique: Teacher uses question-driven dialogues to draw out information from students
Demonstration	High to Moderate	Showing technique: Individual stands before class, shows something, and talks about it
Modeling	High	Showing technique: Teacher or individual behaves/acts in way desired of students. Students learn by copying actions of model
Student-Centered Instructional Approaches		
Discussion	Low to Moderate	Interaction technique: Whole class or small group interact on topic
Panel	Low	Telling technique: Group of students present and/or discuss information
Debate	Low	Telling technique: Competitive discussion of topic between teams of students
Role Playing	Low	Doing technique: Acting out of roles or situations
Cooperative Learning	Low	Doing technique: Students work together in mixed-ability group on task(s)
Discovery	Low to Moderate	Doing technique: Students follow established procedure in an attempt to solve problems through direct experiences
Inquiry	Low	Doing technique: Students establish own procedure to solve problem through direct experiences
Simulations/Games	Low	Doing technique: Involvement in an artificial but representative situation or event
Individualized Instruction	Low to Moderate	Telling/doing technique: Students engage in learning designed to fit their needs and abilities
Independent Study	Low	Telling/doing technique: Learning carried out with little guidance

SOURCE: Moore, K. D. (2001). *Classroom Teaching Skills* (5th ed.). New York: McGraw-Hill. Used with permission

and more effective with certain methodologies than with others. Obviously, you will select the methods that have proven most successful in the past. Because teachers are inclined to select the methodology that makes them feel most comfortable, it is easy to get into a teaching rut. Therefore, you should be prepared to experiment with different methods. You cannot become comfortable or even familiar with methods you have not used.

Your selected methodology must also match the maturity level and experiences of your students. You would not use the lecture method with slower students or young children who have trouble paying attention to verbal messages. Just as teachers often prefer one teaching style, students feel comfortable and learn better when the method fits their abilities, needs, and interests. Keep in mind that when your method is mismatched with students' preferred style, learning does not take place at the maximum level. Thus, you should select the best method for a particular class.

Obviously, your selected method may not always be the best one for all students in a single class, but it should be the best method for the class as a whole. Indeed, to fit the abilities, needs, and interests of every student in a class, you must individualize the instruction. Individualizing instruction does not mean, however, that you leave students on their own at all times. Some direct instruction (active teacher-centered instruction) should be used even when individualizing. After all, you are responsible for organizing the content and directing the learning process.

The environment and related environmental factors also must be taken into account when you select your methodology. Factors such as the space available, time of day, and weather can influence a lesson greatly. For example, you should not select a method such as the discovery method, which requires a great deal of space, when little space is available and when you have a large class.

Finally, how much time should you devote to each of the two approaches to instruction? This is a complex question. This decision varies depending on the subject, the grade level, the amount of time students have available for the lesson, the materials available, and the philosophy of the teacher and school. Indeed, whenever possible, try to vary your method and become skilled in combining a variety of methods into a total lesson strategy.

APPLY AND REFLECT: Teachers should always use appropriate vocabulary. Why is this important? Shouldn't we use the language of our students?

Procedure Selection

As noted earlier, the lesson procedure is your outline, or model, of instruction for the implementation of the lesson and it generally takes one of two basic forms: the teacher-centered or student-centered model. These approaches differ in the amount of structure offered students. The traditional model (teacher-centered) involves all students in all activities at the same time, whereas the interactive model (student-centered)—through its diagnostic-corrective-enrichment activities—provides a high degree of individualization, because it enables students to learn at different paces and to use different materials. These two models will be addressed at length in Chapters 7, 8, and 9.

No matter whether you are an experienced teacher or a novice or how much detail is included in a written lesson plan, the lesson must be well structured to be successful. The structure should incorporate instructional strategies and techniques that will keep students interested and motivated. Some commonly used techniques include

- Making your activities meaningful through active involvement of students.
- Making the content as relevant as possible.
- Keeping the instructional atmosphere as safe and informal as possible.
- Being enthusiastic about the material you are teaching.
- Challenging students by pointing out problems, inconsistencies, and contradictions throughout your lessons.
- Sharing your lesson goals, objectives, and procedures with students, so that they will know where they are going and how they are going to get there.
- Whenever feasible, use the ideas, suggestions, and opinions expressed by students so they will feel you value their input.

Attention to these above suggestions and to the factors that should be considered in selecting an instructional strategy will lead to more effective instruction.

Closure

How will the lesson end? Will the bell ring and the students file out to begin another lesson in a different subject area? Will you simply tell students to put their reading books away and take out their social studies books? These are not very satisfactory ways for lessons to end. A **closure** activity should provide a logical conclusion; it should pull together and organize the concepts learned. Once your lesson has been concluded, the lesson closure consolidates the main concepts and ideas and integrates them within the students' existing cognitive structure.

Closure should be more than a quick review of the ideas covered in the lesson. It should be designed to enable students to organize the new material in relation to itself and to other lessons. It should show the relationship among the major ideas and tie together the parts of the lesson. Closure is a vital, and often overlooked, component in the teaching-learning process. Indeed, it is as vital as your set induction and your lesson itself.

Closure isn't something that takes place only at the conclusion of a lesson: Sometimes you may want to achieve closure during the course of a particular lesson. Closure can be appropriate in the following situations:

- Following up a film, record, play, or television program
- Summarizing the presentation of a guest speaker
- Closing a group discussion
- Summarizing experiences of a field trip
- Consolidating the learning of a new concept
- Ending a science experiment
- Concluding a long unit of study

Many methods of providing closure are available. Having students relate the material learned back to the general theme is one way to achieve closure. Examples of methods that can be implemented to initiate closure discussions include such statements as "The characteristics of this play make it an excellent example of a comedy," "These proofs tend to support our original generalization that a negative number times a positive number results in a negative number," and "This form of government fits our model of a dictatorship."

Cueing is another technique used to provide closure. Have students fill in an outline you have provided that includes the main points of the lesson. Use cueing questions or statements. Examples of cueing questions are "What are some things we found in our study of rocks?" and "Which governmental agencies can we credit with primary involvement in environmental issues?" Cueing statements might include "There are four major environmental issues that society must address, and they are . . ." and "You learned the following things about community helpers: one . . . ." Cueing is an important skill to develop. In a courtroom, cueing is called "leading the witness." In the classroom, cueing is a necessary tool for organizing conceptual learning.

You can also draw attention to the completion of the lesson through the use of summary questions. A question such as "What were the four major ideas covered in today's lesson?" or "Joe, can you summarize today's lesson?" or "Let's see if we can draw any conclusions from our discussion?" can effectively close a lesson.

Connecting new and previously learned material can help students reach closure. A structured statement can be used, such as "Let's relate this to yesterday's study of the nervous system," "This form of art is similar to the other forms of art we have studied," and "Can we relate this example to examples we have studied in the past?"

Another commonly used way for achieving closure is to have students demonstrate or apply what they have learned. If they cannot demonstrate or apply the new concept or skill, then learning is questionable. Examples of this technique include teacher questions such as "Can you give me other examples of verbs and adverbs?" or statements such as "Let's diagram the two sentences at the top of page 123, as the textbook did in its examples" and "Let's do the oral exercises on page 97 together." Demonstrating or applying new information at the conclusion of a lesson has the added advantage of providing needed immediate feedback to the students. Many teachers have students do in-class assignments to achieve closure by application and to provide the needed feedback.

Every student in your class must achieve closure on a lesson. One student's achievement of closure does not indicate that all students have achieved it. Just because one student is able to answer closure questions correctly, it does not mean that all can. Therefore, you must take care to ensure that all students achieve closure. Complete Web Link: Closure to gain additional skill at planning closures for lessons.

WEB LINK **Closure**
Access the lesson plans at URL website www.eduref.org/Virtual/Lessons. Locate five lesson plans relative to the grade and subjects you expect to teach. Analyze and modify the closures to make them more effective for your future students.

Lesson Planning for Everyday Use

The formats described in this chapter are probably more detailed than the formats you will use in the schools. Experienced teachers use an abridged format—commonly found in planning books—like that shown earlier in Figure 4.2.

Figure 4.12
Activities for Class Period

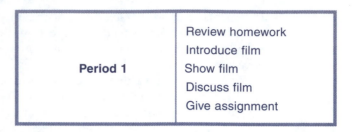

Period 1	Review homework
	Introduce film
	Show film
	Discuss film
	Give assignment

Planning-book formats that are blocked out in terms of days and periods are useful for keeping track of a week's class activities. Because of the limited space available in these books, however, teachers usually list only major activities or topics for a class period, as is shown in Figure 4.12. A quick glance tells the teacher the major activities for the period of the day. This is often helpful in keeping track of where a unit is going.

The use of a planning book does not mean that thorough planning is unnecessary. Every lesson should be thoughtfully planned in detail. The shortened plan can be helpful for communication with school administration; in fact, some teachers submit a copy of this planning-book format for the required weekly lesson plan.

The planning approach typically recommended in textbooks on instruction and by methods-course instructors involves developing objectives, selecting subject matter and associated materials, choosing strategies and methods to be employed, and deciding how to evaluate the achievement of intended outcomes. Preservice students, student teachers, and beginning teachers need to comply with this rational model to develop and/or refine their planning skills. Research indicates, however, that experienced teachers often modify this approach. Objectives, as such, play a very little part in initial planning (although they are subsequently useful for communicating intentions to students and other parties). Instead, experienced teachers focus on the content to be taught and specific instructional activities. Objectives do, however, provide valuable direction for lesson development for experienced teachers.

Planning also goes on more in the mind than on paper for many experienced teachers. Experienced teachers tend to be involved in planning every free thinking moment of the day. They also rely to an extent on incidental planning.

APPLY AND REFLECT: What would you do if a planned lesson went badly? Would you stick with the plan no matter what or improvise? Should teachers always have a backup plan ready in case a lesson doesn't go well?

Reflective Teaching

A model that is receiving much attention is the concept of the teacher as a reflective decision maker. Donald Cruickshank (1987), the primary architect of **reflective teaching,** suggests that reflective teachers consider their teaching carefully and, as a result, are more thoughtful and alert students of teaching. Essentially, according to Cruickshank, careful reflections on past experiences result in teacher growth and lead to more effective planning and teaching. Teaching practices tend to become routine with time and are repeated with very little or no forethought. Through reflective teaching, however, a teacher might examine student satisfaction with a lesson or examine whether all students were actively involved in a lesson. Reflective teachers learn to formulate their own rules, principles, and philosophies that can guide them to better practices. In other words, teachers who reflect on their practices—who submit them to examination—become better decision makers and, consequently, better planners and more successful teachers.

This concludes the discussion of lesson plan structure. Table 4.4 gives a summary of section concepts. Review Table 4.4 and complete Review, Extension, and Reflective Exercise 4.2, which will check your understanding of the concepts presented in this section.

TABLE 4.4 Lesson Plan Structure Concepts

Component	Description
Set Induction	Activity at outset of a lesson to get students' undivided attention, to arouse their interest, and to establish a conceptual framework.
Instructional Strategy	The methodology and procedure. It is the global plan of a lesson.
Methodology	Planned patterned behaviors that are definite steps by which the teacher influences learning.
Procedure	Sequence of steps designed to lead students to the acquisition of the desired learning.
Closure	An activity designed to pull a lesson together and bring it to a logical conclusion.

Review, Extension, and Reflective Exercise 4.2

Discuss lesson planning in terms of set induction, instructional strategy, and closure.

Connections to INTASC Standards:

- Standard 4: Instructional Strategies. The teacher must understand and use a variety of instructional strategies to encourage students' development of critical thinking, problem solving, and performance skills.
- Standard 7: Planning Instruction. The teacher plans instruction based upon knowledge of subject matter, students, the community, and curriculum goals.

Connections to the NBPTS:

- Proposition 2: Teachers must know the subjects they teach and how to teach those subjects to students.
- Proposition 4: Teachers must think systematically about their practice and learn from experience.

Review

- What is the purpose of the lesson set induction and closure?
- What is the lesson instructional strategy?

Reflection

- What kinds of lesson plans would be most appropriate for the grade and/or subject you expect to teach? How will you approach the introduction and closure?

VIEW FROM THE CLASSROOM

What do teachers think about planning? Teacher survey results relative to the planning topics presented in this chapter are expressed below. Review these results and discuss with classmates.

What do you mostly spend your time doing during your teacher preparation time?

Preparing lessons	38%
Grading work	21%
Administrative tasks	15%
Photocopying	11%
Discipline issues	8%
Other	5%
Communicating with parents	1%

(Continued)

VIEW FROM THE CLASSROOM (Continued)

From an educator's viewpoint, what is the best invention ever created?

Copy machines	38%
Computers	36%
White boards	10%
Coffee	7%
Textbooks	6%
Ball point pens	2%

When I am searching for curriculum resources on the Internet, I am most often working at a computer:

At home.	89%
In my classroom.	8%
In none of the locations listed.	2%
In the school media center.	1%
In a school computer lab.	0.4%

What single factor holds you back from using the Internet in your classroom:

I need better access to the Internet or equipment.	52%
I don't have enough time.	34%
I don't feel I have administrative support for Internet use in the classroom	7%
I need more training and/or simple technology how to's.	5%
I don't feel there is relevant information on the Internet for me.	2%

What single change would help you be a more effective teacher this year?

Smaller classes	52%
More classroom resources made available to me	20%
More professional learning opportunities	11%
Fewer class periods to teach	10%
Greater support from the building administrators	7%

SOURCE: Excerpted from *Teach-nology*, available at www.teach-nology.com/poll

THE PUBLIC VIEW OF EDUCATION

What does the public think of our schools in terms of how teachers should plan? Review these results and discuss with classmates.

In your opinion, are student achievement standards in the public schools in your community too high, about right, or too low?

Too high	6%
About right	57%
Too low	33%
Don't know	4%

Where do you think that American public schools rank when compared with schools in the other advanced industrial countries of the world?

Among the best	5%
Above average	14%
Average	37%
Below average	31%
Among the worst	7%
Not sure	6%

SOURCE: Excerpted from *PollingReport.com*, available at www.pollingreport.com/educ2.htm

Summary

- Effective teaching requires planning. Novices, as well as experienced teachers, must plan and plan well.

Planning Instruction

- Teachers engage in four levels of planning: course, unit, weekly, and daily.
- Student-teacher planning is valuable in some situations.
- Course planning is the broadest and most general type of planning.
- Comprehensive unit plans that include a title, goals and instructional objectives, an outline of content, learning activities, resources and materials, and evaluation strategies are necessary for coherent instruction.
- Thematic units are emphasized in many schools.
- The planning of daily lessons should be viewed as one of the most important components of effective teaching.

Lesson Plan Structure

- A strong set induction is crucial for a lesson. It sets the tone and establishes a conceptual framework for the coming activities.
- The methodology and procedure form the lesson instructional strategy. The method used forms the heart of a lesson where you decide which will be most appropriate, a teacher-centered or a student-centered mode of delivery.
- When selecting a lesson method, students should actively respond in some manner or should at least be mentally alert.
- Lessons should have a well-planned ending. This is your lesson closure.
- Teachers should be reflective decision makers. Reflective teachers encompass past experiences in planning their teaching.

Discussion Questions and Activities

1. **Set induction techniques on television.** Watch the beginnings of several television programs, and notice how the concept of cognitive set is used to get viewers interested in the upcoming program. Can you use the same techniques in the classroom environment?

2. **Closure techniques on television.** Watch the endings of several television programs, and notice whether closure is achieved. If so, how?

3. **Textbook.** Examine the teacher's guide for a textbook in your field at the grade level you expect to teach. Are the units and lessons organized as you would like to teach them? How would you change the sequence if you had to use this text for teaching? Are there things you would like to leave out or add?

4. **Research.** Collect as many examples of unit and lesson plan models as you can find in the library. Try to think of one lesson in your field that is particularly suited to each model you discover. Develop a few lesson plans using the models you have collected.

5. **Planning a lesson.** Plan a lesson presentation for the topic of your choice for the grade level or content you expect to teach. Include in the plan the three key ingredients that make up a well-written lesson plan.

Connection With the Field

1. **Classroom observation.** Observe in several classrooms. Note the structure of the lessons being presented. Can you identify the elements that constitute the lesson plan? How is set induction achieved? How is closure achieved? Can you draw any conclusions as a result of your observations?

2. **Teacher interviews.** Interview several teachers. Are they required to write and submit lesson plans? Do they include the three major components of a lesson plan?

Praxis II Connection

The following test preparation exercises are intended to help you prepare for the Praxis II: Principles of Learning and Teaching. The Praxis II may be required by your teacher education preparatory program and for state certification or licensing. These exercises will give you direct access to pedagogical knowledge from Chapter 4 that may be expected of you on the Praxis II and other pedagogical exams that may be required at the end of your teacher education program.

Topic Connections

1. Units and Lessons (II. B1)

Describe the principal components of a unit and lesson. Why is it important to include these components in every unit and lesson?

2. Thematic Units (II. B1)

Thematic learning units that integrate two or more content areas have become common in many classrooms. Describe the principles involved in designing thematic unit activities.

ON YOUR OWN

Log on to the web-based student study site at http://www.sagepub.com/eis for more information about the vignettes and materials presented in this chapter, suggestions for activities, study aids such as electronic flashcards and review quizzes, and research recommendations including journal article links and questions related to this chapter.

Part 3

MONITORING AND
EVALUATING STUDENT LEARNING

Eventually, teachers must evaluate the effectiveness of instruction. Teachers must evaluate results and assign grades. To this end, you must have a clear understanding of evaluation, measurement, and testing. Chapters 5 and 6 cover assessment, information sources, test construction, test scoring, and the conversion of test data into grades. The strengths and limitations associated with various test-item types and grade assignment techniques are explored.

Chapter 5 focuses on the role of evaluation in the instructional process, evaluation types, and various systems of evaluation. It also focuses on the role of evaluation in the instructional process. Measurement accuracy and source of information are covered and considered. Finally, Chapter 5 provides a framework for making accurate observations to be used in planning, evaluation, and during instruction.

Evaluation provides the data to make judgments for grading and assigning grades. Chapter 6 provides a framework for teacher-made test construction and accurately assigning grades. Test design and construction is a major focus of this chapter. Various techniques and systems for assigning grades are presented and discussed. Authentic and portfolio assessment are also covered.

5

EVALUATING AND
MEASURING LEARNING

*If you tell people where to go but not how
to get there, you'll be amazed at the results.*

GEORGE S. PATTON

OVERVIEW

Today, evaluation occurs more frequently in schools than it did 30 years and more ago. The heavy emphasis on evaluation is a result of the accountability and reform movements that have impacted this nation's schools. Therefore, it is critical that beginning teachers build a repertoire of effective evaluation strategies for assessment of knowledge, behaviors, skills, and abilities in the cognitive, affective, and psychomotor domains.

Like every other aspect of the teaching-learning process, assessing the outcomes of teaching and learning is a complex and sometimes confusing endeavor. Nonetheless, teachers, administrators, and parents need information about the general impact of their programs and instruction.

Though the terms *evaluation* and *measurement* are closely related, they are not synonyms. In this chapter you will examine the difference between these terms, as well as some of the kinds of evaluation and measurement techniques. The information presented should make teaching more productive, learning more engaging, and explaining the outcomes more tenable.

Although certain evaluation techniques are beyond the scope of this chapter, many of the basic concepts will be addressed. Thus, it will provide beginning teachers with a basic grasp of evaluative topics and procedures.

OBJECTIVES

After completing your study of Chapter 5, you should be able to do the following:

1. Define *evaluation* and explain the purposes of student evaluation.

2. Distinguish between the concepts of evaluation and measurement.

3. Explain the purposes of evaluation.

4. Compare and contrast pretest, formative, and posttest (summative) evaluation.

5. Create a plan for the appropriate use of the three different kinds of evaluation.

6. Differentiate among the competitive, noncompetitive, and performance assessment systems.

7. Explain what is meant by the possibility of bias in the assessment process.

8. Differentiate among the concepts of reliability, validity, and usability.

9. Describe the various sources of evaluative information.

10. Identify the advantages and limitations associated with the use of the different sources of evaluative information.

11. Explain the purpose of and advantages associated with the use of rating scales, checklists, and questionnaires.

12. Define the following evaluative terms: *competitive evaluation, noncompetitive evaluation, performance assessment, norm-referenced evaluation, criterion-referenced evaluation, standard scores,* and *percentile.*

The Evaluation Process

Evaluation is a vital part of the instructional process. Evaluation must be conducted to determine whether students are learning, to gauge the appropriateness of the curriculum for a given group of students, to identify what must be retaught, to ensure proper placement of individual students within a program of instruction, and to make sure that state guidelines for achievement have been met. Viewed in this context, evaluation performs a dual function in the educational process. Essentially, it provides not only information about student achievement but also information that can be used in future curriculum planning.

As you can see, evaluation serves many roles in the teaching-learning process. It is important to decide the purpose of every evaluation effort prior to implementing a plan of action. The approach to evaluation you would take if you wished to determine the level of student learning differs from the approach you would take if your purpose of evaluation were to determine the effectiveness of a particular teaching technique. Likewise, you would not use a pencil-and-paper test in ascertaining whether a particular performance skill, such as creating a poster using the computer, has been achieved. How you plan for and carry out evaluation and the methods of measurement you use can help determine how effective you are as a teacher.

Evaluation must also be more than a measurement of academic achievement. It will be necessary to determine the quality of student work beyond a minimum standard. You may want to gauge how well students work in small and large groups. You may want to evaluate students' abilities to work with very little supervision on projects of interest to the students. You may need to identify which students display leadership potential in group situations. Perhaps you will need to know your students' attitudes toward a particular learning experience. There are appropriate strategies for finding out whatever you need to know.

The identification of learner difficulties is a basic skill that successful teachers must possess. No matter how much planning goes into your lessons, some students will experience difficulty in mastering desired learning outcomes. Without proper identification and remediation, such difficulties may compound until the student becomes frustrated and turns off to your subject altogether. Thus, evaluation and measurement are essential components to effective teaching.

No process is more central to teaching than evaluation. But evaluation is not just testing. Evaluation is much broader. It demands that you make a qualitative judgment regarding some type of measure. **Evaluation** is the process of making a judgment about student performance; **measurement** provides the data for making that judgment. Valid evaluations depend on accurate measurement. Evaluation often involves more than simply measuring academic achievement. It requires some type of decision. In other words, information is used in making a decision. Thus, in the classroom, evaluation can be related to how well students carry out specific actions (performance) or to what they can produce (product). Sometimes you will be interested only in how well a student performs, whereas at other times you may only be interested in an end product. For example, you may want to evaluate how well your students participate in group work, how well they can perform algebraic equations, or how they go about adjusting a microscope in an experiment. Also, because attitudes and feelings can have an effect on learning, you may want to focus on such subjective factors in your teaching and in your evaluation.

Evaluation must be viewed as a two-step process. First, you must gather pertinent data regarding the desired outcomes. During this step, the tools and techniques of measurement are applied in gathering relevant information about students' acquisition of the intended instructional outcomes. Second, once the data have been gathered, the information is used in making reasonable judgments concerning students' performance.

Measurement comes in different types and with different precision. For example, you can compare the loudness of two sounds or the height of two objects, use a scale to find your weight, use a ruler to find the length of an object, or watch a speedometer on a trip. What these measurements have in common is that the perceptual process of hearing and sight are used in gathering data. These measurements, however, differ greatly in terms of their precision.

As a teacher, you will take hundreds of measurements daily. But, like all measurements, they will differ in type and have varying degrees of precision. For example, you will collect data as you observe your students' behaviors, when you ask questions and hear responses, and when you give and analyze an examination. There will be differences in the accuracy of the data, however, because of the difference in what is being measured and how it is being measured.

Evaluation requires that judgments and decisions be made. TenBrink (1986) suggests that the evaluation process consists of four steps:

1. *Preparation.* Determine the kind of information needed, as well as how and when to collect it.
2. *Information collecting.* Select techniques for gathering a variety of information as accurately as possible.

REFLECTIONS ON TEACHER PRACTICE

Keeping Up With Students

1. How important is homework in the teaching process? Should you grade all homework?
2. Are the benefits derived from the use of rubrics worth the time and effort it takes to develop them? How else might student learning be assessed and evaluated?

Keeping up with all those student papers can be a chore. I find that having a system definitely does help.

Homework Policy: I always make sure that I collect all assignments and let students know that "everything counts." I do want them to take their assignments seriously, so I review all assignments after I collect them, and then assign a letter grade of E, S, or N. If they really appear to get the idea, let's say on a math sheet, they receive an E. If they appear to be doing reasonably well with the assignment, I assign an S. If they miss the point altogether, I assign an N. Most of my students strive for an E. I let them know that homework is part of their grade. Each week, I assign a grade of 1 to 5 for homework completion. If they miss one assignment in the week, they get a 4. If they miss two, they get a 3, and so on. At the end of the marking period, I use homework completion as a means of deciding whether or not a borderline student can be raised up to the higher grade, or should be dropped down a grade. Quality of homework also enters into the picture when it comes to grading. Shoddy work receives a shoddy grade.

Student Writing: This is the most challenging and time-consuming thing to keep up with. You need to obtain or create a rubric for your students' writing exercises. Creating a rubric takes time, but once you have it, you can use it from year to year, and it provides a quick and objective means of grading writing. I created a rubric for each type of writing piece the kids do. I have rubrics for persuasive, expressive, descriptive, narrative, and informative writing. Books like those published by "Teacher's Mailbox" have writing ideas and rubrics to go along with them. These published rubrics can help. I tend to use my own, so that I am meeting state standards. Our students are graded on voice, conventions, organization, and content, so I take these into consideration when I am creating rubrics for my students. In one writing piece, I may not look for *everything*. I may tell the students that they will be graded on organization in a particular writing piece. In another, I may be grading for voice. Toward the end of the school year, I will grade on everything—all domains, and expect them to have the work as "picture perfect" as they can possibly make it.

Tests: I use the tests that come with the text series as often as possible to save myself time, but I do have some of my own quizzes made up. Of course, you probably realize that multiple-choice tests take a great deal less time to grade than essay. But I do believe that students should write in all areas, so I typically assign at least two to three essays with each test I give.

—CAROLYN, *elementary school teacher*

SOURCE: Reprinted with permission from ProTeacher, a professional community for elementary school teachers (http://www.proteacher.net)

3. *Making judgments.* Compare information against selected criteria to make judgments.
4. *Decision making.* Reach conclusions based on formed judgments.

These four steps require that you develop an understanding of the different kinds of evaluation and the different data-collection techniques, and that you sharpen

APPLY AND REFLECT: Is student evaluation really necessary at the grade level you expect to teach? Why or why not? If so, how would you use the information collected?

Evaluation provides essential information regarding how your students are doing relative to intended outcomes.

your decision-making skills. These understandings and skills will be addressed in this chapter and the next.

The ultimate question in the instructional process is whether or not you have taught what you intended to teach and whether students have learned what they were supposed to learn. Can they demonstrate the outcomes specified in your original objectives? That is, do they meet the acceptable level of performance as specified in the criteria of your objectives? These objectives call for the demonstration of cognitive skills, performance skills, and in some cases attitudes or feelings. Thus, you may be required to perform evaluations in the cognitive, psychomotor, and affective domains. These different evaluations call for different evaluation techniques.

Evaluation in the three domains of learning demands that you collect different types of information. Before turning our attention to the gathering of evaluation information in the three domains, however, let us briefly look at the evaluation types and the sources of evaluation information available to classroom teachers.

Evaluation Types

Continuous feedback is needed throughout the planning, monitoring, and evaluation of instruction. This feedback may be obtained through any one of three different types of evaluation: pretest, formative, and posttest (summative;

TABLE 5.1 Characteristics of Pretest, Formative, and Posttest Evaluation

	Pretest	Formative	Posttest (Summative)
Purpose	To identify difficulties and place students	To promote learning through feedback	To assess overall achievement
Nature	Many questions related to general knowledge	Few questions related to specifics of instruction	Many questions related to specific and general knowledge
Frequency of Administration	Varied—usually before instruction	Frequently—usually during instruction	Once—usually final phase of instruction

see Table 5.1). These three primary types of evaluation differ in terms of their nature and chronological position in the instructional process.

Pretest Evaluation

Diagnostic pretest evaluations normally are administered before instruction to assess students' prior knowledge of a particular topic for placement purposes. Diagnostic evaluations, however, may become necessary during the course of study when the teacher feels students are having difficulty with the material. The purpose of pretest evaluations generally is to anticipate potential learning problems and, in many cases, to place students in the proper course or unit of study. A common example of pretest evaluation is the assignment of high school students to basic mathematics or remedial English based on entrance assessment. Such preassessments are often designed for checking the ability levels of students in designated areas, so that remedial work can be planned or an instructional starting point can be established.

Pretest evaluation provides valuable information to teachers about the knowledge, attitudes, and skill of students. The results will assist the teacher in planning effective lessons in terms of appropriate activities and the level and pace of class instruction. Pretest evaluation can be based on teacher-made tests, standardized tests, or observational techniques.

Pretest information gives curriculum planners invaluable information regarding the appropriateness of instruction. Unfortunately, most school districts use pretest information for determining the achievement levels of students rather than for evaluating the curriculum. Achievement test scores, for example, are often devoted to making comparisons of school district group scores with national norms, whereas they could be interpreted for the purposes of making needed improvement in curricula and for redesigning curricula in areas found to be below the national norms.

Pretest information can also be used for the correct placement of students in curricula tracks and courses. One critical piece of pretest information often needed by secondary teachers is reading ability and comprehension. If your students have reading difficulties, modification in instruction must be planned to address these deficiencies.

Formative Evaluation

Formative evaluation is carried out during instruction to provide feedback on students' progress and learning. It is used in monitoring instruction and promoting learning. Formative evaluation is a continuous process. But comparatively little use has been made of formative evaluation.

Pretest information should be revised as formative information is gleaned from students' performance on oral and written work. This permits teachers to monitor and modify their instruction as needed. As individual student deficiencies or program problems are noted, remedial work or changes should be planned that will bring the slower-learning students up to the level of their peers or that will correct program weaknesses. Thus, although pretest evaluation alone usually is considered diagnostic, formative evaluation is also diagnostic in that it provides information about the strengths and weaknesses of students.

Students sometimes require more assistance than you can provide. On such occasions, you should seek outside assistance from a qualified specialist. Finally, the information gained from formative evaluation might lead you to correct any general misconceptions you observe or to vary the pace of your instruction.

Formative evaluation generally focuses on small, independent pieces of instruction and a narrow range of instructional objectives. Essentially, formative evaluation answers your question "How are you doing?" and uses checkup tests, homework, and classroom questioning in doing so. You should use the results obtained from formative evaluation to adjust your instruction or revise the curriculum, rather than to assign grades.

"I can accept and process data, but I have trouble generating it on my own."

Posttest Evaluation

Posttest (summative) evaluation is the final phase in an evaluation program. Because posttest evaluation is primarily aimed at determining student achievement for grading purposes, it is generally conducted at the conclusion of a chapter, unit, grading period, semester, or course. Thus, **posttest evaluation** is used for determining student achievement and for judging teaching success. Grades provide the school with a rationale for passing or failing students and are usually based on a comprehensive range of accumulated behaviors, skills, and knowledge.

Posttest evaluation, as the term implies, provides an account of students' performances. It is usually based upon test scores and written work related to cognitive knowledge and rarely addresses such areas of learning as values, attitudes, and motor performance.

Student performance on end-of-chapter tests, homework, classroom projects, and standardized achievement tests is commonly used in posttest evaluation. Posttest evaluation can be used in judging not only student achievement but also the effectiveness of a teacher or a particular school curriculum. The data collected and instrumentation used in collecting the data differ, depending on the type of posttest evaluation being considered.

Devices such as tests and homework are used most often in posttest evaluation. These devices, however, can also help diagnose learning problems and promote learning. In short, some evaluation devices can be used in diagnosing learning problems, promoting learning, and deriving a grade. For example, tests can identify areas of difficulty (diagnose problems), feedback can be given when you return the examination and discuss the items (promote learning), and test grades should be recorded (derive a grade). Likewise, homework should be analyzed for problem areas; feedback comments written in the margins can promote learning; and, finally, grades can be assigned.

Evaluation should be a continual process as you go about the daily classroom routine. Many times you will gain valuable information regarding achievement, skills, or attitudes prior to or during class. Difficulties can be noted, and on-the-spot feedback can be provided to remedy the situation. Lack of response to questioning, for instance, often reveals that material is misunderstood. Trouble with a written assignment may suggest that students need further instruction. A spot-check of student term papers during seatwork might reveal problem areas.

Systems of Evaluation

Evaluation systems can be grouped into two categories: competitive and non-competitive. **Competitive evaluation** systems force students to compete with other students (norm-referenced), whereas **noncompetitive evaluation** systems do not require interstudent comparisons; rather, they are based on established sets of standards of mastery (criterion-referenced). We will take a closer look at norm-referenced and criterion-referenced tests later in this chapter. Traditionally, many middle and secondary schools have required competition among students because of the belief that it stimulated motivation.

Figure 5.1

Normal Probability
Curve

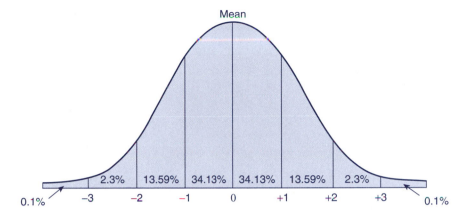

Competitive Evaluation

Most evaluators concerned with students' standing within a group make use of the *normal curve*. This curve is commonly called the *natural curve* or *chance curve* because it reflects the natural distribution of all sorts of things in nature. This distribution is shown in Figure 5.1. Such a curve is appropriately used when the group being studied is large and diversified.

An understanding of the normal curve requires a basic knowledge of the concept of variability; that is, you must understand standard deviation. The **standard deviation** is a measure of the extent to which scores are spread out around the mean. The greater the variability of scores around the mean, the larger the standard deviation. A small standard deviation means that most of the scores are packed in close to the mean. A large standard deviation means that the scores are spread out. When all the scores are identical, the standard deviation is zero.

The **normal curve** is a mathematical construct divided into equal segments. The vertical lines through the center of the curve (the mean) represent the average of a whole population on some attribute. For example, in a large population, the average (mean) IQ would be 100. Because this number represents the mean, it would occur most often and appear at the highest point on the curve. To the left of the highest point, each mark represents 1 standard deviation below the average. To the right of the highest point, each mark represents 1 standard deviation above the average. Neither side of the curve would touch the baseline, thus showing that some extreme IQ scores might exist. As shown in Figure 5.1, about 34 percent of the named population on an attribute will be within 1 standard deviation below the mean, and about 34 percent of that population will be above the mean. About 13.5 percent of the identified population will be in the second deviation below the mean, and 13.5 percent of the population will be in the second deviation above the mean. About 2 percent of the population will fall in the third deviation below the mean, and an equal portion will fall in the third deviation above the mean. Finally, about 0.1 percent of the population will fall in the extreme fourth deviation below the mean, and 0.1 percent will be in the fourth deviation above the mean. Some of the many things that are subject to the normal distribution are weights and heights of

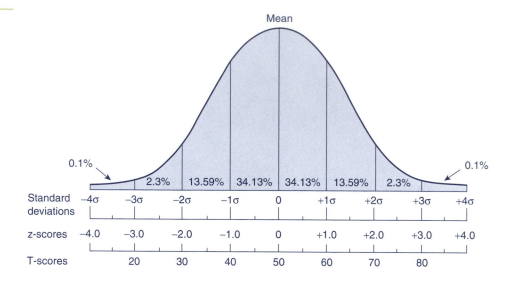

animals, average temperatures over an extended period of time, and margins of error on measurements. Indeed, most schools use normal curve and standard scores when reporting the results of standardized tests.

Standard Scores and Percentile

Most schools report student performances in terms of **standard scores** such as z scores, T scores, and stanine scores, as well as in terms of percentile. These methods use the normal distribution curve to show how student performances compared with the distribution of scores above and below the mean. Standard scores provide a standard scale by which scores on different evaluative instruments by different groups may be compared reasonably (see Figure 5.2). The various standard scores and percentile say the same thing in slightly different ways.

Note that z scores and T scores correspond to the standard deviation of the population scores: They tell us how far above or below the mean in standard deviation units raw scores lie. Both z scores and T scores indicate the number of standard deviations that a particular raw score is above or below the mean of the raw score distribution. Thus, a score falling 1 standard deviation below the mean would have a z score of −1, a score falling two standard deviations above the mean would have a z score of +2, and so on. The use of negative numbers is avoided by converting z scores to T scores. This is done by multiplying the z score times 10 and adding a constant of 50.

$$T = 10z + 50$$

Many schools use stanine (standard nine) when reporting student performance, a stanine of 1 representing the lowest performance and a stanine of 9 the highest. These nine numbers are the only possible stanine scores a student can receive. Stanines use the normal distribution in grouping scores into nine categories, with a mean of 5 and a standard deviation of 2. Figure 5.3 gives the stanine score distribution and the percentage of scores that will fall into each category.

Figure 5.3
Normal Distribution Curve
and Stanine Scores

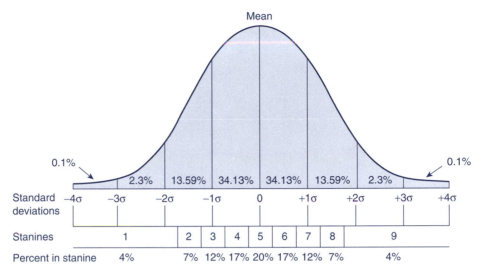

Another type of score is the percentile. Percentile scores are often confused with percentage correct. However, the *percentile score* indicates the percentage of the population whose scores fall at or below that score. A score of 20, for example, would have 20 percent of the group falling at or below the score and 80 percent above the score. Of course, the 50th percentile would be the mean (see Figure 5.2). Equal differences between percentile scores do not necessarily indicate equal differences in achievement.

Converting raw scores to standard scores allows you to compare scores on different assessment instruments. You could compare a student's performance in mathematics with science or reading with English or any other tested areas. For example, if a student obtains a score of 65 on his or her math midterm and 70 on his or her history midterm, on which test did he or she do better compared to the rest of the class? If converting the student's scores to standard score yields a z score of 1.5 in math (T score of 65) and a z score of 1.0 in history (T score of 60), you can conclude that the student did better in math.

Noncompetitive Evaluation

Some researchers suggest that criterion-referenced evaluation (which does not force competition among students) contributes more to student progress than does norm-referenced evaluation (Fantini, 1986). In effect, these researchers suggest that not all students are motivated through competition. In fact, they suggest that competition can discourage less able students who are forced to compete with more capable students. Competition can even be harmful to more capable students, because it often teaches that winning is all-important.

Today, many educators feel grades should reflect a student's efforts. No one should receive an A without really trying, nor should students who are exerting themselves to their fullest potential receive an F. There is now a national call for change in how students are assessed. The feeling is that grades should reflect students' progress. Performance assessment and the use of portfolios show promise as a more viable assessment technique.

"This would be a lot easier if they didn't require such pinpoint accuracy."

APPLY AND REFLECT: What advantages do you see in using competitive evaluation?

Noncompetitive evaluation?

Performance Assessment Using Portfolios

Educators are trying to redesign schools to reflect changing world conditions. An essential element of that redesign is the way student learning is assessed. Simply testing isolated skills or retained fact does not effectively measure a student's capabilities. To accurately evaluate what students have learned, an assessment method must examine their collective abilities. This can be accomplished through authentic assessment. Authentic assessment presents students with real-world situations that require them to apply their relevant skills and knowledge.

Much attention is being directed toward "performance" assessment, a term commonly used in place of, or with, authentic assessment. In **performance assessment**, students demonstrate the behaviors that the assessor wants to measure (Airasian, 2001; Meyer, 1992;). For example, if the desired behavior is writing, students write; or if the desired behavior is identification of geometric figures, they draw or locate geometric figures. Assessment is done by measuring the individual works as well as the portfolio as a whole against specified criteria that match the objectives toward a specific purpose. In effect, samples of students' work are compiled for evaluation. The students, the teacher, or both can select items for assessment of performance. These items are often accumulated in portfolios, thus allowing students to display a variety of evidence of performance. The portfolio is a purposeful collection of student work that tells the story of the student's efforts, progress, or achievement in a given area.

A portfolio can be thought of as a systematic, organized collection of evidence that documents growth and development and that represents progress made toward reaching specified goals and objectives. Portfolios enable students to display their skills and accomplishments for examination by others. Portfolio advocates suggest that portfolios are a more equitable and sensitive portrait of what students know and are able to do. They encourage teachers and schools to focus on important student outcomes.

To make the evaluation of portfolios as objective as possible, most teachers develop a scoring rubric to guide the grading process. A rubric is a summarization of the performance criteria at different levels of performance. Often, teachers label the different levels as "excellent," "good," "fair," and "poor" or with particular grades to summarize the performance. To use a scoring rubric, teachers judge which of the descriptions comes closest to the student's performance. Sometimes teachers use a checklist or rating scale in conjunction with the rubric summary performance levels to increase the accuracy of the assessment. Complete Web Link: Rubrics, which will let you analyze some sample rubrics. Some teachers also require students to include a reflection upon their skills and accomplishments as part of their portfolios. The reflective caption is designed so that the student can explain why he or she chose a particular piece of evidence.

W E B   L I N K   Rubrics
The following websites provide examples of rubrics in different subjects and grades.
http://rubistar.4teachers.org/
http://school.discovery.com/schrockguide/assess.html
http://www.teach-nology.com/web_tools/rubrics/
Analyze the rubric examples relative to their quality. What makes the good ones good and the bad ones bad?

Portfolios also provide students with the opportunity to communicate their learning to their parents (Overturf, 1997). Students can be asked to share their portfolios with parents, and parents can provide a written response regarding the contents. Indeed, student-led parent-teacher conferences can be structured to center around student portfolios (Countryman & Schroeder, 1996).

Due to the bulk of hard-copy portfolios and the limitations associated with paper-based portfolios, there has been movement toward the use of electronic portfolios. Electronic portfolios give students the ability to use electronic artifacts, photographs, and videotapes and clips as performance evidence. Moreover, electronic portfolios have the ability to store multiple media. Graphics, for example, can be incorporated into students' work. Finally, electronic portfolios can be communicated across distances—some distances as short as between classrooms, some as long as from a school to parents or to state education departments.

Efforts to reform education and create a quality teaching force include holding teachers accountable. An approach gaining wide support in many of these accountability systems is the use of teacher portfolios. A teacher portfolio is a collection of work produced by a teacher. Just as artists use portfolios of collected works to illustrate their talents, a teacher portfolio is designed to demonstrate the teacher's talents. Teacher portfolios are developed by teachers to highlight and demonstrate their knowledge and skills as a teacher. A portfolio can also provide means for showing teacher reflections; it offers teachers the opportunity to show how they critique their work and evaluate their teaching effectiveness. What is actually included or related in a teacher portfolio depends on how the portfolio will be used. A teacher portfolio may include teacher background information; results of written examinations—National Teacher's Exam, state licensure tests; a personal statement of teaching philosophy and goals; documentation of effort to improve one's teaching; implemented lesson plans; video- or audiotape of classroom lessons; colleagues' observation records; and written reflections on teaching. A common misconception is that a teacher portfolio is a folder laden with artifacts and evaluation. A teacher portfolio, rather, is a document created by the teacher that reveals and describes the teacher's duties, expertise, and growth in teaching.

APPLY AND REFLECT: Many school districts are now using teacher portfolios to evaluate teachers. What do you think of this process? What should be included in a teacher portfolio?

_____

Accurate information is essential to making sound classroom decisions. Complete Expansion Activity: Accurate Information, which will let you further explore gathering information for your future classroom.

EXPANSION ACTIVITY

Accurate
Information

Accurate information from the teacher is essential for students' academic progress. Distinguish among competitive, noncompetitive, and performance assessment. Describe the purposes of each and which type would be most applicable to the area you expect to teach.

Problems With Evaluation

We all like to view ourselves as fair, even-handed people. We believe it is possible and desirable to fairly evaluate our students' performance. But, for fairness to prevail in student evaluation, we must recognize and plan for biases built into human nature and into the nature of schooling (Lyman, 1991).

A lot of research evidence suggests that certain groups of students are not assessed fairly because of predetermined notions of primarily White, middle-class teachers about what constitutes successful school performance. Girls fare better than boys in the evaluation process partly because the structure of schools and classrooms favors the more passive socialization often demonstrated by girls. At the same time, some evidence suggests that boys begin to perform better than girls, particularly in mathematics and sciences, beginning in the middle-school years (Murphy & Davidshofer, 1991). Many believe that this phenomenon is accounted for partly because boys tend to be given specific feedback regarding their academic performance, whereas girls are more likely to receive nonspecific feedback for both academic performance and classroom behavior (Sadker & Sadker, 1994). Whatever the reasons, girls and boys need to receive equal recognition and feedback for academic performance. Equally important is providing an environment that values individual and group differences within the classroom.

Likewise, poor and minority students often do not fare as well in the classroom setting. Teachers need to be aware of cultural and socioeconomic differences that may negatively influence how students are evaluated and then take every opportunity to reduce the influence of those factors.

Children who are creative, especially in ways not recognized within the ordinary structure of the classroom and the school, are often evaluated unfairly on the basis of pencil-and-paper tests. Children with behavior problems and other special needs are also often assessed unfairly. Poor behavior should never be a factor in determining grades. Special-needs students who have been mainstreamed should be evaluated against their own performance, not against the performance of the class as a whole.

Fairness issues and ethical issues must be considered before methods of assessment are determined. Criteria for evaluation should be related to the learning objectives. Performance standards should be established prior to assessment, not on the basis of the best example you receive. The purpose of the evaluation (pretest, formative, or posttest) should be clear to you and clear to the students before the learning experience takes place. The results of assessment should be shared only with the students and their parents or guardians. Some circumstances will call for sharing results with the principal or a counselor. The point to be made here is that assessment results are not to be shared indiscriminately. Everyone who sees the results of a student assessment should have a legitimate need to know.

Clearly, if you are to make accurate judgments about student performance, you need to have confidence in the data you have collected. In other words, you must develop and/or select measurement devices that provide reliable and valid information and that are usable.

Measurement Accuracy

Reliability, validity, and usability are three important qualities of every measurement device. If a teacher-made test reveals that 50 percent of an algebra class was unable to solve algebraic equations, should the teacher be concerned? The answer depends on the reliability, validity, and usability of the test—that is, the ability of the test to consistently measure what it is supposed to measure: problem-solving ability. Let's take a brief look at the three essential elements of measurement: reliability, validity, and usability.

Reliability

Reliability is the consistency with which a measurement device gives the same results when the measurement is repeated. In other words, it is the measurement device's trustworthiness or dependability. A reliable bathroom scale, for example, gives identical weights for each of three separate weights taken in a single morning. If, on the other hand, the three weights taken differ by 5 pounds, the scale could not be considered very reliable. Likewise, a true/false test that is so ambiguously worded that students are forced to guess would probably yield different scores from one administration of the test to the next. In short, it would be extremely unreliable.

Measurement devices must provide reliable information if they are to be of value in decision making. No evaluation, however, is perfect. There is always some measurement error—for example, (1) poor construction could affect the score (sampling error), (2) the attribute being measured may vary over time (trait instability), (3) scoring or recording inaccuracies will affect scores (scoring error), and (4) variables such as motivation, health, and luck can cause variance. The extent to which such errors can be minimized determines the reliability of the measurement device.

How can teachers increase the reliability of their measurement devices? Basically, the reliability of measurement instruments can be improved by incorporating the following suggestions into their construction.

1. *Increase the number of evaluative items.* Reliability can be improved by increasing the amount of data collected. Because you have a larger sample of the trait being evaluated, chance errors will tend to cancel each other out. Thus, a test of 30 items is more reliable than one of 20 items.

2. *Establish optimum item difficulty.* Reliability can be increased by making the items being evaluated (test or observational) of moderate difficulty. In effect, moderate difficulty gives a moderate spread of scores, which allows you to better judge each student's performance in relation to other students. Conversely, difficult and easy items result in bunched scores, which make it more difficult to differentiate among scores. Thus, tests made up of moderate items spread the data over a greater range than devices composed mainly of difficult or easy items. In the case of observational scales, an item with a 5-point scale would give more reliable information than a 7- or 3-point scale, because it would give more consistent results than would larger or smaller scales.

3. *Write clear items and directions.* Reliability is improved when students clearly understand what is being asked. Ambiguities and misunderstood directions lead to irrelevant errors.

4. *Administer the evaluative instrument carefully.* Reliability is improved when students are not distracted by noises or when they are not rushed.

5. *Score objectively.* Reliability is greater when objective data are collected. With subjective data, internal differences within the scorer can result in identical responses or behaviors being scored differently on different occasions.

Validity

Validity is the extent to which an evaluative device measures what it is supposed to measure. It measures what was taught and learned. For instance, if social studies content knowledge was taught and learned, but students scored low on the test over the content because they could not understand the questions, then the test is not valid. We all have had teachers who taught one thing and tested over something else, or who have made the test so difficult that we performed poorly.

Although there are several types of validity, the most important one to teachers is content, or face, validity. *Content, or face, validity* is established by determining whether the instrument's items correspond to the content that was taught in the course. Teachers sometimes construct tests that seem to address what was taught but, in fact, do not. For example, if instruction focused on developing issues and trends, the test should give students the opportunity to demonstrate their understanding of issues and trends. If the test focuses on names and dates, it does not have content validity. In the case of standardized tests, test inspection is carried out by subject experts. Similarly, the content validity of a teacher-made test should be evaluated by checking the correspondence of the test items with the teacher's stated outcomes. This simple process alone, however, does not guarantee content validity. For example, the objectives may have been prepared by making a superficial examination of the textbook and writing objectives at random, rather than by carefully matching objectives to what was taught in class. In short, content validity requires that a teacher's test items match the actual class instruction.

Any measurement device, whether it is a test or an observation instrument, must be valid to supply usable information. But, an instrument is not simply valid or invalid; rather, its validity is a matter of degree, with each instrument having low, satisfactory, or high validity. Thus, the adequacy of an instrument involves a judgment regarding the usefulness of the information it provides for future decision making. Although most teachers lack the expertise or time to do extensive validity checks, they can at least make sure their test items match their stated learning objectives.

Usability

Usability is how well a measurement device is suited for gathering the desired information. For example, a 2-hour science test would not be suitable for a 50-minute class period. A test should be easy to administer and score, fall within budget limitations, be suitable to the test conditions, and have the appropriate degree of difficulty.

Reliability, validity, and usability are all interrelated. In fact, measurement devices must be reliable and suitable for the purposes they are used for before they can be valid. For example, if you cannot get consistent height measurements from a yardstick (not reliable), you cannot expect it to be accurate. The measurements might also be very consistent (reliable) but still not accurate (valid). A pencil-and-paper test would hardly be suitable for evaluating the ability to hit a tennis ball. Clearly, if a measurement device is to be used in making decisions, it is essential that the information be reliable *and* valid, as well as suitable.

This concludes the discussion of the assessment process. Table 5.2 gives a review of the major assessment concepts. Before you continue, review Table 5.2 and complete Review, Extension, and Reflective Exercise 5.1.

TABLE 5.2 Assessment Concepts

Concept	Description
Diagnostic Evaluation	Evaluation administered prior to instruction for placement purposes
Formative Evaluation	The use of evaluation in supplying feedback during the course of a program
Summative Evaluation	A judgment made at the end of a project that determines whether it has been successful or not, and commonly used to give grades
Competitive Evaluation	Evaluation that forces students to compete with each other
Noncompetitive Evaluation	Evaluation that does not force students to compete with each other
Performance Assessment	Assessment in which students demonstrate the behaviors to be measured
Portfolio	A systematic, organized collection of evidence that documents growth and development and that represents progress made toward reaching specified goals and objectives
Standard Scores	A score based on the number of standard deviations an individual is from the mean
Percentile	The point on a distribution of scores below which a given percentage of individuals fall
Reliability	The extent to which individual differences are measured consistently, or the coefficient of stability of scores
Validity	The extent to which measurement corresponds with criteria—that is, the ability of a device to measure what it is supposed to measure
Usability	The suitability of a measurement device for collecting desired data

Information Sources

Evaluation is the result of measurement. That is, evaluation requires that a judgment be made, and this judgment requires information. Therefore, you must become familiar with the sources of evaluative information.

Cumulative Record

Cumulative records hold the information collected on students over the school years. These records are usually stored in the guidance center office and contain such things as academic records, health records, family data, vital statistics, and other confidential information, as well as scores on tests of intelligence, aptitude, and achievement. Cumulative records also often contain behavioral comments from past teachers and administrators. These comments can prove useful in understanding

Review, Extension, and Reflective Exercise 5.1

Discuss the nature of evaluation and measurement.

Connections to INTASC Standards:

- Standard 8: Assessment. The teacher understands and uses formal and informal assessment strategies to evaluate and ensure the continuous intellectual, social, and physical development of the learner.
- Standard 9: Reflection and Professional Development. The teacher must be a reflective practitioner who continually evaluates the effects of his or her choices and actions on others (students, parents, and other professionals in the learning community) and who actively seeks out opportunities to grow professionally.

Connections to the NBPTS:

- Proposition 3: Teachers are responsible for managing and monitoring student learning.

- Proposition 4: Teachers must think systematically about their practice and learn from experience.

Review

- What are the purposes of diagnostic, formative, and summative evaluation?
- What are some of the features of performance-based assessment?
- How can portfolios be used in assessment?
- What do fairness, reliability, validity, and usability have to do with the quality of evaluation?

Reflection

- How would you go about creating rubrics for assessing answers to the preceding four items?
- Can a test be valid but not reliable? Reliable but not valid? Explain in your own words.

the reasons for students' academic problems and disruptive behaviors. Treat these comments with great care, however, because teachers sometimes let them color their judgment or expectations. Indeed, it is recommended that you consult students' cumulative records only with good reason. An awareness of the information contained in students' files may affect your own observations and may lead to the formation of inaccurate judgments. Moreover, exercise care in interpreting student test scores. Many teachers misinterpret test scores because of insufficient training.

The test scores found in cumulative files are usually those from standardized tests. As such, students' scores are given in terms of how they compare with a large (usually national) group of students used in establishing norms for the test. That is, the scores are generally reported in the form of standard scores, such as z scores, T scores, or stanine scores, or in the form of percentiles.

Individual scores or a group of scores may vary from established norms for many reasons. For example, the content and skills addressed in a course may differ from that examined in the selected standardized test, or the test may be inappropriate for the individual students or a group in terms of difficulty, clarity of instruction, and so forth. Therefore, when you use a standardized test for collecting evaluative information, make sure it is appropriate for the group being evaluated; this isn't always an easy task.

You should also be aware that federal legislation permits the records of any student to be inspected by parents or guardians. Parents or guardians also have the right to challenge any information contained in the file. As a result, some teachers and administrators are reluctant to write comments or reports that may be considered controversial. This reluctance sometimes leads to the omission of important information that would be useful to other teachers and administrators.

Personal Contact

Information can be gathered as you interact with students on a daily basis. Your observations of students as they work and interact and your conversations with students provide valuable information that will be of assistance in planning your instruction. Indeed, observational information is available continuously in the classroom, as you watch and listen to students in numerous daily situations. For example, you can observe your students during guided practice, while they work in small groups, as they use resource materials, and as they participate in questioning sessions.

Accurate observation provides information about work habits, social adjustment, and personality that cannot be collected through pencil-and-paper tests. Observations can help you answer some of your own questions: Are students confused? Can they apply the concepts? Should I plan more activities to teach this concept? Are some students in need of special assistance?

Based on your observations related to your own instruction, you can draw certain conclusions about the academic progress of your students. Your observation during questioning, for example, might reveal that certain students have trouble with a concept, appear to need special help, or need additional activities related to lesson concepts. Therefore, observe your students closely and be alert as they go about their daily activities. In fact, you may want to develop observational devices such as rating scales or checklists to ensure that your observational information is more accurate.

The information obtained through careful observation needs to be recorded and organized in a way that ensures accuracy and ready access, so insights can be gleaned about learning and development. Without a written record, you are often left with only general impressions of classroom actions. Over time, classroom impressions will fade, become distorted, or blend into one another—which will result in an inaccurate and biased picture of what has transpired. The development and use of an anecdotal record form, such as that shown in Figure 5.4, can prove useful in recording some of your observations.

It is important that you include students in the evaluative process. Students can be asked whether or not they understand material or how they feel about a particular topic of discussion. They can also best report on their beliefs regarding the value of what they have learned, of what they are still unsure, and of their readiness for testing on a topic. In fact, information about student problem areas can often be obtained from casual conversations before and after class. Formal and informal

Figure 5.4
Anecdotal Record Form

Student: _____ Date: _____

Description of environment/class: _____

_____

_____

Description of incident: _____

_____

_____

_____

_____

Reported by: _____

conversations with students may be among the best techniques for gaining diagnostic and formative evaluative information. Therefore, pay close attention to students' comments when they want to talk about needed help or academic concerns. Such exchanges and questions will give you the opportunity for gaining valuable information not readily available from other sources. Exercise caution, however, when considering the reliability of the information gleaned from students: They may choose to tell you what they think you want to hear, so combine your observations with the students' self-reports before making instructional judgments.

The use of observation is not without its critics. Many believe that observation is too subjective to provide reasonable evaluation and, further, that keeping good observational records is too time-consuming to be practical. Simple observational instruments, however, can be devised prior to the lesson under observation, which in turn reduces record keeping concerns. The simple instrument of making several copies of the classroom layout could be used for a variety of purposes (see Figure 5.5). You could record the physical movement of students during seatwork time.

Figure 5.5

Seating Chart Record
of Classroom Behaviors

1 – 1 – 1 1 – 1 – 4 Sherry	1 – 1 – 2 2 – 1 – 2 Julie	2 – 1 – 2 1 – 2 – 1 Sue	2 – 1 –2 3 – 3 – 3 Chad	1 – 3 – 1 3 – 3 – 3 Paul	1 – 3 – 1 5 – 1 – 2 Mary
1 – 1 – 1 1 – 1 – 2 Joe	2 – 2 – 2 2 – 2 – 1 Mike	1 – 2 – 1 1 – 4 – 1 Sally	3 – 3 – 2 2 – 3 – 1 Conrad	3 – 3 – 1 1 – 1 – 1 Aaron	1 – 2 – 2 2 – 2 – 2 Scott
Empty Seat	2 – 2 – 2 2 – 3 – 3 Jan	1 – 1 – 1 2 – 2 – 2 Billie	5 – 5 – 1 1 – 2 – 1 Susan	1 – 1 – 1 3 – 3 – 3 Pat	1 – 1 – 1 3 – 3 – 3 Jean
2 – 1 – 1 1 – 1 – 1 Lisa	2 – 1 – 1 1 – 3 – 3 Lila	2 – 1 – 1 1 – 1 – 4 Dawn	3 – 1 – 1 1 – 1 – 4 Skip	3 – 1 – 1 2 – 2 – 5 Ben	Empty Seat

Legend: 1. Quiet and on task
2. Quiet, not working
3. Talked to other student
4. Finished work early
5. Talked with teacher

Who was out of their seats and why? Did they go to the pencil sharpener? The stack of dictionaries? The wastebasket? The teacher's desk for help or materials? In this way, you would be able to analyze potential problem areas that might keep students from remaining on task.

The same instrument (Figure 5.5) could be used to follow the flow of a questioning session. By devising a simple code, you could indicate who answered and who asked questions. You could break it down further by noting whether the questions answered were higher- or lower-order questions. Later analysis could reveal which students demonstrated understanding of the material and at what level of performance. It also might indicate the level of interest in the topic if, for example, the questions were answered on an all-volunteer basis. Thus, once teachers have refined their observational skills, the objectivity of personal-contact information can be greatly enhanced through appropriate instrumentation. (I will address this issue later in the chapter.) Moreover, the time committed to personal-contact record keeping can be kept under control by opening a portfolio for each student and adding a few descriptive phrases periodically. Examples might include such phrases as "Mary has difficulty remembering to bring her book to class," "John must be continuously reinforced to study," and "Ron has trouble with fine motor adjustments in chemistry lab."

The point to keep in mind is that observation is productive only if it has a clear purpose (e.g., determining if students are on task); if all students have the opportunity to be observed equally; if the rating of performance is consistent with previously

Evaluation is a continuous process fostered by daily teacher-student interaction.

established criteria; and if the information gathered is later contemplated, analyzed, and used for improving instruction and learning.

Analysis

Teachers monitor students' work on a regular basis; that is, they analyze it for possible errors. Analysis of students' work can take place during or following instruction, and, as with other techniques we have discussed, analysis has the advantage of not being a formal test with its accompanying pressures. Analysis is, however, more formal than personal contact.

Analysis is important in that it provides the opportunity for correcting faulty beliefs or practice. A teacher can reteach skills during the learning process by analyzing the students' work as it is produced, probing for understanding, and suggesting new approaches to problem solving. This practice can enhance the students' abilities to self-analyze their performances. When combined with observation and inquiry, analysis can provide useful clues into the students' thinking processes and skills acquisition. For this reason, a good rule to follow is not to assign work unless it is going to be graded immediately by the teacher, another student, or the student himself or herself.

Students can and should be involved in the evaluation process. They can be called on to reflect about and critique their own work and the work of their peers.

If this type of evaluation is to be successful, the criteria for performance should be clearly outlined prior to the exercise. The teacher must determine if the students understand the criteria for review before allowing such an exercise to take place. Peer critiques are especially effective in a cooperative-learning exercise. After a peer review session, students should be afforded the opportunity to revise their work before a grade is assigned.

Analysis is a useful tool for demonstrating progress or the lack of progress to parents. Samples of each student's work should be kept in a file. This file can be reviewed periodically, and progress can be noted. Students should have the opportunity to review and critique previous work. Many students enjoy the chance to improve on something they did earlier in the year. Both samples should be kept to show improvement. Any written critique or analysis done by the teacher needs to be as objective as possible. Once again, planning and determining criteria prior to analysis improves the quality of the analysis.

Open-Ended Themes and Diaries

Teachers have long been aware of the influences that peer groups and out-of-school activities have on classroom learning. Therefore, knowledge about the social climate and activities in which students live can be indispensable in the evaluation process.

Assessment information should be shared with students.

This information will make it possible to adjust the curriculum so that it better addresses out-of-school differences in students' lives. For example, if most of the students in your class have after-school jobs, it is not wise to assign a lot of homework.

One technique that can be used for gaining valuable information about students is simply to ask them to write about different in-school and out-of-school topics. You might ask students to react to questions such as these:

1. What profession would you most like to make your life work? What profession would you least like to make your life work?
2. What do you want to do with your life?
3. What is your favorite leisure pastime? Why?
4. With whom do you most like to spend your free time? Why?
5. How do you feel about the students in this school?

Of course, many of the comments and views expressed in students' writing will be distorted to some extent; nevertheless, students' views of reality will often be revealed when their writing is analyzed.

Diary writing on a periodic schedule (for example, once a week) is another method for obtaining evaluative information. A diary can consist of a record book in which students write about their concerns and feelings. Under conditions of good positive rapport, students often communicate their true concerns and feelings openly and freely.

Conferences

Students do not exist in isolation; they are affected by the environment in which they live. Students are influenced first and foremost by their families, but also by neighborhoods and communities. Accordingly, schools must find new ways to involve parents in the education of students. Many times you can understand classroom problems better after observing and visiting with parents. Objective parental discussions can often reveal much.

Parental conferences may be needed for gathering evaluative information. Parents sometimes can shed needed light on students' social and academic problems. Parent conferences, however, are most beneficial when they are scheduled ahead of time and well planned. Table 5.3 offers a helpful framework for approaching parental conferences. Such conferences should not be a time for lecturing parents or for giving them advice on the proper rearing of the student. The overall atmosphere should be positive.

Traditional parent-teacher conferences are 15- to 20-minute discussions about their child. At times, what the parents hear at home from the youngster is quite different from the picture the teacher paints at the conference. Parents are then in the difficult position of wondering whether to believe their child or the teacher. This often places the teacher and/or parents on the defensive, blocking open communications. One solution to this dilemma is to have the student join the conference. This is often not productive, however, because the student becomes nothing more than a silent partner or a martyr chastised for little effort. An answer to this problem is the establishment of student-led conferences (Countryman & Schroeder, 1996). Student-led conferences give teachers and parents a better opportunity to get to know and understand each other.

TABLE 5.3 **Framework for a Successful Conference**	
Step 1	*Plan ahead.* Establish your purpose. Plan what you intend to say, what information you want to obtain, what your concerns are. Plan what your next step will be in the classroom as a result of the conference.
Step 2	*Starting the conference.* Be positive. Begin the conference with a positive statement.
Step 3	*Holding the conference.* Establish a positive sharing relationship. Be an active listener. Be accepting with regard to input and advice. Establish a partnership, so all concerned can work toward a common goal.
Step 4	*Ending the conference.* End the conference on a positive note. Communicate the fact that in working together the common goals will be reached.
Step 5	*Conduct follow-up contact.* Keep all parties informed. Send notes and make phone calls to share successes and/or further concerns.

Information useful in making evaluative judgments can often be obtained from other teachers who have had your students in their classes. These colleagues can share difficulties these students had in their classes, some techniques that were used to correct problems, and evaluative judgments. Like conferences with parents, however, conferences with other teachers should be scheduled and well planned so that sufficient time will be available for productive meetings.

Finally, the school's support personnel—such as counselors, assistant principals, and secretaries—can be an excellent source of information. For example, counselors can help interpret and shed light on test results, as well as on personality factors that might affect student performance.

Testing

All of you have taken tests. You have taken weekly exams in English or history, and you have taken state-mandated achievement tests during most of your school years. If you examine the purposes of tests, then you have some idea of how testing can be used most effectively. You will also develop an understanding of the limitations of testing for determining some aspects of learning.

A **test** may be defined as a task or series of tasks used to obtain systematic information presumed to be representative of an educational attribute or series of attributes. This definition implies that a test must be developed systematically (using specific guidelines) and must provide a specific description of the traits or attributes being measured, as well as an established procedure for responding and scoring. Tests are classified according to (1) how they are administered (individually or in groups); (2) how they are scored (objectively or subjectively); (3) the emphasis of the response (speed or accuracy); (4) the type of response (performance or pencil-and-paper); and (5) the comparison groups (teacher-made or standardized).

Tests are generally constructed to provide one of two types of interpretations: norm-referenced or criterion-referenced. A **norm-referenced test** interpretation is made when you compare a student's score with that of a norm group (a large, representative sample) in obtaining meaning. That is, a norm-referenced test compares individuals with one another. This comparison is made when you need to know how your students perform in relation to others at the same age or grade level. A **criterion-referenced** test interpretation is made when you compare an individual's score against a predetermined standard. In effect, students are compared with an absolute standard, such as 60 percent or 80 percent correct. Teacher-made tests generally belong in the criterion-referenced group, because students are compared with criteria specified by the teacher.

Tests are used for many reasons. The most common reason is for determining cognitive achievement. Tests are also often used to measure attitudes, feelings, and motor skills.

There are many types of tests carried out in the classroom, including pretests, posttests, chapter exams, unit exams, midterms, final exams, standardized tests, and quizzes. The type of testing depends on your needs and the purpose for collecting the data. Because of problems associated with reliability, validity, and usability, however, extra care must be taken in selecting tests that measure attitudes, feelings, and motor skills.

Good tests are carefully constructed and administered, but have certain limitations. For example, most tests do not measure environmental factors or student motivations. Moreover, you must guard against tests that are poorly administered and vulnerable to student guessing. Unless tests are carefully constructed and administered, the danger of testing superficial learning exists. Even under the best of conditions, pencil-and-paper tests—which are used more often than other kinds of assessment techniques—tend to place more value on knowing than on thinking, on verbalizing than on doing, and on teacher expectations than on student beliefs and values. With careful thought, however, you can construct tests that assess thinking ability. The problem is that most teachers lack either the skill or time to construct proper tests. Although important and probably the most common measurement technique used by teachers, testing should be thought of as only one of several techniques that you can implement for obtaining information about student progress. We will deal with test construction in greater detail in Chapter 6.

APPLY AND REFLECT: Teachers should use multiple sources when evaluating student performance. Why is this necessary? Isn't one test enough to judge student performance?

Objective Observation

Observation can be an effective evaluative technique. But, as noted earlier, observation often lacks reliability and validity. For example, you may view students you like differently from those you dislike, let the time of day affect your observation, or allow your perceptions to change with time. Lack of objective observation can be overcome to some extent through the use of rating scales, checklists, and other written guides that help objectify observations.

A **rating scale** is nothing more than a specific set of characteristics or qualities that are arranged in order of quality. Indications are made along the scale in such a way that a judgment can be made about the degree to which the attribute being assessed is present. For example, a scale for assessing student involvement in a group project might have five steps, with the lowest category labeled "uninvolved" and the highest labeled "involved." It might look like this:

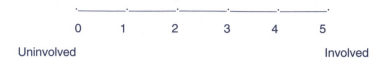

```
._____._____._____._____._____.
0        1        2        3        4        5
```

Uninvolved   Involved

The rater would develop the criteria for what to look for in group involvement and would mark students against the criteria. The scale could be modified and additional scales added to construct a more detailed instrument for assessing total group involvement. This instrument might be similar to the one shown in Figure 5.6.

Checklists are similar to rating scales in that both are used for gathering information about physical kinds of student behaviors. However, a **checklist** differs from a rating scale in that it indicates the presence or absence of identified attributes.

Figure 5.6
Rating Scale for
Group Involvement

RATING SCALE FOR GROUP INVOLVEMENT

Name _____ Date _____

Directions: Rate the student's involvement on each attribute by placing an X on the appropriate position on the scale.

1. Participation
```
._____._____._____._____._____.
0        1        2        3        4        5
```
  Uninvolved   Involved

2. Cooperativeness
```
._____._____._____._____._____.
0        1        2        3        4        5
```
  Inadequate   Adequate

3. Productivity
```
._____._____._____._____._____.
0        1        2        3        4        5
```
  Inadequate   Adequate

4. Self-Discipline
```
._____._____._____._____._____.
0        1        2        3        4        5
```
  Inadequate   Adequate

5. Motivation
```
._____._____._____._____._____.
0        1        2        3        4        5
```
  Inadequate   Adequate

A checklist basically is a list of the criteria against which a student's performance or end product is judged. With a checklist, a teacher simply checks off the criteria items that have been met. For example, a checklist for assessing student readiness for a lesson might look like this:

_____ 1. Reading assignment completed.

_____ 2. Completed homework.

_____ 3. Has book, pencil, and paper.

_____ 4. Demonstrates understanding of related vocabulary.

You would simply check those items that had been demonstrated.

Attitudes, feelings, and opinions are often difficult for teachers to evaluate. Indeed, some attitudinal behaviors may not occur on a daily basis. One technique for overcoming this difficulty is to have students complete a questionnaire. **Questionnaires** call on students to examine themselves and react to a series of statements about their attitudes, feelings, and opinions. Because questionnaires require self-reporting of these attributes, it is important that you recognize the potential for persons to choose socially correct responses rather than to indicate true beliefs. Nonetheless, questionnaires, especially those administered anonymously, can provide valuable information. The questionnaire designer decides what information is wanted and then writes statements or questions that will elicit this information. Questionnaires' response styles can vary from simple checklist-type responses to open-ended statements. For example, a checklist-type questionnaire designed to evaluate a science lesson might include statements such as these:

1. The lesson was   _____ important.
   _____ interesting.
   _____ boring.
   _____ unimportant.

2. I find science   _____ fun.
   _____ exciting.
   _____ boring.
   _____ difficult.

The scoring of the checklist-type of test is simple. The number of negative statements checked is subtracted from the number of positive statements checked. The result is the positiveness of the attribute being measured.

This concludes the formal discussion of information sources and evaluative instruments. Table 5.4 gives a summary of the information sources and evaluative instruments addressed in this chapter. Review Table 5.4 and complete Review, Extension, and Reflective Exercise 5.2.

APPLY AND REFLECT: You should record and organize observational data in a way that ensures accuracy and ready access. How will you do this?

TABLE 5.4 Information Sources and Evaluation Instruments

Concept	Description
Cumulative Record	A file that holds information collected on students during the school years
Personal Contact	The collection of data through daily interactions and observations of students
Analysis	An examination of students' work
Open-Ended Themes and Diaries	The periodic writing of students on in-school and out-of-school topics
Conferences	A meeting between individuals regarding issues of common concern to both parties
Testing	A task or series of tasks used in obtaining systematic observations
Rating Scale	A set of characteristics arranged in order of quality so that performance can be better judged
Checklist	A listing of characteristics used for indicating the presence or absence of identified attributes
Questionnaire	A set of statements to which students react in order to examine their attitudes, feelings, and opinions

Review, Extension, and Reflective Exercise 5.2

Describe some ways to obtain evaluative information.

Connections to INTASC Standards:

- Standard 8: Assessment. The teacher understands and uses formal and informal assessment strategies to evaluate and ensure the continuous intellectual, social, and physical development of the learner.
- Standard 9: Reflection and Professional Development. The teacher must be a reflective practitioner who continually evaluates the effects of his or her choices and actions on others (students, parents, and other professionals in the learning community) and who actively seeks out opportunities to grow professionally.

Connections to the NBPTS:

- Proposition 3: Teachers are responsible for managing and monitoring student learning.

- Proposition 4: Teachers must think systematically about their practice and learn from experience.

Review

- What kinds of information can be obtained from cumulative records, personal contacts, analysis, themes and diaries, conferences, and testing? Which are valid and reliable?
- Why use rating scales, checklists, and questionnaires?

Reflection

- Teachers need evaluative information. In addition to the sources mentioned in this chapter, what other sources of evaluative information would you use in the area you expect to teach? Would rating scales, checklists, and written guides make your evaluative information more accurate.

THE PUBLIC VIEW OF EDUCATION

What does the public think of testing and accountability? Review these results and discuss with classmates.

Pay teachers not based on seniority, but based on the value that they bring to the classrooms, as measured by improvements in their students' test scores. Do you strongly support, somewhat support, somewhat oppose, or strongly oppose this proposal?

Strongly support	66%
Somewhat support	18%
Somewhat oppose	8%
Strongly oppose	6%
Don't know	2%

Offer alternative teacher certification, based on a teacher's abilities rather than his or her degrees or credentials. Do you strongly support, somewhat support, somewhat oppose, or strongly oppose this proposal?

Strongly support	47%
Somewhat support	33%
Somewhat oppose	11%
Strongly oppose	6%
Don't know	4%

Test all teachers periodically to make sure they are competent and qualified to teach. Do you strongly support, somewhat support, somewhat oppose, or strongly oppose this proposal?

Strongly support	83%
Somewhat support	11%
Somewhat oppose	2%
Strongly oppose	2%
Don't know	1%

Public schoolteachers in Arizona, Ohio, and Kansas have been sued by parents because their kids received failing grades. Should individual teachers be exposed to lawsuits for the grades they issue?

Yes	5%
No	90%
Other	4%
Don't know	1%

Students should be required to pass state-wide competency tests to graduate from high school.

Agree strongly	59%
Agree somewhat	22%
Disagree somewhat	7%
Disagree strongly	10%
Other	1%
Don't know	2%

SOURCE: Excerpted from *PollingReport.com*, available at www.pollingreport.com/educ2.htm and *The Internet Party*, available at www.theinternetparty.org

Summary

The Evaluation Process

- Evaluating student learning is a complex endeavor that requires the same careful planning necessary for teaching content.
- Evaluation helps you become a better planner and to better understand students, their abilities, interests, attitudes, and needs in order to better teach and motivate them.

Evaluation Types

- The three types of evaluation are pretest, formative, and posttest (summative).
- Pretest evaluation is carried out prior to instruction for placement purposes. Formative evaluation is used during instruction to promote learning. Posttest evaluation follows instruction and is used to judge the end product of learning.

Systems of Evaluation

- Evaluation can be competitive, noncompetitive, or performance based.
- Competitive evaluation requires that students compete with each other, whereas noncompetitive evaluation requires that students show improvement in their level of achievement.
- Attention is being directed toward "performance" assessment. In performance assessment, students demonstrate the behavior that the assessor wants to measure.

Measurement Accuracy

- Reliability, validity, and usability are three important qualities of every measurement device.

Information Sources

- Evaluation requires information.
- Information can be obtained from cumulative records, personal contacts, analysis, opened-ended themes and diaries, conferences, and testing.

Discussion Questions and Activities

1. **Test-bank critique.** Examine and critique the test materials included in a published program of study for the subject area and grade level you would like to teach. What changes would you make before using the materials?

2. **Evaluation purposes.** List five purposes of evaluation. Why should there be a match between the method of evaluation and the purpose of evaluation?

3. **Conferences.** Plan a general conference with a parent for the first time. Discuss what topics might be important to include in a conference.

4. **Evaluating students.** List all the evaluation practices you think are beneficial to students and their learning. Now list all the practices you think are harmful to students and learning. Reflect on the two lists you have generated.

5. **Testing criticism.** Since paper-and-pencil tests are often criticized as measuring only low-level learning, do you believe that eventually they will no longer be used?

Connection With the Field

1. **Teacher interview.** Interview an elementary and secondary teacher.
   a. How important do they feel assessment is for promoting learning?
   b. How often do they test?
   c. How do they prepare students for testing (such as the day before)?
   d. Do they go over tests with students after they give them?

2. **Evaluation systems.** Study the evaluation system of a teacher in the subject area and grade level you would like to teach. Determine the extent to which the teacher uses norm-referenced and criterion-referenced evaluation.

3. **Observation.** Develop a simple observation instrument to keep track of the questions answered by students in a classroom. Use the instrument in an actual classroom. Did your observational instrument make it easier to keep track of the questioning and answering sequence? How would you modify the original instrument?

4. **Rating scales.** Develop a rating scale for assessing a common classroom behavior problem. Use the scale in an actual classroom. How helpful was your rating scale?

Praxis II Connection

The following test preparation exercises are intended to help you prepare for the Praxis II: Principles of Learning and Teaching. The Praxis II may be required by your teacher education preparatory program and for state certification or licensing. These exercises will give you direct access to pedagogical knowledge from Chapter 5 that may be expected of you on the Praxis II and other pedagogical exams that may be required at the end of your teacher education program.

Topic Connections

1. Types of assessment (II. C1, 4)

What are the purposes of pretest, formative, and posttest evaluation? Explain how teachers can make effective use of the information gathered by each type of assessment.

2. Performance assessment (II. C1, 2, 5)

There has been a recent emphasis on performance assessment and the use of rubrics in evaluation. Describe the characteristics of performance assessment and using rubrics and the potential problems with their use.

3. Valid assessment (II. C2, 5)

Reliability, validity, and usability are important in assessment. How are reliability, validity, and usability, and rating scales, checklists, and questionnaires related?

ON YOUR OWN

Log on to the web-based student study site at http://www.sagepub.com/eis for more information about the vignettes and materials presented in this chapter, suggestions for activities, study aids such as electronic flashcards and review quizzes, and research recommendations including journal article links and questions related to this chapter.

6

CONSTRUCTING AND GRADING TESTS

Experience is the name everyone gives to their mistakes.

OSCAR WILDE

OVERVIEW

Teachers must test. These tests can be commercially produced or teacher-made. Therefore, teachers must be aware of how standardized tests are produced, as well as how to write test items and design tests.

The final step in the evaluation process is the interpretation of collected information in assigning grades. To do so, teachers must be able to arrange information in an objective and impersonal way.

This chapter was designed to help prospective teachers better understand testing, to improve test construction skills, and to better understand grading and the assignment of grades. To these ends, the focus will be on test types, test item construction, and the assignment of grades based upon evaluative data.

OBJECTIVES

After completing your study of Chapter 6, you should be able to do the following:

1. Given the purpose of the test, correctly determine the best type of test for that purpose.
2. Compare and contrast standardized tests and teacher-made tests.
3. Compare and contrast the different types of teacher-made test items and the advantages and disadvantages associated with each.
4. Construct the different types of items that can be included in teacher-made tests.
5. List the purposes for assigning grades.
6. Assign letter grades for participating students and provide a valid rationale for this assignment.

Most schools put their primary emphasis on learning in the cognitive domain. Although there are a number of ways to measure knowledge in the cognitive domain, the most common is through the use of tests. These tests can be published by commercial testing bureaus, or they can be designed and constructed by individual teachers.

Tests are designed and administered for various purposes. Some are given for diagnostic (pretest) purposes, whereas others are given for determining grades. As such, tests are sometimes given before instruction; others, after instruction. Indeed, at times a single test may be given before instruction for diagnosis (pretest) and again after instruction for determining student progress (posttest). Tests are also designed and administered for measuring student achievement. The measured achievement can be used in comparing students' scores with one another (norm-referenced tests) or in comparing students' scores with predetermined criteria (criterion-referenced tests).

As a teacher, you will be responsible for selecting the tests for your classroom. This will not always be easy.

Types of Tests

The compilation of evaluative information requires the use of a data-recording instrument. Of course, the most popular instrument in schools today is the test. Consequently, in this section, we will discuss the general characteristics of two commonly used testing devices: standardized tests and teacher-made tests. Detailed guidelines for constructing these tests are beyond the scope of this book. For more information on test construction, you should consult a basic textbook that details the construction, validation, and administration of tests.

Standardized Tests

Ebel and Frisbie (1991) define a **standardized test** as one that has been constructed by experts with explicit instructions for administration, standard scoring procedures, and tables of norms for interpretation. Standardized tests measure individual performance on a group-administered and group-normed test. Standardization means that the examinees attempt the same questions under the same conditions with the same directions, the time limit for taking the test is the same for everyone, and the results are scored with the same detailed procedure.

The preparation, editing, and analysis of standardized tests are undertaken by experts in the field covered. First, these experts write a battery of content questions related to the subject field that should be answerable by the average, well-informed student at the targeted grade level. These questions are then tried out on a representative sample of students in the subject area at the specified grade level from all kinds of schools in all parts of the country. Based on the results obtained from the representative sample, the test is revised, and a final version of the exam is written. The exam is then administered to a sample of students that is larger and more carefully selected to represent the target subject area and grade level. This latter sample of students forms the norming group against which all subsequent student scores will be compared. The final step in the development of the standardized test is the

Preparing for Standards Assessment

1. Is high-stakes testing beneficial to students, families, and society? Do you support high-stakes testing?
2. How concerned should you be regarding students' reading ability and reading comprehension skills?

We've just completed standards assessment testing for the state. The experience led me to reflect upon my own teaching practice and to wonder about education in lower socioeconomic areas.

No Child Left Behind (NCLB) says that for our school (which is classified as a "failure" at the moment) to be taken off the failure list, we must raise our test scores at least 6 percentage points every year in order to make the 100-percent pass rate at the end of the time period allowed. We are to do this with no additional help from the government and very little from the district. I, personally, have not been given any additional curriculum (e.g., texts, readings, etc.) or administrative tools (e.g., increased copy machine access to run off the items needed) to ensure my classroom success. At least 40 percent of my students read below grade level but do not have a reading class scheduled in their roster (there are not enough reading specialists in my building to accommodate the need).

How can the students be better prepared for taking a standardized test in general? As an eighth grade teacher, I am not sure how much damage I can undo before they leave me and go to the high school, where the performance bar is raised even higher. I want to raise the bar myself, but I am afraid that it is all for naught. I feel caught in a vicious cycle that I am worried will never end.

The students I teach have poor writing, reading comprehension, and math skills. Why is that? I have seen them struggle through exercises that my 12-year-old (a sixth grader) can handle with ease. It has to boil down to what these students have NOT been getting in their past academic lives. It is obvious to me that they have not been getting a "proper" education. I use the term loosely, as it can mean different things depending on where you are coming from. For example, proper reading skills for my eighth graders would not always include being on grade level. For you and the students you teach, that might be different. Proper reading skills for me would include being able to comprehend what you have just read and apply it to a real-life situation. Remember, I teach 13- and 14-year-olds. I would have thought their prior knowledge base would be wider and deeper than it is. I feel as though I have to reteach ideas that they should already know. Let me give you an example of what I am up against.

We are learning about the frontier West, the pioneers, and the westward expansion of the United States during the years 1840 to 1880. In the first lesson, I wanted to "revisit" (note my word of choice) what the country looked like during this time period and how the geography of the United States played a significant role in being able to settle the West. Our task was to label mountains, plains, rivers, and deserts using our textbook and a student atlas. Well, I could not go further because most of my students did not know what a "plain" was, let alone how it might have been an obstacle in travel plans. And some wanted to know if a desert was the same thing as what you eat at the end of your meal (I kid you not). So instead of moving forward, I had to step back (several steps actually) and teach a lesson on United States geography, which, by the way, is in our sixth grade district curriculum. After they learned terms and applied them to a map of the United States, their assessment was to answer the following question: If you were a pioneer traveling on foot or leading a wagon, what kind of obstacle would a mountain present to you? Then substitute the words plain, river, and desert in the place of mountain and answer the question again. We even had difficulty with this. First, I had to define

REFLECTIONS ON TEACHER PRACTICE

Preparing for Standards Assessment

(Continued)

"obstacle" before we could go further. Most still could not answer the question until I set a scene for them.

I painted a picture. "Okay, you are a person who wants to get to the West before the next winter. You come across a river. How are you going to get across it and not lose your supplies like flour and sugar? You know if they get wet they are ruined and you will likely starve." Or "You are driving a wagon pulled by slow oxen. You have come to the start of a steep climb up a mountain. You are in tall grass and the weather is still warm, but when you look straight up at the mountain, all you see is snow. How are you going to get your wagon up and over before the winter comes? What might you experience on the trail that is going to stop you from getting over the top?" This type of banter is ongoing and seems endless to me. Until we've exhausted every angle of every task, the students seem hard-pressed to begin. To me, this comes back to a basic lack of reading and comprehension skills—which bears on their ability to pass the standardized achievement tests.

What can I do in social studies class to help prepare my students for these kinds of tests? First, I have decided that I need to "mock up" a variety of short reading assignments, create multiple-choice questions to test for understanding and then develop an open-ended question that can help determine if the student has internalized the content. These supplemental reading tasks will then "mirror" the kinds of questions students will encounter on the standardized tests.

This is a daunting task. The textbook is a basic form of reading, not a great deal of depth, but a good survey of content. I have not found any books that I could just purchase and include in my curriculum. There are many reading books that will assist in raising student test scores, but after an exhaustive search I have not found even one book that concentrates on social studies readings.

Second, I will need to beef up my reading comprehension strategies and incorporate them more often into my lessons. I have used them sporadically this year, but I really need to focus more on reading in the content area instead of learning the content—a subtle, but very important difference.

I feel as though my main task as a social studies teacher—whether or not I like it—is to help students figure out what to do with the words they see before them that don't make any sense. I didn't go to graduate school to become a reading specialist. But if I don't develop into one (self-taught, because there's no support for my professional development in this area, either), my students are not going to be able to break the cycle of failure. Once again, I need to rethink and remold my teacher-self into something other than what I thought I should be.

I can see why some teachers find a niche and stay put for years and years. Trying to be an effective teacher is exhausting!

—CAROLYN BEITZEL, *eighth grade Social Studies teacher, Beverly Hills Middle School, Upper Darby, PA*

SOURCE: www.middleweb.com. Reprinted with permission.

production of a test manual that provides clear directions for administration and scoring of the test, as well as certain information related to the test characteristics and interpretation of scores.

Standardized tests are particularly useful in comparing the performance of one individual with another, of an individual against a group, or of one group with another group. Such comparisons are possible because of the availability of the norming-group data and the uniformity of the procedures for administration and scoring the test. Thus, you could compare a single school with others schools in a district, compare districts, compare states, or compare students in one state with all students in the nation. For example, suppose a student scored 80 percent on a physics test. For most purposes, this is sufficient information for evaluation purposes, but at times you might want to know how a physics score of 80 percent compares to the physics scores of other students in the district, state, or nation.

Standardized tests come in the form of test batteries and single-subject tests. Some standardized tests are used in assessing personality, but the most commonly used standardized test measures knowledge in specific areas, such as English, social studies, psychology, or chemistry. These tests are usually referred to as *achievement tests,* because they measure how much a student has learned in a particular subject area. Other standardized tests that are commonly used are those that measure students' aptitudes, or abilities, for performing certain activities. These tests are designed to measure an individual's potential in a given field—such as journalism, mathematics, law, drafting, teaching, or auto mechanics—and are given a variety of labels, including general ability test, intelligence tests, or scholastic aptitude tests.

Standardized test results generally include a percentile norm, an age norm, and a grade-level norm, or a combination of these norms. Teachers are often called upon to interpret these norms for parents. Therefore, you need a basic understanding of their meaning. At the most basic level, a percentile rank (see Chapter 5) of 85 indicates that 85 percent of the norm group performed more poorly and 15 percent performed better than the individual in question. An age rank of 15.6 means that, regardless of chronological age, the student got the same number of right answers as did the average 15 1/2-year-old in the norm group: the number to the left of the decimal point represents years and the number to the right of the decimal point represents months. Grade-level norms are the most widely reported and the least useful of the measures. Grade-level norms are reported as grade equivalent scores, with the tenths place representing the months in a ten-month school year. The only real value of grade equivalent scores is to determine if the test was too easy or too difficult for students scoring at a particular level.

Sax (1980) and Ebel and Frisbie (1991) report that standardized achievement tests are most properly used to make decisions about

1. Determining placement in differentiated instructional tracks.
2. Individualizing instruction for remediation or acceleration.
3. Diagnosing areas of strength and weakness.
4. Gauging the effectiveness of an instructional program or group of programs.
5. Evaluating the extent of student progress.
6. Determining teaching emphasis and effectiveness.

Although these reasons present a strong case for the use of standardized tests in educational decision making, it is important to recognize that a too narrow or too broad interpretation of results can lead to oversimplifying a complex situation. For example, one English class performs more poorly on grammar than another. Can you assume that the teacher is doing a poor job of teaching grammar concepts? Probably not, and certainly not without more information about the composition of the two classes. The poor performance could be explained by a large number of mainstreamed special-needs students in the first class, or by the fact that all school assemblies and announcements occur during second period, reducing instructional time during that period.

Standardized tests and teacher-made tests are given for different reasons. Standardized tests generally cover a much broader range of a content area than would a teacher-made test, which is designed to measure achievement in a particular unit of work. Thus, achievement tests in the classroom should supplement teacher-made evaluation. The use of standardized tests will continue to play an important role for educational decision making and for public reporting on the state of school learning, but standardized tests are only one method for evaluating learning. The tests can give valuable information on how well your students are doing overall in comparison with other student groups.

Certain limitations are also associated with the use of standardized tests. For example, their validity is often questionable in situations in which they do not measure what was taught; that is, they may not be consistent with the goals and objectives established by the teacher. Moreover, standardized tests are likely to have some social and cultural bias, which means that the test may discriminate against certain social and cultural groups that lack prerequisite language, background experience, or testing experiences.

APPLY AND REFLECT: Standardized tests are widely used in our schools. Do you think the results should be used to make major educational decisions? Why?

Teacher-Made Tests

Teacher-made tests are the most common of all school evaluative instruments. There are three basic reasons for the popularity of teacher-made tests. First, they can be constructed so they are consistent with classroom goals and objectives. Second, teacher-made tests present the same questions to all students under nearly identical conditions. This means that the test results provide the means and basis for making comparative judgments among students. Third, teacher-made tests generate a product that can be evaluated and easily stored for later use. This means that tests and results can be readily accessible for review by students and parents when explaining how grades were determined. In addition, teacher-made tests are much less expensive to construct and administer.

Although teacher-made tests have their advantages, the bulk of these tests have unknown or low reliability, and most teachers lack the skill for designing valid tests or writing appropriate test items. Teacher-made tests remain, however, an important part of the instructional process. Consequently, you should further develop and refine your skill in test construction.

Teachers have three basic alternatives in constructing tests: They can construct an objective test, an essay test, or a combination. Objective tests comprise

Standardized tests provide valuable information for making curriculum decisions.

alternative-choice, multiple-choice, matching, and completion items, whereas essay tests include supply items. These supply items can be written either as brief- or extended-essay questions; that is, the students must supply short or elaborate responses. Brief-essay items ask students to write a sentence or short paragraph, solve a problem, or give a proof, whereas extended-essay items require that students write at length. The item type or types used in the construction of a particular test depends on your objectives and the nature of the behaviors being measured.

Test items should be written at the taxonomical level of your objectives. Contrary to common belief, this can be accomplished with almost any type of test item—objective or essay. Although it is more difficult to write objective items at the higher levels, it is also difficult to write high-level essay items.

Instructional objectives usually suggest the best type of test item. For example, an objective that involves solving physics problems would probably be best evaluated through the use of brief-essay items, whereas knowledge of the definitions of terms would probably be best evaluated through the use of multiple-choice items. In general, however, when objectives lend themselves to more than one type of test item, most teachers prefer objective items over essay types because of their scoring ease and reliability.

Classroom tests generally should not contain more than two types of test items. Students may have trouble when they must shift to different types of responses. Therefore, if your objectives can be evaluated by one or two test types, then limit your test to these types.

The purpose of testing is to check student mastery of the stated objectives. Therefore, one overall principle applies to the writing of all test items: every item should separate the students who have mastered the objectives from those who have not. Students who cannot respond should not be able to guess or bluff their way to success on a test. Moreover, "test wiseness" (the ability to answer questions through

"I studied for this test, and the ploy paid off."

the use of clues from the question) should be guarded against when constructing a test. Let us now briefly consider the various types of test items commonly used by teachers.

Alternate-Choice Items

The simplest form of objective test item is the alternate-choice type. The true/false format is the most common form of alternate-choice item. Variations on the basic true/false item include yes/no, right/wrong, and agree/disagree items.

Alternate-choice items tend to be popular because they appear to be easy to write. These items, generally, are simple declarative sentences. Unfortunately, writing good alternate-choice items requires skill, if you are to avoid triviality and discourage guessing. Writing good true/false items is difficult because there are few assertions that are unambiguously true or false. Therefore, because of this particular sensitivity to ambiguity, it is especially crucial that your alternate-choice items be stated as clearly as possible. For instance, consider the following:

Poor: The value of pi is 3.14.   T or F

This question is ambiguous; 3.14 is not the exact value of pi, but it is a commonly used value. To be totally clear, the item could be rewritten as follows:

Better: The value of pi is approximately 3.14.   T or F

This question is better because it allows for the small difference between what is commonly used as the value of pi and the exact value. Following are some further suggestions for improving the writing of alternate-choice items:

1. Avoid using negative statements and double negatives. Such statements can be confusing and may cause knowledgeable students to get them wrong.
2. Make sure an item is not dependent upon insignificant facts. Make sure that your items ask something important and worth remembering. For example, a statement should not be false because an individual's seldom-used first name is asked. Do not use trick items that appear to be true but are false because of an inconspicuous word or phrase.
3. Don't make your false items longer than your true items (or vice versa). If you find it necessary to write a few lengthy true items, make sure that you supply approximately the same number of lengthy false items.
4. Watch for item response patterns. Generally, the proportion of true and false items in a test should not be too different. Similarly, guard against correct/incorrect response patterns—such as T T T F F F or T F T F T F—that could help students achieve a misleading number of correct answers.
5. Be clear and concise. Use simple grammar in item construction. Avoid dependent clauses and compound sentences.
6. Limit each statement to only one central idea. Don't mix true and false ideas in a single statement.
7. Be especially sensitive to the use of certain key words that can divulge the correct response. Words such as *always, never, all,* and *none* indicate sweeping generalizations, which are associated with false items, whereas words like *sometimes, often, probably, usually,* and *generally* are associated with true items.
8. Avoid exact quote statements from the textbook or workbook. Quotations can have different meaning when they are taken out of context or may make students think that you prefer rote learning.

Alternate-choice items permit teachers to take a broad sampling of behaviors in a limited amount of time. Moreover, the scoring of alternate-choice items tends to be quick and simple. But it is often difficult to write good items. Also, some kinds of learning cannot be evaluated easily through alternate-choice items. For example, problem-solving situations often are difficult to evaluate using alternate-choice techniques. Finally, students have a 50 percent chance of guessing the correct answer, thus giving the items poor reliability and validity.

Multiple-Choice Items

Probably the most useful and flexible form of test item is the multiple-choice item. It can be used successfully in measuring achievement of almost any objective of interest to the teacher. Moreover, like alternative-choice questions, a multiple-choice test enables a teacher to ask many questions and, thus, cover many objectives on the same test. It can be used for measuring almost any type of cognitive behavior, from factual knowledge to the analysis of complex data. Undoubtedly, the multiple-choice format is the most versatile of all objective item formats. Moreover, it has the added advantage of being easy to score.

The basic form of the multiple-choice item is a *stem* or *lead,* which sets up the problem or asks a question to be completed with one of a number of alternative answers or responses (usually three to five). One of the responses is the correct answer; the other alternatives are called *distractors* or *foils* and should be plausible but incorrect. Writing good multiple-choice items is not as easy as many beginning teachers believe. It often takes a substantial amount of patience and creative ability to write good distractors. Unless you know your course content well, the number of items that can be constructed is limited.

Multiple-choice items should be constructed so they are straightforward, clear, and concise. Consider the following example:

Poor: Who was president during the Civil War?
    A. Jefferson Davis
    B. Abraham Lincoln
    C. Ulysses S. Grant
    D. George Washington

The correct response depends on whether you are asking for the president of the United States or of the Confederacy. In other words, there are two possible correct responses to the question. The question, however, could be reworded as follows:

Better: Who was president of the United States during the Civil War?
    A. Jefferson Davis
    B. Abraham Lincoln
    C. Ulysses S. Grant
    D. George Washington

A summary of the guidelines that can be followed to write better multiple-choice items follows:

1. The central issue or problem should be stated clearly in the stem. It should be stated in the form of an incomplete statement or question, and there should be no ambiguity in terminology.
2. Avoid writing a stem at the end of one page and the alternatives on the next, or placing choices in a linear sequence.
3. Avoid providing grammatical or contextual clues to the correct answer. For example, the use of *an* before the choices suggests that the answer begins with a vowel. Instead, use the form *a(n),* which means "either *a* or *an.*"
4. Use language that even the most unskilled readers will understand. Keep the reading requirement in a question to a minimum. Write concise stems and precise choices.
5. Avoid absolute terms (such as *always, never,* and *none*) in the stem and alternatives. Test-wise individuals are usually sensitive to these terms.
6. Alternatives should be grammatically correct. The use of *is* or *are,* for example, can often help students guess the correct response. All alternatives should fit the stem to avoid giving clues to items that are incorrect.
7. Avoid the use of negatives (such as *not, except,* and *least*) and double negatives in the stem and alternatives. If negatives are used in the stem, put them as near the end of the stem as possible.
8. Avoid giving structural clues. For example, try not to use one letter for the correct response more often than others or create a pattern of correct responses.

9. Use "all of the above" and "none of the above" with care. "All of the above" is usually a poorer response than "none of the above" because all alternatives must be correct answers. It is often difficult to write four or five correct responses to a stem.
10. Avoid pulling statements directly from the textbook. Test students for understanding, not memorization.
11. Alternatives should be plausible to less knowledgeable students. Write distractors that include common errors, errors that are likely, and erroneous commonsense solutions.

Once you have written a pool of multiple-choice items for a unit of instruction, you generally will find it easy to modify the items based on feedback data. Moreover, multiple-choice items are relatively insensitive to guessing; however, they are more sensitive to guessing than are supply items.

Matching

Matching questions are designed to measure students' ability to recall a fairly large amount of factual information. Students are presented two lists of items (phrases, concepts, dates, principles, or names) and asked to select an item from one list that most closely relates to an item from the second list. Essentially, a matching item is an efficient arrangement of a series of multiple-choice items with all stems (sometimes called *premises*) having the same set of possible alternative responses. Thus, matching items can be used anywhere multiple-choice items can be used. They are best suited for measurement of verbal, associative knowledge.

Matching items are relatively easy to construct, especially if they are intended for measuring lower-level learning. Conversely, the chief disadvantage is that they are not effective for evaluating higher-level thinking.

Writing good matching questions is often difficult. Another problem associated with matching items is the tendency for one part of the item to give away the answer to another part. Consider, for example, the following:

Poor:
1. Alex Haley   A. *Wheels*
2. James A. Michener   B. *The Exorcist*
3. William Golding   C. *Lord of the Flies*
4. William Peter Blatty D. *Cujo*
5. Arthur Hailey   E. *Centennial*
6. Stephen King   F. *Roots*

There are exactly six premises and six responses. If each statement is to be used only once, the students need only answer five of the premises correctly to correctly identify the sixth response for the last premise. It is better to allow each response to be used more than once or, even better, to add extra responses—for example,

Better:
1. Alex Haley   A. *The Exorcist*
2. James A. Michener   B. *Wheels*
3. William Golding   C. *The Grapes of Wrath*

4. William Peter Blatty   D. *Lord of the Flies*
5. Arthur Hailey   E. *Cujo*
6. Stephen King   F. *Centennial*
   G. *Roots*
   H. *1984*

Many multiple-choice questions can be easily converted to matching items. In fact, you should think of matching items as a set of multiple-choice items with the same set of alternatives. Each response is then appropriate for each premise. Also, the following guidelines will aid in the construction of better matching items:

1. Indicate clearly and concisely the basis for matching the premises with the responses.
2. Design the entire matching item so it is contained on one page. That is, don't put the premises on one page and the responses on the back or on the next page.
3. Keep the number of items to be matched short. Limit the number of items to 10 or so. The more premises, the more difficult it is to avoid giving inadvertent clues.
4. Put premises and responses in logical order. That is, be sure that premises and responses are easy for students to find.
5. Be sure items include statements, words, or phrases that have a high degree of homogeneity. Both the premises and the responses should fall in the same general topic or category.
6. Make the length of statements consistent. In fact, longer statements and phrases should be listed in the left column and shorter ones in the right column.
7. If names are to be matched, use complete names. Using only last names sometimes causes confusion.

Completion

Completion items require that students write responses in their own handwriting. They generally ask students to supply a recalled word or phrase. A completion test item usually contains a blank, which the student must fill in correctly with one word or a short phrase.

Completion items are not easy to write. Skill is needed to write such items so that there is only one correct response. Some teachers eliminate this problem by providing students with a selection of answers, some correct and some incorrect, from which students select a response.

Completion items are most useful for the testing of specific facts. They are less powerful than essay items, however, in terms of the kinds of thinking they can evaluate.

Placement of the blank is of prime importance in writing completion items. Consider the following glaring error:

Poor:

_____, _____, and _____ are three large cities in _____.

In general, it is best to use only one blank in a completion item, and it should be placed near the end of the statement. Thus, the example would be better rewritten as follows:

Better:
    Dallas, Houston, and Austin are three large cities in the state of _____.

A summary of guidelines associated with writing better completion items follows:

1. Give clear instructions. Indicate how detailed answers should be, whether synonyms will be correct, and whether spelling will be a factor in grading.
2. Be definite enough in the incomplete statement so that only one correct answer is possible.
3. Do not adapt direct statements from the textbook with a word or two missing. Such usage encourages students to memorize the text.
4. Make sure all blanks are of equal length and correspond to the lengths of the desired responses. That is, all blanks for all items should be of equal length and long enough to accommodate the longest response. Young students write big. So, allow sufficient space for your young students to write their answers.
5. Write items that can be completed by a single word or brief phrase.

Some subjects lend themselves better than others to testing through completion items. For example, subjects that focus on the recall of specific unambiguous facts or that require students to perform certain calculations to fill in the blank in the statement are more suited for evaluation through the use of completion items.

Essay

Essay items give students the opportunity to formulate answers to questions in their own words. Essay questions are said to measure what students know because they permit students to select from their own storehouse of knowledge in answering a question. In effect, essay questions can successfully determine students' ability to analyze, synthesize, evaluate, and solve problems. Some specialists advocate using words such as *why, how,* and *what consequences* in essay questions because, they claim, such terms call for a command of essential knowledge of concepts to integrate the subject into an appropriate response. Other test specialists urge teachers to use words such as *discuss, explain,* and *examine* because they prompt responses that provide a glimpse of how students think. Still other specialists advocate more precision and structure through the use of words such as *identify, compare,* and *contrast.*

Essay test items come in two basic forms: brief and extended. The brief-essay item generally requires a short answer or the solution of a problem, whereas the extended-essay item calls for several paragraphs of writing. Because of time constraints, extended essays are seldom used in the classroom. In fact, most teacher-made tests are a combination of objective items and brief-essay items.

Essay items continue to be misused by teachers. Teachers often take less time in writing essay items than objective items. In fact, essay questions appear to be so easy to write that teachers often prepare them too hastily. Consider the following example:

Poor: Discuss Shakespeare's work.

This question is unclear. You should tell students what to discuss, and tell them in descriptive terms. "Describe the use of metaphor in Shakespeare's works" or "Analyze the political ramifications of Shakespeare's works" are more specific statements. Notice that the following phrasing makes the requested task much clearer.

Better: Analyze the use of humor in Shakespeare's *Twelfth Night*.

You should give careful consideration to the construction of essay questions so that students will know what is required of them. The following guidelines should be of further assistance in writing better essay questions:

1. Make directions clear and explicit. If spelling and grammar are to be considered in grading, tell the students. Also, if organization, creativity, and content are to be considered in grading, share this information.
2. Allow ample time for students to answer the questions. If more than one essay question is to be answered during a period, suggest a time allotment for each question.
3. Students should be given a choice of questions. Such choice avoids penalizing students who may know the subject as a whole but have limited knowledge in the particular area of a single question.
4. The worth of each question should be determined as a test is being written. Convey this information in the test instructions, and grade accordingly.
5. Explain your scoring technique to students before you give the test. It should be clear to them what you will be looking for when you grade the test.

A common problem associated with essay tests is content coverage. Because of the time students need to respond to essays, fewer topics can be covered. Realistically, only a few essay items can be included on an exam.

Essay items are difficult to score. There is often no single right answer to a question. Because of this tendency, essay items generally tend to be less reliable and less valid than other types of test items. With care, however, biases associated with essay grading can be controlled to some extent. Several guidelines follow:

1. Write a sample answer to each essay question ahead of time and assign points to various components of your answer.
2. Skim through all responses to a question before beginning the grading of the question. Establish a model answer for each question, and grade each question for all students before proceeding to the next question.
3. Grade essays blindly. Have students write their names on the back of the exam so it can be graded without knowledge of the identity of the respondent.
4. Establish a reasonable page limit and time limit for each essay item. This will indicate the level of detail desired and help students finish the entire test.
5. If time permits, read student responses several times. This will reduce the chances of making serious errors in judgment.

Despite grading drawbacks, unrestricted essay items are usually required to evaluate higher-order knowledge and thinking. Therefore, they should be used, but used with care.

APPLY AND REFLECT: Teacher-made tests can be objective or essay. Which would work best at the grade level you expect to teach? Why?

"It's not easy getting all your homework done between dinner time and prime time."

Authentic Assessment

Authentic assessment is any type of assessment that requires students to demonstrate skills and competencies that realistically represent real-world problems and situations. Students are required to integrate knowledge and to complete tasks that have real-life applications. Authentic assessments can include exhibitions, oral presentations, and other projects. Students might be asked to evaluate case studies, write definitions and defend them orally, perform role plays, or have oral readings recorded on tape. They might collect writing folders that include drafts and revisions showing changes in spelling and mechanics, revision strategies, and their history as a writer.

Perhaps the most widely used authentic assessment technique is the portfolio. Portfolios are a collection of learner work over time. They may include research papers, book reports, journals, logs, photographs, drawings, video- and audiotapes, abstracts of readings, group projects, software, slides, test results; in fact, some of the assessments listed earlier could have a place in a portfolio. Portfolios should represent a documented history of learning and an organized demonstration of accomplishment. They can serve as a catalyst for reflection on one's growth as a learner.

Some guidelines for the development of good authentic assessment are the following:

1. Design meaningful and worthy programs or tasks that match the content and outcomes of instruction.

2. Make sure tasks have real-life applicability.
3. Put emphasis on product and process, conveying that both development and achievement matter.
4. Provide opportunities for learner self-evaluation.
5. Develop scoring procedures and their application. Develop rubrics to help establish consistency and fairness.

APPLY AND REFLECT: Authentic assessment represents an option to objective and essay testing. What problems do you associate with this form of assessment?

Teachers must assess, and this assessment should serve several purposes. Complete Expansion Activity: Classroom Assessment to further explore the validity of assessment.

EXPANSION ACTIVITY

Classroom
Assessment

Think about the following statement and decide whether you agree or disagree with it.

A teacher should never use a single measure to assess learning.

This section has focused on several types of test items. Keep in mind, however, that the different kinds of items can be written to sample almost any behavior. Even so, there are certain advantages and disadvantages associated with the various types of teacher-made test items. Table 6.1 illustrates these advantages and disadvantages.

Although not technically a teacher-made test item type, quizzes represent an important source of evaluative information to teachers. Moreover, quizzes can often be used to motivate students.

Quizzes

Classroom quizzes can be used for evaluating student progress. In fact, quizzes are an excellent way to check homework and find out whether concepts from the preceding lesson were understood.

Teacher quizzes differ from regular teacher-made tests in that they usually consist of three to five questions and are limited to the material taught in the immediate or preceding lesson. They are easy to develop, administer, and grade; thus, they provide prompt evaluative information to both students and teacher.

Quizzes encourage students to keep up with their homework, and they show students their strengths and weaknesses in learning. In addition, quizzes help teachers improve instruction by providing feedback related to their effectiveness. Problems identified through quizzes serve as early warning signals of teaching or learning problems. Early identification allows the teacher to focus on problems before they worsen.

TABLE 6.1 Advantages and Disadvantages Associated With the Different Types of Test Items

Type	Advantages	Disadvantages
Alternate Choice	Large sampling of content Easy to score	Guessing Writing clear items difficult Tends to test memorization
Multiple Choice	Large sampling of content Scoring simple and fast Measures wide range of cognitive levels Reduces guessing	Question construction time-consuming Often used to test trivial content
Matching	Large sampling of content Can test associations Easy to construct and score	Tests for recognition Guessing
Completion	Large sampling of content Easy to construct Limited guessing	Tests for memorization Writing good items difficult Difficult to score
Essay	Measures higher cognitive levels Less time needed to construct	Difficult to score Questions sometimes ambiguous

Valid tests are not always easy to construct. It takes time and knowledge of evaluation.

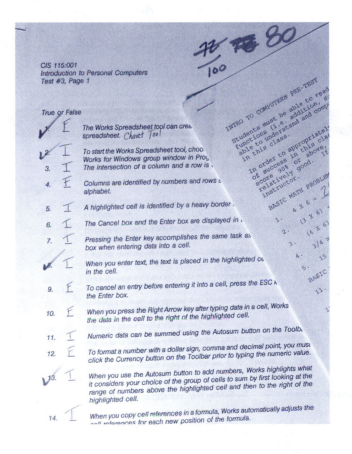

Published Test Banks

Many textbooks and programs of study include publisher-produced test banks. These test banks vary in quality. Some test banks are provided in the form of masters for copying and typically include chapter and unit tests. Many of these tests are geared to factual information and, consequently, ease of grading. If you have planned a set of instructional objectives independent of those suggested in the textbook, it is likely that the published test will fall short of serving your needs.

A more promising development is the advent of test bank databases. Schools that purchase this service for teachers are provided with a phone number that allows teachers to order customized tests from the test bank. Use of this tool certainly requires advance planning. Complete Web Link: Computer Use in Assessment to identify other resources that will help you in your assessment efforts.

WEB   LINK   Computer Use in Assessment

Do an Internet search relative to the use of computers in classroom assessment. What are some appropriate computer uses at the grade level you expect to teach? Share your findings with your class.

A summary of the testing concepts covered to this point is given in Table 6.2. Study Table 6.2 and complete Review, Extension, and Reflective Exercise 6.1 to check your understanding of the concepts presented in this chapter.

TABLE 6.2 Evaluative Instruments

Type	Description
Standardized Test	A commercially developed test that samples behavior under uniform procedures
Teacher-Made Test	An evaluative instrument developed and scored by a teacher for classroom assessment
Alternate-Choice Item	A statement to which respondents react either positively or negatively
Multiple-Choice Item	A test question with a stem that poses a problem or asks a question to be answered by one of several alternative responses
Matching Item	An arranged series of premises, each of which is matched with a specific item from a second list of responses
Completing Item	A statement with a missing word or phrase, which must be supplied by the respondent
Brief-Essay Item	A question to which respondents formulate a short-answer response in their own words or solve a problem
Extended-Essay Item	A question to which respondents formulate responses of several paragraphs in their own words

Review, Extension, and Reflective Exercise 6.1

Describe the different types of tests.

Connections to INTASC Standards:

- Standard 8: Assessment. The teacher understands and uses formal and informal assessment strategies to evaluate and ensure the continuous intellectual, social, and physical development of the learner.
- Standard 9: Reflection and Professional Development. The teacher must be a reflective practitioner who continually evaluates the effects of his or her choices and actions on others (students, parents, and other professionals in the learning community) and who actively seeks out opportunities to grow professionally.

Connections to the NBPTS:

- Proposition 3: Teachers are responsible for managing and monitoring student learning.
- Proposition 4: Teachers must think systematically about their practice and learn from experience.

Review

- What is a standardized test? How is it developed?
- Why do most classroom teachers use teacher-made tests?
- Name and describe the kinds of teacher-made tests.

Reflection

- What would be the best type of test to use in the area you expect to teach? Why?

The gathering of data is not the end of the evaluative process. You then must interpret these data and assign grades. The importance of grades cannot be overemphasized because of their influence on students' lives. For example, grades are often used for college entrance, courses of study, and job recommendations.

Grading Systems

Assigning grades is a responsibility most teachers dislike and feel uncomfortable doing. There is no way to assign grades that is fair to all students. Most school districts assign grades of A, B, C, D, and F. Regardless of the system used, however, assigning grades to students' work is inherently subjective.

You will be required to make judgments when grades are assigned. How many tests should be given? How many As, Cs, and Fs should be given? Will grading be absolute or on a curve? Will students be allowed to retake exams? Can students use extra-credit assignments to modify grades and to what extent?

Homework is a special consideration. Should it be counted in the grading system? Who should grade homework—students or teachers? The grading of homework by students provides immediate feedback and allows the teacher to decide what materials need to be retaught. On the other hand, when the teacher grades the homework, work loads are increased and feedback to students is delayed. Moreover, there is some question as to whether homework should be counted in the grading system. Some say no. Indeed, it is generally not a good idea for a teacher to assign a grade to work that has been graded by students; instead, only the fact that the work was completed should be recorded.

A distinction must be made between the grades you give to students on tests, quizzes, and classroom activities and the grades you issue for grade cards. As a teacher, you must grade students' examination and quizzes. Basically, these grades can be assigned in one of two ways: an absolute grading system or a relative grading system.

Absolute Grading Standards

Grades may be given relative to performance against an established set of grading criteria. An illustration of an **absolute grading standard** is shown in Table 6.3. In this system, grades are assigned based on the number of items answered correctly. This system, in theory, makes it possible for all students to make high grades. In fact, each student is potentially capable of achieving any grade; that is, no one needs to fail, and all students can make good grades if they put forth the effort. Grading is simple: a student either does get an established percentage of the responses correct or does not. Student scores depend on the difficulty of the test.

TABLE 6.3 Examples of Absolute Standards of Grading

Grade	Percentage Correct		Percentage Correct
A	90 to 100		85 to 100
B	80 to 89		75 to 84
C	70 to 79	OR	65 to 74
D	60 to 69		55 to 64
F	less than 60		less than 55

There are major limitations associated with an absolute grading standard: (1) the establishment of a standard for each grade is often difficult; (2) the standard established for each grade may vary from time to time, according to the content being taught and with respect to curriculum changes; (3) teaching effectiveness may vary; and (4) the level of examination difficulty may vary. Despite these limitations, however, most teachers use the absolute standard of grading. The major advantage of such a system is that it puts the control of test scores in the hands of students.

Relative Grading Standards

Teachers frequently use a relative grading standard, in which they assess student performance with respect to the performance of other students. Accordingly, they often use a curve when assigning grades. In this type of system, students are compared with each other. Of course, the best-known curve is the normal curve (see Chapter 5). When this curve is used, you would expect to give 3.5 percent As, 23.8 percent Bs, 45 percent Cs, 23.8 percent Ds, and 3.5 percent Fs. The normal curve, however, is applicable only when the group is large and diversified. Moreover, when the normal curve is used, some student must get As, some students must fail, and most of the students must be given Cs.

Because of its lack of flexibility, few teachers use the normal curve. Instead, they implement a relative grading system based on a simple ranking system. In a ranking system, the teacher establishes a fixed percentage for each assigned grade. For example, you might set up the following curve:

A = Top 10 percent

B = Next 20 percent

C = Next 40 percent

D = Next 20 percent

F = Next 10 percent

Another common method of grading with curves is the inspection method. When using this method, a frequency distribution of raw scores is set up on a vertical or horizontal line, as shown in Figure 6.1. Grades are then assigned according to natural breaks in the distribution. It is possible that this type of system will not yield A or F grades. For example, if the lowest grade in Figure 6.1 had been 14, few teachers would assign an F grade for this work. As you see, the inspection method yields different grades for different individuals. There is no correct or incorrect division. Figure 6.2 shows three possible inspection grading patterns for grade distribution.

Figure 6.1

The Inspection Method

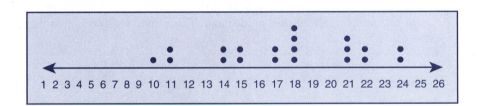

1 2 3 4 5 6 7 8 9 10 11 12 13 14 15 16 17 18 19 20 21 22 23 24 25 26

Figure 6.2

Examples of Inspection Grade Distributions

100			100			100		**A**
95		**A**	95		**A**	95		
94	(1)		94	(1)		94	(1)	**B**
91	(1)		91	(1)		91	(1)	
90	(1)		90	(1)		90	(1)	
85		**B**	85			85		
81	(2)		81	(2)	**B**	81	(2)	
75		**C**	75			75		
74	(4)		74	(4)		74	(4)	**C**
70	(3)		70	(3)		70	(4)	
65		**D**	65		**C**	65		
64	(2)		64	(2)		64	(2)	
60	(1)		60	(1)		60	(1)	
55		**F**	55			55		**D**
50			50		**D**	50		
45			45			45		
44	(1)		44	(1)		44	(1)	
43			43			43		
42			42		**F**	42		**F**

The relative grading standard has a major limitation in that it does not take into account differences in overall ability of students. Thus, some students will always receive As, and some always get Fs.

Assuming one of the previously mentioned methods is used in arriving at grades, the next task you will face as a teacher is to assign nine-week, or term, grades. As you might imagine, this can represent a real challenge.

Assigning Final Grades

Final term grades are generally determined by combining all the results of students' work for a grading period. There are three major ways of accomplishing this end: a point assignment system, a weighted assignment system, and a percentage assignment system.

Point Grading System

A **point grading system** is fairly simple and easy to use. The importance of each assignment, quiz, or test is reflected in the points allocated. For example, you may decide that assignments will be worth 10 points, quizzes 25 points, and tests 100 points. At the end of the grading period, the points are added up and grades are assigned according to the established grade range. This system is illustrated in Figure 6.3.

Figure 6.3

Example of a Point Grading System

Student Work	Points
Assignments	250 (25 × 10 pts.)
Quizzes	150 (6 × 25 pts.)
Tests	300 (3 × 100 pts.)

Total points possible = 700

Grade Range

A 650 to 700

B 600 to 649

C 550 to 599

D 500 to 549

F Less than 499

Figure 6.4

Example of a Weighted
Grading System

Student Work	Weight
Homework assignments	25%
Quizzes (6)	25%
Tests (3)	50%
Total	**100%**

Weighted Grading System

A **weighted grading system** is more complex than the point grading system. Every assignment is given a letter grade, and all grades are then weighted to arrive at a final grade. An example of this system is illustrated in Figure 6.4.

The determination of a final grade can be made simpler and more objective by changing grades to numerical values: A = 4; B = 3; C = 2; D = 1; F = 0. Once numerical values are assigned, an average score is calculated for homework, quizzes, and tests. For example, you would calculate a homework average for seven homework assignments with the grades of A, B, B, C, C, D, and A by carrying out the following computation:

$$(4 + 3 + 3 + 2 + 2 + 1 + 4) / 7 = 19 / 7 = 2.71$$

A quiz average for four quizzes graded B, B, C, and D would be computed as follows:

$$(3 + 3 + 2 + 1) / 4 = 9 / 4 = 2.25$$

Calculation of a test average for three tests with grades of C, C, and D would result in the following computation:

$$(2 + 2 + 1) / 3 = 5 / 3 = 1.67$$

Applying the weights outlined in Figure 6.4, you would calculate a final grade as follows:

$$\text{Homework:} \quad 2.71 \times 25\% = 2.71 \times .25 = .68$$
$$\text{Quizzes:} \quad 2.25 \times 25\% = 2.25 \times .25 = .56$$
$$\text{Tests:} \quad 1.67 \times 50\% = 1.67 \times .50 = .84$$
$$\text{Total numerical grade} = 2.08$$

Thus, the final grade for the student would be 2.08 or a C. Of course, if other student exercises—such as class projects, term papers, and group projects—were included in a grading period, they would also be part of the grading system and be accounted for in the weights.

Percentage Grading System

The **percentage grading system** is probably the simplest of all grading systems and the most widely used. The system typically relies on the calculation of the percentage correct of the responses attempted. For example, a student who gets 20 of 25 correct on a homework assignment has a score of 80 written in the grade book; 6 of 8 correct on a quiz has a 75 recorded in the grade book; and 40 of 60 correct on an examination has a 67 written in the grade book. You typically calculate an average of these and other term scores in arriving at a final score on which to base the term grade. The problem with this system is that all student exercises carry the same weight, even though the type of exercises are markedly different—homework, quiz, and examination.

Even with the noted flaw, teachers tend to use the percentage system extensively for two reasons. First, it is simple to use and understand. Second, parents and students prefer the system because of its simplicity and their ability to understand it. Before I finish this chapter on test construction and grading with a discussion of contracting for grades, complete Expansion Activity: Grading, which will help you develop your philosophy on grading.

EXPANSION ACTIVITY

Grading

Construct a sound approach to grading. What criteria did you establish for making **the approach sound? Share it with your class.**

APPLY AND REFLECT: Because teacher-made tests are seldom designed to give a normal distribution, it usually is unwise to give grades based on the normal curve. Do you agree with this statement? What is your rationale for your decision?

Contracting for Grades

Most schools give teachers considerable freedom in establishing grading standards. Some teachers have used this flexibility in implementing a contract approach to grading. With a contract, the teacher promises to award a specific grade for specified performance. Students know exactly what they must do to receive a certain grade; depending on the amount of work they wish to do, they receive a particular grade. For example, a simple contract follows:

To receive a grade of D, you must satisfactorily complete activities 1 through 6, satisfactorily complete half of the homework, and pass the posttest.

To receive a grade of C, you must complete activities 1 through 6, satisfactorily complete 60 percent of the homework, do one of the optional activities satisfactorily, and receive at least a C on the posttest.

To receive a grade of B, you must complete activities 1 through 6, satisfactorily complete 80 percent of the homework, do two of the optional activities very well, and receive at least a B on the posttest.

Assigning grades
is not an easy task.

To receive a grade of A, you must complete activities 1 through 6, satisfactorily complete 90 percent of the homework, do four of the optional activities excellently, complete at least one of the major project activities satisfactorily, and receive at least a B+ on the posttest.

Even though this contract outlines the requirements for a D, it is unlikely that students will want to contract for the low grade. It sets the baseline, however, for the activities required for a higher grade.

When you establish a contract system, you must develop sets of objectives that correspond to specific letter grades. You then decide the activities and assignments that will be required at each level. These objectives, corresponding letter grades, and requirements are shared with students in writing, so students can study them and make decisions on a contract grade.

Some teachers like to write a more detailed contract, which is signed by both student and teacher. A detailed sample contract is illustrated in Chapter 12, Figure 12.2.

This section has described grading systems and the assigning of grades. But, as noted earlier, grading is a very subjective undertaking. It should be carried out with care and planning. Review Table 6.4 and complete Review, Extension, and Reflective Exercise 6.2.

APPLY AND REFLECT: You should make grading procedures explicit. They should be written down and communicated clearly to students early in the year. What procedure and system do you feel best fits the grade level you expect to teach?

TABLE 6.4 Assigning Grades

System	Description
Absolute Grading Standard	Performance compared with established set of criteria
Relative Grading Standard	Students' performance compared with that of classmates, including grading on the curve
Point Grading System	Student work is allocated points, and grades are assigned according to established grade range
Weighted Grading System	Assignments are given a letter grade, and all grades are weighted to determine final grade
Percentage Grading System	Percentage correct is recorded for each assignment, and an average is calculated to determine final grade
Grade Contract	Written agreement between student and teacher as to what students will do to earn a specific grade

Review, Extension, and Reflective Exercise 6.2

Outline techniques for assigning grades.

Connections to INTASC Standards:

- Standard 8: Assessment. The teacher understands and uses formal and informal assessment strategies to evaluate and ensure the continuous intellectual, social, and physical development of the learner.
- Standard 9: Reflection and Professional Development. The teacher must be a reflective practitioner who continually evaluates the effects of his or her choices and actions on others (students, parents, and other professionals in the learning community) and who actively seeks out opportunities to grow professionally.

Connections to the NBPTS:

- Proposition 3: Teachers are responsible for managing and monitoring student learning.
- Proposition 4: Teachers must think systematically about their practice and learn from experience.

Review

- What is the purpose of assigning grades?
- Describe the two basic grading systems.

Reflection

- Reflect on how the teachers you had over the years assigned grades. Were the systems fair? How would you have changed them?
- How do you plan to assign grades in the area you expect to teach?
- Do you feel comfortable assigning grades?

VIEW FROM THE CLASSROOM

What do teachers think about testing and grading? Teacher survey results relative to topics presented in this chapter are expressed below. Review these results and discuss with classmates.

When preparing the majority of your lessons, what single variable is at the forefront of your mind?

Learning standards	41%
Student interest	39%
Norm-referenced achievement tests (state/national assessments)	10%
Criterion-referenced tests (knowledge/skills-based assessments)	10%

SOURCE: Excerpted from *Teach-nology*, available at www.teach-nology.com/poll

THE PUBLIC VIEW OF EDUCATION

What does the public think of testing and grading? Public trends and attitudes toward education tend to give education a high national importance. Review these results and discuss with classmates.

In your opinion, will the current emphasis on standardized tests encourage teachers to "teach to the test," that is, concentrate on teaching their students to pass the tests rather than teaching the subject, or don't you think it will have this effect?

Will encourage teaching to the tests	66%
Will not have this effect	30%
Don't know	4%

If the current emphasis on results is encouraging teachers to "teach to the tests," do you think this will be a good thing or a bad thing?

Good thing	39%
Bad thing	60%
Don't know	1%

SOURCE: Excerpted from *The 35th Annual Phi Delta Kappa/Gallup Poll of the Public's Attitudes Toward the Public Schools* (2003) by Lowell C. Rose and Alec M. Gallup, available at www.pdkintl.org/kappan/k0309pol.htm

Summary

Testing and grading represent two important, but unpopular, challenges for teachers.

Types of Tests

- Teachers generally use either standardized tests or teacher-made tests in the classroom.
- Standardized tests are tests prepared and published by assessment specialists, whereas teacher-made tests are developed by teachers to address specific classroom situations.
- Standardized tests are used for providing some indication of how individual students and classrooms compare with local, regional, or national averages.
- Teacher-made tests are used for gathering information and making judgments regarding the achievement of students.
- Widely used teacher-made test formats include: alternative-choice tests, multiple-choice tests, matching tests, completion tests, essay (brief and extended) tests, and combinations of these.

Grading Systems

- The absolute grading system and relative grading system are the two principal grading systems commonly used in schools.
- An absolute standard compares student performance against an established set of criteria, whereas the relative standard compares students with one another.
- Three systems are available to teachers for assigning grades: the point system, the weighted system, and the percentage system.
- Teacher contracts can be used effectively in the grading process. With contract grading, the teacher outlines exactly what students must do to earn specific grades.

Discussion Questions and Activities

1. **Standardized tests.** Describe three important characteristics of commonly used standardized tests. Briefly describe at least three standardized tests for a subject area.

2. **Test items.** Make up several examples of alternate-choice, multiple-choice, matching, completion, and essay test items. Ask your class to critique them. Discuss which types of items were most difficult to construct and the least difficult to construct.

3. **Grading systems.** Compare the major advantages and disadvantages associated with absolute and relative grading standards. Do you prefer one system over the other? Defend your choice.

4. **Grading objectivity.** Can a teacher be objective in assigning grades? Explain.

5. **Grading procedures.** Outline a grading procedure you expect to follow and use as a teacher.

Connection With the Field

1. **Teacher interviews.** Interview several classroom teachers about their tests and homework. How do the teachers deal with the following issues?

   a. Test construction
   b. Test and homework scoring and grade assignment
   c. Test and homework make-up for absences
   d. Homework for extra credit
   e. Late or missing homework

2. **Test construction.** Examine a standardized test and then visit with several classroom teachers relative to their tests. Compare the tests in terms of construction, clarity, and readability. Are there major weaknesses in either test?

Praxis II Connection

The following test preparation exercises are intended to help you prepare for the Praxis II: Principles of Learning and Teaching. The Praxis II may be required by your teacher education preparatory program and for state certification or licensing. These exercises will give you direct access to pedagogical knowledge from Chapter 6 that may be expected of you on the Praxis II and other pedagogical exams that may be required at the end of your teacher education program.

Topic Connections

1. Types of tests (II. C1, C2)

Distinguish among standardized tests and teacher-made tests. Describe the purposes of each.

2. Test formats (II. C1, C2, C4)

Distinguish among objective tests and essay tests and describe the appropriate use of each.

3. Assigning grades (II. C6)

Distinguish between absolute grading standard, relative grading standard, point grading system, weighted grading system, percentage grading system, and contracting for grades and explain the use of each.

ON YOUR OWN

Log on to the web-based student study site at http://www.sagepub.com/eis for more information about the vignettes and materials presented in this chapter, suggestions for activities, study aids such as electronic flashcards and review quizzes, and research recommendations including journal article links and questions related to this chapter.

DESIGNING INSTRUCTION TO MAXIMIZE STUDENT LEARNING

E ffective teaching methods often make or break a lesson. Chapters 7, 8, 9, and 10 focus on helping you choose and use appropriate methods for specific learning intent. The strengths and limitations of various teaching strategies and methods are the focus of these chapters.

Effective teachers must keep students involved in their lessons if they are to accomplish their intent. Thus, teachers must master a variety of teaching strategies. They must be able to establish and maintain student attention. They must be able to elicit responses from students so as to keep them involved. Therefore, Chapters 7, 8, 9, and 10 focus on selecting teaching strategies, reinforcement, and questioning that will help accomplish this task.

Chapters 7, 8, and 9 focus on using the direct, integrated, and indirect teaching methods for instructional delivery. The importance of thinking skills is stressed in Chapter 10. Chapter 10 focuses on developing thinking skills as part of the school curriculum.

7

USING DIRECT TEACHING METHODS

*Not only is there an art in knowing a
thing, but also a certain art in teaching it.*

CICERO

OVERVIEW

I will now engage in a study of actions and skills that produce learning. In this chapter, you will study direct approaches that can be used to organize and present integrated bodies of knowledge for instruction. Direct teaching and exposition approaches to teaching integrated bodies of knowledge provide us with direct instructional alternatives.

Effective questioning patterns have long been associated with good teaching. As such, it is important that prospective teachers recognize and use behavior patterns related to the productive use of the different levels of questions, as well as the different kinds of questions and proven questioning techniques. Thus, in this chapter, I will focus special attention on questioning and its effective use in the classroom.

OBJECTIVES

After completing your study of Chapter 7, you should be able to do the following:

1. Discuss factors that should be considered in selecting teaching techniques and strategies.
2. Define *direct teaching* and *exposition teaching* and discuss the strengths and weaknesses of the various methods within these teaching strategies.
3. Describe the *direct teaching* format and its appropriate uses.
4. Explain the importance of and techniques for improving the lecture method.
5. Explain the importance of incorporating different levels and types of questions.
6. Identify and differentiate between the different categories of questions, as well as the levels within these categories.

7. Identify and differentiate between focusing, prompting, and probing questions.

8. Define wait-time 1, wait-time 2, halting time, and silent time.

9. Define and explain the benefits derived from the use of the redirecting technique, wait times, and halting time.

10. Identify guidelines that should be followed in effective questioning.

Successful teachers draw from a variety of strategies (methods and procedures) in accomplishing their instructional purposes. Strategies should be selected that best serve the delivery of content and achievement of the purposes and objectives. If strategies are just arbitrarily chosen, then their emphases are on themselves, rather than on content, purposes, or objectives.

Strategies, then, should be viewed as utilitarian: They achieve the instructional intent. For example, if the intent of a social studies lesson is to share views on some controversial issue, it is obvious that the discussion method and applicable procedures should assist in achieving this objective. The lecture method, or simply showing a film, would not support the intent of the lesson.

With all the possible strategies, how do you decide which is best? Experience can often be the best basis for selection; however, other factors often must be considered in your selection of strategies:

- What are the students' needs?
- What age are the students?
- What are the students' intellectual abilities?
- What are the students' physical and mental characteristics?
- What are the students' attention spans?
- What is the lesson purpose?
- What content is to be taught?

You should take such factors into account when you consider teaching strategies and, above all, select those strategies that should best serve the teaching situation.

Some strategies influence students directly, whereas others influence students indirectly; that is, some strategies emphasize focused, teacher-directed instruction, whereas others involve students actively in their own learning. Thus, there are two major ways of delivering instruction: directly or indirectly. The direct delivery of instruction ("telling") is the "traditional" or didactic mode, in which knowledge is passed on through the teacher, the textbook, or both. The indirect avenue of instruction ("showing") provides students with access to information and experiences whereby they develop knowledge and skills.

How much time should be devoted to each of the two modes of instruction? This is a complex question. At this point, suffice it to say that the amount of time spent varies, depending on the subject, grade level, students, time, and material available, as well as the philosophy of the teacher and the school. Experience suggests, however, a compelling relationship between method of instruction and student retention, depicted in Table 7.1, in which a blend of "telling" and "showing" techniques results in greater retention. Furthermore, varying the strategy can positively affect student

Table 7.1 Relationship Between Method of Instruction and Retention

Methods of Instruction	Recall 3 Hours Later	Recall 3 Days Later
Telling When Used Alone	70%	10%
Showing When Used Alone	72%	20%
Blend of Telling and Showing	85%	65%

motivation to learn. It is a fortunate situation when you have a choice of equally effective strategies for achieving your instructional intent. In such instances, it is possible to choose a method and procedure (strategy) that will foster motivation, improve classroom control, or cost less to implement. Indeed, you should become skilled in combining various strategies into a total lesson package.

The remainder of this chapter will elaborate on the direct modes of instruction: direct teaching, exposition teaching, and exposition with interaction teaching. These are modes of instruction with which you have had much experience. I will review some of the integrated direct approaches and procedures in Chapter 8 and the more indirect modes and procedures in Chapters 9 and 10.

APPLY AND REFLECT: How much time should be devoted to direct teaching and to indirect

teaching at the grade level you expect to teach? Which mode of delivery do you favor?

Direct Teaching

Direct teaching, sometimes called systematic teaching or active teaching, is a teacher-centered, skill-building instructional model with the teacher being a major information provider. The teacher's role is to pass facts, rules, or action sequences on to students in the most direct way possible. This usually takes a presentation with explanations format (modified lecture), examples, and opportunities for practice and feedback. The direct teaching format calls for teacher-student interactions involving questions and answers, review and practice, and the correction of student errors. The direct teaching strategy works best with teaching skill subjects such as reading, writing, mathematics, grammar, computer literacy, and factual parts of science and history. Young children, slower learners, and students of all ages and abilities during the first stages of learning informative material or material that is difficult to learn will benefit most from direct teaching.

Different authors describe the specific elements of direct teaching differently (see Evertson, Emmer, Clements, Sanford, & Worsham, 1994; Hunter, 1995; Rosenshine & Stevens, 1986). They generally agree, however, as to the sequence of events that characterize effective direct teaching lessons. First, the teacher brings students up-to-date on any skills they might need for the lesson and tells them what they are going to learn. Then, the teacher devotes most of the lesson time to teaching the skills or information, giving students opportunities to practice the skills or express

REFLECTIONS ON TEACHER PRACTICE

Answering Questions

1. Should students be encouraged to find their own answers to all questions?
2. Is it important that teachers work on improving students' listening skills? Are listening and questioning related?

I teach sixth grade and was going home each and every day mentally wiped out because I think I answered 9,000 questions. Questions like "Should I put my name on my paper?" (Of course.) "Can I write in red pen?" (Never.) I started calling these "self explanatory questions" because they pertained to policy that they should have had under control by now—and I think some of them just liked to hear themselves talk. Anyway, I started with discussing strategies of how they could find answers to their questions before asking me—basically just wanting to work on their listening skills (Hey, isn't that a standard?!) I even went so far as to give them each three tickets for the day—if they had a question to ask me (not content related) that they could have found the answer for themselves, I took a ticket away in exchange for an answer. Some kids didn't even make it through first period.

As a result, I had a parent COMPLETELY flip out and call our assistant principal. She totally supported me to this parent, but I had to write a "letter of explanation" about why I had to use the ticket system in my classroom. I made sure that I filled it with things like "listening is a skill that will benefit all students" and "by answering fewer self-explanatory questions I have more time for one-on-one instruction with students" and so forth and so on. It just made me angry that they would even waste time questioning it. At any rate, the ticket system has worked. If students make it to the end of the day with a ticket, they get a piece of candy. Now, we have stretched it to three tickets for the week—make it to Friday and you get candy. My days go much much smoother!

Michelle, sixth grade teacher

SOURCE: Reprinted with permission from ProTeacher, a professional community for elementary school teachers (http://www.proteacher.net)

the information, and questioning or quizzing students to determine whether or not they are learning what is intended. The general lesson structure will vary in different subject areas and at different grade levels. Teachers of older students may take several days for each step in the process, ending with a formal test or quiz. Teachers of younger children may go through the entire process in one instructional period, using informal assessments at the end.

A brief description of the parts of direct teaching follows:

1. *State learning objectives and orient students to lesson.* Tell students what they will learn and what will be expected of them. State the goals and objectives of the lesson. Establish a mental set or attitude of readiness to learn in students. This is your set induction.

2. *Review prerequisites.* Go over any skills or concepts students will need to understand the lesson. Provide advance organizers to give students a framework for understanding the new material.

3. *Present new material.* Teach the lesson, presenting information, giving concrete and varied examples and nonexamples, demonstrating concepts, and so on. Present the material in small steps. Present an outline when material is complex.

4. *Provide guided practice and conduct learning probes.* Pose questions to students to assess their level of understanding and correct their misconceptions. Give students practice problems and check for misconceptions and misunderstanding. Have students summarize in their own words. Reteach as necessary.

5. *Provide independent practice.* Give students an opportunity to practice new skills or use new information on their own, in seatwork, or in cooperative groups.

6. *Assess performance and provide feedback.* Review independent practice work or give a quiz. Give feedback on correct answers, and reteach skills as needed.

7. *Provide distributed practice and review.* Assign homework to provide distributed practice on the new material.

Madeline Hunter's "Mastery Teaching" contains many of the features of the direct teaching strategy and has been implemented in many parts of the country. Keep in mind, however, that not all elements of the direct teaching strategy belong in every lesson, although they will occur in a typical unit plan composed of several lessons.

Let's now look at the various components of direct instruction in more detail. Expository teaching (lecture and explanations) and questioning hold key roles in the success of direct instruction.

Exposition Teaching

Exposition teaching is considered to be the best way to communicate large amounts of information in a short period of time. Exposition techniques comprise the methods in which an authority—teacher, textbook, film, or microcomputer—presents information without overt interaction between the authority and the students.

Lecture

The **lecture** is probably the most widely used exposition teaching method. Virtually every teacher employs it to some degree, and some use it almost exclusively. Though much criticized by current educators, the lecture does possess some unique strengths.

Strengths of the Lecture

The lecture is an excellent way of presenting background information when building a unit frame of reference or when introducing a unit. Indeed, it often can be just the tool for setting the atmosphere or focusing for student activities. Moreover, a short lecture can effectively wrap up a unit, an activity, or a lesson. Finally, the lecture is time-efficient; that is, planning time is devoted to organizing content, rather than to devising instructional procedure. Thus, the lecture affords the teacher ample opportunity to collect related materials, assemble them into a meaningful framework, and present the information to students in a relatively short period of time. The teacher simply plans a lecture for the entire instructional period.

Weaknesses of the Lecture

The lecture has several serious flaws, however. First, it is passive learning, with very low student involvement. Students are expected, and even encouraged, to sit quietly, listen, and perhaps take notes. Thus, it is not a good approach for helping students develop skills in thinking, problem solving, and creativity.

Second, lectures are often boring and do not motivate. For this reason—except in unusual cases—very little of a lecture is retained by students. Indeed, because lectures tend to focus on the lowest level of cognition, understanding and transfer are often limited.

Finally, the lecture method may lead to the development of discipline problems. Most lectures generate little interest and student attention soon wanes and turns to more stimulating and often undesirable activities. Thus, not only does the lecture lose the attention of those involved in these unwanted activities, but the lecture itself is often disrupted. The wise teacher should always remember that most students are easily bored and usually have a low tolerance for boredom.

"It's difficult to reprimand some children for inattention in class."

TABLE 7.2 **Sample Table of Contents Used in Textbook Lecturing**	
Chapter 1	The Science of Biology
Chapter 2	The Nature of Living Matter
Chapter 3	The Beginning of Life on the Earth
Chapter 4	Units of Living Matter
Chapter 5	The Classification of Living Things
Chapter 6	The Bacteria
Chapter 7	Microbes and Disease
Chapter 8	The Seed Plants
Chapter 9	The Higher Plant Body
Chapter 10	One-Celled Animals—The Protozoa
Chapter 11	The Mammals
Chapter 12	Muscles and Their Actions
Chapter 13	Life of the Past
Chapter 14	Human Life of the Past

Textbook Lecture

Lecturing from the textbook could well be the most common teaching method used in today's schools. The content of such lectures usually is structured directly from the course textbook, progressing from Chapter 1 to the end of the book without deviation, as illustrated in Table 7.2.

Textbook teaching requires very little teacher preparation when the structure of the textbook is strictly followed. Indeed, when one is teaching in a content area without adequate academic preparation in that area and one does not wish to spend the time to become content-competent, textbook teaching is an ideal technique. Thus, the lack of time needed for preparing lesson plans and lack of content mastery are reasons for the popularity of this method of instruction.

Textbook teaching suffers from all the problems of lecturing, but it has a couple of unique flaws. First, the content of the course often becomes rigid; normally, no new content is added to the lecture and the course content is determined entirely by an external author who is not in complete harmony with the needs of students, school, and community. Second, the lectures can get extremely boring, because the teacher usually is lecturing about the material students were assigned to read. If no new content is added to the lesson, students tend to either read the text or listen to the lectures—seldom both.

Planning the Lecture

Planning is essential for a good lecture. Lectures must be well crafted to be clear and persuasive. The lecture must be designed to gain—and maintain—student attention throughout the lesson, to instill motivation, and to accomplish lesson objectives. Let's now look at some techniques that can help achieve these ends.

The most successful lectures should be relatively short. Even older, brighter students probably won't listen to a lecture for more than about 20 minutes. Therefore, limit your lectures to short periods of time and periodically change to other activities (preferably to those that require active student involvement). For example, the subdivisions of a lesson (with time allotted for each activity) might be as follows:

1. Overview of topic (10 minutes)*
2. Show a film (20 minutes)
3. Discussion of film (10 minutes)
4. Demonstration (5 minutes)
5. Wrap up and review (5 minutes)*

*Denotes activities where the teacher is lecturing.

Although this plan uses lecturing where appropriate, it relies on other techniques to augment the learning—namely, discussion and demonstration. Only three-tenths of the time is devoted to lecturing; most of the time allows for more student involvement.

In planning, give careful attention to the start of your lecture. Determine the specific objectives of the lecture and share them with students at the beginning. Research (Wulf & Schane, 1984) shows that, when objectives are shared, intentional learning tends to increase. Moreover, your lecture introduction should arouse student interest, should be motivational, and should establish a framework for the lesson (see Chapter 4 for a review of these topics).

In preparing the lecture, you must decide what students are to do while you lecture. Will students be asked to take notes? Will students be involved in some assigned seatwork? If yes, instructions and guidelines must be planned accordingly. Using the chalkboard and passing out written instructions are often the best ways for establishing these guidelines.

A lecture must have closure (see Chapter 4). Once given, the lecture theme should be related to the course and/or to what has already been taught. This can be accomplished through a review of the major points of the lecture.

In summary, a good lecture must be well planned if it is to be clear and persuasive. Try following this good planning formula:

- Tell students what you are going to tell them.
- Tell them.
- Tell them what you have told them.

The proper application of this formula will result in a logical, well-organized lecture with a firm introduction and a well-planned wrap-up.

Presenting the Lecture

An effective lecture must maintain student interest and attention from beginning to end. Factors such as the tempo, audiovisual aids, stimulus variation, and language can exert major influence on student interest and attention.

Tempo

The tempo, or pacing, of your lecture should be moderate (not too slow or too fast). If the pace is too fast, students become discouraged with their inability to understand and keep up; if the pace is too slow, they become bored and look elsewhere for stimulation. Use feedback checks to ascertain whether students understand your material and adjust your pace according to the feedback you obtain.

Instructional-Media Learning Tools

Visual aids should accompany all lectures. The use of the chalkboard, models, pictures, transparencies, diagrams, and PowerPoints can greatly enhance a lecture. Use any media that can be used to help convey your message; they should stimulate and maintain student interest. Indeed, make your lectures as multisensory as is feasible. Multisensory input will usually result in better learning.

When appropriate, teach students to take notes. A good lecturer, for example, outlines the major points on the chalkboard or on an overhead projector. Such outlines provide students with the structure and time needed for developing their note-taking skills. Once students have become skilled note takers, the practice of supplying an outline can be discontinued.

Stimulus Variation

As you plan your lecture, create an introduction that will grab students' attention and augment your lecture with actions that will maintain this attention.

The use of instructional materials and media enhances most lectures and stimulates student interest.

Stimulus-variation techniques, such as gestures, pauses, and teacher movement, can help keep student attention directed toward your lecture. As student attention wanders, a tap on the board, a hand gesture, sudden silence (a pause), or physical movement often will refocus attention back to your lecture.

Enthusiasm is contagious. If you express a high level of interest and sense of importance about your topic, students often become spellbound, anxious to find out what is so interesting. But be a bit careful: too much enthusiasm can direct attention toward you, the teacher—and away from the lecture topic.

Humor and rhetorical questions can also attract and keep student attention. Humor can help reduce anxiety, whereas rhetorical questions, used in conjunction with pauses, give students the opportunity to consider and think about the information presented.

Finally, eye contact can help maintain attention. Eye contact gives students the feeling that you are addressing each of them personally. Indeed, eye contact can provide a teacher with valuable feedback on how well a lecture is being received. Look at your students; glance around and move about the room, based upon what you see.

Voice and Language

Delivery can make the difference between a boring lecture and a stimulating one. Keep your voice low-pitched, be expressive, and make sure all students can hear. Your voice can bring words to life. Voice volume, rate, tone, inflection, and pitch can all communicate valuable information.

Deliver your lectures in Standard English, and use vocabulary that students will understand. That is, don't talk over your students' heads. Also, avoid using slang expressions and street language in your lectures. Such language will only confuse your students.

Balancing the Lecture

Lecturing to students is inevitable for most teachers; however, it should be used sparingly, especially with younger students, and mixed with other appropriate methods. For example, a teacher could follow up a short lecture by having students complete a worksheet, by conducting a small-group discussion, or by asking students to conduct an investigation.

Indeed, a lesson or 50-minute class period can often be divided into a number of short lectures, with a distinct change in modality between lectures. These changes retain students' attention and hold their interest for the instructional period. Above all, adjust your lecture time and style to students' attention span. Break up your lecture with other methods and activities. Devise a questioning sequence, give students a problem to solve, or give students a short break.

APPLY AND REFLECT: Lectures can be boring. How have your past teachers that used the lecture method made them more interesting? If you plan to use the lecture method extensively, how will you keep your students interested and involved?

Variants of the Lecture

Let's now examine some of the commonly used variants of the lecture. Two such variants are: telelecture and prerecorded lecture.

Telelecture

Normally, the lecturer and students are in the same room. In some rural areas, however, an insufficient number of students needing or desiring a course in one district may not warrant the hiring of a teacher for that course. Through technology, however, it is possible for several districts to "hire" a needed teacher and to transmit lectures from a studio classroom to other locations by means of telephone, cable, or microwave. This **telelecture** enables students who are not in the immediate classroom to hear the lectures. The remote students may talk to the lecturer and ask questions by means of a telephone link. Special science, mathematics, and language courses are being taught in this manner across the nation.

Prerecorded Lecture

A lecture is easily captured on tape or film. Such tapes and films often are prepared by local school districts and by commercial publishers. Prerecorded lectures, however, have several disadvantages when compared with live lectures. First, and perhaps most important, there is *no* direct contact between students and lecturer; no minute-by-minute adjustments can be made based on feedback and questions. Additionally, student attention becomes a major problem when the lecture is on tape or film; attention lags more quickly than when a person is actually present. Finally, tapes and films quickly become obsolete as new information is gleaned regarding content and teaching techniques.

Despite the flaws, prerecorded lectures have some merits. Most important is their capacity for individualized instruction, because a tape or film can be played as many times as desirable. I will address individualization of instruction in greater detail in the next chapter.

Table 7.3 summarizes the different direct teaching and the exposition teaching methods. Review the summary and complete Review, Extension, and Reflective Exercise 7.1.

Exposition With Interaction Teaching

Exposition with interaction teaching is a method of teaching in which an authority presents information and follows it up with questioning that determines whether that information has been understood. Essentially, this method is a two-phase technique: First, information is disseminated by the teacher or through students' study of written material. Second, the teacher checks for comprehension by asking questions to assess student understanding of the material explained or studied.

The comprehension-monitoring phase of this teaching technique requires that the teacher be knowledgeable and an effective questioner. Because questioning is so essential to the overall success of exposition with interaction, let's first analyze this important skill in some detail.

Lectures need not be
passive learning. They can
be made stimulating.

TABLE 7.3 Exposition Teaching

Method	Description
Direct Teaching	Teacher controls instruction by presenting information and giving directions to the class; associated with teacher-centered, teacher-controlled classrooms; an instructional procedure for teaching content in the most efficient, straightforward way
Lecture	Teacher presents information, with no overt interaction with students
Telelecture	Lecture transmitted from central-studio classroom to distant classrooms
Textbook Lecture	Lecturing directly about material presented in the textbook
Prerecorded Lecture	Lecture that has been recorded on videotape or film

Review, Extension, and Reflective Exercise 7.1

Describe direct teaching and the lecture method.

Connections to INTASC Standards:

- Standard 1: Subject Pedagogy. The teacher must understand the central concepts, tools of inquiry, and structures of the discipline(s) he or she teaches and be able to create learning experiences that make these aspects of subject matter meaningful for students.
- Standard 2: Student Development. The teacher understands how children learn and develop and can provide learning opportunities that support their intellectual, social, and personal development.
- Standard 3: Diverse Learners. The teacher understands how students differ in their approaches to learning and creates instructional opportunities that are adapted to diverse learners.
- Standard 4: Instructional Strategies. The teacher must understand and use a variety of instructional strategies to encourage students' development of critical thinking, problem solving, and performance skills.
- Standard 6: Communication. The teacher uses knowledge of effective verbal, nonverbal, and media communication techniques to foster active inquiry,

collaboration, and supportive interaction in the classroom.
- Standard 7: Planning Instruction. The teacher plans instruction based upon knowledge of subject matter, students, the community, and curriculum goals.

Connections to the NBPTS:

- Proposition 1: Teachers are committed to students and their learning.
- Proposition 2: Teachers must know the subjects they teach and how to teach those subjects to students.
- Proposition 4: Teachers must think systematically about their practice and learn from experience.

Review

- What are the strengths and weaknesses of direct teaching and the lecture method?
- How can you make the lecture method more effective?

Reflection

- Reflect on the teaching methods used by your past teachers. Did they use direct teaching? The lecture method? Was it effective?
- Do you plan on using direct teaching or the lecture method in the area you expect to teach? How will you make them effective?

The Art of Questioning

Proper questioning is a sophisticated art at which many of us are less than proficient even though we have asked thousands of questions in our lives. Research indicates that questioning is second only to lecturing in popularity as a teaching method. Teachers spend anywhere from 35 to 50 percent of their instructional time conducting questioning sessions. Teachers ask questions for a variety of purposes, including

- To develop interest and motivate students.
- To evaluate students' preparation and check on homework.
- To develop critical thinking skills.
- To review and summarize previous lessons.
- To assess achievement of objectives.

Questioning is an important part of the teaching-learning process because it enables teachers and students to establish what is already known, to use and extend this knowledge, and then to develop new ideas. It also provides a structure to examine ideas and information. Questioning is important to developing reflective and metacognitive thinking. It requires students to reflect on their understandings and can lead to changes and improvements in learning, thinking, and teaching.

Good questioners must be skilled in formulating good questions: Questions must be asked at the appropriate level, they must be of the appropriate type, and, above all, they must be worded properly. Moreover, the art of questioning requires mastery of techniques for follow-up to students' responses—or lack of response— to questioning. The kinds of questions asked, the way they are asked, and the responses given affect both the self-esteem of the students and their participation. Let's now look at the different levels at which questions may be asked.

Levels of Questions

Questions may be categorized as being "narrow" or "broad." Narrow questions usually ask for only factual recall or specific correct answers, whereas broad questions seldom can be answered with a single word. Moreover, broad questions do not have one correct answer and call on students to reach beyond simple memory. Broad questions prompt students to use the thinking process in formulating answers. Both narrow and broad questions contribute to the learning process. Too often, however, teachers rely too heavily on narrow questions when learning would be greatly enhanced through the use of both types of questions.

You must adapt the level of your questions to the purpose for which they are being asked. Consequently, ask questions that reveal whether students have gained specific knowledge, as well as questions that stimulate the thinking process. Because thinking can take place at several levels of sophistication, it is important that you as a teacher be able to classify—and ask—questions at these different levels.

Many effective classification systems have been developed for describing the levels of questions. Most of these systems are useful only to the extent that they can provide a framework for formulating questions at the desired level within a classroom environment. Consequently, some teachers may want to use only a two-level classification system, whereas others may want to use a more detailed system.

This discussion will focus on two systems that will be of most benefit to you as a classroom teacher. The first widely used system classifies questions as either *convergent* or *divergent;* the second categorizes questions according to the mental

"Mirror, mirror, on the wall, who's the most sensitive,
open, student-centered, and innovative teacher of all?"

operation students use in answering them. These two classification systems are only two of the many systems to which you can refer in your classroom. When you prepare questions, however, evaluate them according to some classification system. By so doing, you will significantly improve the quality of your questions.

Convergent and Divergent Questions

One of the simplest and easiest ways of classifying questions is to determine whether they are convergent or divergent. **Convergent questions** allow for only a few right responses, whereas **divergent questions** allow for many correct responses.

Questions regarding concrete facts that have been learned and committed to memory are convergent. Most who, what, and where questions are also classified as convergent:

"What is 2 + 2?"

"Who was the 25th president of the United States?"

"What type of equation is $x^2 + 3x + 3 = 0$?"

"Where is Stratford-upon-Avon located?"

"What was the major cause of the Great Depression?"

Convergent questions may also require students to recall and integrate or analyze information for determining *one expected* correct answer. Thus, the following questions would also be classified as convergent:

"Based on our discussion, what is the major cause of water pollution?"

"By combining the formulas for a triangle and a rectangle, what would be the formula for finding the area of a trapezoid?"

"Based on our definition of a noun, can you name three nouns?"

Most alternate-response questions, such as yes/no and true/false questions, would also be classified as convergent, because the responses available to students are limited.

Conversely, questions calling for opinions, hypotheses, or evaluation are divergent in that many possible correct responses may be given:

"Why do you suppose we entered World War II?"

"What would be a good name for this painting?"

"Can you give me a sentence in which this word is used correctly?"

"Why is it important that we speak correctly?"

Divergent questions should be used frequently because they encourage broader responses and, therefore, are more likely to engage students in the learning process. They prompt students to think. Convergent questions, however, are equally important in that they deal with the background information needed in dealing with divergent questions. In the classroom, it is generally desirable to use convergent questions initially and then move toward divergent questions.

Mental Operation Questions

Based on the work of J. P. Guilford and Benjamin Bloom, Moore (2001) developed the Mental Operation system for classifying questions. Table 7.4 shows the relationship between the Mental Operation system, Guilford's Structure of the Intellect model, and Bloom's Taxonomy. The **Mental Operation system** is basically a four-category system that combines the cognitive and memory categories of the Guilford model into a single factual category. In addition, it combines four of Bloom's categories into two categories. The categories of questions that make up the Mental Operation model are factual, empirical, productive, and evaluative.

Factual questions test the student's recall or recognition of information learned by rote. That is, it tests the student's recall or recognition of information that has

TABLE 7.4 Categories of Questions

Mental Operation Questions	Guilford's Structure of the Intellect	Bloom's Taxonomy
1. Factual	Cognitive/memory	Knowledge/comprehension
2. Empirical	Convergent thinking	Application/analysis
3. Productive	Divergent thinking	Synthesis
4. Evaluative	Evaluative thinking	Evaluation

been committed to memory through some form of repetition or rehearsal. Some examples of factual questions are listed here:

"Who drilled the first oil well?"

"Joe, can you define the short story?"

"Which of these is the chemical formula for salt?"

"What is the formula for the volume of a cylinder?"

Empirical questions require that students integrate or analyze remembered or given information and supply a single, correct *predictable* answer. Indeed, the question may call for quite a lot of thinking, but, once thought out, the answer is usually a single, correct answer. Empirical questions are also narrow questions. Some examples of empirical questions include the following:

"Based on our study of California, what conditions led to its becoming a state?"

"Given that this circle has a radius of 5 centimeters, what is its area?"

"According to the information provided in the text, what is the most economical source of energy presently being used in the United States?"

"Which of these two forms of government is most like the British?"

Note that when answering these questions, students must recall learned information and carry out a mental activity with that information to arrive at the correct answer. There is, however, only one correct, predictable answer.

Productive questions do not have a single, correct answer, and it may be impossible to predict what the answer will be. Productive questions are open-ended and call for students to use their imaginations and think creatively. These questions ask students to develop a unique idea. Although the broad nature of productive questions prompts students to go beyond the simple recall of remembered information, students still need the basic related information to answer them. Following are some examples of productive questions:

"How can we improve our understanding and use of English?"

"What changes would we see in society if we were to eliminate unemployment in the world?"

"What are some possible solutions to the problem of world hunger?"

"What do you suppose the painter's intent was in this painting?"

Finally, **evaluative questions** require that students put a value on something or make some kind of judgment. Evaluative questions are special cases of productive questions in that they, too, are often open-ended. They can, however, be more difficult to answer than are productive questions in that some internal or external criteria must be used; that is, some criteria must be established for making the judgment. The responses to evaluative questions can often be predicted or limited by the number of choices. For example, the question "Which of these two short stories is the best?" limits the responses to two, whereas the question "What is the best automobile made today?" allows a variety of responses. Other examples of evaluative questions are these:

"Who was our greatest scientist?"

"How would you rate our success in controlling government spending in this nation?"

"Do you think the author of the play developed the characters sufficiently?"

"Are Native Americans portrayed accurately in the movies?"

These questions call on students to make judgments based on internal criteria. When student responses are formally evaluated and bear directly on grades, however, you must establish evaluative criteria. The alternative is to rely on students' internalized criteria, which you cannot evaluate, confirm, or refute. You can establish evaluative criteria for your evaluative questions by following them up with an empirical or a productive question that asks for the reasons behind the stated judgment or value, or by making sure you develop and ask evaluative questions in a way that includes external criteria.

Use of the Mental Operation system of classifying questions (Table 7.5) should give you the needed framework for improving your questioning skill. You should be asking questions at all four levels of the system, instead of at the factual level only, as many teachers do. To this end, you should plan and ask more productive and evaluative questions than is commonly done by teachers. These questions will give your students the opportunity to think and reason.

Types of Questions

As an effective teacher, you must ask the right types of questions. That is, you must adapt the type of question to the specific purpose for which you are asking the question. For example, you may want to ask questions to determine the level of

TABLE 7.5 Levels of Classroom Questions

Category	Type of Thinking	Examples
Factual	Student simply recalls information	"Define . . ." "Who was . . ." "What did the text say . . ."
Empirical	Student integrates and analyzes given or recalled information	"Compare . . ." "Explain in your own words . . ." "Calculate the . . ."
Productive	Student thinks creatively and imaginatively and produces unique idea or response	"What will life be like . . ." "What's a good name for . . ." "How could we . . ."
Evaluative	Student makes judgments or expresses values	"Which painting is best?" "Why do you favor this . . ." "Who is the best . . ."

Questions can often give a lesson life and arouse student interest.

your students' study, to increase student involvement and interaction, to increase clarification, or to stimulate student awareness. These purposes call for different types of questions.

Focusing Questions

Focusing questions, which may be factual, empirical, productive, or evaluative, are used to direct student attention. Focusing questions can determine what has been learned by students, can motivate and arouse student interest at the start of a lesson or during the lesson, can stimulate involvement and check understanding during a lesson, and can check students' understanding of lesson material at the close of a lesson.

Was the assigned chapter read by students? No use discussing the material if it wasn't read! Did the students learn and understand the material assigned? Can students apply the information? Focusing questions can provide valuable information regarding these concerns. Ask factual questions to check on basic knowledge at the beginning of or during a lesson. Use empirical questions to have students figure out correct solutions for problems related to assignments or issues being discussed. Pose productive and evaluative questions for motivating and stimulating thinking and interest in the topic.

When opening a lesson or discussion with a question, it is good practice to use a productive or evaluative question that focuses on the upcoming topic. The question should be such that it arouses students' interest and thinking:

"What do you suppose would happen if I were to drop these two objects at the same time?"

"How could we test the hypothesis suggested by the results?"

"Should we do away with the income tax in the United States?"

These questions should then be followed with questions at all levels to develop understanding and to maintain interest.

Prompting Questions

What should you do when a student fails to answer a question? Most teachers answer the question themselves or move on to another student. This technique will get your question answered, but it fails to involve the original student in the discussion. Rather, it leaves that student with a sense of failure, which, more than likely, will result in even less participation in the future. A better way to address this problem is to use a prompting question as a follow-up to the unanswered question.

Prompting questions use clues that help students answer questions or correct initially inaccurate responses. Thus, a prompting question is usually a rewording of the original question—with clues added. Consider this example of a prompting questioning sequence:

Teacher: What is x^2 times x^3, Pat?

Pat: I don't know.

Teacher: Well, let's see if we can figure it out. What do we do with the exponents when we multiply variables?

Pat: Multiply?

Teacher: No.

Pat: Add!

Teacher: Right! So, if we add 2 + 3, what will our answer be?

Pat: [*Pause*] 5.

Teacher: So what would x^2 times x^3 be?

Pat: x^5.

Teacher: Very good, Pat.

Your use of prompting questions with students should lead to a sense of success when they finally answer correctly. Indeed, the successes could even act as reinforcers to students, which result in even greater participation.

Probing Questions

Up to this point I have discussed focusing questions and prompting questions. The former can be used for determining the level of learning and understanding and for increasing student participation, whereas the latter can be used when no response to a question is forthcoming. Another situation with which a teacher must contend occurs when the student's response is incorrect or correct yet insufficient because it lacks depth. In such cases, you should have the student correct the mistake or ask that he or she supply the additional needed information. This is accomplished through the use of probing questions.

Probing questions aim at correcting, improving, or expanding a student's initial response. They compel the student to think more thoroughly about the initial response. Probing questions can be used for correcting an initial response, eliciting clarification, developing critical awareness, or refocusing a response.

You may want to ask a probing question for the purpose of clarification. Students sometimes give flimsily thought-out answers or give only half-answers to questions. These responses should be followed up with probing questions that force the student to think more thoroughly and urge him or her to firm up the response. Here are examples of such probing questions:

"What are you saying?"

"What do you mean by the terms . . . ?"

"Would you say that in another way?"

"Could you elaborate on those two points?"

"Can you explain that point more fully? It lacks clarity."

You sometimes may want students to justify their answers; that is, you may want to foster their critical awareness. This also can be accomplished with probing questions. Probing questions that could be used to develop critical awareness include these:

"What is your factual basis for these beliefs?"

"Why do you believe that?"

"What are you assuming when you make that statement?"

"What are your reasons for those assumptions?"

"Are you sure there isn't more evidence to support that issue?"

Finally, you may want to probe to refocus a correct, satisfactory student response to a related issue. Examples of questions that could serve this function follow:

"Let's look at your answer with respect to this new information."

"Can you relate your answer to yesterday's discussion?"

"What implications does this conclusion have for . . . ?"

"Apply these solutions to . . ."

"Can you relate Mary's earlier answer to this issue?"

The different types of questions will be invaluable to you as a teaching tool. When used effectively, they can increase student participation and involve students in their own learning. You should practice these different questions and become proficient in their use.

APPLY AND REFLECT: You can use focusing, prompting, and probing questions to determine what has been learned, to arouse interest, and to stimulate involvement. Are these different question types more effective at specific grade levels? If so, what grade level?

Questioning Techniques

Certain techniques associated with asking questions tend to increase the quantity of and enhance the quality of the students' responses. Let's now look at four such techniques.

Redirecting

Redirecting is a technique that is useful for increasing the amount of student participation. It allows you to draw students into a discussion by asking them to respond to a question in light of a previous response from another student. Because this technique requires several correct responses to a single question, the question asked must be divergent, productive, or evaluative. The following is an example of how you might redirect a question:

Teacher: We have now studied the administrations of several presidents. Which president do you think made the greatest contribution? [*Pause. Several hands go up.*] Cindi?

Cindi: Lincoln.

Teacher: Jeff?

Jeff: Washington.

Teacher: Mary, what is your opinion?

Mary: John Kennedy.

You should note that, if you are using redirecting correctly, you do not react to the student responses. You simply redirect the question to another student. Thus, it is hoped that this technique will lead to greater student participation and involvement and, consequently, to greater learning and increased interest.

The redirecting technique can also be used effectively with students who are nonvolunteers. You should try to involve these nonvolunteers as much as possible because, as noted earlier, participation enhances learning and stimulates interest.

It is important to remember, however, that nonvolunteers should never be forced to answer; rather, they should be given the opportunity to contribute to the discussion. In addition, you should give nonvolunteers ample time to consider a response. This time needed for students in considering their responses to questions is referred to as **wait-time**. Let's now look at the appropriate use of wait-time in questioning.

Wait-Time

Students need time for thinking and pondering the responses they will give to your questions. Research by Rowe (1974a, 1974b, 1978), however, has shown that teachers on the average wait only about *one* second for students to give an answer. Rowe's research also revealed that, when teachers learned to increase wait-time from 3 to 5 seconds, the following results occurred:

1. Student response time increased.
2. Failure to respond tended to decrease.
3. Students asked more questions.
4. Unsolicited responses tended to increase.
5. Student confidence increased.

Basically, there are two types of *wait-time. Wait-time 1* is the time provided for the first student response to a question. *Wait-time 2* is the total time a teacher waits for all students to respond to the same question or for students to respond to each other's response to a question. Wait-time 2 may involve several minutes. If you are to engage students more in your lessons, you must learn to increase your wait-time tolerance, so students have more opportunities to think and to ponder their answers.

The typical pattern of questioning in the average classroom can be depicted as follows:

Teacher————————————-> Student A

Teacher————————————-> Student B

Teacher————————————-> Student C

This pattern represents nothing more than a question-and-answer period. The teacher asks a question of a student, the student answers, the teacher moves to the next student and asks a question, the student answers, the teacher moves to the next student, and so on. Students often receive little time for thinking and expressing themselves and usually no time for reacting to each other's comments. In fact, most of the questions are typically at the lower level. Appropriate use of questioning techniques, higher-level questions, and wait-time can and should change this sequence to:

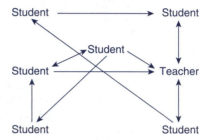

This pattern facilitates student discussion, welcomes extended responses, and provides opportunities for commenting on other students' questions and for asking questions. There is real involvement! Indeed, you will find that extending the time you wait after a question from 3 to 5 seconds—and giving students time to react to your questions and other students' responses—is well worth the added effort.

Halting Time

When presenting complex material, you need to learn to halt in what you are saying and give students time to think. This pause is referred to as **halting time**. No questions are asked, and no student comments are elicited. In using the halting-time technique, you present some complex material or complicated directions and then stop momentarily, so students have time to consider the information or carry out the directions. During this pause, you visually check with the class to see whether they are with you and understand what you are trying to communicate. If your observations are positive, you continue. If students appear to be confused, you may want to redo the explanation or directions.

Reinforcement

Once you have asked a question and have received an acceptable response, you must react to the response. Should you merely accept the response without comment and continue with the lesson or should you offer praise for a job well done? Your reinforcement—that is, your pattern of positive reaction—will have a powerful effect on the direction of the interaction in the classroom.

Rewards and praise often encourage students to participate. Phrases such as "Fine answer," "Great," "What an outstanding idea," and "Super" may be used when rewarding students' correct answers.

Reinforcement is often a good idea, but the too-frequent application of reinforcement can negate the benefits of using wait-time. If reinforcement is given too early in an answering sequence, other students may decide not to respond because they fear their answer could not match an earlier response. After all, didn't you say the earlier response was "great?" Rather than give reinforcement early in the questioning-answering sequence, you should allow as many students as possible to respond to the question, then reinforce all of them for their contributions. You can always return to the best answer for further comment.

APPLY AND REFLECT: You can keep students focused on your lesson through the use of the redirecting technique, wait-time, halting time, and reinforcement. Have your past teachers used these techniques? Were they effective? Why or why not?

Tips On Questioning

Asking good questions is an art. It is an art, however, that can be mastered with practice. The improper use of questioning can negatively impact learning. Teachers who strive for higher-level questions, for example, may lose interest in the just as important bread-and-butter memory questions. They may even tend to cater to the capacities of superior students. Let's now look at some questioning tips that may prove helpful in avoiding questioning pitfalls.

Questions should be clear, and you should ask the question before designating who is to answer. Ask the question, wait for the class to think about it, and then specify an individual to answer. As usual, there are exceptions to this rule. When you call on an inattentive student, it is often wise to designate the individual first, so that the student is sure to hear the question. Similarly, you should call the name first of slow or shy students, so that they can prepare themselves.

Distribute your questions about the class fairly. Avoid directing all questions to a selective few bright students. Also avoid using a mechanical system for asking questions, because students soon catch on to such systems—such as going by alphabetical order or row by row—and they will pay attention only when it is their turn.

Do not ask more than one question at a time. Asking too many questions at once often confuses students. Simultaneous questions permit no time to think, and, when several questions are asked, students are not sure which question to answer first.

Do not ask too many questions. Often, you need to establish a knowledge base before initiating a questioning sequence. This is especially true when the questions require thinking and reasoning.

Ask questions at all ability levels in the class. Some questions should be easy, whereas others should be more difficult. Also, use questions to help students modify their inaccurate responses. Use prompting and probing questions to help students think more thoroughly about their responses. This approach will increase involvement, will develop better thinking skills, and will reinforce student successes.

Finally, listen carefully to student responses. Wait at least 3 seconds following a student response. This allows the student time for making further comments and gives other students time to react to the initial student's response.

The key to the effective use of exposition with interaction is good questioning. Therefore, you must refine your ability to think, plan, and ask questions throughout your lessons. Let's now look at some methods that contain many of the features of the exposition and exposition with interaction strategies.

APPLY AND REFLECT: Do you consider effective questioning an art? What are your strengths and weaknesses as a questioner? What types and levels of questions will be the most useful to you as a classroom teacher?

Lecture Recitation

Lecture recitation is an instructional method in which the teacher presents information by telling and explaining, and follows up with question-and-answer sessions at periodical intervals. Thus, questions are used for summarizing the content of the lecture and for helping students consolidate and organize the presented information.

The lecture-recitation method is often efficient in terms of time, flexibility, and learning, while actively involving students in the lesson. Its basic structure of teacher talk/teacher question/student response/teacher talk makes questioning the key component to the method. Moreover, this method is highly adaptable to a large variety of topics and frequently is used as a companion to the lecture method or to the study of a textbook. Indeed, it is a form of recitation.

A hybrid form of the lecture-recitation method, in which questions are interspersed throughout the lecture, has proven to be the most popular among classroom teachers (Goodlad, 1984). When proper lecturing is executed and when questions are strategically used, this method is an effective and efficient way of teaching content. That is, the questions can and should be designed to provide feedback on understanding, to add variety to the lecture, and to maintain the students' attention. Moreover, questions from students can also help clarify the content and shed light on how well the lecture is being understood.

Textbook Recitation

The **textbook recitation** method is relatively simple: You assign students content to read and study in their textbook and then question them on what they have read and studied. Textbook recitation is an effective technique for teaching basic information simply because students are often motivated to read and study the assignment in anticipation of being called on to recite the information. However, this method does not foster true understanding and the application of the assigned content.

On the other hand, textbook recitation has the added advantages of giving students feedback on the accuracy of the content learned and of providing them with the opportunity to learn from the replies of fellow students. Indeed, these ends can be accomplished by planning higher-level questions in advance, with an emphasis on questioning sequences that will develop thinking and reasoning skills.

APPLY AND REFLECT: You must make sure a knowledge base has been established prior to questioning. How can this knowledge base be established?

The various direct instruction models have strengths and weaknesses. Complete Web Link: Direct Instruction to explore some of these strengths and weaknesses.

W E B   L I N K   Direct Instruction

Choose one of the direct instruction models found in this section and do an Internet search relative to the strengths and weaknesses of the model. Share the results with your class.

This concludes our discussion of various direct teaching methods. Apply the concepts developed in this chapter in Expansion Activity: Direct Instruction.

EXPANSION ACTIVITY

Direct
Instruction

List the sequence of steps that would characterize a direct instruction lesson.

Share your steps with several classmates. Do they agree?

Table 7.6 gives a review of the direct teaching methods. Review the table and complete Review, Extension, and Reflective Exercise 7.2.

TABLE 7.6 Exposition With Interaction Teaching	
Method	**Description**
Lecture Recitation	Teacher presents information and follows up with questions
Textbook Recitation	Students are assigned content to read and study and are later questioned over information

Review, Extension, and Reflective Exercise 7.2

Describe the effective use of questioning in the classroom.

Connections to INTASC Standards:

- Standard 1: Subject Pedagogy. The teacher must understand the central concepts, tools of inquiry, and structures of the discipline(s) he or she teaches and be able to create learning experiences that make these aspects of subject matter meaningful for students.
- Standard 2: Student Development. The teacher understands how children learn and develop and can provide learning opportunities that support their intellectual, social, and personal development.
- Standard 3: Diverse Learners. The teacher understands how students differ in their approaches to learning and creates instructional opportunities that are adapted to diverse learners.
- Standard 4: Instructional Strategies. The teacher must understand and use a variety of instructional strategies to encourage students' development of critical thinking, problem solving, and performance skills.
- Standard 6: Communication. The teacher uses knowledge of effective verbal, nonverbal, and media communication techniques to foster active inquiry, collaboration, and supportive interaction in the classroom.

- Standard 7: Planning Instruction. The teacher plans instruction based upon knowledge of subject matter, students, the community, and curriculum goals.

Connections to the NBPTS:

- Proposition 1: Teachers are committed to students and their learning.
- Proposition 2: Teachers must know the subjects they teach and how to teach those subjects to students.
- Proposition 4: Teachers must think systematically about their practice and learn from experience.

Review

- Describe the exposition with interaction instructional method of teaching. What are the strengths and weaknesses of this instructional approach?
- Why is questioning an art?
- Describe two questioning classificational systems.
- Describe the different types of questions.

Reflection

- Do you consider yourself a good questioner? How can you improve your skills?
- Should teachers use a question classification system? Why? What system do you plan to use in the area you expect to teach?

VIEW FROM THE CLASSROOM

What do teachers think about teaching approaches? Review these results and discuss with classmates.

The type of teaching style I prefer can be best described as:

Facilitator: Teacher facilitates and focuses on activities.	43%
Demonstrator: Teacher demonstrates and models what is expected.	30%
Delegator: Teacher places much of the control and responsibility for learning on learner(s).	14%
Formal authority: Teacher feels responsible for controlling the flow of content.	13%

SOURCE: Excerpted from *Teach-nology*, available at www.teach-nology.com/poll

Summary

- There is no best teaching strategy.
- There are two basic approaches to teaching: direct and indirect.

Direct Teaching

- Direct teaching is a teacher centered skill-building model.
- Although different authors describe the key elements of direct teaching differently, they tend to agree as to the sequence components.

Exposition Teaching

- Exposition teaching offers an effective way to convey a great deal of information in a short period of time.
- Exposition teaching should generally be short, lively, and to the point.

Exposition With Interaction Teaching

- Exposition with interaction teaching is often more effective than exposition teaching.

- Exposition with interaction teaching tends to bring student and teacher involvement in the learning process to a better balance.
- The key to exposition with interaction teaching is questioning.
- Asking good questions is an art that is essential to the lecture recitation and textbook recitation methods.
- The recall of information requires the use of narrow questions (convergent) while the desire to stimulate thinking and reasoning calls for the use of broad (divergent).
- The Mental Operation question system categorized questions as factual, empirical, productive, or evaluative.
- Focusing, prompting, and probing questions can be used to arouse interest and increase involvement.
- Redirecting questions, using wait-time and halting time, and using reinforcement can enhance questioning skills.

Discussion Questions and Activities

1. **Strategy selection.** You have been assigned a 10th grade social studies class. This class consists largely of slow learners. The class is restless, not interested, and hard to manage. What teaching strategies and methods would be best to use with this class? Give a valid rationale for your selection.

2. **The lecture method.** When would it be appropriate to use the lecture method? Consider objectives and purpose. How would one plan an effective lecture? Consider motivation, length, aids, clarity, and interest. How could you tell whether a lecture has been successful?

3. **Preparing questions.** Prepare examples for each level within the following question categories.

   a. Convergent and divergent
   b. Mental Operation system

4. **Textbook questions.** Obtain the teacher's edition of a textbook for a subject you expect to teach. Analyze the questions contained in the text. What levels and types of questions are most frequently suggested?

Connection With the Field

1. **Questioning in the classroom.** Attend a class in a public school or college classroom. Keep a tally of the levels of questions, and types of questions, used by the instructor. Did you see any patterns? What other questioning techniques did you observe? Were they successful? Why, or why not?

2. **Teaching.** Prepare and teach a minilesson using a direct methods approach. Use the miniteaching guidelines and forms in Appendix B to plan and analyze your minilesson.

3. **Teaching analysis.** Make a videotape of your miniteaching lesson; then critically analyze it with your peers.

Praxis II Connection

The following test preparation exercises are intended to help you prepare for the Praxis II: Principles of Learning and Teaching. The Praxis II may be required by your teacher education preparatory program and for state certification or licensing. These exercises will give you direct access to pedagogical knowledge from Chapter 7 that may be expected of you on the Praxis II and other pedagogical exams that may be required at the end of your teacher education program.

Topic Connections

1. Direct Instruction (II. A2, A3)

Describe the basic format of direct instruction. When is it appropriate to use the direct instruction format?

2. Asking Questions (III. C)

Identify the different forms/classification of questions. What kinds of questions are used to promote learning?

ON YOUR OWN

Log on to the web-based student study site at http://www.sagepub.com/eis for more information about the vignettes and materials presented in this chapter, suggestions for activities, study aids such as electronic flashcards and review quizzes, and research recommendations including journal article links and questions related to this chapter.

8

USING INTEGRATED TEACHING METHODS

In doing we learn.

GEORGE HERBERT

I will now engage in a study of techniques for giving students access to information and allowing them to examine the content and help produce their own learning. I will examine instructional approaches that can be used to organize and integrate bodies of knowledge for direct instruction with students engaging in a form of guided learning.

In this chapter, I will focus on the use of the various integrated directed teaching strategies in the classroom. Demonstrations, the Socratic method, concept attainment, cooperative learning, simulations and games, individualized instruction, independent study, and mastery learning provide integrated direct teaching alternatives.

After completing your study of Chapter 8, you should be able to do the following:

1. Describe the integrated directed teaching concept.
2. Describe the purpose, structure, and function of the demonstration method, Socratic method, concept attainment strategy, and cooperative learning method, valid reasons for their use, and techniques for their effective implementation.
3. Identify and explain the three-step procedure for role-playing and suggest ways to use role-playing in the classroom.
4. Explain the purposes of simulations and games and the benefits and limitations associated with their use.
5. Differentiate between human and person-to-computer simulations as well as between simulations and games.
6. Describe the three fundamental individualization strategies: individualized instruction, independent study, and mastery learning.

7. Identify the benefits and limitations associated with individualization of instruction.

8. Describe the purpose of drill and practice, as well as techniques for their effective use.

The teacher's task in the classroom is to deliver instruction. This task may be accomplished through strategies that influence students directly, indirectly, or by a combination of these. Thus, the teacher may deliver instruction by telling, by showing, and by providing access to the information to be learned. A combination of these options can be viewed as integrated directed teaching. The teacher provides access to information by working with students. Together, teacher and students can blend telling, showing, and self-exploration into a meaningful intrinsically motivational approach. This approach tends to give students more control over their own learning. To a degree, students become self-directed. The teacher provides access to learning and it is up to students to engage in the learning. Students become aware of their own learning. They learn to think critically, and to derive their own patterns of thought and meaning from the content presented. Self-directed learning is an approach to both teaching and learning that engages students, actively and/or mentally, in the learning process to acquire higher-order thinking outcomes. Students learn to construct their own understanding and meaning and learn to reason, problem-solve, and think critically.

The way teachers deliver instruction is changing. Technology and the Internet have the potential for effecting fundamental changes in the design of the learning process. Students and teachers will have ubiquitous access to all forms of information sources, demonstrations, library and research materials, and tutorials over high-speed networks from anywhere at any time. Effective use of the Internet as a teaching tool requires that the concept of self-directed learning be understood and developed. Teachers, who have learned through direct teaching methods and have been successful in using the direct methodologies, must gradually blend teacher-directed and self-directed learning. Students must learn that they can be in charge of their own learning some or most of the time.

Teachers must nurture student self-direction by providing students with opportunities before, during, and after instruction to exercise some control over their own learning. An emphasis on self-direction means that students must be taught and engaged in strategies that offer them opportunities to make decisions and solve problems on their own without being told what to do at all times. It means providing students with strategies designed to help them process information effectively and be self-confident, believing that they have the ability to succeed. And perhaps most important, teachers need to help students become more reflective about their thinking and learning processes.

APPLY AND REFLECT: Do you see potential uses for the newer technologies (smart boards, the Internet, online instruction, etc.) in the area you expect to teach? What technologies will be the most useful to you? Discuss your ideas with your classmates. Are their selections similar to yours?

Self-direction depends on who makes the learning decision—what is to be learned, who should learn it, what methods and resources should be used, and how the success should be measured. As such, only degrees of self-directness are possible. Complete Expansion Activity: Self-Directness to further explore the levels of self-directness.

EXPANSION ACTIVITY

Self-Directness

Is the level of self-directness that students can handle age related? How much self-directed learning do you plan to use at the grade level you expect to teach? Share your thoughts with classmates. Do they agree?

An excellent starting point for developing self-directed learning is through demonstrations, the Socratic method, concept attainment, and cooperative learning. These initial experiences can be followed with simulations and games and individualized instruction, which give students even more control over their own learning.

The Demonstration Method

The **demonstration** is the method in which the teacher or another designated individual stands before the class, shows something, and tells what is happening or what has happened, or asks students to discuss what has happened. A demonstration, then, is a process of teaching by means of using materials and displays to make information accessible to students. Even though the only person usually directly involved with the materials is the teacher or individual conducting the demonstration, students like demonstrations because they are actively engaged in a learning activity rather than merely talking about it. Information and concepts are made accessible to students; it is up to the students to learn. It is often good procedure, however, to have a student conduct the demonstration. This often arouses even more interest and student involvement.

The demonstration can be effective in many subject fields. For example, a teacher could demonstrate the steps in doing a science activity, the steps in writing a business letter, the steps in solving a mathematics problem, or how to adjust a microscope. Essentially, the technique deals mostly, but not totally, with showing how something works or with skill development. The demonstration may be by the teacher, by a student, by film or videotape, by Internet, or even by a sequence of pictures. Whatever technique is chosen, a demonstration should be accompanied by a verbal explanation or follow-up discussion. In an ordinary demonstration, the explanation accompanies the demonstration. One type of demonstration, however, asks students only to observe in silence. This method is referred to as the **inquiry demonstration**.

The inquiry demonstration is similar to the Socratic method (see next section of this chapter) in that students observe the demonstration in silence. These observations are then followed up with teacher questioning or with a discussion of what was observed. Students are asked to think logically, make inferences, and reach conclusions.

Seeking Quality

1. How can you help students take responsibility for their own learning and behavior?
2. Can students be trusted to objectively evaluate each other and themselves?

How do we get kids to work toward quality rather than just completion? I struggled with this for a long time, and this year I finally really and truly got it: AUDIENCE and REFLECTION.

The journey started with a series of PowerPoint presentations to the class. After each group presented, I asked the audience to share each presentation's strengths and areas that needed improvement. It was slow going at first; I had to remind them time and again that their critiques had to be specific so the presenters would know what to repeat and what to avoid in another situation.

I went through this process several more times with various pieces of work. My kids developed better on task behavior, became more likely to use the rubric while they were working, and my students' comments were more specific. Better yet, more students were completing projects, and the projects themselves were of higher quality. The only thing I was not happy with was presentation skills; though the kids would point out lack of eye contact, volume, and so on in their critiques, I didn't see the same sort of improvement as in the projects themselves.

As a result, with the last presentation I had kids work with their partners to score each presentation with the rubric. While content was included, the bulk of the points were focused on volume, enthusiasm, eye contact, speaking clearly, and so forth. The kids filled out the rubrics, made comments at the bottom, and then we shared our thoughts in discussions. As a result, I saw more kids actively working on volume, eye contact, and enthusiasm, among other things.

They have become very good evaluators, and no one wants to be evaluated poorly by their peers. We've developed a common language and understanding of what makes quality work, and the kids are judging solely on the work and not who the presenter is. As

they work, I push them to answer the question, "Is this good enough?" themselves, using the scoring guide and their own experiences. I can honestly say it has helped AND, if we don't present something we've done in class, they always want to know why. We put those items on the wall, and the discussion continues after class.

It is a process. I did A LOT of modeling, demonstrating the appropriate way to give praise and make suggestions. If a student made a particularly insightful/interesting/appropriate comment, I'd point to their comment as the type we were looking for. I ALWAYS start with the positive, no matter how dreadful the presentation is; we found good things to say about students with one slide out of the required eight, incomplete work, and so on. There is always a strength, a place to start, and while I had to connect the dots for them at first, they've gotten really good at doing it themselves. Of course, they still really enjoy pointing out the flaws, BUT they do it in a completely objective, supportive manner. I wonder if they zero in on the negatives so easily because that's what they've seen modeled for them by their teachers through the years?

It is just not Okay to treat others poorly in my classroom or in my presence. I've tried to model what I want from them at all times. We sometimes believe kids know how to act, and while they might be able to describe it, putting it into practice is an entirely separate matter. We must teach, model, and practice how to talk with each other thoughtfully.

As I've thought all of this over, I've realized how important it is to teach kids to become their own evaluators. They came in so dependent on me to tell them what was good and what needed improvement. If I am *really* going to teach them, I need to teach them to evaluate themselves and hold themselves to high standards. In the end, it's not about me, it's about them learning how to recognize and work for quality—for themselves.

—ELLEN BERG, *sixth grade teacher, English/language arts, St. Louis, MO*

SOURCE: www.middleweb.com. Reprinted with permission.

Students should be directly involved in classroom demonstrations and, whenever possible, should perform the actual demonstration.

There are at least five major reasons for teachers to use the demonstration in conveying a concept or the content in a subject: Among other things, demonstrations are useful when there is danger involved in students' using equipment or materials, they save time when absolutely necessary, they can show proper use of equipment, they can detail the steps in a particular procedure, and they can get a point across that is not easily expressed in words.

A good demonstration begins with an introduction (cognitive set) that indicates what students are to learn and/or are to look for and, perhaps, defines terms you will use in the demonstration. It is essential that you establish a strong cognitive set prior to conducting an inquiry demonstration. Your introduction should result in a focus of attention on what is to follow, but it should not give the details of what is to take place.

Following the introduction, the demonstration should be completed as simply and as much to the point as possible. If equipment or a procedure is being demonstrated, you should follow the desired action step-by-step, with pauses and explanations offered as needed in clarifying the actions. Occasionally, when the mere process of listening could interfere with students' observations, you might want to hold comments to a minimum or conduct an inquiry demonstration. In fact, in such cases, you might even want to proceed through the demonstration silently the first time and repeat it with explanations. Finally, in conducting classroom demonstrations, the following guidelines should be followed:

1. Go slowly so students can follow.
2. When procedures are complex, break down the demonstration into small components and demonstrate them separately; once students understand the components, conduct the demonstration in its entirety.
3. Repeat steps of the demonstration until students understand.
4. Remember, left and right are reversed, so set up the demonstration from the students' perspective.

After the demonstration, you should do a follow-up to check for understanding. It may be advantageous to have the students walk through the steps with you to test their competency at using equipment or in using a demonstrated procedure. In fact, you might wish to use the Socratic method (see next section of this chapter) to determine the effectiveness of your demonstration.

Plan your demonstration for success. Try your demonstrations before trying them in class to be certain that they will work and that they take a reasonable amount of time. Set up demonstrations so that they are visible to all students; seating students in a semicircle around the demonstration often works best. You should plan techniques for keeping students attentive. In most cases, presenting demonstrations that are exciting will keep students' interest and attention. But, if needed, questions are often effective at regaining wandering attention.

APPLY AND REFLECT: Demonstrations can be used in most subject areas and at most grade levels. Demonstrations, however, are more applicable to some areas than others. How useful will demonstrations be as a teaching method in the area(s) you expect to teach?

The Socratic Method

The **Socratic method** derives its name from its ascribed adherent, Socrates. It is a technique of using a questioning-and-interaction sequence designed to draw information out of students, rather than pouring it into them. This method is purely verbal and interactive. Most teachers use the Socratic method to develop content information.

The Socratic method, in general, involves teaching by asking questions and, in so doing, leading students into a logical contradiction. Essentially, the Socratic method follows a general pattern:

1. A broad, open-ended question that most students can answer is asked first.
2. A second questioning sequence begins to narrow the range of responses and focuses the students' thinking onto the topic of the questioning strategy.
3. Review lectures and/or statements are interspersed among the questions in order to keep the salient points in the forefront.
4. A concluding question then brings students to the desired end point.

The techniques as originally developed by Socrates must be adapted to the reality of the classroom. The method Socrates conceived requires a one-to-one relationship between the student and teacher, with the teacher posing a series of questions that gradually tangle the student up to the point where ideas and thinking must be carefully scrutinized. In the classroom, the teacher generally does not focus the questioning sequence on one student but, rather, questions one student first, then another, and then another—moving slowly throughout the class. Although this technique usually works well, the pure essence of the Socratic technique is often difficult to capture. Still, the Socratic method can be quite effective, and it works best in small-group sessions and in tutorial sessions.

Richard Paul (1993) outlines the types of questions that can be used in the Socratic dialog sequence to probe the underlying logic or structure of student thinking and enable them to make reasonable judgments. Example questions might include the following:

- **Questions of clarification**
  - What do you mean by that?
  - Can you give me an example?
  - Why do you say that?

- **Questions that probe assumptions**
  - What is being assumed?
  - Why would somebody say that?
  - Is that always the case?

- **Questions that probe reason and evidence**
  - What are your reasons for saying that?
  - What criteria do you base that argument on?
  - Could you explain your reasons?

- **Questions that probe implications and consequences**
  - What might be the consequences of behaving like that?
  - Do you think you might be jumping to conclusions?
  - How can we find out?

- **Questions about viewpoints or perspectives**
  - What would be another way of saying that?
  - How do Judy's ideas differ from Mike's?
  - What is an alternative?

- **Questions about the question**
  - How is that question going to help us?
  - Can you think of any other questions that might be useful?
  - What is the question?

A Socratic dialog is a collective attempt to find the answer to a fundamental question or issue. The question or issue is the center of the dialog. Consider this dialog relative to choice.

Teacher: Suppose your school is having a science fair and you can get class credit for presenting a project. Someone offers to do the necessary science project for you for a price. You know that wouldn't be right. What do you do?

Mike: I would pay them and let them do it for me.

Teacher: What would you do if a science judge asked if it was your work?

Mike: I paid for it. I would say it was mine.

Teacher: But wouldn't that be a lie?

Mike: I did pay for it. So it is mine.

Teacher: All right, but you know it wasn't really your work. Suppose the judge asks you to verify that you did the actual work.

Mike: I'd have no choice but to say I didn't.

Teacher: Suppose it wasn't the science judge, but rather your science teacher who asked "Mike, did you do all this good work?"

Mike: I might say, "Yes, I did it."

Teacher: Okay, why would you say that?

Mike: Fear of getting no credit.

Teacher: Does that mean it is all right to have someone else do your work and lie? Then, doctors should be able to do it, your classmates, the president, and your parents?

Mike: [*Long pause*] Well, no.

Teacher: Then it is okay for you, but not others? Are there different rules for you?

Mike: [*Longer pause*] No.

Teacher: What would you think of yourself now that you've said that you would lie to your teacher out of fear? Are you that kind of person? You would pay someone else to do your work. What vision would you have of yourself?

Mike: Well, what with the thought I have given it today, I would feel bad. Before today, I wouldn't have cared.

Teacher: Do you have a different image of yourself now?

Mike: Yes. I think more of myself today than I would have yesterday. Because I know there's a better me and I should do the right thing.

When conducting such a dialog, you must have a clear vision of what you want students to learn from it. It is essential to have your end point in mind so that you can always be angling toward it.

APPLY AND REFLECT: Can the Socratic method be used effectively at the grade level you plan to teach?

Concept Attainment

Concept attainment is an instructional strategy that uses a structured inquiry process. The strategy is based on the research of Jerome Bruner (1977) and his associates, who investigated how different variables affected the concept-learning process. In concept attainment, students figure out the attributes of a group or category that has been provided by the teacher. To do so, students compare and contrast examples that contain the attributes of the concept with examples that do not contain those attributes. By observing these examples, students discuss and identify the attributes of each until they develop a tentative hypothesis (definition) about the concept. Next, students separate the examples into two groups, those that have the attribute and those that don't. This hypothesis is then tested by applying it to other examples of the concept. Examples could be symbols, words, passages, pictures, or objects. This strategy can be used in all curriculum areas. Finally, students demonstrate that they have attained the concept by generating their own examples and nonexamples. Concept attainment, then, is the search for and identification of attributes that can be used to distinguish examples of a given group or category from nonexamples. With carefully chosen examples, it is possible to use concept attainment to teach almost any concept in all subjects.

To illustrate the concept attainment process, consider the concept *proper noun.*

- First, the teacher chooses the concept to be developed (i.e., proper noun).
- Begin by making a list of both positive "yes" and negative "no" examples: The examples can be put on sheets of paper or flash cards or written on the chalkboard.
- *Positive examples:* Positive examples contain attributes of the concept to be taught (e.g., Jane, Houston, John, Settle, United States, George Washington, Honda, Old Testament). Your list of examples should include the idea that a proper noun means a specific person, place, or thing.
- *Negative examples:* Next present negative examples of the concept (i.e., run, is, and, boy, heavy, slowly, town, chair). Note the negative examples differentiate *proper nouns* from *common nouns.*
- Designate one area of the chalkboard for positive examples and one area for negative examples. A chart could be set up at the front of the room with two columns—one marked YES and the other marked NO.
- Present the first card by saying, "This is a YES." Place it under the appropriate column (e.g., Settle is a YES).
- Present the next card and say, "This is a NO." Place it under the NO column (e.g., run is a NO).
- Repeat this process until there are three examples under each column.
- Ask the class to look at the three examples under the YES column and discuss how they are alike. Ask, "What do they have in common?"
- For the next three examples under each column, ask the students to decide if the examples go under YES or NO.
- At this point, there are six examples under each column. Students should begin to hypothesize a name for the concept. These hypotheses are tested with further examples and nonexamples provided by the teacher. Students determine which hypotheses are acceptable and which ones have to be rejected based on the examples. They also can suggest additional hypotheses at this point. The process of presenting examples, analyzing hypotheses, presenting additional examples, and continuing to analyze hypotheses continues until all the hypotheses but one are eliminated.
- Discuss the process with the class. Students should be asked to explicitly define the hypothesis and identify the characteristics. Students are then asked to define a proper noun.
- Next, students are asked to apply the concept by classifying examples or generating examples of their own.
- Students analyze their own thinking (metacognition). Ask questions such as, "Did anyone have to change his or her thinking?" or "What made you change your mind?" or "When did you begin to see this concept?"

The concept attainment strategy is based on the assumption that one of the best ways to learn a concept is by seeing examples of it. Because examples are central to the concept attainment activity, special attention must be paid to their selection and sequencing.

APPLY AND REFLECT: The concept attainment strategy takes more time to plan, prepare materials, and carry out than some of the other strategies. Do you think the time is well invested or should this time be used for other more pressing classroom activities? Share your thoughts with your classmates. Do they agree with you?

Cooperative Learning

The evolving constructivist perspectives on learning have fueled interest in collaboration and cooperative learning. As a result, **cooperative learning** has emerged as a promising instructional approach. Several approaches to cooperative learning have been developed (Davidson & O'Leary, 1990; Kagan, 1990); however, most of them share certain characteristics.

Cooperative learning is more than simply putting students in groups. Cooperative learning generally requires that students work together in mixed-ability groups in accomplishing a set of tasks. Students are placed in groups that are mixed in performance level, gender, and ethnicity. The percentage of high, middle, and low learners in each group should represent the appropriate population of each group in the whole class. Rewards to individual students are often based on the performance and accomplishment of the team. Accountability of individual students for the whole group builds an incentive for students to work productively together.

The size of the cooperative-learning group varies, depending on the task to be accomplished. The common group size tends to be four. In general, cooperative-learning groups are given considerable autonomy. Team members are allowed a great deal of freedom as they decide how to deal with the assigned task.

Individual accountability is an essential characteristic of all cooperative learning. Accountability means that the success of the group is based on the individual learning of each team member. Individual accountability occurs when each student in the group is held responsible for the required learning goals.

Some teachers assign roles and responsibilities to students to encourage cooperation and full participation. Assigned student roles might include recorder, encourager, materials monitor, taskmaster, quiet captain, and coach. If you do decide to assign roles, be sure the roles support the desired learning and that students understand their roles.

Cooperative learning takes many forms. The most common approaches include Peer Tutoring, Student Teams Achievement Division (STAD), Group Investigation, and the Jigsaw Strategy.

Peer Tutoring. One of the simplest forms of cooperative learning uses students as supplementary instructors in basic-skills areas. The teacher presents material as he or she normally would. Pairs of students then use structured exercises and worksheets with answer sheets to reinforce the new material. Students take turns being the tutor and provide each other with immediate, one-to-one feedback (Miller, Barbetta, & Heron, 1994).

Student Teams Achievement Division (STAD). In Student Teams Achievement Division (STAD), students are paired on evenly matched teams of four or five, and team scores are based on the extent to which individuals improve their scores on skills tests. Rewards are given to teams whose members improve the most over their past performances, thus encouraging group cooperation. The steps involved in implementing STAD are (Slavin, 1995):

1. Pretest. This can be a unit pretest or work from previous units.
2. Rank students in descending order.
3. Divide students so each team of four has high-, medium-, and low-ability students and those groups are diverse in terms of gender and ethnicity.
4. Present lesson as you normally would.
5. Students study worksheets that focus on the goals and content covered by the teacher.
6. Monitor groups relative to progress on goals.
7. Administer individual quizzes to students.
8. Assign team scores based on individual score gains.

STAD is a popular cooperative learning strategy because of its wide applicability across a variety of subject matter areas (including math, reading, and social studies) and grade levels.

Group Investigation. Cooperative learning can be used to promote higher-level learning. Group investigation involves a combination of independent learning and group work. It places students together in teams of three to six to investigate or solve some common problem. Examples might include social studies or a science experiment, a community project, or construction of an art collage. Students are responsible for developing group goals, assigning individual responsibilities, and bringing the projects to completion. Cooperation is encouraged and fostered through common group goals, and grades are assigned to the total project. Designers of group investigation identify six steps in implementing group investigations: (1) topic selection, (2) cooperative planning, (3) implementation, (4) analysis and synthesis, (5) presentation of final product, and (6) evaluation. To accommodate diversity, the teacher should ensure that groups are heterogeneous and the different groups' members all contribute to the goals and final product. The teacher's role is to facilitate investigation and maintain cooperative effort.

Jigsaw Strategy. The jigsaw strategy is a cooperative learning plan in which six-member teams work to investigate a common topic. The topics are typically broad enough in scope (for example, the country of Canada in geography, islands in science, and the body in health) that individual members of the team can be assigned subjects within the topic. Individuals are responsible for researching and learning their part. Members of different teams who have studied the same part convene, discuss their part, and then return to their teams, where they take turns teaching their part to other team members. All students are expected to learn all the information on the topic, and comprehensive quizzes can be used to supplement group reports to measure if this happens.

Researchers have found that cooperative learning can be an effective strategy for improving achievement, especially when two essential conditions are met (Johnson & Johnson, 1999, 2002; O'Donnell, 1996; Slavin, 1995):

- Some type of recognition or small reward is provided to groups that do well so that the group members can sense that it is in their best interest to help group mates learn.
- Some method of evaluating each student's individual contribution, such as an individual quiz or individual work, needs to be used. For example, groups might be evaluated on the basis of the average of their members on individual quizzes or students might be individually responsible for a unique portion of a group task. Without this individual accountability, some students might let others do their work.

When the conditions of group rewards and individual accountability are met, cooperative learning improves achievement across different grades, in tasks ranging from basic skills to problem solving, and in all types of schools (Ellis, 2001; Johnson & Johnson, 1999, 2002). In addition to boosting achievement, cooperative learning fosters a positive impact on intergroup relations, self-esteem, attitude toward school, and acceptance of children with special educational needs (Slavin, 1995).

Group work gives students the opportunity to learn important social and cognitive skills from each other.

APPLY AND REFLECT: The cooperative learning strategy is being used by many teachers. Based on your experiences and educational observations, what advantages associated with cooperative learning are behind the recent interest in cooperative learning?

Cooperative learning is appropriate in many situations. It can be an effective technique for reviewing for tests, for completing laboratory work, and for practicing skills. Remember, however, that you are rewarding cooperative learning. All students are involved in their group grade, and the better students are expected to help pull up the team grade. To get a better perspective of the uses and attributes of cooperative learning, complete Web Link: Cooperative Learning.

WEB   LINK   Cooperative Learning
Go to the following cooperative learning websites:

www.co-operation.org
http://jamaica.u.arizona.edu/ic/edtech/strategy.html
http://edtech.kennesaw.edu/intech/cooperativelearning.htm

Review the sites relative to cooperative learning uses and techniques. Write a summary of your findings. Share the summary with your classmates.

Table 8.1 summarizes the teaching approaches presented in this section. Review the summary and check your knowledge of this section by completing Review, Extension, and Reflective Exercise 8.1.

TABLE 8.1 **The Demonstration**

Method	Description
Ordinary Demonstration	Individual shows and explains something to class
Inquiry Demonstration	Individual shows class something without explanation, students observe, make inferences, and reach conclusions
Socratic Method	Questioning-and-interaction to draw information out of students
Concept Attainment	Teaching strategy designed to help students learn concepts and practice analytical thinking skills
Cooperative Learning	Students work together as a team on assigned tasks

Review, Extension, and Reflective Exercise 8.1

Describe integrated directed instructional strategies.

Connections to INTASC Standards:

- Standard 4: Instructional Strategies. The teacher must understand and use a variety of instructional strategies to encourage students' development of critical thinking, problem solving, and performance skills.
- Standard 5: Learning Environment. The teacher must be able to use an understanding of individual and group motivation and behavior to create a learning environment that encourages positive social interaction, active engagement in learning, and self-motivation.
- Standard 6: Communication. The teacher uses knowledge of effective verbal, nonverbal, and media communication techniques to foster active inquiry, collaboration, and supportive interaction in the classroom.
- Standard 7: Planning Instruction. The teacher plans instruction based upon knowledge of subject matter, students, the community, and curriculum goals.

Connections to the NBPTS:

- Proposition 1: Teachers are committed to students and their learning.
- Proposition 2: Teachers must know the subjects they teach and how to teach those subjects to students.

Review

- What are some good demonstration strategies?
- What challenges do demonstrations pose for teachers?
- Describe the Socratic method. What are the strengths and weaknesses of this method?
- Describe the concept attainment and cooperative learning methods of teaching. How do they differ?

Reflection

- During a demonstration, how can teachers give students a sense of ownership?
- Is the Socratic method a viable teaching method for the grade level you plan to teach? Why or why not?
- The concept attainment and cooperative learning strategies could result in the development of social skills. How would you use these strategies to develop social skills at the grade level you expect to teach?

Simulations and Games

Simulations and game activities can be most useful as teaching tools. Indeed, they provide a variety of learning opportunities in the classroom. Such activities can create interest and relieve tension in difficult curriculum areas. Furthermore, students often find simulations and games fun.

"I like educational toys. I like educational TV.
I like educational reading material. It's education I don't like."

Simulation is the presenting of an artificial situation or event that represents reality but that removes risk to the individual involved in the activity. Simulations can be viewed as models of what exists or might exist under manageable and controlled conditions.

Two basic types of simulations can be used in the classroom: human simulations and person-to-computer simulations. Human simulations are usually conducted in the form of role-playing and sociodramas, whereas person-to-computer simulations often take the form of simulation games.

What is the distinction between a *simulation* and a *game*? There is no clear-cut answer to this question. Usually, games are played to win, whereas simulations need not have a winner. In fact, in some simulations, it is difficult to determine whether there are winners or losers. Regardless of the label, simulations and games are similar in that there are roles that must be assumed and specific types of activities for the participants. In addition, the purpose of a simulation is to encourage students to act out the behaviors and express in their own words the actions and arguments behind an issue. Thus, whether an activity is a simulation or a game is often a matter of semantics.

Role-playing is the acting out of roles in recreating historical or future events, significant current events, or imaginary situations (Gilstrap & Martin, 1975, p. 87). The role-playing student tries to "become" another individual and, by assuming the role, to gain a better understanding of the person, as well as the actions and motivations that prompted certain behaviors. Role-playing usually involves a structure, a stated issue to be resolved, and in some cases a winner or loser. Essentially, the idea is to become the individual being played as much as possible and, by recreating the person's actions, to gain a better understanding of the person and the related motivations. A role-playing simulation may involve a limited number of individuals in one-to-one interactions or several students in small-group interactions.

Role-playing is often used for teaching citizenship responsibilities and for group counseling. It gives students opportunities to study human behavior. Students can explore their feelings, gain insights into the perceptions and attitudes of others, and develop their problem-solving skills. Teachers often use role-playing to facilitate learner involvement and interaction in the process of decision making. It teaches the process of decision making. It teaches students to learn through dramatization.

Role-playing can also be a group technique that may include almost any number of participants, depending on the purpose. Role-playing commonly consists of three components: the situation, the role-playing, and the follow-up discussion.

The role-playing episode should be a spontaneous acting out of a situation or an incident, which in the process fosters a deeper understanding of the associated actions, motives, and behaviors. You should give students a thorough briefing or detailed preparation regarding the situation prior to the episode. For example, students can assume the role of Einstein and reenact the development of his theories, or they can reenact the writing of the Declaration of Independence, or they can assume the role of Shakespeare in the Globe Theater. Indeed, students can bring to life scenes from scientific discoveries, scenes from short stories or plays, events from the lives of different people, courtroom dramatizations, legal-ethical situations, mock town meetings, or United Nations sessions. Whatever the episode, describe the situation in detail to your students and set clear guidelines.

A debriefing session should follow any role-playing episode. The class should analyze the episode with respect to the values and behaviors of the participants, as well as the consequences of the actions.

The *sociodrama* is a form of role-playing. But it differs in that it focuses on how the group solves a problem; that is, alternative solutions to problems of concern to the total group are explored. For example, the problem may be related to an issue before a town meeting, a family problem, or a United Nations problem.

Educational games involve students in decision-making roles in which they compete for certain objectives according to specified rules. Thus, educational games should reflect society; they should offer students the opportunity to experience roles that are common in life. The competitive nature of games, however, should be kept in perspective. One of the best-known educational games is Monopoly, a simulation board game of the real-estate business.

The use of computer simulations and games is increasing. Computer games are now familiar to everyone; they are often played on home computers and in many classrooms. They come in a myriad of formats, with the majority of those appropriate for the classroom involving hand-eye coordination (such as Pac-Man) or problem-solving abilities (such as Dungeons & Dragons). Indeed, computer games can function as an excellent motivational device when the chance of playing a game is contingent on doing one's work.

The use of simulations and games offers many benefits:

1. They actively involve students in their own learning.
2. They provide immediate feedback to students.
3. They enable students to practice communication skills.
4. They create a high degree of interest and enthusiasm.
5. They allow teachers to work with a wide range of student capabilities at the same time.
6. They promote and reward analytical and critical thinking.
7. They allow experimentation with a model of the real environment.

Basic to any teaching strategy is its motivational value. Simulations and games appear to be quite effective as motivational tools. Students think they are fun, and they even learn.

Several limitations have also been voiced regarding the use of simulations and games:

1. They demand a great deal of imagination on the part of the teacher and students.
2. They often screen out critical elements; for example, the driver education simulator often does not include traffic, noise, and the presence of others.
3. The expense involved in obtaining commercially produced simulations and games can be great.
4. Relationships often develop between the teacher and students that are too informal, which can lead to management problems.

These limitations can be overcome with proper planning. The use of simulations and games offers too many special opportunities to be ignored.

Some of the best simulations and games are those designed by teachers, who develop and adjust the activities according to their own students' needs. Even better, students can develop their own simulations and games.

APPLY AND REFLECT: Are games really appropriate for the school classroom? Discuss

this issue in class.

In using simulations and games, you must be familiar with the desired roles, rules, and conflicts to be followed or addressed. In the case of games, you would be wise to play the game yourself first. In addition, it is a good idea to prepare handouts, materials, and guides for students. Complete Web Link: Educational Games to further explore the use of games at the grade level you expect to teach.

WEB   LINK   **Educational Games**

Conduct an Internet search on educational games that would be appropriate for the grade level you expect to teach. Make a resource file of the best games and their sources. Are there any cautions teachers need to be aware of when using games for teaching? If there are, describe them. Share your resource file and cautions with your classmates.

Individualized Strategies

Students do not learn or master skills uniformly. Therefore, individualization is often required in maximizing the potential of each student; this is especially important when students come from different backgrounds and have varying abilities. In this section,

I will address three fundamental techniques for individualization: individualized instruction, independent study, and mastery learning. Later, I will take a brief look at the somewhat related topic of drill and practice.

Individualized Instruction

Individualized instruction can take several forms. Ideally, **individualized instruction** engages students in learning plans tailored to meet their interests, needs, and abilities. Accordingly, you might vary one or more of the following: (1) the learning pace, (2) the instructional objectives, (3) the learning method, or (4) the learning materials. Students do not learn at the same pace. Some need more time to attain understanding. Thus, one—and perhaps the simplest—method to individualize instruction is that of permitting students to work on the same assignments at their own pace. This is accomplished by breaking down the instructional materials into a series of short and related activities or lessons. The faster students or high achievers can move through the lessons rapidly without having to wait for classmates to catch up. Students experiencing difficulty can move through the materials at a slower pace, reworking troublesome areas, and seeking assistance when unable to master the material.

Another technique that can be used for individualizing instruction is varying your objectives. If you pretest your class on the intended instructional outcomes (objectives), you may find that some have already mastered these outcomes. Thus, instead of insisting that all students work on the same outcomes, you tailor the activities to the needs and abilities of different students or groups of students. Low-ability students might need to work on all your objectives, whereas better students might need to work on a small number. Clearly, you need to break down your instruction into a variety of objectives and related activities to accommodate this type of individualization.

A third individualization technique is to vary the method used in accomplishing the desired outcome. Even when students are working on the same outcome, they can use different means of achieving mastery. One student may rely on a textbook, whereas another may work with tutors. Still other students with learning difficulties may need to work with special teachers. Self-instructional packages, learning centers, and computer-assisted instruction (CAI) are other possible methods that could provide individualized instruction.

The final technique, of varying the materials used in accomplishing your objectives, can also lead to individualized instruction. As just noted, textbooks can be used in individualizing instruction. Some students, however, may read at lower reading levels than their classmates. In fact, some may have severe reading problems, which would hamper the use of any textbook. If reading is a problem, textbooks at different levels can be made available, as can other modes—such as films, audiotapes and videotapes, overheads, and models.

Essays and research projects are also an excellent way of individualizing instruction. They allow students or small groups of students to pursue areas of interest. For example, essays can be assigned on broad topics such as farming, the space program, teenage suicide, or the national debt, whereas research projects can be given in such areas as creating an air car, building classroom models, or writing and/or performing a play. Research projects usually are more challenging than essays; however, students involved in research often gain needed practice in finding and developing materials.

Although the classroom is normally viewed as a place for housing and teaching a class of students, you can often introduce a certain amount of individualization by forming learning groups or through the use of mastery learning. Group organizational structures—sometimes referred to as cooperative or team learning—enable and encourage students to learn and to assist each other, whereas mastery learning can be achieved through individual learning or group learning (see mastery learning section of this chapter). Students often learn and retain more when taught by peers. Thus, groups can be formed so that a range of ability levels and skills is represented within the groups. Also, student assistants can be assigned to work with specific groups on problems, to lead seminars, to demonstrate equipment, or to direct discussions.

Independent Study

There is no reason for you to do what students can do for themselves. Older students can often be involved in independent study. **Independent study** can be defined as any educational activity carried out by an individual with little or no guidance. Essentially, independent study is a pure form of self-directed learning.

Teachers often need time for working with individual students or with small groups. Independent study can provide this time. One way to provide this time is structuring the time for students to engage in interesting, creative tasks of their own choosing. For example, students can be allowed to research a topic of personal interest. Other possibilities include reading and reviewing books of interest, acting as tutor to other students, working at learning or interest centers, and working on classroom models. Such activities should be available for students who finish their seatwork quickly. They should not be punished indirectly for their rapid completion of an assignment with more of the same work. You might also want to carefully structure long periods of independent study. Self-directed library-research studies on topics of personal interest, for example, make excellent learning experiences. Most students enjoy working independently on gathering facts on concrete problems. These topics need not always be traditional, content-centered topics. Attitude and awareness sometimes can be stimulated by combining factual knowledge with student interests and values.

Mastery Learning

Before focusing on the mastery learning model, let's look at the traditional model of instruction. This traditional model of instruction is shown in Figure 8.1. When you use this model, all of your students are involved in all activities at the same time. The instruction begins with an identification of the unit objectives, and then you present the primary instruction to the entire class. The primary instruction comes in the form of lectures, discussions, reading, media presentations, seatwork, or a combination of these techniques. After the primary instruction, you evaluate student achievement relative to your objectives.

Like the traditional model, the **mastery learning** model takes a group approach to teaching. This model, through its diagnostic-corrective-enrichment activities, provides a high degree of individualization, because students often learn at different

Figure 8.1

The Traditional Instructional Model

Figure 8.2

The Mastery Model of Instruction

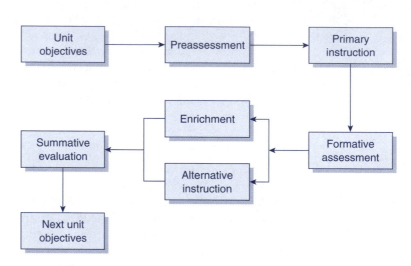

paces and use different materials. As depicted in Figure 8.2, the mastery learning model essentially represents a six-step pattern.

As with the traditional model, your first step in using the mastery model is identification of your objectives. Before the primary instruction is delivered, however, a preassessment step is carried out. The purpose of this second step is to determine where students are with respect to the objectives. Some students may lack unit prerequisite skills and need to work on them prior to receiving the primary instruction. Other students may have already mastered the unit objectives and should be directed to enrichment activities or to the next unit.

The third step in the mastery learning model is the delivery of the primary instruction. This instruction, as with the traditional model, involves all students except those who have demonstrated mastery in the activities, and it is presented through lectures, discussions, readings, and so on.

At this point—the fourth step—the mastery model parts from the traditional model: A formative assessment (progress check or diagnostic test) takes place. The purpose of this evaluation is to determine which students have achieved the desired mastery level and which students are in need of further instruction. Those at the mastery level are directed to enrichment activities, whereas those below the mastery level are involved in further objective-related activities. These fifth-step enrichments and alternatives can be structured as group or individual activities. Further formative evaluations should be an integral part of the alternative instructional sequence.

Once the initial alternative activities have been completed, student progress should be checked once again; this cycle is repeated until mastery is achieved. During this sixth and final phase, all students are given a final, or posttest, evaluation.

The basic structure of the mastery learning model can take two forms. In the first, the enrichments and alternatives parallel each other, with the posttest evaluation providing closure for the unit. As students achieve mastery, they are routed to the enrichment component until the class is ready for the formal evaluation. The sixth step, the posttest evaluation, also may be administered to students at different times. In such situations, students can be tested when the formative evaluation indicates mastery has been achieved. The students who test early can be involved in other types of individualized strategies, or they can work on the next set of unit objectives on an individualized basis.

Effectiveness of Individualization

The evidence supporting the value of the various individualized strategies is mixed. Under certain conditions, for example, research suggests that the mastery learning approach does lead to higher student achievement. When used as the only method of instruction, however, such methods have not proven superior to traditional methods.

Individualized strategies tend to leave students on their own too much. Only the most motivated and self-directed students stay on task for extended periods of time. Therefore, with most students, a lot of time is wasted. Also, most students lack skill at analyzing and thinking reflectively about studied materials. They need the direct teaching and explanations provided by the teacher. Instead, the teacher's time is too often devoted to the preparation of materials and correction of individual assignments.

If carefully designed and monitored, individualization can be effective at providing needed remediation or enrichment. Students can work at their own pace on assignments geared to their ability, for example, but receive direct instruction from the teacher with the rest of the class. This more active involvement in their own learning generally results in a higher level of interest, better motivation, and a feeling of independence and self-discipline.

Efforts at improving individualization will continue. Students can only benefit from such techniques. Therefore, you will want to individualize your instruction at times. Study the various techniques and other self-directed methods and determine how you can incorporate them into your class. Complete Expansion Activity: Self-Directed Learning Methods to explore the use of individualization and other self-directed techniques at the grade level you expect to teach. But be sure to remember that students need a teacher: They need your expertise and guidance.

EXPANSION ACTIVITY

Self-Directed
Learning Methods

Would individualization and self-directed learning work at the grade level you expect to teach? Why or why not? If it would, what forms and techniques would work?

APPLY AND REFLECT: How much individualization do you feel comfortable with in terms of your future classes? What forms would you support?

Drill and Practice

Drill and practice provide (or should provide) exactly what their names indicate—systematic and repeated "workout" in the intended skill areas, with the purpose of achieving automatic accuracy and speed of performance. **Drill** is concerned with the fixation of specific associations for automatic recall, whereas **practice** is concerned with improvement. Thus, one drills on writing the different shorthand symbols but practices on the basic multiplication facts.

Individualized problem-solving processes are the key to drill and practice. They are based on further development of initial whole-class learning. Seen in this light, drill and practice should be a basic part of the curriculum, not merely a time filler. As such, they should give students opportunities to apply their knowledge in solving problems or refining their skills. Such practice and/or drill, when designed properly, will give you good feedback on how students are progressing. Therefore, you should plan your drills and practice carefully and communicate their importance to students.

Students should not have to interrupt drill or practice frequently to get help. Students who are supposed to work independently must understand what they are to do with little or no help. First, make sure assigned drills and practices are appropriate and not too difficult. Next, give clear expectations about what students should do when they finish their work. Last, make sure students are held accountable; when applicable, all seatwork should be checked.

Computers, with their nearly limitless patience and endurance, can be quite effective at providing drill and practice. Computers can drill students as long as the students can hold up. Math programs, for example, use a random-number generator to create new problems—as long as students make requests.

"We're going to need a new computer in our class today. I hope I'm the one it replaces."

Computer labs as a supplement to classroom teaching offer students opportunities for practical application of instruction.

This completes the discussion of the various individualized techniques. Table 8.2 summarizes these techniques as well as the related drill and practice. Review Table 8.2 and check your knowledge of this section by completing Review, Extension, and Reflective Exercise 8.2.

TABLE 8.2 **Individualization**	
Method	**Description**
Simulations and Games	Models of artificial situations and events designed to provide no-risk experiences for students
Individualized Instruction	Instruction tailored to interests, needs, and abilities of students
Independent Study	Activities carried out with little or no guidance
Mastery Learning	Diagnostic-corrective-enrichment model where students work on objectives until mastery is achieved
Drill and Practice	Development of automatic and/or improved performance

Review, Extension, and Reflective Exercise 8.2

Describe integrated directed instructional strategies.

Connections to INTASC Standards:

- Standard 4: Instructional Strategies. The teacher must understand and use a variety of instructional strategies to encourage students' development of critical thinking, problem solving, and performance skills.
- Standard 5: Learning Environment. The teacher must be able to use an understanding of individual and group motivation and behavior to create a learning environment that encourages positive social interaction, active engagement in learning, and self-motivation.
- Standard 6: Communication. The teacher uses knowledge of effective verbal, nonverbal, and media communication techniques to foster active inquiry, collaboration, and supportive interaction in the classroom.
- Standard 7: Planning Instruction. The teacher plans instruction based upon knowledge of subject matter, students, the community, and curriculum goals.

Connections to the NBPTS:

- Proposition 1: Teachers are committed to students and their learning.
- Proposition 2: Teachers must know the subjects they teach and how to teach those subjects to students.

Review

- What is individualized instruction?
- Discuss important features of individualized instruction.
- What are some pros and cons of individualized instruction?

Reflection

- How would you go about teaching individualized learning skills to students?
- Did any of your past teachers involve you in individualized instruction? If so, how successful was it? Did you like this instructional approach?

VIEW FROM THE CLASSROOM

Do teachers use integrated direct teaching? Review these results and discuss with classmates.

How many computers do you have in your classroom?

3 to 5	28%
1	27%
2	17%
20 or more	9%
6 to 10	8%
None	6%
10 to 20	5%

SOURCE: Excerpted from *Teach-nology*, available at www.teach-nology.com/poll

Summary

- The integrated directed strategy gives students some control over their own learning.
- Technology and the Internet have the potential for changing the fundamental design of the learning process.

The Demonstration Method

- Demonstrations can be effective when used appropriately.
- Before conducting a demonstration, you should practice it in class, have all materials at hand, go slowly, often repeat components, and above all make it simple and to the point.

The Socratic Method

- The Socratic method of teaching is designed to draw information from students through the use of questions.
- Application of the Socratic teaching method calls for the teacher to focus the questioning sequence on a single student, then another, and then another.

Concept Attainment

- The concept attainment strategy uses a structured inquiry process.
- Students learn concepts by comparing and contrasting examples and nonexamples of the concepts.
- With carefully chosen examples, it is possible to use concept attainment to teach almost any concept.

Cooperative Learning

- Cooperative learning has emerged as a promising instructional approach.
- Forms of cooperative learning include peer tutoring, student teams achievement division, group investigation, and the jigsaw strategy.

Simulations and Games

- Simulations are problem situations that are intended to represent reality.
- Role-playing is useful in getting students to look at the motives behind actions and behaviors.
- Educational games involve students in decision-making roles.

Individualized Strategies

- Individualized strategies include individualized instruction, independent study, mastery learning, and drill and practice. They represent techniques tailored to fit students' needs and abilities.
- Individualization can be provided by students working at their own pace on different objectives, working with different materials, and working on essays or projects.
- Mastery learning represents a model of instruction where students continue their work on unit objectives until mastery is achieved.
- Mastery learning represents a diagnostic-corrective-enrichment approach to instruction.

Drill and Practice

- Drill and practice provide students with needed accuracy and/or speed.
- Drill is usually concerned with the recall of associations, whereas practice is more often concerned with improvement.

Discussion Questions and Activities

1. **Demonstration topics.** Generate a list of demonstrations that would be appropriate at the grade level you expect to teach. Once you have compiled your topics, separate them as appropriate only for teachers to do and those that students could do.
2. **Integrated directed methods.** When is it appropriate to use integrated directed teaching methods? Consider your instructional intent, as well as the students themselves. Would mastery learning be appropriate for the students you expect to teach?
3. **Diversity.** Could you use cooperative learning at the grade level you expect to teach? What form would work best? How would you accommodate diversity?
4. **Role-playing.** Identify some core values (American, school, community, etc.) that could be taught using role-playing (for example: honesty, fairness).
5. **Educational games.** Suppose a parent criticized your use of games in the classroom; prepare a response entitled "Why Our School Uses Games."
6. **Individualized strategies.** If individualized strategies are so important and beneficial, why are they not implemented by all teachers? Give your reasons and justify them.

Connection With the Field

1. **Teacher interviews.** Visit with several classroom teachers and discuss with them how they use integrated directed instruction. Do they use individualized strategies extensively? Why or why not?
2. **Classroom observation.** Visit several public school classrooms. Keep a record of the different methods used. What integrated directed methods did you observe? Was there a pattern? Was drill and practice used?
3. **Teaching.** Prepare and teach a minilesson using the demonstration method. Use the microteaching guidelines and forms in Appendix B to plan and analyze your minilesson.
4. **Teaching analysis.** Make a videotape of your miniteaching lesson; then critically analyze it with your peers.

Praxis II Connection

The following test preparation exercises are intended to help you prepare for the Praxis II: Principles of Learning and Teaching. The Praxis II may be required by your teacher education preparatory program and for state certification or licensing. These exercises will give you direct access to pedagogical knowledge from Chapter 8 that may be expected of you on the Praxis II and other pedagogical exams that may be required at the end of your teacher education program.

Topic Connections

1. Integrated direct instruction (II. A1, A2, A3)

Describe the basic format of integrated direct teaching approaches. When is it appropriate to use the integrated direct instruction format?

2. Integrated direct instruction (II. A2, A3)

Describe the teacher's roles in integrated directed instruction. Compare these roles with the roles of the teacher in the direct teaching approaches.

3. Cooperative learning (II. A1, A2, A3)

Outline the basic cooperative learning structure and strategies. Describe the two essential cooperative learning characteristics.

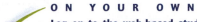

ON YOUR OWN

Log on to the web-based student study site at http://www.sagepub.com/eis for more information about the vignettes and materials presented in this chapter, suggestions for activities, study aids such as electronic flashcards and review quizzes, and research recommendations including journal article links and questions related to this chapter.

9

USING INDIRECT
TEACHING METHODS

What we learn to do, we learn by doing.

ARISTOTLE

OVERVIEW

Many theorists argue that learning is an active process. Indeed, they suggest that your function as a teacher is to act as a facilitator, a guide. They view your function as provider of participatory experiences that will result in the desired learning. This chapter will examine indirect approaches to instruction. Discussions, discovery, and inquiry are indirect participatory alternatives.

OBJECTIVES

After completing your study of Chapter 9, you should be able to do the following:

1. Discuss reasons for using various participatory-teaching techniques as well as advantages and disadvantages associated with their use.
2. Describe the primary roles associated with various discussion techniques and the respective responsibilities.
3. Explain the four areas that must be addressed in effective discussion planning.
4. Identify strengths and limitations associated with various small-group discussion structures.
5. Compare and contrast the purpose and function of the small-group structures of brainstorming, buzz groups, task groups, and panels.
6. Describe the major purpose, characteristics, teacher role, and desired environment associated with heuristic modes of instruction, namely, discovery and inquiry.
7. Differentiate between discovery and inquiry learning.
8. Define *problem solving* and distinguish between the three levels of problem solving.
9. Outline and explain the five-step discovery model, or general scientific method of investigation and the three-step inquiry approach.
10. Identify strengths and weaknesses associated with various heuristic methods.

11. Explain the basic features of Richard Suchman's inquiry learning and the procedures associated with its use.

12. Describe the teacher's function and the appropriate environment conducive to effective implementation of the heuristic methods.

Two major functions of education are the development of students' ability to think critically and the development of their ability to perform independent inquiry. This is often difficult, if not impossible, with the more direct teaching strategies. Fortunately, as a teacher you have at your disposal a wide range of methods of a more participatory nature. These indirect methods typically are less teacher-directed, but they are more time-consuming.

The Discussion Method

An important, but infrequently used indirect teaching method is the classroom **discussion**. What all too frequently passes for a classroom discussion is really nothing more than a lecture with periodic questioning-answering sequences. In a true discussion, students should talk more than the teacher. A discussion is not a "bull" session, however, but a carefully structured exchange of ideas directed toward a specific goal.

Two kinds of classroom goals are conducive to the discussion method. First, many subjects pose questions that have no simple answers. For example, is there a simple answer to the cause of war? What can be done about the rising cost of medical care? How was the work of Ernest Hemingway influenced by the politics of that period? Questions of this type are open to interpretation. Through discussion of issues from history, government, economics, literature, and science, students develop understanding of the issues, rather than simply receiving and rehearsing factual information. Thus, discussing controversial issues often increases knowledge about the issues, as well as encouraging deeper understanding of the various sides of an issue (Johnson & Johnson, 1985).

The second type of goal that lends itself to the use of the discussion method involves situations in which issues from the affective domain are being addressed. Indeed, the discussion method usually is far more effective than the lecture method at changing attitudes, values, and behaviors. A discussion about drug use, for example, would likely tap into students' attitudes more than a lecture would. Similarly, discussions on issues such as voting, AIDS, poverty, types of music, and art can lead to the establishment of such attitudes as civic duty, patriotism, public-health concerns, and a commitment to the arts.

Open communication and a supportive atmosphere are keys to effective discussions. The classroom should serve as an open forum in which students can feel free to express their opinions as well as review factual material. Certain roles and procedures, however, are essential to the success of the discussion procedure.

First, the teacher's role becomes less a director of learning and more a facilitator of or guide to learning. But an active purposeful leader is needed in guiding the discussion. This individual can be the teacher or, even better, a student. Leaders should not dominate the discussion but, instead, should see that the discussion starts smoothly by making sure that everyone understands the purpose and topic of the discussion. Once introduced, the discussion must be kept moving and on track. Thus, discussion leaders occasionally must pose questions to the group and to individuals. These questions should be designed for keeping the discussion on track, preventing individuals from dominating the discussion, getting various individuals involved if they are not participating, and making sure alternative viewpoints are addressed. Finally, the discussion leader should be prepared to summarize periodically the major point of the discussion.

Second, discussions need a recorder (or secretary), who will keep notes on the key points made, create a summary of results, and record the group's conclusions. Occasionally, the teacher may want to assume the recorder role and designate a student group leader. The record can even be displayed on the chalkboard or on an overhead projector, which makes it possible for the participants to see and use the record for reference purposes.

Third, the participants are expected to be prepared, and they should peruse the materials provided for the discussion. They should be ready to listen, give each other the opportunity for expressing differing opinions, and ask questions.

Finally, in a discussion, as the teacher, you can assume the role of leader, recorder, or a consultant—ready to provide needed resources or advice. Whatever role you assume, you must plan the discussion and make sure the plan is executed. Let's now look at the planning phase of the discussion method.

APPLY AND REFLECT: Can the discussion method be used effectively at any grade level? In any subject? Is it more suitable for certain grade levels and/or subject areas? If so, what grade levels and subject areas?

Planning the Discussion

Although few actual materials are usually required in implementing the discussion method, lessons that emphasize the technique must be well organized. If not, most discussions will disintegrate into a sharing of ignorance or into chaos. Basically, four areas must be addressed when planning a discussion activity.

First, you must carefully consider your goals and student preparation needed to achieve these goals. Your goals most likely will be the acquisition of content knowledge or the exploration of attitudes or values. Unlike other methods in which the content or background information is an integral part of the lesson, however, discussions will require that students be thoroughly conversant with the related information prior to the discussion. That is, students must have something to discuss if the discussion method is to work. Thus, it is essential that you direct your students to be prepared with regard to content knowledge or background information prior to the discussion. This preparation may require that they read an assigned chapter, conduct research, or, in the case of attitudes and value-issue discussions, form a personal position to support.

Learning by Doing

1. If students learn best by doing, can we teach all subjects, attitudes, and skills "by doing"? Why or why not?
2. Is "learning by doing" more applicable to the elementary, middle school, or high school classroom?

It is unfortunate that Columbine High School has changed the reputation of our young people. All the stereotypes of "sex, drugs, and violence" are, after all, true, and we must change our schools to prevent such a disaster from ever taking place again! Fortunately, Columbine is merely an aberration—tragic, but in no way typical of today's young people.

At Shawnee Mission Northwest High School just the opposite has been true since the day it opened in 1969. The students have collected food, clothing, and even presents for all the men at the state prison. In 1991, it was decided to make this an autonomous class. It was eventually called "Cougars Community Commitment." It is a social science offering for a half-credit per semester. It is open to juniors and seniors, and, with approval of the sponsor, students may enroll for as many as four semesters.

Seventeen students were enrolled the first year, and those 17 set a standard few classes have met. Few in the community took the class seriously: Rake the lawn, mow my grass at no charge?! The class motto was simply "THE DOER OF GOOD BECOMES GOOD!" It was and is our opinion that what we used to take for granted now has to be taught. Goodness needs to be nurtured but never taken for granted.

—RONALD W. POPLAU, *High School Social Studies Teacher, Shawnee Mission Northwest High School, Shawnee, Kansas*

SOURCE: Randi Stone's Best Practices for High School Teachers: What Award-Winning Secondary Teachers Do. Reprinted by permission.

Second, you must decide whether the discussion should be a large-group (whole-class) or small-group activity. Small-group activities might take such forms as buzz groups, brainstorming sessions, or task groups. The particular type of group used is related to the lesson goals. If the goals are the development of better content understanding or abilities to analyze, synthesize, and evaluate, a large-group activity would be most appropriate. The development of leadership skills, social skills, listening skills, or other related skills, however, would probably call for a small-group activity. Whole-group discussions have some definite advantages—the primary one being the ability to keep the discussion focused on the topic. In addition, it is often much easier to maintain control with whole-class discussions. Unlike small-group techniques, however, whole-class discussions do not give students the opportunity for practicing active listening, editing of ideas, idea building, communication, and turn taking. Thus, if such skills are your goals, small-group work might help you accomplish these goals.

Third, seating must be considered. A productive discussion requires interaction, which often is directly related to the seating arrangement. Seating should

Figure 9.1

Large-Class Discussion Seating Arrangements (To maximize interaction, students should be seated in a circular or hollow-square arrangement. Arrows pointing through the center indicate that the individual was speaking to the total group. Leader and recorder positions are marked with an X.)

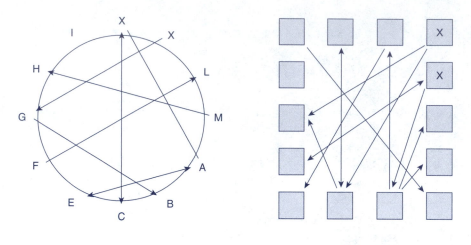

Figure 9.2

Small-Group Discussion Seating Arrangements (Leader and recorder positions are marked with an X.)

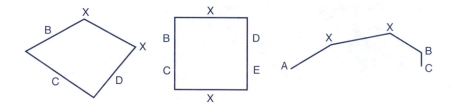

be arranged so that students can look directly at each other when they interact. Figure 9.1 shows two possible whole-class arrangements. Note that any student can make eye contact with any other student without turning. Similarly, Figure 9.2 shows three possible small-group arrangements that should maximize interaction.

Finally, you must consider the time allotted for the activity. Plan for about 45-minute discussion periods with older students, shorter periods with younger students. In general, the time given for small-group discussions depends on the type of small group and its function. Small-group discussion time, however, generally is relatively short. Indeed, a good format to follow is to give students very explicit directions as to what is to be accomplished and a time limit for the discussion.

Only careful planning will result in a successful discussion activity. This planning requires that you have a thorough understanding of the characteristics and function of the two basic discussion forms: whole class and small group.

Whole-Class Discussions

Whole-class discussions are similar in some respects to the class-recitation method. You or a designated discussion leader pose questions, listen to student answers, react, and probe for more information. In the true whole-class discussion, however, you try to assume a less dominant role. Rather, you should assume the role of passive moderator and create a pleasant atmosphere conducive to free interaction. Neither you nor any class member should dominate the discussion. Your major task is to make the total class session more interactive.

When carrying out a whole-class discussion, you first should make sure your topic is appropriate for whole-class discussion and that the class has an adequate knowledge base. Next, make up a plan for the discussion that lays out a procedure (agenda), time limits, and discussion ground rules. For example, your procedure might include a teacher introduction session, followed by a 30-minute discussion, followed by a teacher-directed wrap-up. In addition to your 30-minute discussion time limit, you also might set a 2-minute time limit for each student to speak. You also could lay down ground rules such as these: (1) give a summary of the last student's comments before making your own; (2) sarcasm is not allowed; (3) no one will make fun of another student's ideas or comments; and (4) only the discussion topic will be addressed in making comments.

Plan a lively springboard or set that will get the discussion started. For example, you might start the discussion with a short film, a role-playing exercise, an open-ended question, or a contrived situation. Once the discussion has begun, it is the leader's function to keep it on track, summarize as needed, and involve all class members through the use of questions, the redirecting technique, and reinforcement. Finally, the discussion points must be brought to a logical conclusion.

Textbooks are an essential part of most classes, but their value usually suffers through a lack of integration into various teaching strategies. Indeed, in most classrooms, the textbook is integrated into the lecture method only. An effective way of improving student learning, however, is through whole-class discussions built around textbook content. One such strategy, called *listen-read-and-discuss,* begins with a teacher's short overview lecture of the textbook material, which is to be read by students (Alvermann, Moore, & Conley, 1987). This short introductory lecture should serve as an advance organizer and should set the framework for the material subsequently read by the class. A discussion of the content material follows. This procedure allows students to compare their understanding of the reading with the teacher's presentation. Further, it gives the teacher the opportunity for evaluating and getting feedback on students' understanding of the concepts covered.

APPLY AND REFLECT: Name some topics that would be appropriate for whole-class discussions.

Small-Group Discussions

As with any discussion, *small-group discussions* should follow the presentation of information through teacher-directed lessons, assignments, books, or films. When students are adequately prepared, they should form their groups and start to work.

Successful small-group learning requires very careful planning. The different groups will probably gather and work in different parts of the classroom. Under such conditions, it is impossible for you to be with each group. Therefore, you must provide students with clear guidelines regarding their task and responsibilities. You

Leadership can often be developed through involvement in small-group activities.

should appoint a responsible, well-organized student as leader for each group. The leader's function is to keep the group on task, to guide them toward completion of that task, and to ensure that all group members participate. An appointed group recorder should also write down the group's ideas and conclusions. Upon completion of the group activity, each group should be required to report to the rest of the class.

What is the optimal size for small-group learning? There is no easy answer to this question. But some literature suggests that groups of five to seven work best (Dillion, 1987). In larger groups, it is too easy for students to hide and not participate in the interaction, and smaller groups lack the diversity of opinions needed in the interaction.

Small-group instruction has several strengths, chief among which are the development of communication skills, leadership abilities, open-mindedness, persuasive arguing, and other interpersonal skills. In addition, group work often leads to a stronger sense of personal commitment to decisions made by the group than those made by the whole class or individuals. Finally, students involved in small-group work are usually given more opportunity for active verbal participation and, in some cases, for physical movement.

Small-group discussion has its limitations as well as strengths. One of the primary problems is the tendency for students to quickly drift off task and the activity too often disintegrates into bickering and becomes a waste of time. Another danger of small groups concerns the group composition. It is possible—and quite likely—that some groups cannot work together cooperatively, or that they include students with very similar (or very different) points of view or interests. Such groups often have difficulty reaching conclusions. Careful teacher planning and supervision, however, can combat the limitations associated with small groups.

Groups are often formed and structured for achieving specific purposes. The kinds of groups and functions that can be formed in your classroom are limited in scope only by your own creative design capabilities. Let's now look at four such small-group types.

Brainstorming

Brainstorming is a small-group activity used to generate ideas. The brainstorming session is started by the leader, who introduces a topic or problem and asks each small group to generate ideas, solutions, or comments. The topic can be as simple as "What topics should the class study for enrichment?" or as complex as "What can we do about the low class test scores?" All answers, no matter how wrong, should be accepted as possible solutions. No comments about or reactions to contributions should be allowed until all groups have reported their ideas.

Brainstorming sometimes results in a mood of delightful quest. Therefore, you should emphasize the need for decency and decorum. At the same time, participants need to realize that quantity of suggestions is paramount.

Brainstorming is an excellent initiating process for another activity, such as another discussion, research, problem solving, or small-group activities. For example, the brainstorming suggestions can be evaluated, and those deemed worthy of further study can be addressed in follow-up activities.

Buzz Group

A **buzz group** is a work group of relatively short duration. Such a group is established quickly to share opinions, viewpoints, or reactions. The group can be formed easily by counting off or by having those in proximity form a group.

Buzz groups usually consist of from four to seven members and rarely meet for more than 15 minutes. They can be established for a brief discussion of certain ideas or course content. The buzz session then should be followed up with a whole-class discussion of the conclusions or findings.

Task Group

A **task group** sets out to solve a problem or complete a project. Unlike other types of discussion, however, task groups involve students in some kind of work or activity, and each group member has a role or an assignment that is clearly defined for all group members. Their size usually ranges from four to eight members, depending on the problem or project.

Task groups tend to be teacher-directed. The teacher selects the tasks and assigns the group members specific responsibilities. The teacher may also find it beneficial to establish a work schedule and monitoring system. In addition, the teacher should make available any resources needed in accomplishing the identified tasks.

Task groups are best suited for a small number of students who are, or can be, fairly self-directed. The students should be able to create an uninhibited, but productive, environment in which discussion can be free and open.

Panels

Panels, which also are referred to as *round tables*, are a special form of the small-group approach. A group of students—usually five to eight—prepare in advance an informal discussion about an assigned issue to be presented in front of the class. One student usually serves as panel chair and directs the discussion. Each panel member makes an informal opening statement; however, no speeches as such are made. A give-and-take session between panel members and members of the class follows the opening statement and discussion.

The topics for panel discussions can evolve from ongoing class activities, or they can be anticipated and planned by the teacher. Identification of controversial areas within a given unit is often a relatively simple matter; however, the best panel discussions come from issues that are important and meaningful to the students.

Most students will need teacher assistance in preparing for their panels. For most panel issues, the group should be given about a week's preparation time. Part of this preparation time should be given in class, so that you can oversee the development of their presentations.

You should brief students carefully on the panel procedure to be followed. The initial-panelist presentations should be limited, for example, to about 15 minutes. After this more formal portion of the panel presentation, the discussion should be opened up for a class discussion of the topic or for a question-and-answer session from the audience. This open-ended session then should be followed by a summary of the important points by the panel chairperson.

APPLY AND REFLECT: Name some topics or tasks that would be appropriate for small-group discussions. What type of small-group structure would be best for each topic or task?

Planning and conducting a discussion lesson can be challenging. Complete Web Link: Discussions to further explore discussion techniques.

W E B   L I N K   **Discussions**

Search the Web and locate a discussion lesson plan appropriate for the grade level you expect to teach. Dissect the lesson's component parts. Describe the quality of your chosen lesson and how you think it could be improved.

This concludes the examination of the various discussion techniques. Table 9.1 summarizes the different discussion teaching methods. Review the summary and complete Review, Extension, and Reflective Exercise 9.1.

TABLE 9.1 Discussion Methods

Method	Description
Whole-Class Discussion	All students in class exchange and share ideas regarding an assigned topic
Small-Class Discussion	Five to eight students interact and/or work together in reaching conclusions, generating ideas, or completing a task
Panels	Five to eight students prepare and discuss topics in front of class

Review, Extension, and Reflective Exercise 9.1

Describe the various discussion techniques and their strengths and limitations.

Connections to INTASC Standards:

- Standard 4: Instructional Strategies. The teacher must understand and use a variety of instructional strategies to encourage students' development of critical thinking, problem solving, and performance skills.
- Standard 5: Learning Environment. The teacher must be able to use an understanding of individual and group motivation and behavior to create a learning environment that encourages positive social interaction, active engagement in learning, and self-motivation.
- Standard 6: Communication. The teacher uses knowledge of effective verbal, nonverbal, and media communication techniques to foster active inquiry, collaboration, and supportive interaction in the classroom.

- Standard 7: Planning Instruction. The teacher plans instruction based upon knowledge of subject matter, students, the community, and curriculum goals.

Connections to the NBPTS:

- Proposition 2: Teachers must know the subjects they teach and how to teach those subjects to students.
- Proposition 4: Teachers must think systematically about their practice and learn from experience.

Review

- Describe the characteristics of the true discussion.
- What are some pros and cons of the discussion teaching method?
- Describe the different discussion formats.

Reflection

- Can the discussion approach to learning be adapted to any grade level? Why or why not?

Heuristic Methods

Teaching can be organized so that it is active, somewhat self-directed, inquiring, and reflective. Such modes of instruction are referred to as *heuristic* teaching methods. In this section, I will address some modes that are designated as heuristic approaches: discovery, inquiry, and the Richard Suchman inquiry methods of instruction.

Confusion often is expressed when the discovery and inquiry methods are discussed. Some educators use the terms interchangeably, whereas others feel they represent subcategories of each other. For the purposes of this textbook, the discovery and inquiry methods will be considered as unique, yet somewhat related, techniques. Because the **heuristic approach** actively involves students in problem solving, let's begin our study of the heuristic modes by looking at the problem-solving process.

Problem Solving

A problem exists whenever something gives rise to uncertainty. The literature generated by John Dewey from 1884 to 1948 advocated a curriculum that was based on problems. Some contemporary curricula and a large number of textbooks rely heavily on Dewey's problem-solving approach, along with direct experiences. That is, students are required to solve problems through direct experiences provided by the teacher. Therefore, a good working definition of **problem solving** is the intentional elimination of uncertainty through direct experiences and under supervision.

Because preparing students to solve everyday problems is an important function of schools, curricular specialists who advocate a problem-solving instructional approach suggest that schools should develop traits (or behaviors) that enable individuals to be effective problem solvers. Furthermore, the experiences provided by the school should articulate the content and processes needed to produce successful problem solvers.

Problem solving actively involves students in their own learning. The amount of decision making performed by students, however, can be classified according to three levels of involvement. As depicted in Table 9.2, Level I is the traditional teacher-directed method, in which the problem, as well as the processes and procedures leading to an intended conclusion, is provided for students. This level of problem solving can also be referred to as guided problem solving. Level I problem solving is highly manageable and predictable. It is probably best for students without the ability to engage in higher mental operations and best for teaching basic concepts.

In Level II, problems are usually defined by the teacher or the textbook, whereas the processes for solving the problems are left for students to develop. Level II problem solving gives the learners the opportunity, often for the first time, to find out something by themselves through their own independent skills.

Level III represents almost total self-direction. Students generate the problems and then design ways to solve these problems. This level is often referred to as open problem solving.

Ideally, you should have students independently identify some of their class problems and the procedures for solving them. Student-identified national problems, for example, are an excellent source of issues for supplemental inclusion in a

TABLE 9.2 Levels of Problem Solving

Level	I	II	III
Problem Identification	Generated by teacher or textbook	Generated by teacher or textbook	Generated by student
Processes for Solving Problem	Decided by teacher or textbook	Decided by student	Decided by student
Establishment of Tentative Solution to Problem	Determined by students	Determined by students	Determined by students

"Earth science, close up."

social studies, civics, or government class. Care should be taken, however, in the amount of independence given students. Some students will be unable to benefit from such freedom and, therefore, such an activity should be delayed until a later date.

APPLY AND REFLECT: What level of problem solving would work best at the elementary level? Middle school level? Secondary school level?

Discovery Learning

Discovery learning is a means by which students engage in problem solving in developing knowledge or skills. A good working definition of *discovery learning* is intentional learning through supervised problem solving following the scientific method of investigation. Thus, with discovery, the learning must be planned, it must be supervised, and it must follow the scientific method of investigation (see Figure 9.3). As noted earlier, discovery learning is frequently confused with inquiry.

Actually, both discovery and inquiry are specific kinds of problem solving. Whereas discovery follows an established pattern of investigation, inquiry has no such established pattern: Discovery learning follows the general scientific method

Figure 9.3

General Scientific Model of Investigation

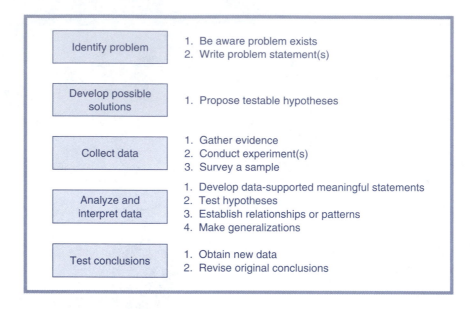

Identify problem	1. Be aware problem exists 2. Write problem statement(s)
Develop possible solutions	1. Propose testable hypotheses
Collect data	1. Gather evidence 2. Conduct experiment(s) 3. Survey a sample
Analyze and interpret data	1. Develop data-supported meaningful statements 2. Test hypotheses 3. Establish relationships or patterns 4. Make generalizations
Test conclusions	1. Obtain new data 2. Revise original conclusions

for conducting an investigation, shown in Figure 9.3. There is no such method for inquiry learning.

Discovery learning can take place at three levels, depending on the level of problem solving (review Table 9.2). At Level I, discovery learning is carefully guided (*guided discovery*); at Level II, a moderate amount of guidance is administered (*modified discovery*); and at Level III, it is very casually supervised (*open discovery*).

The collection of data is a significant component of discovery learning.

Discovery Learning Strategies

The degree of success of discovery learning depends in a large part on your ability to plan and execute the problem-solving process effectively. Your role is to provide a situation that lets students identify a contradiction or uncertainty and then to guide and assist them in finding a relationship between what they already know and the newly discovered knowledge. Essentially, you direct the planning, organization, and execution of the general scientific method of investigation (review Figure 9.3).

Selecting the Problem. Although problem solving is emphasized in discovery learning, students often lack the sophistication to identify their own problems (open discovery); that is, students usually lack the expertise for involvement in Level III problem solving (review Table 9.2). Therefore, you must be prepared to suggest problems or areas in which students may seek problems.

Discovery learning works well with many subjects. Science, geometry, social studies, art, and mathematics all provide many opportunities for discovery learning. For example, in a science class, you might suggest an examination of pollution in the local river; in a social studies class, you could suggest an investigation of voter apathy; in an art class, you might have students mix colors; in a mathematics class, a discussion of societal mathematics needs might suggest an examination of the mathematics skills needed by individuals in various occupations.

Language arts and other subjects that are not as obviously discovery-oriented can still be presented with the discovery method. Completing crosswords or other puzzles, using a computer spell checker, discussing recently read literature, presenting dramatic plays with specified situations but without scripts, following maps created by a partner, working in small groups to solve a common problem, and creating and operating puppets are just a few examples. Another example of discovery learning for social studies would be during a lesson about another culture. You could select a traditional cultural recipe. The difficulty of the recipe would depend upon the age and ability of the students. The ingredients, tools, and written recipe would be made available to students. You could allow students to make the food according to the recipe directions. Figure 9.4 offers some additional discovery learning activities.

Suitable problems should not be left to chance. Left alone, students often flounder or select problems that are not suitable for your course or they may select problems whose solution requires materials and equipment that are not available or problems that are too large and unyielding.

Once students have a general grasp of the problem, you must help them clarify and state the problem in clear, precise terms. You should be prepared to make suggestions or ask questions that will assist students in knowing exactly what they want to find out. These suggestions or questions should be such that students are forced to think and analyze the problem situation for clarity; that is, you should help students make sure they are clear on what problem is to be studied.

Clarification of the problem is a crucial step in finding a solution. If this crucial step is neglected, students often have difficulty in knowing exactly where to start in attempting to find a solution.

Proposing Possible Solutions. Once students clearly define the problem, hypotheses and solutions must be generated. Accomplishment of this task requires that data be collected and analyzed. Your function will be to provide materials or make

Figure 9.4
Discovery Learning
Activities

Flashlight Fixing

Materials:

- Shoe boxes
- Working flashlights with bulbs and batteries
- Paper and pencil

Take the flashlights apart. For younger children simply remove the batteries. For older children also remove the light bulb. Put the flashlights and the various parts into the shoe boxes. Instruct the children to put the flashlights together so they will work. Children should record their discoveries.

Car Design

Materials:

- Books about automobiles, transportation, and/or simple machines such as the wheel
- Several small boxes such as shoe boxes, tissue boxes, or gift boxes
- Items to create wheels and axles such as paper towel tubes, cardboard, dowel rods, plastic coffee can lids, rubber balls, spools, etc.
- Scissors
- Glue
- Tape
- Crayons, watercolor markers, or paints—optional

Read to the children or have the children read one or more of the selected books. Instruct children to use the craft items or others they find to create cars with wheels that roll.

Baking Bread

Materials:

- A gingerbread or cornbread recipe or for younger children a mix
- The ingredients for making the bread and all the bowls and utensils
- Adult supervision for the baking

Provide children with all the ingredients and tools needed to make the mix and ready it for the oven. Supervise the baking, placing into and removing the bread from the oven if need be. Once it has baked and is sufficiently cool, have the children serve and taste the results.

suggestions about where data can be located and to provide resources where information related to the problem area can be obtained.

When students are proposing possible solutions, you should encourage guessing and intuitive thought. Also, encourage healthy skepticism and practice in suspending judgment. Ideally, you want to give students the opportunity to express all their ideas in a nonthreatening environment.

Collecting of Data. Proposed solutions must be tested; that is, each of the generated hypotheses must be checked for validity. Thus, additional data must be amassed. Data collection sometimes requires that experiments be set up and carried out. At other times, surveys must be conducted. Students often need guidance and assistance with their data-collection tools and techniques. Experiments must yield valid results, and surveys must provide usable data, which often calls for planning and the development of appropriate instrumentation. Students may need your assistance with such planning and instrumentation.

Data Analysis and Interpretation. Once collected, data must be analyzed and interpreted. Criteria must be established, and the validity of hypotheses must be judged against these criteria. You might need to guide students in making such judgments and in determining their validity. Students often think they have proven a hypothesis, when, in fact, they have not.

Based upon the interpretation of data, conclusions must be established. Thus, the data must be carefully examined and evaluated so that conclusions are supported by the data. Although you should not establish conclusions for students, you can help in this process by pointing out patterns, showing relationships, and asking questions. With your help, students should develop skill in reaching plausible conclusions to their identified problems.

Testing Conclusions. Once established, conclusions must be tested and revised. Consequently, the final step in the problem-solving component of discovery is the generation of data that will lend support to the identified conclusions or that will lead to revisions of the conclusions.

Benefits of Discovery Learning

Discovery learning is active rather than passive learning. **Active learning** tends to result in a higher degree of intrinsic motivation. With verbal teaching methods, motivation comes only from your comments following class contributions, following correctly answered questions, or from grades received on assignments. In discovery learning, motivation comes from the activity itself and the excitement of direct involvement. This activity and excitement have the added advantage of increased learning and better retention. Students tend to learn more and retain information longer when they are actively involved in the learning process. Explore further benefits of discovery learning by completing Expansion Activity: Discovery Learning.

EXPANSION ACTIVITY   **Write a short essay explaining how discovery learning is related to constructivist theory.**

Discovery
Learning

___

Discovery learning also fosters the development of positive social skills. Obviously, discovery learning requires that students work cooperatively. They must develop skill in planning, following established procedures, and working together toward the successful completion of common tasks.

Limitations of Discovery Learning

The greatest limitation associated with discovery learning probably is the demand it places on you and your students. Because discovery learning is a cooperative process rather than a competitive one, it calls for an adjustment—by students and teacher alike—to the very nature of discovery. With the lack of competition, there is little feedback as to how well students are doing and how much learning is taking place. This lack of feedback often leads to uncertainty for you and for students.

Discovery learning can also be an inefficient system for covering large amounts of material. This limitation is a major concern to teachers who feel they are expected to cover all the material in the textbook.

Inquiry Learning

Like discovery, **inquiry** basically is a problem-solving technique. Unlike discovery, however, the emphasis is placed on the process of investigating the problem, rather than on reaching a correct solution. In fact, although inquiry is concerned with problem solving, it does not require solutions to the problems being investigated. Thus, whereas with discovery learning a set pattern is followed by reaching a solution, no established pattern exists with inquiry learning. Indeed, different students may use different strategies in obtaining information related to a problem. Students may even take intuitive approaches to problems.

As with discovery learning, there are three levels to inquiry learning: guided inquiry, modified inquiry, and open inquiry. Thus, you may want to identify the problem and then decide how to investigate it (guided inquiry), you may want to identify the problem and then have students decide how to go about finding out about it (modified inquiry), or you may want the students to identify the problem and then design ways for obtaining information (open inquiry).

Inquiry Learning Strategies

The inquiry approach is flexible yet systematic. It is systematic in that a basic, three-step problem-solving procedure is followed (review Table 9.2), yet it is flexible in that the activities used in addressing the problem may vary. Let's now look at this three-step procedure.

Identifying the Problem. Inquiry learning is closely related to discovery learning. Thus, the problem-selection processes are essentially identical, with either the teacher deciding (as in guided or modified inquiry) or the students deciding (as in open inquiry) the problems or issues to be addressed. This decision, of course, depends on the sophistication of the students. In short, you must decide whether students are ready and have the skill to identify suitable problems for study. In most cases, however, you must continually monitor the problem-identification process and provide guidance or suitable alternatives for consideration.

Working Toward Solutions. The second task in an inquiry lesson is to work on a solution to the problem. Again, there should be no set prescription or rules governing the procedure for finding a solution. In fact, decisions regarding strategies directed toward a solution can be teacher-orchestrated (guided inquiry) or student-orchestrated (modified and open inquiry).

The emphasis in inquiry learning should be placed on the process of finding a *problem's* solution, not on the solution itself. Whenever appropriate and within limits, students should be given the opportunity to devise their own strategies for addressing problem situations. Some may want to attack a problem through the literature and a search of textbooks, whereas others may want to interview experts in the problem area, and others may want to design and carry out experiments. In a word, the teacher should provide the freedom to enable students to develop creative approaches to problem solving. These opportunities show students how inquiry works in the real world.

Establishing Solutions. The success of inquiry learning is not necessarily dependent on reaching a predetermined conclusion. Even when directed by the teacher, inquiry learning should be a highly personal experience for each individual involved. Individuals should be given the opportunities for applying themselves totally—so they may put their fullest talents, ideas, skills, and judgments to work in reaching their own conclusions.

Unfortunately, our traditional educational system has worked in a way that discourages the natural process of inquiry. Students become less prone to ask questions as they move through the grade levels. In traditional schools, students learn not to ask too many questions; instead they are trained to listen and repeat the expected answers. Figure 9.5 offers an example of an inquiry lesson for young children.

Figure 9.5

Inquiry Lesson for Young Children

Grade level: K–1

Description: Young children should explore an awareness of themselves in a social setting. This lesson lays the foundation for the study of school and family life.

Prior to this lesson the children learned about *families* so they have an understanding about different types of families. In this lesson, children will speculate about where families live, examine pictures of different types of houses and locations, and draw conclusions.

Materials: Dollhouse, flip chart, pictures of different types of homes

Instructional Objectives:

Students will:

- Speculate about where families might live.
- Describe different types of homes based on a set of pictures.
- Describe simple differences and similarities among ways people live in different locations.
- Develop a general statement indicating that families live in a variety of homes that provide for family needs.

Figure 9.5
(Continued)

Procedures:

1. Introduction and motivation
   a. Place the class dollhouse in the center of the classroom. *Ask: If this were a real house, how would a family use it?*
   b. Allow children to describe how the rooms might be used. *Ask: Why is it important for families to have a place to live?* Important reasons may include: sleep, eat, keep warm, and play.

2. Have students develop some guesses
   a. *Ask: Where do people live?*
   b. Students may respond that people live in houses. If so,
      i. Write the word houses on the flip chart.
      ii. Stimulate guessing. *Ask: Does everyone live in the same type of house?*

3. Looking at pictures
   a. *Say: Those are really good ideas. Let's look at some pictures of houses and see if we can get some more ideas.*
   b. Show pictures: (a) suburban house, (b) complex in city, (c) trailer house, (d) apartment house, (e) farmhouse. After each picture, *Ask: Tell me about this house.* Point out differences in style and location.
   c. Possible problem: Children unfamiliar with apartments may be confused about how families live in these buildings. Use the school as a comparison with the classrooms as apartments. Houses have rooms; apartments have rooms.

4. Adding to our list
   a. *Ask: Did we learn about some new houses?*
   b. *Say: Let's add those homes to our list.*

5. Conclusion
   a. Let's go back to our BIG question. Where do people live?
   b. *Ask: What can we say about where people live?*
   c. Outcome: People live in a variety of homes that provide for family needs.

6. Assessment
   a. Did the class develop the conclusion?
   b. Who participated in the discussion?

7. Possible follow-up activities
   a. Have children find and cut out pictures from magazines, brochures, catalogs, and old books that show different homes.
   b. Have children draw a picture of their home and have them talk about it with the class.

Suchman Inquiry Learning

J. Richard Suchman (1961, 1966) developed a junior high school-oriented program designed entirely around the concept of inquiry. This program, the Inquiry Development Program (IDP), placed emphasis on physical science and was

"Mrs. Broderick isn't as user-friendly as our teaching machines."

designed for developing the basic processes associated with inquiry. These processes varied, with some associated with data generating, some with data organizing, and some with idea building.

The basic feature of the **Suchman inquiry** is the concept of "discrepant event." These discrepant events were filmed physics demonstrations—originally presented in short, silent, color, loop cartridges—whose outcomes were contradictory to what was expected. A common example showed a teacher filling a collecting bottle to the brim with water and placing a 3-by-5-inch piece of cardboard over the mouth of the bottle. The bottle was then inverted, with the cardboard held firmly over the mouth. The hand supporting the cardboard was then taken away. The water remained in the bottle—and the cardboard firmly attached—even though the cardboard was not supported in any way. The title of each of these filmed demonstrations asked why the outcome of the demonstration occurred. The teacher's role was to develop an environment where inquiry could take place.

The original Suchman inquiry approach has changed in two ways. First, the episodes to be considered are usually shown directly through materials by the teacher rather than through films. Second, students receive more guidance from the teacher than did the students in the original program. But the basic purposes of the inquiry program, which were the development of skills in searching and data processing and the development of concepts through analysis of concrete problems, have not changed.

The Suchman inquiry approach focuses on the process by which information is acquired, rather than on the final information. The problem-solving process associated with this approach occurs in three steps: analyzing the episode, gathering information, and reaching conclusions.

Analyzing the Episode. A Suchman session is initiated by having students view a discrepant event. The event can be presented by the teacher or by playing one of the Suchman film loops. After the discrepant event has been presented, the teacher asks the class for ideas, guesses, or hypotheses as to what has transpired. Students are allowed to ask the teacher as many questions as they wish in their attempt to develop these explanations. There are three rules, however, that must be followed.

1. All questions to the teacher must be worded so that they can be answered with a yes or no.
2. One student has the floor at a time and can ask as many questions as he or she wants without being interrupted by the class.
3. The teacher will not respond to a question that asks for support of a student-originated theory or hypothesis.

These rules give students the freedom of establishing a sequence and pattern of questions that, in turn, will help lead them to possible hypotheses.

Gathering Information. Once a hypothesis has been presented, it is the class's responsibility to gather data that support or refute this hypothesis. Thus, students formulate their own hypothesis and then collect their own supporting or refuting data. The questions asked during this phase have to be phrased in such a way that allows tests to be set up to verify an answer. "Would the object sink in a different kind of liquid?" and "Would a heavier object sink in the liquid?" are examples of such questions. Also, during this phase, students attempt to determine what conditions were necessary for the final outcome to occur.

The Suchman inquiry approach requires a supportive atmosphere. Students must be given the opportunity to conduct any reasonable tests or experiments to check on the validity of their proposed hypotheses. Although the teacher does provide some information for assistance to students, the class is encouraged to seek data individually or in small groups without help from the teacher. Thus, in the typical Suchman inquiry session, students work independently, conducting experiments, reexamining the discrepant event, engaging in questioning sessions with the teacher, and involving themselves in an evaluation of data.

Reaching Conclusions. Based upon the data obtained, students draw their own conclusions and attempt to explain the cause of the observed phenomenon. In addition, they try to determine why the conditions identified were necessary for the final outcome.

The Suchman inquiry technique can be a valuable tool in a teacher's repertoire. By seeing how problems are solved in the classroom, models are provided that can be followed in solving problems in other areas of their lives.

Benefits of Inquiry Learning

The inquiry method of teaching has several unique benefits. First, it encourages students to develop creative solutions to problems: There are no rigid guidelines, so the imagination can be used without penalty. In fact, students sometimes can go off on tangents and address problems that have little to do with the original problem. Thus, investigations can be as original and limitless as students' imaginations. They are allowed to solve a problem any way they can.

Inquiry often stimulates interest and urges students to solve problems to the very limits of their abilities. They are not penalized for lack of content knowledge. Students are free to use the skills they do possess to reach their own solutions.

Last, because of the individuality possible in carrying out the problem-solving procedure, it is impossible to fail in inquiry learning. Students carry out the approach to the best of their abilities, and then stop without being penalized for not reaching a predetermined solution. Thus, students' self-confidence is enhanced.

Limitations of Inquiry Learning

Inquiry tends to appear, and sometimes tends to be, chaotic. It is possible in a class of 25 students to have as many as 25 different activities that address a single problem. Although the students involved generally cause few problems, inquiry can appear to be an undisciplined process in which little learning is taking place. Anticipating and locating materials can be a major problem. It is impossible to anticipate all the resources that students will require in one inquiry lesson. Indeed, some students may want to conduct experiments, whereas others may want special reference books in carrying out a literature search. Whatever the need, you must try to anticipate students' needs and make the materials available. This isn't an easy task.

As with discovery learning, a problem associated with inquiry learning is time: Giving students the freedom to engage in problem solving is time-consuming. Moreover, because students investigate to their own limits, some will finish quickly, whereas others will not want to stop their investigations.

A problem unique to inquiry is evaluation. Because you must provide grades, you need some criteria on which to base your evaluation. This problem can be overcome, to some extent, by having students keep records of their activities. From such reports, you can determine your students' progress.

APPLY AND REFLECT: What problems would you encounter in implementing the discovery learning method? Inquiry learning method? Are they appropriate for the grade level(s) you expect to teach?

Systemic Problem Solving

Problems that teachers and students face in and out of the classroom are seldom presented in a clearly defined form. Therefore, teachers must undertake a process to solve problems in a systematic, purposeful manner. The International Technology Education Association identified a process used for technological design that can be implemented in the classroom to help teachers and students alike learn how to solve a problem in a procedural-type approach. This technological design and problem-solving process has specific steps to initially follow, similar to the process when using the scientific method. This process, however, allows for criteria, constraints, efficiency, and trade-offs to be intertwined with human creativity. Although this process has steps to follow, it should be understood that the process is iterative. The steps in the design and problem-solving process are

1. Defining the problem.
2. Brainstorming.
3. Researching and generating ideas.
4. Identifying criteria and specifying constraints.
5. Exploring possibilities.
6. Selecting an approach.
7. Developing a design proposal.
8. Making a model or prototype.
9. Testing and evaluating the design using specifications.
10. Refining the design.
11. Creating or making the solution.
12. Communicating the processes and results.

The defining characteristics for the design and problem-solving process are that it is purposeful, based on certain requirements, systematic, and contains many possible solutions. Teachers have often thought that only one answer or solution can be the "right one" to solve a problem. In fact, there can be many different solutions to solve the same problem. Balancing the solution with the criteria, constraints, efficiency, and trade-offs of the design, will allow the teacher and the student to solve the problem in the most appropriate manner for the situation. Using problem solving as a teaching method can be a powerful approach to teaching and learning that draws on what students currently know and can explain about a given situation. The problem-solving approach as a teaching methodology used in conjunction with constructivist process may allow the teacher and students to reach a deeper level of understanding for not only the task at hand, but for lifelong learning.

This completes the discussion of the various heuristic teaching methods. Table 9.3 summarizes these methods. Review the summary and complete Review, Extension, and Reflective Exercise 9.2.

Since the teacher and environment are so important to the success of the indirect approaches to instruction, let's take a brief look at these two factors before we go on to thinking skill development.

TABLE 9.3 Heuristic Methods

Method	Description
Discovery	Intentional learning through supervised problem solving following the scientific method
Inquiry	Flexible yet systematic process of problem solving
Suchman Inquiry	Inquiry approach whereby students are presented with and asked to explain discrepant events

Review, Extension, and Reflective Exercise 9.2

Outline discovery and inquiry learning and the strengths and limitations associated with each.

Connections to INTASC Standards:

- Standard 4: Instructional Strategies. The teacher must understand and use a variety of instructional strategies to encourage students' development of critical thinking, problem solving, and performance skills.
- Standard 5: Learning Environment. The teacher must be able to use an understanding of individual and group motivation and behavior to create a learning environment that encourages positive social interaction, active engagement in learning, and self-motivation.
- Standard 6: Communication. The teacher uses knowledge of effective verbal, nonverbal, and media communication techniques to foster active inquiry, collaboration, and supportive interaction in the classroom.
- Standard 7: Planning Instruction. The teacher plans instruction based upon knowledge of subject matter, students, the community, and curriculum goals.

Connections to the NBPTS:

- Proposition 2: Teachers must know the subjects they teach and how to teach those subjects to students.
- Proposition 4: Teachers must think systematically about their practice and learn from experience.

Review

- Contrast discovery and inquiry learning.
- Describe the three levels of problem solving.
- What are the strengths and limitations of discovery and inquiry learning?
- What are the teacher's roles in discovery and inquiry learning?

Reflection

- Can all students be given the freedom needed to make discovery and inquiry learning successful? If not, why not? If yes, what are some areas of concern for you that must be overcome?

Teacher's Role

When using indirect approaches to instruction, you should function as a facilitator. Accomplishment of your goals, however, will usually call for continuous monitoring of students.

Active participatory methods require a close working relationship between you and your students. You must constantly be alert for hang-ups and stumbling blocks. Students must not simply be turned loose and allowed to flounder around or follow their own whims.

Although the various indirect participatory approaches to instruction are good preventive techniques against discipline problems, there are students in every school who, sometimes because of factors outside your control, will cause you difficulty. If these students won't meet you halfway, there's not much you can do about it. An interactive, constructivist approach that engages students in relevant, meaningful experiences is likely to be good preventive medicine against even the most difficult students. Indeed, this approach can often encourage and empower the most disheartened students. You must take every opportunity to interact with your students one-on-one and to really get to know them as individuals. Find out as much as you can about their experiences/interests, and try to connect to these whenever possible. This will be a challenge, but students who are turned off to school often have special interests and talents that you can tap.

Problem solving often requires special attention. You must help students constantly in their systematic investigation of problems. You must make sure that you or the students define the problem precisely, and then you must make sure problem-solving methodologies focus on and are appropriately applied to the various aspects of the problem. Indeed, the problem must be established, related issues must be clarified, ways of obtaining information must be proposed, and conclusions and discoveries must be formed. In fact, you would be wise to demand that students submit periodic progress reports related to their investigative progress.

A participatory approach to teaching requires in-depth planning. Don't expect to step into the classroom and wing it and be successful. If you don't plan thoroughly and thoughtfully, you will likely have major problems. Don't be discouraged when things don't work as well as you hoped. Make adjustments and try again. Don't fall into the student-blaming trap.

APPLY AND REFLECT: How would you make problem solving successful? What role would you assume?

Classroom Environment

Now that I have addressed the basic tenets of the various indirect methods and the respective teacher's roles, let's look at the kind of classroom environment that promotes such methods. First, the participatory methods imply a certain amount of freedom for exploring problems and arriving at possible solutions. Such freedom takes time—with a corresponding reduction in the amount of material that can be covered. Indeed, problem-solving episodes may last for a period of days or even weeks. At times, you may opt to conduct ongoing problem-solving episodes and regular, more teacher-directed lessons.

Active, self-directed, inquiring learning requires that students be directly involved in the quest for their own knowledge. To this end, the classroom must contain the necessary materials and equipment needed by students in testing their ideas and hypotheses. In fact, as noted earlier, the classroom may even appear somewhat chaotic at times, what with all the different activities that can be taking place simultaneously.

Indirect methods require openness. Encouragement must be readily available when mistakes are made and diversity must be encouraged at all times. Permissiveness and sloppy work, however, must not be tolerated. Indirect methods are most effective in classrooms where there is cooperation, trust, self-control, and conviction. This requires that you plan carefully and emphasize systematic skill building.

Summary

- Traditional classroom methods often stress structure too much and are not oriented to critical thinking and independent inquiry.

The Discussion Method

- Discussions can be used to stimulate students' thinking, to help them articulate their own ideas, and for teaching them how to listen to the ideas of others.
- The teacher's role in discussion sessions is to be less directive and less obtrusive. Simply set discussions into motion and monitor their progress.
- Discussions can be whole class or small group.
- One of the major problems of whole-class discussions is that a few students tend to dominate.
- Small-group discussions result in more student-to-student interactions.

Heuristic Methods

- Heuristic methods actively involve students in their own learning and result in higher degrees of intrinsic motivation.

- The heuristic modes of discovery and inquiry essentially represent different types of problem solving.
- Systemic problem solving represents a systematic, purposeful problem-solving process.

Teacher's Role

- The teacher's role in using indirect methods is to act as a facilitator.
- Active participatory methods require a close working relationship between teacher and students.

Classroom Environment

- Indirect methods require a certain amount of student freedom.
- Indirect methods require openness.

Discussion Questions and Activities

1. **Indirect methods.** When is it appropriate to use indirect methods? Consider the objectives and purpose of the instruction as well as the students themselves.
2. **Discussion topics.** Generate a list of topics that would be appropriate for discussions. Once you have compiled your topics, separate them as appropriate for whole-class or small-group discussions. Give your reasons and justify them.
3. **Textbook examination.** Examine a textbook or curriculum guide and identify several possible topics for a discussion lesson. What kinds of questions would you use to (1) begin the lesson, (2) keep the discussion rolling, and (3) wrap up the lesson?

Connection With the Field

1. **Classroom observation.** Visit several public school classrooms. Keep a record of the different methods used. What indirect methods did you observe? Was there a pattern?
2. **Inquiry lesson.** Design a lesson for an inquiry lesson. How in the lesson will you initiate the following phases?

   a. Identifying the problem
   b. Working toward solutions
   c. Establishing solution
   d. Teaching the lesson

3. **Teaching.** Prepare and teach a minilesson using an indirect method. Use the microteaching guidelines and forms in Appendix B to plan and analyze your minilesson.
4. **Teaching analysis.** Make a videotape of your miniteaching lesson; then critically analyze it with your peers.

Praxis II Connection

The following test preparation exercises are intended to help you prepare for the Praxis II: Principles of Learning and Teaching. The Praxis II may be required by your teacher education preparatory program and for state certification or licensing. These exercises will give you direct access to pedagogical knowledge from Chapter 9 that may be expected of you on the Praxis II and other pedagogical exams that may be required at the end of your teacher education program.

Topic Connections

1. Classroom discussions (II. A1, A2, A3)

Classroom discussions can often provide effective learning experiences. Describe the characteristics and principles of effective discussions.

2. Discovery and inquiry (II. A1, A2, A3)

Describe the basic structures of discovery and inquiry learning. What are their strengths and limitations? What are the teacher's roles?

ON YOUR OWN

Log on to the web-based student study site at http://www.sagepub.com/eis for more information about the vignettes and materials presented in this chapter, suggestions for activities, study aids such as electronic flashcards and review quizzes, and research recommendations including journal article links and questions related to this chapter.

10
TEACHING EFFECTIVE THINKING STRATEGIES

The person with big dreams is more
powerful than the one with all the facts.

ANONYMOUS

OVERVIEW

It is necessary, and even desirable, to provide students with a sound education in basic skills. A complete education, however, must emphasize thinking skills that enable students to function responsibly and to solve problems in ways that are sensitive and caring of others, society, and the world. Undoubtedly, this goal requires teachers of all disciplines explicitly teach the thinking skills deemed necessary for a lifetime of continuous learning.

In the 1923 work *The Prophet,* Kahlil Gibran tells us, "If the teacher is indeed wise, he does not bid you enter the house of his wisdom, but rather leads you to the threshold of your mind." These words suggest that thinking skills must be placed high on our agenda as one of the most basic of all skills needed today. In fact, thinking skills can be regarded as essential skills.

This chapter will focus on teaching students how to think. A wide variety of thinking skills will be examined; however, critical and creative thinking will be emphasized. I will attempt to examine some of the ideas, methods, and issues related to critical thinking and creative thinking.

OBJECTIVES

After completing your study of Chapter 10, you should be able to do the following:

1. Define *thinking* and differentiate among the various categories of thinking skills.
2. Explain creativity as a process and product and describe the four stages of creative thought.
3. Describe various difficulties that can hinder the creative process.
4. Define and describe *metacognition*.
5. Describe different approaches and activities that can be used in teaching thinking skills.
6. Explain the eight behaviors that exemplify "nonthinking."
7. Explain the role of the teacher and how modeling is used in the teaching of thinking skills.

Research (Sadler & Whimbey, 1985) has led educators to question the meaning of "basic skills" for learning, and many have suggested that "thinking skills" are the basis on which all other skills are developed. That is, individuals need thinking skills for remembering information, incorporating knowledge, learning and using motor skills, and developing values and attitudes. Some of these skills are generic and can be taught as general learning strategies, without reference to content.

The research findings tend to confirm that when thinking skills become an integral part of the curriculum and instructional practice, test scores in academic areas increase. It is now widely accepted that teachers of every discipline must teach thinking skills explicitly in addition to their content area. It is also generally agreed, however, that students must assume much of the responsibility for developing these skills. Students must take an active role in the learning process, but the teacher must provide opportunities for using thinking skills and not inhibit such activity.

Implicit within the notion of thinking is the concept of decision making, which involves making choices from among a number of competing appropriate responses. Not all problems have answers that are clearly "correct." In such situations, a person must choose from among a variety of acceptable alternatives. This process of making choices involves skill at thinking (Beyer, 1988).

To further explore the concept of thinking, complete Expansion Activity: Thinking.

EXPANSION ACTIVITY

Thinking

Schools should develop a well-balanced program of personal development for all students. This program should balance academic, social, and personal growth. Can all types of school experiences be accepted as part of the development of student thinking skills? Are school experiences designed to develop thinking skills? If so, have they been successful?

Thinking Skills

What are thinking skills? How does one go about teaching them? These are difficult questions to answer. Indeed, there are as many definitions of *thinking* as there are thinkers. Do not all cognitive acts require thinking? Although it is true that all cognitive acts require thinking, it is also important to distinguish between the ability to use one's mind in simply reproducing rote facts and the creative ability to use higher thinking skills to generate new information.

Many believe that it is possible to teach students the skills that will enable them to produce the creative thoughts that lead to finding solutions to problems—a skill much needed in preparing the youth that will be tomorrow's leaders. In fact, authorities in the field of education have expressed strong feelings about what it means to "think" beyond the mere level of replication of information. For example, in a 1990 Association for Supervision and Curriculum Development (ASCD) video, David Perkins of Harvard University says that **thinking** is "problem solving, it's decision making, reading, reflecting, making predictions about what might happen." In the same video, Matthew Lipman (ASCD, 1990) suggests that thinking is processing your experiences in the world; to edit, or rearrange, or examine

Students must learn
to be responsible for
their own learning.

experiences; and to think about the process of thinking about your experiences. On the other hand, Ernest Boyer (1983), president of the Carnegie Foundation, stated that thinking cannot be separated from good language. Finally, *Webster's Twentieth Century Dictionary* (2nd edition, unabridged) defines thinking as follows: "A bringing of intellectual faculties into play; of making decisions, and the drawing of inferences; it is to perform any mental operation, or to reason, judge, conclude, to choose, hold an opinion, to believe, or to propose, or to muse over, to mediate, to ponder, to reflect, or to weigh a matter mentally." All of these reflective thoughts describe many important aspects of the operation of thinking, and there are, indeed, many areas to approach in the teaching of thinking.

There appear to be many views of thinking. To clearly define *thinking* for teachers searching for ways to create thinking students, this discussion will encompass all of the definitions cited and summarize *thinking* as the act of withholding judgment to use knowledge and experience to find new information, concepts, or conclusions. Let us now look at the different types of thinking.

Thinking Games

1. What is "thinking" ability?
2. Is thinking an ability everyone possesses and uses everyday? Why might we need to address thinking in school?

To engage my students in thinking, I have my class work in pairs to construct a game about our state. I give them a rubric when I explain the lesson that outlines what they are expected to include (for example: game pieces, strategy, at least 15 cities mentioned, at least 15 facts about the state, etc.). An old clothes box makes a great box for storage of the game! The game construction worked out great and the kids had fun working on the project.

I was really impressed with some of the game ideas students came up with. On the day they were due, each pair had to present their game to the class. Then we had a "game day" and I let them play their games for part of the afternoon. We also kept them in the room for extra things to do during indoor recess. I plan to use the same idea again and students will get to pick different states.

—TRACY, *elementary school teacher*

SOURCE: Reprinted with permission from ProTeacher, a professional community for elementary school teachers (http://www.proteacher.net)

Categories of Thinking

Your first task in teaching thinking skills is to determine which skills are appropriate for your class. In doing so, you should consider the maturity level of your students, along with the special needs of your subject. It is commonly believed that it is better to teach a few skills well and thoroughly rather than many skills superficially.

APPLY AND REFLECT: You should show students that they can be successful thinkers.

How could you do this at the grade level you expect to teach? Share your ideas with

your class.

All teachers teaching thinking skills should refer to Bloom's Taxonomy of thinking levels for assistance in the formation and understanding of various thinking levels. Indeed, almost all content areas can provide instruction at six levels of thinking: knowledge, comprehension, application, analysis, synthesis, and evaluation.

- At the knowledge level, most thinking tasks require students to recognize or remember key facts. The knowledge level calls on students to be attentive to information, or repeat information verbatim, and to recite facts, such as math facts and formulas. Activities that ask students to recall, define, recognize, practice drills, or identify concepts are a few knowledge-level thinking skills.

- Students translate, interpret, and explain given information at the comprehension level. Comprehension thinking tasks involve interpreting the meaning of a graph or diagram or decoding a word. Knowledge and comprehension levels are not representative of the higher-order thinking-skill levels because students are not required to come up with new information, but are called on to translate the information that has been given.

- Students at the application level can transfer known information to applicable situations. In effect, they must think and decide how information can be applied to situations other than those presented. Students are given generalizations and are required to make application and explain relationships. For example, students could be asked to solve equations by applying a correct formula or transfer known skills to another area in solving a problem.

- At the analysis level, students must think about how to divide a whole into component elements. Generally, this level includes finding comparisons and relationships between the parts to the whole concept. Students are required to break down complex information or ideas into simpler parts. Thinking tasks that call on students to identify the underlying structure of complex ideas or information and to compare similarities and differences fall into the analysis level.

- Thinking tasks at synthesis levels require that students take parts of previously learned information and create completely new products, or wholes. Both inductive and deductive thinking and reasoning fall in this category. With inductive thinking, students are provided evidence or details and then asked to use thinking skills to make generalizations. Conversely, students using deductive thinking are given a generalization and are asked to provide evidence that explains the generalization. Hypothesizing, predicting, and concluding are examples of deductive thinking.

- Finally, evaluation level thinking tasks are those in which students judge quality, credibility, worth, and practicality. Student thinking at this level generally must provide evidence, logic, and values in support of conclusions. It is easy to make swift judgments that do not require the evaluation level of thinking. Tasks at this level, however, also demand that students use all the previous levels of thinking. The key in determining whether students are actually at this level lies with their ability to withhold judgments until they are able to explain the logic or provide evidence in support of their judgments.

Critical Thinking

Critical thinking is not the same as intelligence; it is a skill that can be improved in everyone (Walsh & Paul, 1988, p. 13). Also, many educators differentiate between ordinary thinking and thinking critically. According to Lipman (1988b), ordinary thinking is usually simple and lacks standards, whereas critical thinking is more complex and is based upon standards of objectivity and consistency. He suggests that students must be taught to change their thinking (1) from guessing to estimating, (2) from preferring to evaluating, (3) from grouping to classifying, (4) from believing to assuming, (5) from inferring to inferring logically, (6) from associating concepts to grasping principles, (7) from noting relationships to noting relationships among relationships, (8) from supposing to hypothesizing, (9) from offering opinions without reasons to offering opinions with reasons, and (10) from making judgments without criteria to making judgments with criteria.

Open-ended activities, with no single correct answer, can be used to develop thinking skills.

"Cafeteria duty."

Critical thinking tends to require higher levels of thinking—that is, more evaluation and synthesis than application or analysis. Indeed, it should be remembered that Bloom's Taxonomy is hierarchical; therefore, operation at the evaluative level requires the use of the previous thinking levels as well.

Creative Thinking

All people have the potential for experiencing those feelings of "Aha!" or "Wow, guess what I just figured out?" Such thinking is creative thinking. It occurs as the result of questioning and learning beyond the gathering of rote information. Research indicates that the "creative" right brain generates ideas and images, whereas the "logical" left brain critiques and evaluates. It is during the creative processes that the two halves of the brain seem to communicate best. Before we can decide how to develop creativity, however, we must discuss what, exactly, creativity is.

Some degree of **creativity** occurs whenever a person assembles information to discover something not previously taught or understood. To the individual, this may be the discovery of a new relationship between two unlike concepts. This concept of creative thinking is often associated with creative thinking as a process.

When creativity is defined as a product, the result embraces the idea of the production of a new invention or theory. This type of creative thinking is associated with the realization of an original concept. For the student, this could be the creation of a poem, a song, a game, or an unusual use for a common item. Ideally, all creative thinking takes people "beyond where they have ever gone before."

Curiosity, imagination, discovery, and invention are all equated with creative thinking. Although it may not be possible for one person to teach another person how to be creative, it is possible to provide activities that enhance opportunities for thinking. Frequently, there is a high level of frustration associated with creative thinking as individuals travel through the four stages of creative thought.

Creative thinking is generally thought of as putting together information to come up with a whole new understanding, concept, or idea. The four stages generally identified with the development of creative thought are preparation, incubation, illumination, and verification. Numerous thinking skills are used during each of these stages of the creative process. In fact, the greater the flexibility in thinking, the greater the possibility for creative thinking.

During the first stage, preparation, the creative thinker collects information and examines it, using many of the thinking processes previously mentioned. The creative thinker, however, questions and investigates until a major relationship seems to appear among events, objects, or ideas. Usually a hypothesis emerges in the thinker's mind, which causes the individual to ponder and meditate in a questioning manner. This begins what is known as the second stage of creative thought, incubation. The individual may spend quite some time allowing images from the unconscious to surface. At other times, this stage may be very short-lived, moving the creative thinker into the "Aha!" or illumination stage. Suddenly, the "I've got it" or "Now I know" may emerge. At this stage, the individual may feel confident and regain equilibrium, which can be followed by new questioning and a need for elaboration. Next, the individual begins to seek out ways of verifying and testing the idea. This is called the stage of verification. Figure 10.1 summarizes the four stages of creative thinking.

Figure 10.1
Stages of Creative
Thinking

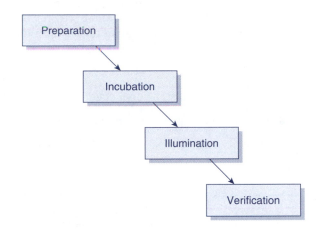

Eminent creative persons, and others less prominent but no less creative, have expressed frustration and disconcerting feelings while struggling with a puzzling concept that later led them to a discovery or "Eureka!" feeling. The following types of difficulties have been reported (Torrance, 1983) by many who have studied the creative thinking process.

1. Difficulty in finding words to describe original images is one of the frequently reported frustrations given by creative thinkers. Sometimes ideas or images are too complex for them to put into words. Certainly, not all creative insights must be expressed in words; they can also be expressed visually or kinesthetically.

2. An inability to let the imagination "go" can be a problem. Many cannot permit themselves to "let go" in childlike play even momentarily. The ability to relax, laugh, and play with new ideas with an unrestricted attitude is an important characteristic of creative thought.

3. A tendency to analyze rather than synthesize is a common mistake that can hinder creative thinking. Whereas analysis is helpful during the early stages of creativity, synthesis is necessary in pressing forward through the development of new, original ideas.

4. Creative thinkers sometimes "jump the gun" to synthesize before analysis of the facts is complete. This can create "thinking blocks," which hinder the consideration of other valuable possibilities.

5. Many have communicated fears of expressing new ideas they were generating in their own minds. Some are afraid to let others see their inventions and express doubt that others will appreciate their ideas. It takes courage to be an independent thinker. This does not mean, however, that independent thinkers never experience doubt or misgivings. Even the most eminent creative thinkers of our time have experienced these feelings.

6. A frequent complaint of creative thinkers has been that they get too many ideas at one time. The flood of information becomes a form of stress and gives the individual an "avalanche effect." Successful completion of one or more of these ideas requires the thinker to shelve some of the ideas and focus on what is needed for the moment.

If you are to confront and overcome these difficulties, you must provide students opportunities for creative successes in the classroom. Moreover, you should avoid judging students' creative endeavors and provide support and encouragement for their attempts.

APPLY AND REFLECT: You should provide instructional materials and support for students' creative endeavors. Generate some ideas for materials and support that would help your future students develop their thinking skills. Share your ideas.

Few people would argue with the importance of improving critical thinking and creative skills of students in subjects such as mathematics, English, and history. Of course, some students will develop learning skills on their own, but most students need assistance.

Metacognition

Metacognition can be simply defined as "thinking about thinking." Thinking skills and study skills are examples of metacognitive skills. They include invisible thinking skills such as self-interrogation, self-checking, self-monitoring, and analyzing, as well as memory aids (called mnemonics) for classifying and recalling content.

Metacognition consists of two processes occurring simultaneously: monitoring progress when engaged in learning, and making changes and adapting corrective strategies when problems occur during learning. It involves overseeing whether a cognitive goal has been met. It is about self-reflection, self-responsibility, and initiative. Metacognitive skills include monitoring the progress of learning, correcting errors, analyzing the effectiveness of learning strategies, and changing learning behaviors when necessary. Metacognitive strategies come into play when cognitions fail, such as the recognition that one did not understand what one just read. Such an impasse should activate metacognitive processes as the learner attempts to rectify the situation.

Metacognition enables students to better benefit from instruction. Students don't often stop to evaluate their comprehension of material. They don't generally examine the quality of their work or stop to make revisions as they go along. They too often don't attempt to examine a problem in depth. They don't make connections or see the relevance of material in their lives. Take reading, for example. Students often read a page (or a whole chapter!) in a textbook without comprehending a single thing. They simply go on to the next page, thinking that merely reading the words on a page is enough. They need to learn to re-read difficult pages until the main concept is understood, or flag difficult pages until the main concept is understood, or flag a difficult passage to ask for clarification from the teacher.

Students can be taught strategies for assessing their own understandings and how to choose effective plans of attack to study or solve problems. For example, in reading a book, students are bound to come across a paragraph that they don't understand on first reading. What do they do? Perhaps they could re-read the paragraph more slowly. Perhaps they should look for other clues, such as pictures, graphs, or glossary terms, to help them understand. Perhaps they should read farther back in the chapter to see whether the difficulty arose because they did not fully understand something that came earlier. These are all examples of metacognitive skills; students need to learn how to know when they are not understanding and how to correct themselves (Schunk & Zimmerman, 1997). Another important metacognitive process is the ability to predict what is likely to happen or to tell what is sensible and what is not. Other metacognitive strategies that students can be taught to use include

- Consciously identifying what they already know.
- Determining how performance will be evaluated.
- Estimating the time required to complete a task.
- Planning study time into their schedule and setting priorities.
- Making a checklist of what needs to happen when.
- Organizing materials.
- Taking the necessary steps to learn by using strategies like outlining, mnemonics, diagramming, and so on.
- Reflecting on the learning process, keeping track of what works and what doesn't work.
- Monitoring learning by questioning and self-testing.
- Providing their own feedback.
- Keeping concentration and motivation high.

APPLY AND REFLECT: Use and teach students mnemonic devices for remembering information. Have you used such devices before? If not, research some common ones. Share your findings with your class.

Although many students will develop adequate metacognitive skills, some will not. Teaching metacognitive strategies to students can lead to a marked improvement in their achievement (Alexander, Graham, & Harris, 1998). Students can learn to think about their own thinking processes and apply specific learning strategies to think themselves through difficult tasks (Bulter & Winne, 1995; Schunk, 2000). Self-questioning strategies are particularly effective (Zimmerman, 1998). Essentially, students can be taught to talk themselves through activities they are engaged in, asking themselves or each other the questions you would ask.

As students become more skilled at using metacognitive strategies, they gain confidence and become more independent as learners. Students realize they can pursue their own intellectual needs and discover a world of information is at their fingertips. The task for you as a teacher is to acknowledge, cultivate, exploit, and enhance the metacognitive capabilities of all your students.

APPLY AND REFLECT: You should be a model of critical and creative thinking. How would you do so?

The concepts regarding thinking skills are summarized in Table 10.1. Review the summary and complete Review, Extension, and Reflective Exercise 10.1.

Students should be given the opportunity to ponder issues related to classroom instruction and to present alternative ideas.

TABLE 10.1 Thinking Skills

Concept	Description
Thinking	The act of withholding judgment to use knowledge and experience in finding new information, concepts, or conclusions
Critical Thinking	The ability to analyze complex situations critically, using standards of objectivity and consistency
Creativity	The capacity for producing imaginative, original products or ways of solving problems
Metacognition	The skill of thinking about thinking

Review, Extension, and Reflective Exercise 10.1

Define thinking and describe several types of thinking.

Connections to INTASC Standards:

- Standard 2: Student Development. The teacher understands how children learn and develop and can provide learning opportunities that support their intellectual, social, and personal development.
- Standard 4: Instructional Strategies. The teacher must understand and use a variety of instructional strategies to encourage students' development of critical thinking, problem solving, and performance skills.
- Standard 5: Learning Environment. The teacher must be able to use an understanding of individual and group motivation and behavior to create a learning environment that encourages positive social interaction, active engagement in learning, and self-motivation.
- Standard 7: Planning Instruction. The teacher plans instruction based upon knowledge of subject matter, students, the community, and curriculum goals.

Connections to the NBPTS:

- Proposition 1: Teachers are committed to students and their learning.
- Proposition 3: Teachers are responsible for managing and monitoring student learning.

Review

- What is thinking?
- What is the focus of critical thinking?
- What is creative thinking? How can teachers foster creative thinking?
- What is metacognition?

Reflection

- Some experts contend that few schools teach students to think critically and creatively. Does your own experience support this view? If you agree with the experts, why isn't critical and creative thinking more widely or effectively taught? Do you think you can teach critical and creative thinking at the grade level you expect to teach?

Thinking-Skills Instruction

The teaching of thinking skills requires open-mindedness on the part of those that teach them. Every rock of information must be turned over; every avenue of learning must be explored. You must be willing to explore, question, take risks, and experiment; otherwise, how can you lead students through the same processes?

Many suggest that you begin the teaching of thinking skills by selecting only a few individual lessons that focus on particular skills. Then, as experience and confidence grow, you should consider extending the emphasis on thinking skills and integrate these skills into your content area.

Should you teach thinking skills separately or infuse them into your content area? There are pros and cons to both approaches. Those favoring the separate approach maintain that, like reading and writing, thinking skills are enabling disciplines and deserve separate instruction (Lipman, 1988a, p. 43). Conversely, advocates of the infusion approach argue that certain cognitive skills are specific to particular disciplines and, therefore, should be taught in context (Ashton, 1988, p. 4). Perhaps the answer to this issue is to use both separate instructional programs and infusion programs. Let's look at these two approaches.

The Separate Approach

Reuven Feuerstein (ASCD, 1990), an internationally known cognitive psychologist, points out that many students lack the basic skills and abilities for seeing relationships or comparisons between ideas. He suggests that these students need special programs of focused instruction upon specific skills—that is, separate instruction on thinking skills. Many educators prefer the **separate approach** when introducing a new skill because it may be difficult for students who are unfamiliar with a skill to focus on the learning of a new skill and on learning of content at the same time.

Modeling is an important component in the separate approach. In fact, when using this approach, you should always begin the teaching of a skill by modeling it. For example, when teaching students about classification, you should demonstrate the skill by doing a whole-class classification activity. Although you may demonstrate how to classify, you would be wise to create a thinking exercise wherein the students' answers diverge. Guidance can be provided, for instance, by presenting the classification steps on the overhead projector or chalkboard—for example:

1. Skim over all the objects to find two that have something alike.
2. Choose two that are alike and label them as a group.
3. See if any others fit into that group.
4. Find two more that have similarities and label them a group.
5. Skim over the others to see if they fit into this group.
6. Continue the process until all items have been classified.

You should call for whole-class responses to each of the steps, which in turn will demonstrate that the skill allows for many correct responses. Class input is one of the most important aspects of teaching the classification skill as a thinking skill. As students make suggestions and form their own classified groups, you gradually need to release responsibility to students by allowing them to arrive at answers. Afterwards, students should give explanation to the logic that led to their conclusions. Once the initial introductory activity has been completed with the group, you should provide students an opportunity for practicing the skill individually, so their understanding of the modeled skill can be evaluated.

The Infusion Approach

The **infusion approach** calls for the use of the desired skill in conjunction with the regular curriculum. In effect, this approach requires that students transfer the newly acquired skill to the regular content being studied. If teaching students the skill of classification, for example, after the skill has been taught, it would be applied to the regular curriculum. That is, once students are taught to classify through introductory activities, they are asked to apply it to the content being studied. You might simply ask them to synthesize different ways the content being studied can be classified. If necessary, direct them toward items in your content area in which classifying may be of use. For example, the outlining of a chapter requires grouping information under headings and categories. Once another use has been established, go through the whole-class collaboration steps once again—using the skill in this new context. Afterwards, the procedure of infusing the thinking skill into your content needs can be finalized by assigning students a situation in your content area in which they can apply the skill.

Critical-Thinking Instruction

Stephen Brookfield (1987) purports that there are two activities central to critical thinking: (1) identifying and challenging assumptions and (2) exploring and imagining alternatives. Moreover, Brookfield defined *assumptions* as the unquestioned rules that individuals have assimilated into their value system as self-evident truths—"taken-for-granted" truths established by the culture that individuals have accepted as their own. These assumptions influence how we interpret situations and how we perceive solutions to problems. Consequently, one of the basic behaviors we develop through critical thinking is open-mindedness and a willingness to explore other possibilities. In effect, we must teach students to examine old ideas in new ways and to consider alternatives to old ways of thinking. This task is not an easy one because it is often inherently disruptive to personal values and beliefs. This personal disruption may be one reason critical-thinking activities are at times so strongly resisted.

Direct, specific instruction is often useful in critical thinking and should be used in assisting students in dealing with assumptions so that a more open-minded attitude toward new modes of thinking can be developed. Without such instruction, there is little hope for dismantling the concepts our society has outgrown—for example, previously held conceptions about racism and sexism. Although many misconceptions about areas such as these still exist, an important aspect of teaching thinking is the modeling of the open-minded attitude you hope to foster. This will not be possible if you become a dictator of your most comfortable ways of thinking and behaving. Indeed, you must provide opportunities for students to think about their views and the views of others; yet, the final decision should be left to students as respected thinkers. Without this atmosphere of respect, it is impossible to model the concepts you desire to teach.

One good way of providing opportunities for students to examine assumptions is by having them work in small groups with a list of "loaded" questions—statements about which the groups must gather responses from each member and then report their areas of agreement and disagreement during a whole-class discussion. The following statements are examples of loaded questions:

1. When we see a person who is wearing shabby clothes, what assumptions might we make about him or her?
2. When we see a picture of a rock star, what assumptions might we make about his or her lifestyle?

3. When we see a classmate get a D on his or her report card, what assumptions might we make about him or her?
4. When we see a woman running for the presidency of the United States, what assumptions might we have about her abilities?
5. If a substitute teacher is in the classroom on a particular day of school, what assumptions might you make about how to conduct your behavior for the day?
6. When we hear someone has AIDS, what do we think?

Developing societal consciousness is a starting point in developing a line of reasoning skills needed for producing thoughtful citizens for our future. Certainly, one of the critical aspects of critical thinking is the challenge of the basic assumptions. A word of caution is in order, lest we isolate the very foundation we desire to develop. Indeed, Stephen Brookfield (1987) points out that challenges of the assumptions underlying our value systems can be both "liberating" and "threatening." He further suggests that questioning internalized truths, whether actually true or not, is a part of one's personality. It may seem demeaning to our capacity for valuing, believing, and developing moral codes, however, when we discover that the absolutes we hold to be true are not necessarily absolutely true. The development of completely new thought patterns that differ from past thinking structures can even create momentary imbalance. Therefore, you might find it necessary to implement ways to help students broaden their thought structures beyond the confines of their own culture, without weakening their desire to believe in, and form, values. The goal is not to destroy but to refine. Above all, remember that, sometimes you, too, will pass through these disruptive processes as a teacher-learner.

APPLY AND REFLECT: Develop a plan for integrating direct instruction of critical and creative skills, techniques, and processes into your teaching. Share your plan.

Regardless of the approach you choose for teaching critical-thinking skills, there are eight nonthinking behaviors (Raths, Wassermann, Jonas, & Rothstein, 1986) frequently reported by classroom teachers. These eight behaviors will negatively impact the development of thinking skills. As such, you must learn to diagnose and prescribe appropriate thinking activities that will enable your students to overcome the following behaviors:

1. *Impulsiveness.* Students may respond before the question is completed. They do not take time to consider the problem or alternatives. In other words, they "leap before they look" without adequate thought. These students think, but they fail to consider consequences of their inferences, hypotheses, or decisions on information presented. They blurt out the answer without having enough information, or they impulsively base their decision on the first thing that enters their minds.
2. *Overdependence on the teacher.* Students sometimes raise their hands as soon as the teacher finishes explaining the assignment and begins the independent work. These students won't try the concept first but, rather, say, "I don't understand this"—before even attempting to read the instructions. These

students often fail to pay attention during group instruction and insist that the teacher provide individual instruction at their desks.

3. *Inattentive behavior.* These students start working but don't stay on task. They need constant prompting; their attention span is short; and their attention constantly wanders, seemingly into "space." These students rarely finish assignments and demonstrate a lack of self-motivation.

4. *Restless rusher.* Restless rushers get very little meaning out of assigned tasks; rather, they rush through their work concentrating only on turning in the assignment. These students frequently finish the work first but lack accuracy. When asked questions pertaining to the assignment just finished, they pause and reply, "I don't know." If the student is prompted further to redo the work, he or she usually rushes through the second time just as quickly as the first time. These students differ from impulsive students in that they usually don't base their responses on past or similar experiences and jump the gun as impulsive students do; instead, they concentrate only on turning in the work.

5. *Dogmatic, assertive behavior.* These students fail to consider another's point of view. Basic assumptions are never questioned, and they always think their perceptions are the only correct ones. Because they think their views are already perfect, they see no reason for considering or listening for other possibilities.

6. *Rigidity, inflexibility of behavior.* These students are reluctant to give up old strategies that have worked for them in the past, even when they prove inadequate in the new situation. For example, students might be requested to perform a certain task, and they may reply that it's not the way they learned to do it last year.

7. *Fearful, lack of confidence.* These students rarely respond to questions that require anything other than one right answer. They are fearful of expressing their own views and opinions, as they lack confidence in their own thinking. When asked to answer a question that calls for higher-order thinking skills or to voice their thoughts during a brainstorming activity, these students are afraid to express themselves. They seem to be the opposite of the overdependent student in that they usually won't seek extra help.

8. *Responsibility forfeiture.* These students want the teacher to provide one right way of accomplishing all learning tasks. Again, fear of taking risks or assuming responsibility is evident. These students are grade-conscious individuals who are not afraid to approach their teacher for specific guidelines; by obligating the teacher in this way, the students shift responsibility to the teacher and relieve themselves from thinking for themselves.

Often, you will need to prescribe thinking activities that alter these behaviors and promote self-confidence and mental growth. Let's now look at some of the activities that could be used in correcting faulty thinking habits.

APPLY AND REFLECT: It is suggested that teachers build into their lessons time for students to reflect on their learning. Is this a good idea for students at the grade level you expect to teach? Why or why not?

Thinking Skills Activities

Teaching thinking skills requires open-ended activities in which no single, correct answers are sought. Although there are many areas, categories, and thinking operations that could be approached, let's examine some of the concepts that could be prescribed for the eight nonthinking behaviors.

Brainstorming

Brainstorming is an excellent way of promoting fluent thinking (see Chapter 9). The goal of brainstorming is to produce as many responses as possible. It is crucial that all responses be accepted and appreciated during the activity. Withhold praise or judgment and provide an accepting atmosphere throughout the activity. Encourage your students to "hitchhike" on each other's ideas. Emphasize that not all responses will be of high quality because the aim is for quantity, and hitchhiking on each other will generate additional ideas. Brainstorming activities of this type can also encourage flexible thinking.

Flexible Thinking

With flexible thinking, activities stretch the mind into considering possibilities beyond the usual responses. During these activities, you need to define the area for examination. Ask students to put their five senses to work in thinking about how many different ways a concept could be used. For example, ask your students questions that help them consider alternate possibilities—perhaps, for the use of a water hose should they be stranded on a deserted island. Inspire them to ask themselves questions that take forms such as these:

What if _____?

Suppose that _____?

How is _____ like _____?

If you were _____?

Such questions and statements help define new possibilities and produce flexible thinking.

Another outstanding thinking skill that improves students with impulsive behaviors is cause-and-effect considerations. Forecasting activities can help students generate causes and effects of a given situation.

Forecasting

Instruct students to brainstorm all possible causes and effects of getting good grades. This requires that students make inferences about cause and effect. The idea, once again, is to forecast what could be or might be. Afterwards, students should examine the quality of each prediction and choose the best cause and effect, and then they should provide reasons for their choice. Providing explanations for choices that students determine to be the best helps promote inductive thinking.

Inductive Thinking

Inductive thinking activities can be helpful for students who frequently fail to check their responses to determine whether their generalizations can hold up against data. During **inductive thinking**, students collect, organize, and examine data; then they identify common elements; finally, they make generalizations based on common or general elements. Once students have examined the data, they should be encouraged to state generalizations that are based on inferences found in the data. For example, encourage students to "read between the lines" when reading a selected newspaper article and then to state a generalization based on information known about the article. If possible, provide students with newspaper articles from different areas and by different authors to further check the generalization against data. Making inferences is closely related to finding generalizations.

Inference Making

When a person makes an inference, he or she must provide a possible consequence, conclusion, or implication from a set of facts or premises. Inference making requires that thinkers provide a rationale for their thoughts. These thoughts are personal beliefs about a situation based on similar associations with past experiences. Basic assumptions people hold play a key role in the inferences they make. Questions that call for inference making ask students to provide their personal opinion. "Why do you suppose?" and "What do you think someone should do?" and "What do you suppose was meant by . . . ? Why?" are all questions frequently used in promoting inference making. As with forming generalizations, however, it is important that you ask students to supply evidence or provide reasons for the inference they make. Even when basic assumptions are examined, it may be necessary to determine whether or not inferences are based upon clear, meditative thinking or whether they are the product of assertive, dogmatic rigidity. Therefore, students also need practice in logical thinking.

Logical Thinking

Logical thinking is believed to be a left-brain function that organizes and associates ideas. Activities that require logical thinking begin with assumptions or concepts and generate ideas step-by-step to arrive at an end point or a solution. Logical thinking is based on previous knowledge or acquired patterns of thinking. Logic requires that students interpret information in deriving the intended meaning from a source. Students must examine the main idea presented and follow the supporting details to arrive at a conclusion. For example, samples of logic skills can be taught, and then students can develop thinking activities, such as the one shown in Figure 10.2. Indeed, such activities can be developed by students and exchanged with classmates for solving.

Deductive Thinking

Whereas inductive thinking calls on a student to make generalizations based on data, **deductive thinking** asks the student to consider the generalizations given and provide supporting data. Most thinking activities will be incomplete until students provide a rationale for their responses.

Figure 10.2

Sample Logical-Thinking
Activity

CRAWLING CATERPILLARS

1. The caterpillar crew is enjoying an out-of-school crawl.

2. Read the clues below carefully. Then write each crew member's name in logical sequence.

ASSUMPTIONS:
(Clues)

1. Rick Reader loves to read.

2. Rick Reader is between Duff and Shades.

3. Shades is following Carrie the Carrier.

4. Carrie the Carrier is following Headphones Hector.

SOURCE: Raul Acosta, seventh grade, Anadarko Junior High. Used with permission

Deductive thinking is crucial in a democratic society that demands a responsible citizenry in decision making. Deductive thinking often requires that students evaluate the merit of an activity, object, or idea. Therefore, teaching students to identify possible outcomes, define standards of appraisal, and make judgments based on careful consideration are all-important elements of instruction. When students are called on to decide among objects or alternatives, decision-making and problem-solving steps will be helpful to them in reaching their conclusions.

Problem Solving

Complex thinking processes often involve problem solving and decision making. Problem solving involves six steps: (1) defining the problem, (2) collecting data, (3) identifying obstacles to the goal, (4) identifying alternatives, (5) rating alternatives, and (6) choosing the best alternative. Problem-solving models can be developed that guide students through these important steps. For example, divergent questions might be developed that discourage students from supplying one "right" answer. Also, brainstorming should be an important aspect of each step. Students should consider the following questions as they carry out the problem-solving steps:

1. What is fact and what is opinion?
2. Is there only one right way?
3. Do the examples presented prove the rule?

4. Just because two things happened together, does this prove one is the cause of the other?
5. Is it possible that personal feelings are causing you to rule out possibilities?

Sometimes guides with similar questions help new problem solvers organize problem-solving activities. In using such a guide, students should be asked to record alternatives, and then asked to critically consider their choices.

Decision Making

Decision making involves the thinking skills needed in choosing the best response from several options. It involves examining advantages and disadvantages, considering all of the steps of problem solving, and evaluating the final decision in relationship to available alternatives and consequences. Basic to decision making are the abilities to observe, interpret, compare, classify, and analyze information.

Observation

Observation demands that students watch for a purpose and note objective changes, details, or procedures. Students must use their five senses if they are to record data accurately. This activity can help students check the accuracy of a match between what is seen, heard, smelled, and so on. The proposition that you can't believe anything you hear and only half of what you "think you see" becomes a reality, as students not only examine their own perception of things, but also attempt to understand the point of view of others. A good way of practicing careful observation techniques is by observing television commercials for underlying messages developed and conveyed through various techniques. Close observations of this type lead students to recognize the power of effective persuasion and help them develop open perceptions when attempting to interpret information.

Interpretation

Interpreting requires that students use their perceptions in examining their assumptions when making a judgment or reaching a conclusion. Perceptions are developed through associations with personal experiences and are, therefore, unique to each individual. Interpreting is an important skill to teach directly, as people tend to generalize on the basis of insufficient evidence in our repertoire of basic assumptions. Our interpretations sometimes become hazy when we experience doubt in our attempts to attribute causation and validity to data. Causation and validity must be closely examined before deriving conclusions. Explain to students that the skill of interpreting depends on drawing inferences from *valid* data. Warn them about the tendency to generalize on the basis of insufficient evidence. Guide them in critically examining information and in differentiating between what is true and what they may believe to be true. Students' first interpretation activities might begin with your presentation of a large poster with a graph or picture. Begin by asking students to list at least four statements that can be made through observing the picture. Afterwards, ask them to share with the class their interpretation of what the picture was telling. After the first student gives personal responses of interpretation, search for other responses that might represent different interpretations. This particular activity prompts examination of the many ways individuals perceive and interpret information. It can further develop students' ability to withhold judgments of absolutes and to consider other alternatives. Thinking-skills instruction must include training that fosters open-mindedness, so that students understand that what seems to be unconditionally true in one situation may not be completely true in another.

Comparison

Comparison requires that students examine two or more situations, objects, ideas, or events and seek out relationships, similarities, or differences. The degree of thinking (or level of Bloom's Taxonomy) needed varies with the assignment of tasks for comparison. Once differences and similarities have been determined, designate opportunities for the students to practice the skill independently. Above all, link the thinking skill taught to some practical use and encourage students exhibiting non-thinking behaviors to keep an open mind and compare their answers and beliefs with the opinions expressed by others.

WEB   LINK   Critical Thinking
Select an on-line lesson plan (www.lessonplanspage.com) and "remodel" it as a critical-thinking activity. Describe elements of the remodeled lesson that will develop and reinforce students' critical thinking skills.

Analysis

During analysis, students examine the problem to be solved, taking it apart, identifying its elements, and finding relationships. Instruct students to identify useful ways of breaking problems into parts, ask them to define each part clearly, and request that they organize the data related to each part and examine relationships in determining their conclusions. If you prefer the infusion method of instruction, you should ask students to consider each of these elements in relation to the problem needing solving. If, however, you prefer to step your students through the skill of analyzing before asking them to apply the skill to a real problem for solving, you might simply present an item for analysis and give them four steps to follow—for example: first, identify the whole; second, define each part of the whole; third, organize data related to each part; fourth, state a conclusion based on your analysis. Keep in mind the difference between asking an analysis question and asking a knowledge-level recall question.

While analysis is an important aspect of problem solving and decision making, it is not intended for confining the individual to categorizing only presented information. That is, students should be encouraged to analyze information for relationships that might otherwise go unnoticed.

Again, the teacher's role in developing students' skills in decision making is to create an atmosphere of acceptance and support in the forming of values and beliefs, lest students experience despair and turn off from a feeling of "overloaded" disequilibrium. Let's look at one scenario in which a teacher successfully shared classroom decision making responsibilities with students. This teacher felt so overwhelmed by the demands of record keeping needed in the classroom that she formulated a shared-responsibility system with her students. Each class was divided into three groups, and student elections were conducted. Each group elected an officer, who handled record keeping for their group.

Students quickly learned to value honesty and accountability. As a result, each group requested additional officers so they could ensure more of a "check and balance" system. Each of the groups elected three officers—governor, assistant, and secretary—and assigned them each specific responsibilities. For example, the secretary of each group recorded and collected all makeup work for absentees in the group. When students returned after being absent, they were directed to see their secretary for makeup work. Thus, the group held the secretary accountable for all makeup work. Subsequently, another interesting occurrence with this system was that peer responsibility began to expand and be expected among students. Often, secretaries talked with a group member when absenteeism was frequent or was affecting the member's performance in class. Moreover, whenever an officer failed to provide a student member with accurate records, other issues evolved. For instance, should a student be "impeached" from office when found in error? To what extent should peers be tolerant of shortcomings? The classroom teacher in this situation continued to insist on a shared-responsibility role and required students to use problem-solving and decision-making skills in resolving these problems. Thus, the system provided students with opportunities to practice and refine responsibility learning.

APPLY AND REFLECT: Plan a sequence of learning activities that will lead to successful thinking skills. Share your activities.

When you convey to your students that you view them as responsible persons, you give them an "I can!" sense that helps them view themselves as successful thinkers and, so, nurture different ways of thinking, believing, and acting. Help them develop the vital sense of responsibility for their own accomplishments and for finding solutions to complex problems.

You need to reassure students constantly that, even though it is important to withhold judgments temporarily, it is important to never "bail out" until they feel comfortable with their personal interpretations and perceptions. You, too, may feel some disequilibrium and may be tempted to shut down or bail out because the challenges your students present have become intense. Complete Web Link: Critical Thinking and Web Link: Creative Thinking, which will give you some experience at planning for critical and creative thinking.

W E B   L I N K   Creative Thinking

Evaluate an on-line lesson plan for its creative value. Discuss aspects of the lesson that foster students' creative skills with your classmates. Explain how the lesson could be improved to increase its creative value.

This completes the examination of various activities for developing students' thinking skills. Table 10.2 summarizes the two thinking-skills instructional approaches. Review the summary and complete Review, Extension, and Reflective Exercise 10.2.

Creativity should be encouraged in the classroom.

TABLE 10.2 **Thinking-Skills Instruction**	
Concept	**Description**
Separate Approach	Program that focuses instruction on thinking-skill development without regard to content
Infusion Approach	Development of thinking skills in conjunction with regular curriculum; thinking-skill instruction is followed by applying the skill to the content being studied

Review, Extension, and Reflective Exercise 10.2

Describe how teachers can foster thinking skills.

Connections to INTASC Standards:

- Standard 2: Student Development. The teacher understands how children learn and develop and can provide learning opportunities that support their intellectual, social, and personal development.
- Standard 4: Instructional Strategies. The teacher must understand and use a variety of instructional strategies to encourage students' development of critical thinking, problem solving, and performance skills.
- Standard 5: Learning Environment. The teacher must be able to use an understanding of individual and group motivation and behavior to create a learning environment that encourages positive social interaction, active engagement in learning, and self-motivation.

- Standard 7: Planning Instruction. The teacher plans instruction based upon knowledge of subject matter, students, the community, and curriculum goals.

Connections to the NBPTS:

- Proposition 1: Teachers are committed to students and their learning.
- Proposition 3: Teachers are responsible for managing and monitoring student learning.

Review

- Differentiate between the separate and infusion approaches to teaching thinking skills.
- Describe the eight nonthinking behaviors reported by teachers and activities to overcome them.

Reflection

- Should you teach thinking at the grade level you expect to teach? If so, which approach to teaching thinking skills would work best? If not, why?

Summary

- Thinking can be viewed as the act of withholding judgment to use knowledge and experience to find new information, concepts, and conclusions.

Thinking Skills

- The ability to think at a level beyond the recall of factual information requires planned experiences and practice.
- Thinking can take place at any one of Bloom's Taxonomy levels: knowledge, comprehension, application, analysis, synthesis, and evaluation.
- The thinking level most appropriate to a specific class depends on the maturity of the students and the needs of the content area. The most commonly taught thinking skills are critical and creative thinking.
- Metacognition can be simply defined as thinking about thinking.

- Metacognition skills enable students to better benefit from instruction.

Thinking-Skills Instruction

- The teaching of thinking skills requires open-minded teachers.
- Thinking skills can be taught separately (separate approach) or by infusing them into the content (infusion approach).
- Direct, specific instruction often proves useful in fostering critical- and creative-thinking skills.
- Eight behaviors have been identified that negatively impact the development of thinking skills impulsiveness; overdependence on the teacher; inattentive behavior; restless rusher; dogmatic, assertive behavior; rigidity, inflexibility of behavior; fearful, lack of confidence; and responsibility forfeiture.

Discussion Questions and Activities

1. **Teaching methods.** What teaching methods and procedures can be used to improve students' critical thinking abilities? Creative thinking abilities?
2. **Thinking.** What type of thinking is emphasized in most schools? Is critical thinking rewarded? Creative thinking? Is school success based upon students' ability to think critically? Creatively?
3. **The environment.** What type of classroom environment would be conducive to developing critical thinking? Creative thinking? What problems can you foresee in establishing this environment?

Connection With the Field

1. **Classroom observation.** Visit several public school classrooms at the grade level you expect to teach. Keep a record of the techniques used to develop student critical thinking and creative thinking. Share your record with your class.
2. **Interviews.** Interview several teachers at different grade levels. How do they incorporate critical thinking and creativity into their everyday teaching activities? Make a list of ideas you can use when you become a teacher.

Praxis II Connection

The following test preparation exercises are intended to help you prepare for the Praxis II: Principles of Learning and Teaching. The Praxis II may be required by your teacher education preparatory program and for state certification or licensing. These exercises will give you direct access to pedagogical knowledge from Chapter 10 that may be expected of you on the Praxis II and other pedagogical exams that may be required at the end of your teacher education program.

Topic Connections

1. Thinking Skills (II. A1, A3)

Describe various thinking skills. What can teachers do to cultivate these skills in the classroom?

2. Creativity (II. A1, A3)

What is creativity? Describe techniques that teachers can use in the classroom to foster creative thinking.

ON YOUR OWN

Log on to the web-based student study site at http://www.sagepub.com/eis for more information about the vignettes and materials presented in this chapter, suggestions for activities, study aids such as electronic flashcards and review quizzes, and research recommendations including journal article links and questions related to this chapter.

LEADING THE
DYNAMIC CLASSROOM

O nce lessons have been planned, they must be implemented. Even the best-laid plans, however, can fail in the classroom. A successful teacher is one who can ably communicate, motivate, diagnose, and manage a classroom. Therefore, teachers must be aware of the influences that the communication process, motivation, and management skills have on the success of a lesson. Part 5 focuses on these implementation issues.

Without communication and motivation, there would be no teaching or learning. Chapter 11 deals with the important process of communication. Various verbal and nonverbal techniques are addressed, as well as the often-overlooked skill of listening.

Chapter 12 focuses on motivation. Learning will take place only when there is a desire to know, to understand, to learn. Thus, teachers must develop students' desire for learning. They must motivate!

Skillful classroom management is indispensable to a career in the classroom. The establishment of an environment conducive to learning will not be an easy task. If you are to do well, you must have a repertoire of management techniques from which to choose. Chapter 13 outlines several approaches to classroom management. In addition, Chapter 13 looks at leadership and the classroom atmosphere and their effect on behavior.

11
COMMUNICATING WITH STUDENTS AND PARENTS

I have often regretted my speech, never my silence.

XENOCRATES

OVERVIEW

Communication is essential in helping students learn. As a teacher, you must be sensitive to cultivating excellent communication skills and to monitoring the effectiveness of your interactions with students and parents.

Unfortunately, teachers often do most of the talking in classrooms, and students do most of the listening. Perhaps because of this, teachers tend to not really listen to what students are saying or not saying.

Experienced teachers know the importance of open communication and positive dialogue with parents. They make it a point to open channels of communication with parents at the beginning of the school year.

This chapter is about communication. As such, it will address both the sending and receiving of information and messages.

OBJECTIVES

After completing your study of Chapter 11, you should be able to do the following:

1. Explain the importance of the communication process.
2. Diagram a model of the communication process.
3. Differentiate among the verbal, vocal, and metaverbal components of a message.
4. Identify variables associated with the verbal and vocal components of a message.
5. Explain the role nonverbal communication plays in the classroom and provide examples of various nonverbal behaviors commonly used in the classroom.
6. Identify and explain the four spatial distances.
7. Explain how color communicates.

8. Explain the importance of listening and define the different types of listening.

9. Identify and describe variables that interfere with listening.

10. Explain the importance of feedback in the communication process.

Of all the knowledge and skills you possess as a teacher, those concerning communication will be among the most significant and the most useful. Through communication, you interact with students and parents, you teach, and students learn. Without communication, teaching could not occur and a school would not function.

As a practical skill, communication consists of the ability to speak, write, and read. Of equal importance in the communication process, however, is the ability to listen. Most teacher preparatory programs place a great deal of emphasis on the ability to read and write, with little attention put on speaking, and almost no attention being given to nonverbal communication and listening. The most persuasive teachers do not rely exclusively on reading and writing; they talk, they observe, and they listen. Thus, the skills I will examine here are verbal and nonverbal communication, as well as the art of listening, which serves an important function in the classroom.

Classroom Communication

Communication is the act, by one or more persons, of sending and receiving messages that are distorted by noise, have some effect, and provide some opportunity for feedback. The communication act, then, would include the following components:

1. Source(s)—receiver(s)
2. Messages
3. Noise
4. Sending, or encoding, processes
5. Receiving, or decoding, processes
6. Feedback
7. Effects

These elements are the universals of the communication process. They are present in every communication act, regardless of whether the communication is with oneself, parents, colleagues, or students. As a teacher, therefore, you will be intimately involved in this communication process as you interact with students and colleagues on a daily basis. This process is illustrated in Figure 11.1.

As shown in Figure 11.1, classroom communication can be viewed as a five-phase process, with teachers and students performing two functions: sending and receiving. First, you, as a teacher, encode (compose) a desired message into a form that you hope will be understood by your students. Second, you transmit this message, which can be sent by speaking, writing, gesturing, smiling, and so on. Third,

Figure 11.1

Communication as
a Five-Phase Process

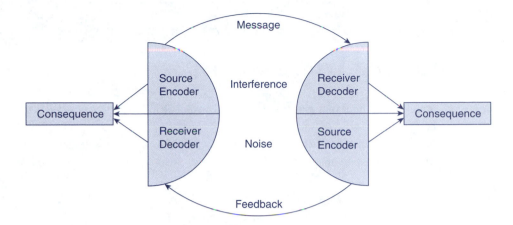

your transmitted message is accepted and decoded by students. The message can be received by listening, reading, seeing, smelling, and so on. Fourth, students then become a source and encode reactions to your message. Most student reactions are nonverbal. Fifth and finally, the nonverbal message (feedback) tells you whether the received message was understood or not. Thus, as you send messages, you are also receiving messages in the form of feedback and must constantly decode and react to this feedback. Your reaction may be to continue with your lesson, to clarify the original message, or to repeat the message.

A typical classroom situation will illustrate the communication model. Suppose you want to emphasize specific information for your students. Therefore, you encode and send this message: "This information should be included in your notes." The transmitted message is received and decoded by students to mean that you will ask about the information on the next exam. Therefore, they add it to their notes for future reference. Because you observe (feedback) the information being written in the students' notes, you feel your communication has been successful and continue with your lesson. If, on the other hand, you were to observe that students did not add the information to their notes, you might want to reemphasize its importance with a message such as this: "That information is so important that I had better write it on the board!" This example illustrates the importance of accurate messages, and it points to how critical your attention to feedback is to classroom communication.

Classroom communication always has some effect or consequence. In fact, there are three classes of classroom communication consequence: Students can acquire new information or awareness (cognitive effect), can change attitudinal or emotional states (affective effect), or can learn a new skill (psychomotor effect). Often, however, the consequences involve all three types of effects.

Noise and interference sometimes distort or interfere with classroom communication. The hum of an air conditioner, hall noise, the sunglasses a person wears, cars passing in the street, student movements, clothes students wear—these all may be regarded as classroom noise because they can interfere with the effective transmission of your messages to the class. Noise can also be psychological. Biases and prejudices, for example, can distort or interfere with getting an accurate message across. These sources of noise and interference must be overcome if students are to accurately receive and decode your messages.

Working With Parents

1. Should the school year and student time in school be extended?
2. Are parents unrealistic about the function of schools and what schools can accomplish?

As an educator, I am familiar with the old "boredom" tale from parents. I listen politely without comment. Then I ask them nicely what I can do to make my class more interesting for their child. Usually, they don't have an answer. The real problem is that in this age of instant results, many parents today expect their child's entire education to occur within the 6-hour school day. And they expect it to be individually tailored to their child. Whereas teachers should consider individual needs, it is unrealistic to individualize instruction for all students. I think many parents and educators have lost sight of the original intent of public education in the United States. Public education was set up to provide students with a foundation of skills and opportunities for education. It was assumed that truly interested students would continue learning at home. Now, with most parents working to make ends meet, I believe they have an absolute right to expect more from their child's school. But because most kids are only in school for about 1,200 hours per year, it is unrealistic to expect schools to work miracles. So much has changed in society, but our country's educational system has not yet caught up.

Perhaps we need to restructure our country's educational system to better address the needs of today's parents, who, just trying to survive, are often spread too thin to educate their children at home. If individualized instruction is what we need to have, then perhaps all students should be designated for "special education," with smaller classes of students working toward individual goals. After all, every student has his or her own special needs. As our system works now, only certain "identified" students are having their "special" needs met. Is that really fair?

Perhaps students should be in school for more hours. I feel like I have so much to "cover" for standardized tests that my students don't get the opportunity to practice newly learned skills as much as research says they need to. Of course, changes in our educational system will not happen until teachers are seen (and ultimately paid) as the highly specialized professionals that we are.

—MARY, *elementary school teacher*

SOURCE: Reprinted with permission from ProTeacher, a professional community for elementary school teachers (http://www.proteacher.net)

Messages may be sent and received in many forms: verbal, vocal, physical, or situational. Thus, you must be skilled at sending messages through any one or combinations of these modes. But of equal importance is your ability to decode messages (feedback) transmitted by students. This ability is directly related to your listening skill. Before I address listening, let's look at verbal and nonverbal communication.

Cell phones in the classroom can be a problem. Many schools do not allow cell phones in school.

Verbal Communication

Teachers communicate information to students by talking, that is, through **verbal communication**. Learning, however, does not take place only through teacher talk and words. Nonverbal variables sometimes determine whether or not something is learned.

Goodall (1983, pp. 14–15) breaks spoken messages into three components: verbal, vocal, and metaverbal. The **verbal component** refers to the actual words spoken and their meanings; the **vocal component** includes such variables as voice firmness, modulation, tone, tempo, pitch, and loudness; and the **metaverbal component** refers to what may be implied, or intended, by the spoken words.

The Verbal Component

Words can be interpreted in many ways, and these interpretations can be the basis for misunderstandings. Indeed, the message communicated in any interaction depends on both the words and the meanings attached to the words spoken. These meanings are learned as a result of experiences and, thus, are arbitrary. For example, a class discussion of terms such as *ghost, fear, feminism, religion,* or *democracy* will have varying outcomes, depending on students' experiences. Despite the formal dictionary definitions of such terms, you must make sure that your verbal instructions are related as much as possible to the learners' experiences. This determination calls for your assessment of what students bring to the learning situation—for example, intelligence, learning history, and learning ability. This information may show that the verbal aspects of your messages are outside the experience base of your students. (A word of caution: Don't let your assessment of students influence your expectations of their ability. Students tend to behave in a way congruent with how they are viewed.)

Another problem associated with the use of words is their misuse, which may stem from a lack of knowledge of their meanings. Indeed, it is often possible to talk endlessly about a subject and sound quite knowledgeable when, in fact, you haven't the slightest idea of the word meanings. These bluffing behaviors with words should be avoided in the classroom. Students will usually see through the lack of knowledge, and you will lose their respect.

Hurt, Scott, and McCroskey (1978, p. 76) suggest several other variables that may have some effect on whether a message is received and decoded accurately:

1. *Organization.* Good or well-organized verbal information tends to be learned more thoroughly, as does the information presented first or last in a lesson.
2. *Message sidedness.* Two-sided messages that present opposing views tend to be learned best.
3. *Language intensity.* Verbal information that deviates from a neutral position appears to be learned best.
4. *Concreteness and ambiguity.* The more concrete a message, the better. You must take care, however, that your message isn't made so concrete that the basic concept is lost.

Generally, variables such as those discussed earlier and those suggested by Hurt et al. (1978) tend to increase students' attention, which is your primary aim in the classroom. The increased attention should result in increased learning. Join some classmates to react to Expansion Activity: Talking to further explore teacher talk in the classroom.

EXPANSION ACTIVITY Talking	**Talk "with" people, not "to" people. What does this statement imply? Should you talk "with" or "to" students? Form groups** of four or five and react to the statement above. Share your group's reaction with the class.

The Vocal Component

How you say words is extremely important. The voice brings words to life. Changes in tone, voice loudness or strength, rate, inflection, or pitch can change a message emphasis, as well as its very meaning. For example, messages such as "I agree!" or "Yes!" can communicate different meanings, depending on the tone and modulation.

As a teacher, you will interact with groups and will often want to emphasize points with your voice. Therefore, it is essential that you develop and project a strong voice, so that you are heard by all students. This will take practice, but is well worth the effort. Often, the practice of talking over a little distance or the practice of inhaling and exhaling air will improve both the strength and projection of your voice.

The rate at which you speak will impact students as well. When you speak rapidly, you might convey the message that the subject isn't really important and should be finished with as soon as possible. In contrast, words spoken at a slower rate can indicate their importance and, therefore, indicate that they should be considered carefully. This fact is important to remember because you might be required to teach subjects that interest you little or to teach in areas in which you lack preparation. With such subjects, you must carefully watch your rate of presentation.

The tone, inflections, and pitch of the voice often impact words. Tone or inflection can communicate word seriousness or validity. For example, the seriousness of such messages as "I mean it!" or "Be quiet!" or even "I am losing my patience!" is affected by your tone and inflection. Moreover, as Hennings (1975, p. 17) points out, "the high-pitched voice can grate on a decoder's nerves so that the listener turns off to words spoken; the very deep voice can distract from the message." Therefore, you must guard against using an incorrect tone, inflection, or pitch, which might distract from your messages.

Voice volume, rate, tone, inflection, and pitch send emotional information. High levels of loudness, rate, and pitch can communicate excitement or enthusiasm, whereas a slow rate and even pitch can communicate disinterest. Joy, eagerness, anger, wonder, awe, displeasure, determination, and indecisiveness can be communicated through variations in the voice. Skill at using your voice can assist you greatly in keeping students on task and with the general management of the classroom environment. Therefore, practice with your voice; it will continue to serve you in your instruction if you know how to use it effectively.

You must be aware of the effect that a monotone voice can have on students. It can put them to sleep, cause their minds to wander, and, in general, result in a loss of student attention. Diversity in the voice can overcome these negative effects to some extent. Indeed, you can be a more effective teacher and keep students' attention by varying your voice volume, rate, tone, inflection, and pitch.

Classroom communication is a multichannel process. When you communicate with students all the expressive cues (verbal and nonverbal) converge to communicate one message, positive or negative. Sometimes, however, what is said is not what students are expected to understand.

The Metaverbal Component

When you speak, there is often an implied, or intended, message that cannot be directly attributed to the meaning of the words or the way they are spoken. This is referred to as the metaverbal component of a message. You may, for example, ask a student to drop by after school for a visit about an issue brought up in class, when actually you want to discuss the student's falling grades.

Metaverbal messages are often tricky, because you are trying to communicate an implied message. That is, students are being asked to hear beyond the words. Sometimes what you mean to imply when you speak is not how your words and actions are interpreted.

As you teach or listen, all basic components of verbal communication contribute to the messages received by students. Thus, students are hearing what you say at three levels: what is said, how it is said, and why (implied) it is said. Therefore, exercise care in the act of communicating and match your intent with your message.

APPLY AND REFLECT: More communication is not always best; some things are best left unsaid. What is implied in this statement? Discuss your interpretation with that of your classmates.

Technology can have an impact on a teacher's ability to communicate. Complete Expansion Activity: Communicating With Technology, which will let you explore this issue.

EXPANSION ACTIVITY

Communicating
With Technology

Technology is having a tremendous impact on education and our schools. How can e-mail and technology be used to improve communication within a school? With parents? With students?

Nonverbal Communication

Communication can be nonlinguistic. That is, you can send messages without using words. This form of communication is referred to as **nonverbal communication**. Because some researchers in the area of communication claim that more than 80 percent of our communication is nonverbal in nature, it is important that teachers be proficient with its use (Miller, 1986; Sathre, Olson, & Whiney, 1977).

You constantly send messages through the way you dress; your posture; the way you look, move, work your voice, and use space; and the way you use words. These

Teacher gestures and movement can improve the communication of classroom concepts.

"First, you have to get their attention."

nonverbal messages can reinforce, modify, or even contradict your verbal messages, as, for example, when you say with a sigh of relief, "I wish you could stay longer." In fact, the nonverbal part of communication often is more important than the verbal part, in that it expresses real feelings. Sometimes nonverbal information plays a role in determining what our reaction will be in certain situations or in deciding what our future behavior will be. For example, when a friend says, "I'd like to get together again soon," that person may state it in such a way that you suspect otherwise. Thus, actions often do speak much louder than words.

Sometimes nonverbal communication is designed very carefully for evoking a particular response, whereas at other times it occurs naturally or accidentally. In either case, it can influence perceptions, attitudes, and feelings. These nonverbal cues are often not taken at face value; rather, inferences are made from them in determining what to believe. Thus, teachers and students often unwittingly reveal attitudes and feelings toward each other and toward school in general through nonverbal cues. In other words, you must be alert to your nonverbal expressions and the effects they can have on students. An awareness of nonverbal communications and their consequences is a step toward controlling them. I will now look at some elements of nonverbal communications.

Facial Language

The face and eyes are probably the most conspicuous parts of our body, and, as such, we communicate a great deal of information through our facial expressions. In fact, according to Miller (1986), the face is second only to words in communicating our feelings. Miller further suggests that these facial expressions can be readily visible or fleeting, involuntary or voluntary. Whatever the type, facial expressions can reinforce, modify, and contradict what is said verbally.

Facial expressions that are readily visible are usually intentional. They send a message (e.g., a smile of pleasure) or are used to mask true feelings (e.g., a stern look of displeasure to cover pleasure). These expressions are formed by the movement of facial muscles around the forehead, mouth, eyebrows, chin, cheeks, or nose. Wrinkling the forehead, for example, communicates deep thought, lifting the eyebrows reveals wonder or surprise, a sneer shows anger or displeasure, and a jutting chin demonstrates firmness. Conversely, fleeting facial expressions are often unintentional and are usually quickly covered up with other expressions. For example, you may feel sudden disgust, anger, or dislike for someone you meet, but do not want to communicate this to the individual. Therefore, you quickly mask your true feelings or emotions with other, intended expressions.

Involuntary facial expressions usually take place under traumatic or delightful circumstances. Such microexpressions can flash across your face in situations where you are fearful, angry, happy, or surprised. In the classroom, these expressions are often fleeting in that you attempt to cover them up with other expressions as soon as possible. Under certain circumstances, however, you may want to retain such expressions to convey a message to students. For example, teachers often use expressions of displeasure or anger for controlling misbehavior in the classroom and expressions of humor for relieving tension or improving student attention.

Teachers commonly use voluntary facial expressions when communicating with students. In fact, effective teachers have perfected their facial expression. They convey a message with a look—for example, a smile of approval or a frown of displeasure.

The eyes can send several kinds of messages. As Miller (1986, p. 13) notes, your eyes "can be shifty and evasive, conveying hate, fear, and guilt, or they can express confidence, love, and support." Also, with eye contact you can open communication, prolong communication, or cut off communication entirely.

As most teachers know, eye contact can be used in controlling interaction in the classroom. When they want a student to speak, they make direct eye contact with that individual. Conversely, when they want to continue talking, they refrain from making direct eye contact with anyone who may want to speak. Moreover, most of us can remember trying to avoid a question we couldn't answer by glancing away from the teacher. At such times, we became very interested in our textbook or our assignment. Thus, teachers sometimes gauge eye contact in determining when students are lying, when students can't answer a question, or when students have failed to complete their homework. Indeed, you probably have heard it said that, when students are lying or when they haven't done as they should, they avoid direct eye contact. This hypothesis, however, generally hasn't been supported by research. In fact, watch your use of such unproven generalizations, for they may influence you inappropriately. For example, you may tend to distrust students who do not make direct eye contact when speaking to you. But a shy student who does not like or finds it difficult to make direct eye contact may be completely trustworthy.

Very direct eye contact—a stare—can change student behavior. A stare used with silence can be quite effective in gaining the attention of misbehaving or inattentive students. Indeed, the stare alone can result in appropriate student behavior.

Body Language

Kinesics, or the study of body movements and gestures in communication, represents an important source of information. Indeed, gestures with the head, arms, hands, and other body parts are pervasive as nonverbal communicators. Gestures may provide information, as when you point when giving directions; they may communicate feelings, as when you nod your head in agreement as a student speaks; they may emphasize a point, as when you tap something you have written on the chalkboard; they may call for attention, as when you stomp your foot. Indeed, we often interpret an individual's body movements as an indication of his or her character (as in an authoritative or nonchalant walk). Our physical actions, then, are sending information constantly to those who are observant and attentive.

The overuse of body movement and gestures can be a deterrent to effective communication. When you use too many gestures too often, students find it difficult to discern the peaks and cannot really tell what is important in a message. Also, too many gestures can prompt students to attend to the gestures themselves rather than to the message.

Stance and general posture are another type of kinesics communication. A tense, rigid body tends to communicate the desire for distance and insecurity, whereas a relaxed body denotes strength, openness, and friendliness. The way you stand can also communicate information. A body orientation toward the listener tends to suggest security and comfort in the communication interaction.

The use of touch is a very powerful nonverbal communicator. Touch in communication is influenced by who does the touching. Teachers of young children, for example, often use hugs as reinforcement, whereas touch is often inappropriate for use with middle and secondary school students.

Although it is usually unwise for you to touch a student of the opposite sex, remember that an appropriate pat on the back is a good reinforcer for students. You should use your best judgment as to whether or when to use touch in communicating with your students.

The way you dress sends a variety of messages. It is often difficult to take a speaker seriously, for example, if he or she is dressed in ill-fitting, wrinkled clothing. Conversely, we tend to pay attention to an attractively dressed speaker. Teachers, then, would be well-advised to dress as befitting their roles as classroom leaders.

The Language of Space and Motion

The arrangement of your classroom and your use of the space can shape communication. How you place objects within your classroom, as well as where and how you choose to move within the confines of the space, are significant.

The Environment

The physical makeup of the learning environment can create moods and, in doing so, affect the interaction within the environment. Indeed, the attractiveness of a room appears to influence the happiness and energy of people working in it. Such findings are supported by Miller (1986, p. 23) in his summary of research related to student reactions in ugly and beautiful classrooms. He states that "subjects in the ugly room had reactions of monotony, fatigue, headache, irritability, and hostility, while subjects in the beautiful room responded favorably with feelings of comfort, pleasure, importance, and enjoyment for completing the assigned tasks." Thus, Miller's findings suggest that a well decorated, pleasing classroom is more conducive to open communications and is more effective at keeping students on task.

Colors can affect the behavior of students. For example, it has been shown that blue is more soothing and red more active than other colors (Snider & Osgood, 1969). Perhaps color can be used in influencing actions within the classroom. It may be that a combination of such colors as blue and red will result in more productive communication patterns.

Territoriality

Territoriality is commonly observed in the classroom. Indeed, learning environments are too often arranged into territories, with the teacher's desk forming the teacher's territory and each student's seat or desk forming the individual student's territory. Such arrangements can lead to the understanding that each is to remain in his or her own territory. This, too, often leads to a restricted environment, with little interaction. Also, such restricted environments can convey messages of teachers wanting to keep their distance from students.

Territoriality can also be observed in classrooms or other areas where seats are not assigned. For example, when a student takes the seat normally occupied by another student, the regular occupant often becomes disturbed and resentful. Likewise, in a library, you may mark your territory with a jacket or books when you leave the room.

Teacher Motion

Teacher movement within the classroom can aid or hinder the communication process. Movement toward a student who is speaking can, for example, convey a message of interest, whereas movement away from the student can communicate lack of interest. A teacher's movement, then, can often prolong interaction. Indeed, teacher movement throughout different areas in the classroom often helps keep student attention directed toward the teacher (see Chapter 12 for a more detailed discussion of this topic).

Proxemics

Proxemics is the study of the use and meaning of space. Studies (Hall, 1959; Montagu, 1977) indicate that people engaged in interaction tend to choose a particular separation distance, depending on their feeling toward the other person or persons at the time, the context of the conversation, and their personal goals. For example, conversations between intimate people usually take place within 18 inches (intimate distance). Friends in conversation usually stand 3 to 4½ feet apart (personal distance). Business and social interactions usually take place with a separation of 4 to 7 feet (social distance). For most presentations, a distance of 15 feet or more is most common (public distance).

Even though the generalizations about "appropriate" interaction distances are tentative, you should recognize the value of the use of space in your interactions with students. In general, teachers want to work within the personal and social distance ranges in their interactions with students. Interactions with individual students should take place at a personal distance, whereas whole-class interactions usually occur at the social distance.

The Language of Time

Time and its subtleties can be wisely used for successful communication. How you decide to spend class time conveys important attitudinal information. When you spend little time on a topic, or pass it by completely, you communicate that the topic is unimportant or that you have little interest in it. Such actions can unintentionally translate into similar attitudes by students.

Pauses and silence represent another way that time can be used in communicating. For example, pausing just before or after you make a point signifies that the point is important. In addition, pauses can cue students that an important point is going to be made or that the last point made was important enough for them to reflect on it.

Time can also be used to communicate a variety of emotional responses. Silence, for example, can reflect fear, a determination to be uncooperative, or an attempt at defiance. And, of course, silence is often used for showing lack of interest. In fact, your discussions will often result in silence when your topic lacks interest or when you fail to motivate.

Teachers ask many questions; however, they may find it difficult to allow for sufficient time between the asking of their questions and the reception of a student response. Teachers often expect almost instant responses to their questions, and, when not forthcoming, they tend to answer the questions themselves. These teachers must learn to increase their wait-time so they can improve classroom interaction (see Chapter 7 for a detailed discussion of wait-time).

Finally, reverence for silence and the sense of time vary with different cultures, subcultures, and regions (Berger, 1991; Gilliland, 1988). The Apache, for example, encourage silence. For some African cultures, time is only approximate. The Midwest has a reputation for punctuality. In New York, people are on the go, and time is money; however, punctuality is perhaps not as revered as in the Midwest. Indeed, lateness can be "fashionable" for social gatherings. On the notoriously laid-back West Coast, on the other hand, being late is not a serious problem. Teachers then should take a close look at their students' concept of time before they react to situations that involve time. Perhaps their students are running on different clocks.

The Language of the Voice

As mentioned earlier in this chapter, the vocal cues that accompany our spoken language exert a great deal of influence on a listener's perception. Indeed, vocal intonation can reveal prejudices, emotions, and background information about a speaker; it can communicate excitement, fear, or some other strong emotions. These perceptions are generally based on experiences and stereotypes associated with various vocal qualities, intonations, characteristics, and so on.

The adage is often true: "It's not what you say. It's how you say it." A vibrant "That's an excellent idea!" conveys a different message than does a simple monotone "That's an excellent idea." As noted earlier, when a contradiction occurs between a verbal and vocal message, the vocal message is usually believed.

As a teacher you must watch your vocal messages. Your vocal intonations sometimes will communicate meanings different from those you intend. Your messages can be modified by varying the loudness or softness, by using high pitch or low pitch, and by varying the tone or the quality of speech. You must be aware of and pay attention to the effect of these voice intonations. That is, you must learn to speak so your verbal and vocal messages are congruent.

APPLY AND REFLECT: Make sure your verbal and nonverbal messages are congruent when you interact with students. Do you have any habits that might negatively impact this ability?

This concludes the discussion of verbal and nonverbal communication. Table 11.1 summarizes the material presented in this section. Before moving on to communicating with parents, review the summary and complete Review, Extension, and Reflective Exercise 11.1.

TABLE 11.1 Communication Process

Type	Description
Verbal Communication	Communication with the spoken word through verbal, vocal, or metaverbal components
Nonverbal Communication	Nonlinguistic communication, or the sending of messages without words

Review, Extension, and Reflective Exercise 11.1

Identify good approaches to communication.

Connections to INTASC Standards:

- Standard 2: Student Development. The teacher understands how children learn and develop and can provide learning opportunities that support their intellectual, social, and personal development.
- Standard 6: Communication. The teacher uses knowledge of effective verbal, nonverbal, and media communication techniques to foster active inquiry, collaboration, and supportive interaction in the classroom.

Connections to the NBPTS:

- Proposition 1: Teachers are committed to students and their learning.

- Proposition 3: Teachers are responsible for managing and monitoring student learning.

Review

- Describe the components of the communication process.
- What are some barriers to effective communication?
- What are some important aspects of nonverbal communication?

Reflection

- What are your own communication strengths and weaknesses? What might you do to improve them? How does your ability to speak affect your view of the world?

Communicating With Parents

Veteran teachers stress the importance of communicating with parents and families, but good communication between you and parents will not just happen. It requires work and special skills such as good listening techniques, tact, kindness, consideration, empathy, enthusiasm, and an understanding of parent-child relationships.

You should not wait for parent-teacher conferences to begin communicating with parents. Effective teachers start communicating with parents at the beginning of the school year. This will be a major investment of time, but one that will pay off in the long run. Send a letter of introduction to parents (see Figure 11.2). It doesn't need to be personal, just an overview of what you think the semester or year will look like, an introduction of yourself and a general invitation to the parents to be involved in your classroom. Make sure to include how parents can best get in contact with you and encourage them to feel free to do so. If you can find out from the students (This is something you should include on their information sheets.) what their parents' last names are, it is nice to use a computer to put "Dear Ms. Alvarez" at the top instead of "Dear Parent or Guardian." It is also a good idea to send these letters through the mail rather than via the black holes of students' backpacks and lockers.

Invite parents to your classroom. In most schools, there is an open house near the beginning of each year or semester. Take full advantage of this and share your expectations with them. Invite them at other times, too. Invite them to hear student presentations or performances. Have students organize a night at the end of the year to showcase their work and have a little party for their parents.

Use progress reports to really report student progress to parents. While it is much easier to simply average grades and write "85" on a progress report, parents will appreciate it much more if you add a few sentences at the bottom. These should always include some good things before any bad ones. "Mike has turned in almost every assignment and is making good progress, but he did not do quite enough to prepare for his presentation on Mexico. We will be working on research skills before we begin our next unit."

As more and more school districts across the United States implement school-based management, teachers communicating with school administrators and community leaders will assume greater importance. Indeed, teachers are now finding themselves with the power to be involved in making decisions about how money should be spent at school sites, what the staff mix should be, and what should be taught in classrooms and how. School-based management decentralized control from the central district office to individual schools as a way to give school constituents—principals, teachers, parents, and community members—more control over what happens in schools.

This completes my brief discussion on communicating with parents. But before moving on to the next section, complete Web Link: Communicating With Parents. In the next section, I will consider another very important topic related to the communication process: the art of listening.

W E B   L I N K   Communicating With Parents
Research suggests that it is important to have strong family communication with the school. Access Internet sites www.ncpie.org/Resources/and wwwtools.cityu .edu.hk/news/newslett/parents.htm for ways to improve family communication with schools. Share your findings with the class.

Jones Elementary School
2004 Elementary School Road
Wichita, KS

September 5, 2004

John and Mary Miller
5555 Springdale Drive
Wichita, KS

Dear Mr. and Mrs. Miller:

I am Larry's new [fourth grade] teacher. I am excited about this year and look forward to working with you to accomplish your child's academic needs. I will use several methods to give feedback to you and your child about his progress. Please note that I use the following:

1. quarterly grade reports will give your child's progress to date

2. graded homework assignments weekly

3. graded quizzes and tests

4. our [fourth grade] Internet school site

I hope you will ask Larry about his homework and weekly grades. Please have him share his work with you. I do schedule parent conferences as needed. If you wish to schedule an appointment with me, please call 471-1234. I am available before and immediately after school. Those hours are 7:30 a.m. to 8:00 a.m. and 3:00 p.m. to 4:00 p.m.

So you will be able to talk with your child about his work this first 9 weeks, the objectives we will cover include

-

-

-

I look forward to meeting you at the open house on September 11 at 7:00 p.m. My room number is 28 and I am located in the north wing.

I look forward to the opportunity of working with you and your child this year. Together we will make a terrific team.

Sincerely,
Jane Zimmerman
Teacher

Communication comes in many forms and can send a variety of messages to different individuals.

Components of Listening

Hearing and listening are not the same thing. Hearing is an automatic, physical component of listening. **Hearing** occurs when eardrum vibration caused by sound impulses is transmitted to the brain. **Listening** occurs when the brain assigns meaning to the transmitted impulses. Thus, listening is an active process, an art.

Many times, you hear but do not listen. You hear boring lectures, for example, but seldom listen to them. It is hard work to *really* listen—and it is much harder than talking. Although listening takes effort and discipline, the dividends that result will continue to reward you as a teacher, both inside and outside the classroom.

Virtually everyone listens; however, few do it well. Basic to the improvement of your listening ability is awareness of the need for improving the skill. When you compare all the training you receive in reading, writing, and speaking with that provided in listening, you will find your listening training to be lacking. This is ironic when you realize that 60 percent of your communication involves listening (DeVito, 1985; Friedman, 1986).

Listening requires that you first learn to cut down on your talking. Although when we were younger we tended to ramble on and on, oblivious to what others around us were saying, we soon learned from adults that others did not look favorably toward those who talked continuously. But cutting down on our talking is only the beginning to becoming a good listener.

Listening is more than just being silent. Like thinking, listening is an intense, active process. It takes concentration and self-discipline. In fact, Barker (1971, p. 4) describes the listening process as having four components: hearing, attending, understanding, and remembering.

Hearing

As previously mentioned, *hearing* is physiological. It is the nonselective process of sound waves striking the eardrums, with the resultant electrochemical impulses being transmitted to the brain. Therefore, any aural information you wish to process and understand is accompanied by noise. This noise masks the desired message. In fact, hearing can be affected by exposure to continuous loud tones or noise. Loud music and city noises can lead to auditory fatigue, a temporary loss of hearing, and even to a permanent loss of hearing.

Attending

Although listening starts with a physiological process of hearing, it quickly becomes a psychological one as students decide whether to focus on, or *attend* to, what you say. This decision is directly related to their needs, wants, desires, and interests, as well as the relevance of the message, the setting, the intensity of the message, the concreteness of the message, and the duration of the message.

Listening involves focusing on the speaker and the message being transmitted. In some cases, listeners may not like what the speaker is saying, or they may not see the importance of the message, but they will never truly know unless they sit it out and listen. Although you cannot control all the variables that affect listening in your classroom, your awareness of such variables can enable you to take a step toward controlling them. You must teach students to focus their attention, stop talking, stop fidgeting, and stop letting their minds wander. You must teach them to "lock in" on what you are saying while blocking out everything around them.

Blocking out external stimuli is not an easy task for you and students and, in fact, is not always desirable behavior for teachers, who must be aware of everything that is happening in the classroom. Indeed, teachers must learn to both be aware of what is going on in the classroom and pay attention to students when the situation calls for it.

The way we view a speaker also affects our willingness to listen. If a speaker is described as being very intelligent or as someone of importance, we tend to listen with greater intensity. This tendency also applies to speakers who are attractive and who hold ideas, attitudes, and values similar to our own. Other factors such as size, dress, and name may also have an effect on our capacity for listening. You must control these affecting variables as much as possible if you are to enhance listening in your classroom.

Listening, like talking, consists of both a verbal and nonverbal component. The words we hear are only one aspect of listening. We also gain information through nonverbal means—that is, through the constant interplay of gestures, feelings, body movements, and so on inherent in human interaction. Thus, teachers sometimes believe they are sending one message (verbal), but their voice, choice of words, and gestures (nonverbal) send a completely different message.

Sokolove, Sadker, and Sadker (1986, p. 232) identify four nonverbal cues that will affect communication in your classroom. These writers suggest that attentiveness can be improved by giving special attention to the following:

1. *Eye contact.* Focus your eyes directly on students when they speak, while taking care that the direct contact does not make them uncomfortable.

2. *Facial expressions.* Let your facial expressions show that you are really listening. These expressions should give feedback (positive and negative) to students as to whether the message is being received as intended.
3. *Body posture.* Relax as a listener. This will relax your students and stimulate them to say more. In fact, the teacher who is relaxed and leans toward students when they are speaking communicates interest and involvement.
4. *Physical space.* Locate yourself so that you and student speakers have comfortable separation.

Although much of the nonverbal information you receive will be on a conscious level, you will also glean information from students at the subconscious level—for example, when you know they aren't really interested in what you are saying. This subconscious information will play an important part in shaping your impressions and helps in developing a response to the messages being sent, even though students may not be aware of them. Indeed, inferences—sometimes inaccurate—regarding students are often formed based on the subconscious information you receive.

Understanding

Understanding involves the mental processing of received information. During this phase, students must actively judge the worthiness of the message and the relevance of the information, as well as select and organize the information received (Friedman, 1986). They must consider the information and decide "Am I really interested?" This judgment is based on several elements. First, it involves recognition of the rules of grammar that were used to create the message. Second, judgment is often based upon their knowledge about the source of the information—whether the source is reliable, the teacher, a professional, and so on. Third, understanding can hinge on the social context. For example, the same message delivered in the classroom and on the playground would most likely elicit different judgments. Finally, students often judge the merit of a message by their ability to organize it into a recognizable form.

Remembering

Remembering is the fourth component of the listening process. The recall of information is directly related to how the information is evaluated. In other words, before students send the information to long-term memory, they must decide that it is worthy of remembering. In this evaluation process, they are "weighing the message against personal beliefs, questioning the speaker's motives, challenging the ideas presented, suspecting the validity of the message, holding the speaker's ideas up to standards of excellence, wondering what has been omitted, thinking how the message could have been improved, and in other ways evaluating what is being said" (Friedman, 1986, p. 7). This evaluation generally takes place with respect to the internal beliefs and values they hold. They must learn, however, to evaluate information on its own merit. This ability is difficult, and it takes self-discipline, but, it will be well worth the effort.

Experiences and internal feelings often have an effect on student evaluation. They all have emotional filters, which affect how they evaluate what they hear. These filters may block words or phrases or, conversely, allow certain words or phrases to rush in and overly impress them. They may at times even change what they hear, as with such words as *homework, test,* or *play.* Like observing, listening can be selective to some degree.

Nichols and Stevens (1957) offer three guidelines for helping students reduce the effects of filters on evaluation. They should do the following:

1. Be self-disciplined. Withhold evaluation until they receive the total message.
2. Hunt for negative evidence related to the received message. Don't take what they hear at face value.
3. Make a realistic self-analysis of the information they hear. Test the information against their biases, values, and feelings.

APPLY AND REFLECT: Be careful not to filter out difficult or undesirable messages. Do you have a tendency to do so? If so, how can you overcome this tendency?

The ability to recall information is also related to how often students hear the information and to whether the information has been rehearsed. Of course, the more times they hear any piece of information, the better they will retain it; similarly, rehearsed information is more often remembered.

Some students are poor listeners because they have developed bad listening habits. These bad habits include the following:

1. *Pseudolistening.* Pseudolistening is an imitation of listening. Good pseudolisteners look you in the eye, nod and smile in agreement, and even answer questions occasionally. In other words, they give the appearance of attentiveness, but, in reality, they are thinking about other things.
2. *Insulated listening.* Some students avoid listening when they do not want to deal with an issue or when it takes mental exertion to understand what is being said. If they have such a habit, you must make special efforts to have them practice listening to difficult-to-understand information.
3. *Selective listening.* Selective listeners attend only to a teacher's remarks that interest them. Such students automatically cease listening when the message is of little interest. They equate "interest" with "value." The fallacy associated with this habit is that the message is often worth listening to. Of course, all students are somewhat selective at times—for instance, when they screen out the class next door and background noise.
4. *Attribute listening.* Attribute listeners are more interested in the delivery and/or the physical appearance of the teacher. These students are often more concerned with criticizing the teacher's style of delivery or physical appearance than with listening to the message. They associate the importance of the message with the way it is delivered or with the appearance of the teacher or speaker. They should remember that the content of most messages is more important than the method of delivery or the appearance of the deliverer.
5. *Stage hogging.* Stage hoggers want to talk. They are interested only in expressing their own ideas. If they allow others to speak, it seems to be only while they catch their breath. Some students and many teachers, for example, want to do all the talking in the classroom. These students and teachers seldom give other students the opportunity to voice their opinions; when they do, they often cut off these student remarks. Teachers must be especially sensitive to the habit of stage hogging. Remember: Stage hogging isn't really conversing; essentially, it's speech making.

6. *Defensive listening.* Defensive listeners take innocent remarks as personal attacks. Teenagers are notorious for being defensive listeners. They often take parental or teacher remarks about their behaviors as being distrustful snooping, and teachers must be aware of this. Similarly, teachers must also realize that many students will be overly sensitive and defensive regarding remarks about their appearance and physical attributes. Children and teenagers can be extremely cruel to each other at times.

In most cases, an awareness of the bad habits associated with the listening process is enough in itself to assist students in overcoming their effects. Still, students should practice working on such bad habits if they are to become better listeners.

Thinking often affects listening. It is a well-established fact that we can process information at a faster pace than it can be delivered to us. Therefore, when students listen they have time for taking in their environment and for thinking—for meandering off on mental tangents. This extra thinking time would be better used in reflecting on and analyzing what is being said.

Although teachers want students to be better listeners, they often lack the skill. These needed skills might be better understood through an examination of the different styles of listening.

Styles of Listening

We listen for different reasons and with different ends in mind. Indeed, listening does and should vary from situation to situation. Listening to a student recitation, for example, calls for a different style of listening than does helping a student with his or her problems. Here I will address three styles of listening: one-way, two-way, and empathic.

One-Way Listening

One-way listening occurs when you are not actively taking part in the exchange of a message. In a word, it is passive listening. You listen without talking and without giving nonverbal directions to the speaker. One-way listening gives speakers the opportunity to develop their thoughts and ideas without being unduly influenced by the listeners. Common examples of one-way listening are watching television and taking in a lecture.

One-way listening gives a speaker free rein. The listener becomes a sounding board for the speaker's ideas or problems. Students often need such a person, who will just hear them out without giving a reaction. The occasional need for a sounding board explains why some people enjoy talking to inanimate objects or pets.

You are also taking part in one-way listening when you just sit back, relax, and let the auditory input stimulate your senses. Listening to music for the pure enjoyment is an excellent example of this type of listening.

One-way listening has limited value to teachers. Indeed, except for the few cases we have addressed, it isn't very effective for the simple reason that students often misunderstand at least some of a teacher's ideas. For example, messages that are overly vague will often be interpreted incorrectly by students. In other cases, teachers can send incorrect information or a student can simply get the information wrong. Thus, a teacher can say "8 grams" instead of "5," or a student can transform 8 grams into 5. On the whole, although one-way listening has its uses, complete understanding of your message isn't always a sure thing. Fortunately, there are other, better listening styles.

Two-Way Listening

Two-way listening actively involves the listener in the exchange of information. In practice, listeners provide feedback to the speaker by asking for more information or by paraphrasing the speaker's message.

Asking for additional information when a message is unclear is a valuable tool in seeking understanding. Often, you simply ask the student to elaborate on the information presented. For example, you might want a student to provide more details on the method used to solve a math word problem, a student might ask you to repeat your directions for writing a theme, or students might ask you for clarification on how to use a piece of laboratory equipment.

Restating the student's message in your own words is another technique for providing feedback. One example of paraphrasing might be "So you're telling me that you have problems with your parents because they are too restrictive." The thing to remember in restating the student's message is to paraphrase the words, not parrot them.

Although active listening usually involves verbal feedback, the feedback can be nonverbal—for example, a smile or nod of comprehension, or a frown that shows a lack of understanding. If you are observant, active nonverbal listening techniques can be as effective as the more common verbal techniques.

Two-way listening offers some real advantages for teachers. First, it boosts the odds that you will accurately and fully understand what students are telling you. In effect, active listening serves as a double check on the accuracy of your interpretation of student statements. A second advantage of active listening is that it often stimulates students to explore issues in greater depth. Last, your use of listening encourages students to solve their own problems by giving them the opportunity to talk through them.

Empathic Listening

Empathic listening is listening with feeling. It is an earnest attempt to experience what the speaker is experiencing or feeling and to respond to those feelings. Only through such listening can you fully understand another's meaning. Empathic listening calls for careful attention to the speaker's verbal and nonverbal cues. The listener gleans the full meaning of the speaker's message by putting these cues together into a statement that reflects the content as well as the associated feeling.

During the response portion of empathic listening, the listener is attempting to avoid misinterpretation of the speaker or to clarify the message. Sokolove, Sadker, and Sadker (1986, p. 230) suggest that the teacher's function in empathic listening is like holding up a mirror for the student's words, feelings, and behaviors. Through the process of empathic listening, you try to provide direct feedback regarding the success of student communication. This response can take the form of simple paraphrasing of the student's words, or can be an actual interpretation of the student's message as reflected in the verbal and nonverbal behaviors. For example, if a student conveys that he or she dislikes your science class, your reflective response to the content of this message might be, "I believe you are saying that you dislike science because you find the experiments too difficult."

Your response to a student statement can be related to the content component of the message or the affective component of the message. For example, your response to the content of a message might begin with phrases such as "I believe you are saying" or "You appear to think," whereas, with responses that reflect the affective component of a message, you might begin with "I think you are feeling" or "You appear to feel."

There are no quick methods for achieving empathy with your students. But it is important to work toward this end. You must learn to see the student's point of view. For example, if students turn in their work late, you should attempt to put yourself in the students' place in understanding the reasons for the lateness. You will often see behaviors that you will consider foolish and ridiculous. What you need to do, however, is consider such situations from the viewpoint of the students.

In summary, skill in the various types of listening is an essential tool for effective teaching. Indeed, the importance of good listening on the part of teachers has become more acceptable and recognizable today than ever before. Listening skill is now acknowledged as directly related to teacher effectiveness. All teachers must be proficient listeners.

APPLY AND REFLECT: Listen with an open mind. Withhold judgment until you have all the information. Why is it important that teachers do this? Discuss your reasons with the rest of the class. Do they agree?

Listening Feedback

Classroom communication requires that the specific messages you encode and transmit are received and accurately decoded by students. This is generally continuous and two-way. Students continuously decode the information you send and send you messages in return. These student-feedback messages, in general, are usually nonverbal.

Students are continuously sending nonverbal messages of understanding or uncertainty, agreement or disagreement, liking or distaste, concern or lack of concern, attention or inattention. When you receive this feedback, you should interpret it and incorporate it to modify or clarify your original message; namely, you should respond by reexplaining, offering further examples, or changing your mode of instruction. Identifying and responding to such student feedback is a skill you must master.

The successful use of feedback in the learning environment is an effective way to improve instruction. Many teachers, however, indicate that they rarely, if ever, use feedback as part of their teaching strategy. But feedback is so important to the total learning process that it must not be avoided or ignored.

APPLY AND REFLECT: Interpretation of feedback isn't always accurate. Check the validity of the feedback you receive. What are some techniques for doing this?

Table 11.2 summarizes the different types of listening. Review the summary and complete Review, Extension, and Reflective Exercise 11.2.

TABLE 11.2 Listening

Type	Description
One-way	Passive listening with no interaction between speaker and listeners
Two-way	Active listening with exchange between speaker and listeners
Empathic	Listening with an effort to experience speaker's feelings

Review, Extension, and Reflective Exercise 11.2

Identify the components and styles of listening.

Connections to INTASC Standards:

- Standard 2: Student Development. The teacher understands how children learn and develop and can provide learning opportunities that support their intellectual, social, and personal development.
- Standard 6: Communication. The teacher uses knowledge of effective verbal, nonverbal, and media communication techniques to foster active inquiry, collaboration, and supportive interaction in the classroom.

Connections to the NBPTS:

- Proposition 1: Teachers are committed to students and their learning.
- Proposition 3: Teachers are responsible for managing and monitoring student learning.

Review

- Describe the components and styles of listening.
- Differentiate between one-way and two-way listening.
- What is empathic listening?

Reflection

- How difficult do you find it to stop talking and really listen? What does it mean to listen with an open mind? How does your ability to listen affect your view of the world?

VIEW FROM THE CLASSROOM

What do teachers think about communicating with students and parents? Teacher survey results relative to communicating are presented below. Review these results and discuss with classmates.

Which method of communication do you find most helpful to keep in contact with parents?

Telephone	43%
E-mail	25%
Notes sent home with students	17%
Class newsletters	11%
Notes sent via the postal system	3%
Teacher/school websites	1%

SOURCE: Excerpted from *Teach-nology*, available at www.teach-nology.com/poll

Summary

- Communication is central to the learning process, for without it, learning could not take place.

The Communication Process

- Classroom exchanges consist of both spoken and nonverbal messages, with the spoken message comprising the verbal, vocal, and metaverbal components.
- The verbal component of a message is the actual words spoken; the vocal component is the meaning attached to the words, depending on such things as pitch, loudness, tone, and rate; and the metaverbal component is the implied, or intended, message.
- Students also learn through nonverbal communication; that is, they learn from a teacher's facial language, body language, use of space and motion, use of time, and use of the voice.

Components of Listening

- Teachers and students alike need to develop better listening skills.
- Effective teachers communicate with parents.
- Communicating with school administrators and community leaders is assuming greater importance.
- Listening is a four-step process: hearing, attending, understanding, and remembering.
- Many people have developed bad habits that must be overcome if they are to be effective listeners.
- Teachers must overcome bad habits and become proficient at one-way, two-way, and empathic listening.
- Teachers generally do most of the talking in the classroom.
- Teachers have not learned to use nonverbal communication effectively, and rarely—if at all—have they learned to use feedback and to *really* listen to students.

Discussion Questions and Activities

1. **The communication process.** Even when effectively carried out, communication can have good or bad results. Recall several incidents in which communication improved a situation and several in which communication made a situation worse.
2. **Listening habits.** Use the bad habits described in this chapter to describe faulty listening behaviors you use daily. In what circumstances are you guilty of these habits? Around whom? In what settings? At what times?

Connection With the Field

1. **Vocal communication.** Listen to the audio portion only of a videotape instructional episode from a classroom at the level that you expect to teach. List information being exchanged through vocal communication.
2. **Nonverbal communication.** Play the tape in activity 1 with only video (no audio). List information being exchanged by the teacher or the students through nonverbal communication.
3. **Metaverbal communication.** Play the tape again with audio and video. Did you notice any implied messages? If so, what were they? Give your reasons for making these conclusions.

4. **Classroom observation.** Complete several observations at the grade level you expect to teach. Collect data related to communication acts such as these:

   a. The effective use of verbal communication
   b. The different nonverbal languages used by the teachers
   c. The teachers' listening skills

Praxis II Connection

The following test preparation exercises are intended to help you prepare for the Praxis II: Principles of Learning and Teaching. The Praxis II may be required by your teacher education preparatory program and for state certification or licensing. These exercises will give you direct access to pedagogical knowledge from Chapter 11 that may be expected of you on the Praxis II and other pedagogical exams that may be required at the end of your teacher education program.

Topic Connections

1. School Communication (II. A)

Describe the various communication components and types. What might you do to become a better communicator? How might you improve communication with students? Parents? School administrators?

2. Listening (II. A)

Describe the components of the listening process and the different listening styles. How can teachers develop better student listening skills?

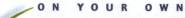

ON YOUR OWN

Log on to the web-based student study site at http://www.sagepub.com/eis for more information about the vignettes and materials presented in this chapter, suggestions for activities, study aids such as electronic flashcards and review quizzes, and research recommendations including journal article links and questions related to this chapter.

12
MOTIVATING STUDENTS

Whether you think that you can, or
that you can't, you are usually right.

HENRY FORD

OVERVIEW

One of your greatest teaching challenges will be to develop students' desire to learn—that is, to motivate students. The traditional approach to motivation was one of preaching to students about learning and the benefits they would derive as well-informed citizen. Needless to say, this approach was ineffective.

Lack of motivation and problems with classroom management are often cited as the major causes for the apathy. Thus, motivation and classroom management are two keys to effective instruction. Classroom management will be addressed in Chapter 13.

This chapter will focus on the meaning of motivation and will consider three basic orientations: cognitive, stimulation, and reinforcement. Through these three orientations, I will address internal and external factors that affect motivation. Emphasis will be put on techniques that will help keep students interested, involved, and on task.

OBJECTIVES

After completing your study of Chapter 12, you should be able to do the following:

1. Describe the concept of motivation from the cognitive, stimulation, and reinforcement points of view, as well as explain the interrelationship among the three viewpoints.
2. Identify examples of intrinsic and extrinsic motivation.
3. Discuss student attitudes and needs and their motivational effect on learning.
4. Explain the possible effects of stimulus variation on learning, as well as techniques for varying the stimuli in the teaching-learning environment.
5. Define *reinforcement* and describe the types of classroom reinforcement.
6. Differentiate between the concepts of positive and negative reinforcement.

7. Identify and discuss three techniques that can be used in providing feedback to students.
8. Describe the characteristics of reward-mechanism systems and explain the advantages associated with their use.

9. Describe common ways to identify viable reinforcers for use with students.
10. Describe contingency contracts and their appropriate classroom use.

Children and adolescents today have been raised with television, high-production movies, and highly stimulating musical productions. Having grown accustomed to such highly stimulating experiences, children often expect such experiences when they enter the classroom. Needless to say, they are usually disappointed and often find the classroom less than exciting. Consequently, there is limited motivation to learn in many classrooms.

All teachers will undoubtedly agree that motivation is a critical factor in classroom learning. Some students will be naturally enthusiastic about learning, but many need—or expect—their teachers to inspire, challenge, and stimulate them. But what is motivation, and, more important, how do you go about developing students' basic physiological drive to learn? Attempts to explain motivation have led to disagreement because of the complexity of the concept. Let's begin our study of motivation by looking at its source.

Intrinsic Versus Extrinsic Motivation

Motivation can be defined as something that energizes and directs our behaviors. That is, motivated behavior is behavior that is energized, directed, and sustained. In plain language, motivation is what gets you going, keeps you going, and determines where you're trying to go. Motivation can vary in both intensity and direction. Obviously, such influences can come from within (internal) or outside (external) the individual. Internal, or **intrinsic, motivation** is what learners themselves bring into the learning environment—that is, their internal attributes (attitudes, needs, personality factors, and values). I shall refer to the emphasis on these internal factors as a *cognitive* approach to motivation. Essentially, this view is concerned with the unique internal attributes that direct individual behaviors. In contrast, external, or **extrinsic, motivation** originates in the learning environment, where persons are offered the right incentives for doing certain things. This use of rewards represents a *reinforcement* approach to motivation.

Internal motives often are difficult to change, and, when change does occur, it occurs slowly. Indeed, what with the short time you will have with students, the likelihood of your changing students' internal motivational patterns will be slim at best. Thus, you must learn to stimulate the motivational attributes that already exist.

Keeping students on task is a challenge in the instructional process.

External motivation makes use of incentives in getting students to modify behaviors. These incentives represent artificially devised techniques for prompting students to work harder. Ideally, incentives should never become the primary reason for doing classroom work; that is, you should use incentives only sparingly and phase them out as soon as possible.

Current evidence strongly favors establishing a classroom climate in which students are intrinsically motivated to learn (Hennessey & Amabile, 1998; Wigfield & Eccles, 2002). Students are more motivated to learn when they are given choices, become absorbed in challenges that match their skills, and receive rewards that have informational value but are not used for control.

Many theorists assume that intrinsic and extrinsic motives are interrelated and will interact. This viewpoint, referred to as the *stimulation* approach to motivation, suggests that external, environmental factors can be used in influencing internal factors. Figure 12.1 shows how the different motivational viewpoints interact to influence student motivation. Let's look at these approaches more closely.

Establishing a Token Economy

1. What are the ethical implications of a token economy system?
2. Would a token economy system work with elementary school children? Middle school students? High school students?

Last year was the first time I used this type of system, and the class loved it! The way I used it required a lot of start-up work, but after that it ran quite smoothly. First of all, I made up a list of classroom jobs, enough for each student to have at least one job. Then the jobs were posted as Mrs. _____'s classified ads. The kids filled out applications that were made to resemble real job applications, with strengths, references, and so on. Then I notified them that they were to come in (usually at lunch or other "free" times) for an interview. They are instructed to dress up a bit, and be polite and businesslike. It's so cute, they get so nervous. Then they are notified about which job they are getting. They are then asked to read and sign a contract, which includes a $10.00 signing bonus.

They are paid every week. Usually each job pays $5.00 or $10.00 per week. I have payroll people (students) who write out the paychecks, with taxes deducted (10 percent to keep it simple). The following day we do our banking. I go to a local bank and get check book covers, and account registers. Each child gets one; they feel so grown up. I copy real bank deposit slips, and the kids fill them out. This takes some time

and weekly reinforcement, but once they understand how to do it they are responsible for filling out the deposit slip correctly. If the banker finds an error, the student's bank account is charged a $5.00 fee. I have one or two parents help out on banking day. We also have a cash system I made up—"Starbucks" in the amounts of $1.00, $5.00, $10.00, and $20.00. The kids can earn money for things such as a good test or quiz score, exceptional behavior, caught being good, asking a really good question, and so on. And they each get $20.00 on their birthday. They can also lose money for things like forgetting homework, needing to go out to their locker, or to their book bag, excessive talking, being out of their seat at inappropriate times, and so on. Throughout the year, the parents are asked to send in anything that they think the kids would like, and we have an auction at the end of each semester (twice a year). Most of the stuff is new, and some is just stuff that their kids don't play with or use anymore. These things don't have to be expensive, just things that kids would like. Some of my most popular and highest auction items came from the dollar store. Grab bags with pop, candy, and chip-type things are really popular, too.

I think our token economy system is a wonderfully worthwhile endeavor; the kids love it and are learning some real-life skills in the process.

—LIBBY, *Fifth Grade Teacher*

SOURCE: Reprinted with permission from ProTeacher, a professional community for elementary school teachers (http://www.proteacher.net)

The Cognitive Approach to Motivation

Like most people, students have a tendency to react according to their perceptions of events. These perceptions result in differing desires, based on variations in their

Figure 12.1
Motivational Interactions

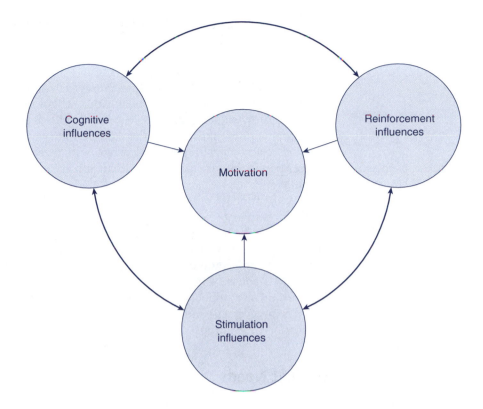

attitude, need structure, curiosity level, task interest, satisfaction with learning, and sense of well-being. According to the cognitive perspective, students' thoughts guide their motivation. The focus is on such ideas as students' internal motivation to achieve, their attributions (perceptions about the causes of success or failure, especially the perception that effort is an important factor in achievement), and their beliefs that they can effectively control their environment. The cognitive perspective also stresses the importance of goal setting, planning, and monitoring progress toward a goal (Schunk & Ertmer, 2000; Zimmerman & Schunk, 2001).

APPLY AND REFLECT: You should urge your students to think about and select realistic

long-term goals. What kinds of goals do you hope to instill in your students? Will you

involve parents in setting student goals?

Students' Attitude

Some students will love school and your subject at the outset, whereas others will hate it all. These predetermined **attitudes**—or mind-sets toward certain persons, places, and things—are the results of prior experiences with school and similar subjects: Some will love school and your subject because they find it interesting or easy, whereas others will hate school and your subject because they find it boring or difficult. Your job is to deal with negative attitudes and to bring about change. Because you cannot force students to like school or your subject, this task will not be an easy one. Indeed, you cannot compel students to change their attitudes against their will. Your best strategy is to entice change through the use of innovative motivational techniques.

First, it is important that negative mind-sets regarding school and learning be reversed. Thus, you must show students that school is worthwhile. In other words, you must show students that the learning acquired in school is important to the development of life skills and of the skills necessary for accomplishing career goals. One way of accomplishing this task is by inviting respected community leaders and businesspeople into the school for discussion about the importance of school and learning.

Second, students often are concerned with subject relevance. Therefore, you should be prepared to respond to those age-old questions: "Why do we have to learn this stuff?" or "What good is this stuff going to be for me?" If you cannot answer such questions convincingly, perhaps you should reevaluate your course content. You, of all people, should know why your subject is worthwhile.

Finally, if you are going to develop positive attitudes toward school and learning, you must involve students in their own learning and stimulate their interest. We will consider involvement and interest techniques in the next section, when we discuss stimulation motivation.

Student Needs

A **need** can be defined as "any type of deficiency in the human organism or the absence of anything the person requires, or thinks he requires, for his overall well-being" (Kolesnik, 1978, p. 149). Obviously, students will enter your class with a wide variety of needs. Indeed, Maslow (1970) has suggested that human needs function on seven hierarchical levels. The first four, lower-level needs, labeled **deficiency needs**, are the need for survival, safety, belonging, and self-esteem, whereas the three higher-level **being needs** are the need for intellectual achievement, aesthetic appreciation, and self-actualization. The being needs, unlike the deficiency needs, are never truly satisfied; that is, the quest for their fulfillment only motivates individuals to seek further fulfillment.

Maslow's needs hierarchy can provide valuable insight into the reasons for some students' behaviors. In a word, students' desire to fulfill lower-level needs may interfere with your desire that they achieve higher-level goals. A student's longing, for example, to belong to the peer group and maintain self-esteem within the group may interfere with achievement. Indeed, students sometimes break rules, or even openly defy a teacher, simply for peer recognition. Furthermore, the intensity of various needs varies from individual to individual and even changes with time and circumstances.

The need for safety has important ramifications for teachers. Essentially, because it is usually more difficult to learn when there is a feeling of insecurity, you should avoid using fear and excessive anxiety as a motivating device. That is, avoid shaming students when they make mistakes or judgment errors, and avoid overemphasizing tests and grades. Indeed, students are often motivated when they feel secure enough to share their ideals and opinions. An atmosphere tempered with a little anxiety can motivate students, but exercise care when you use fear and anxiety with your students.

Schools now recognize that if students' basic needs are not met, learning will suffer. They have responded by providing free breakfast and lunch programs. The most important deficiency needs, however, are those for love and self-esteem. Students who do not feel that they are loved and that they are capable are unlikely to have a strong motivation to achieve the higher-level growth objectives.

All students have the need to achieve and the need to avoid failure. Consequently, the overall tendency (resultant motivation) of students will be to take risks to achieve or to avoid threatening situations that might lead to failure. Therefore, when you plan, consider which students have high achievement needs, low achievement needs, and fear of failure. You may want to provide challenging optional assignments for high achievers and provide encouragement and reinforcement for students with an acute fear of failure.

Natural Motives

By nature, people are curious, are stimulated by suspense, and have a natural desire for action, adventure, and interesting experiences. Therefore, you should harness these **natural motives** in planning your learning activities. For example, educational games, puzzles, computers, and simulations represent viable strategies for capturing the natural motives of most students. Finally, as much as is feasible, select activities that will give students the opportunity to pursue individual interests and desires.

Other incentives include giving students recognition—for example, by displaying their work, giving them a certificate of achievement, placing them on the honor roll, or verbally mentioning their accomplishments. Another type of incentive focuses on allowing students to do something special, such as a desirable activity, as a reward for good work. This might include extra time at recess, playing computer games, a field trip, or even a party.

APPLY AND REFLECT: Make sure your students have sufficient opportunities for fulfilling their need for affiliation and belonging. What kinds of activities and interactions would you use to help you accomplish this task?

To this point, I have focused on the internal motives of students. Table 12.1 offers a review of the major concepts.

What can you do to influence students' perceptions of events? How can you stimulate the internal motives of your students? To answer these questions we must turn to the stimulation approach to motivation. Before you continue, however, complete Review, Extension, and Reflective Exercise 12.1, which will check your understanding of the concepts presented to this point.

The Stimulation Approach to Motivation

It is rather easy to teach when students are internally motivated to learn. This, however, is usually not the case; most students are not overly excited about learning.

TABLE 12.1 Cognitive Approach to Motivation

Factor	Description
Attitude	Mind-set toward person, place, or thing
Need	Deficiency, real or imaginary, that a person requires for well-being
Natural Motives	Internal desires of individual; many are believed to be innate

Review, Extension, and Reflective Exercise 12.1

Discuss the key factors in the cognitive view of motivation.

Connection to INTASC Standards:

- Standard 5: Learning Environment. The teacher must be able to use an understanding of individual and group motivation and behavior to create a learning environment that encourages positive social interaction, active engagement in learning, and self-motivation.

Connections to the NBPTS:

- Proposition 1: Teachers are committed to students and their learning.

Review

- What is motivated behavior?
- What is the difference between intrinsic and extrinsic motivation? How can extrinsic motivation be used to support achievement?
- Define motivation from the cognitive perspective and describe its key components.
- How would you summarize the cognitive perspective to motivation?

Reflection

- Recall a school situation in which you were highly motivated to accomplish something. How would you describe your motivation in terms of the cognitive view of motivation?
- How do motives tend to change as children progress from elementary through high school? Why is intrinsic motivation considered to be more desirable or powerful than extrinsic motivation?

Thus, you must learn to stimulate the desire to learn. Let's look at some techniques that can be used in accomplishing this end.

Classroom Atmosphere

The school and classroom atmosphere often set the tone for learning. Such factors as the physical environment and classroom communication can often make the difference between a motivated learner and a bored, reluctant learner (see Chapter 11).

Will your classroom be attractive and colorful with open communication, or will it be bleak and drab with limited communication? Many classrooms tend to be on the bleak side with little or no communication. An attractive room, however, is more conducive to learning. Compelling bulletin boards and displays can add much to the atmosphere of your classroom. Indeed, they can be designed to be both informative and colorful; and when students are allowed to design and construct them, classroom bulletin boards and displays can be quite motivating.

The arrangement of the classroom, coupled with the seating of students can also be an effective motivating device. That is, your room arrangement can foster group cohesiveness, which can lead to a high level of group belongingness. Because a sense of belonging is a basic need, it has a positive influence on motivation. Even better, give students an occasional opportunity to rearrange their own seating. When arranging your classroom, however, remember that distractions and disruptions can often occur in high-traffic areas. These include group work areas, students' desks, the teacher's desk, the pencil sharpener, bookshelves, computer stations, and storage location. Separate these areas from each other as much as possible and make sure they are easily accessible.

APPLY AND REFLECT: Make your classroom physically and psychologically safe.

How would you accomplish this task?

_____

Modeling

Modeling is a motivational technique in which people whom students admire demonstrate, through their actions, the values and behaviors you want students to acquire. These actions usually take the form of subtle suggestions that are communicated through noted nonverbal body language. For example, students who role-play or observe others role-play political leaders, musicians, poets, and scientists sometimes develop related interests. Furthermore, students at times serve as role models for each other. That is, when students see certain desirable behaviors in respected or admired peers, they may learn these behaviors themselves. Consequently, group work sometimes results in the transfer of desirable behaviors.

The most notable model in most classrooms will be you, the teacher. Indeed, the enthusiasm and sense of wonder you show for your subject will often be passed on to students. Consequently, if you appear interested and excited about a lesson, students often become transfixed, eager to find out what is so interesting. Indeed, research suggests that enthusiastic teachers produce higher academic achievement by students (Silvernail, 1979, pp. 27–28). Thus, teacher enthusiasm appears to be directly related to students' need for achievement.

Be enthusiastic about your subject. A teacher's enthusiasm is a crucial factor in student motivation. If you become bored or apathetic, students will too. Typically, a teacher's enthusiasm comes from confidence, excitement about the content, and genuine pleasure in teaching. If you find yourself uninterested in the material, think back to what attracted you to the field and bring those aspects of the subject matter to life for your students. Or challenge yourself to devise the most exciting way to present the material, however dull the material itself may seem to you.

Teacher enthusiasm is a compelling source of motivation.

APPLY AND REFLECT: Are you enthusiastic? How would you demonstrate this enthusiasm to your students?

Stimulating Interest

Students naturally seek stimulation as they constantly search for interesting things to do, for variety, for challenge. Thus, students prefer environments rich in stimuli to those that are monotonous and dull; doing *something*—no matter how trivial— generally is more interesting than doing nothing.

The human need for stimulation has important motivational implications. The learning environment typically is under continuous bombardment from such external stimuli as street traffic, hall traffic, and schoolyard conversation. All these stimuli take students' attention and interest away from the classroom to some degree. Therefore, you must compete continuously with irrelevant external stimuli for students' attention. If the students view the irrelevant external stimuli as more interesting or novel than the learning activity, more than likely they will direct their attention and interest toward the external stimuli.

Students are notorious for their inattentiveness and short attention spans. If periodic changes in stimuli do not occur in the learning environment, students lose interest. In other words, unless students are extremely engaged in the class proceedings, their attention soon turns to external stimuli or to their own thoughts. Thus, you must learn to vary your behaviors or your learning activities, so students receive new stimuli that will keep their attention directed toward the lesson. In effect, you must consciously incorporate *stimulus variation* into your lessons for the purpose of gaining, maintaining, and increasing student attention and interest. Allen, Ryan, Bush, and Cooper (1969a) suggest several behaviors or behavior patterns that can accomplish this end: gestures, focusing techniques, varied interaction styles, shifts in sensory channels, and movement.

"Of course I believe that a teacher should offer a positive role model; however . . . "

Gestures can capture and focus our attention. A tap on the desk, a hand movement, or a shift of body position, for instance, is often all that is needed to refocus attention back on a lesson. Such gestural movements represent a change in stimuli to the students, which usually prompts them to direct their attention back to the lesson. Indeed, an added emphasis can be communicated through various general movements of the body, head, and hands. A snap of the fingers or a nod of the head can focus student attention on you as you teach.

Focusing is the technique of directing students' attention to what you have said or will say through verbal statement or gestures. Verbal focusing can be used effectively in directing students to pay closer attention to specifics in a lesson presentation, or it can be used when you notice that student attention is beginning to wander. Examples of verbal statements that are commonly used in focusing students' attention are "This point is well worth remembering!" and "These are today's major issues!" or even "Make sure you include this point in your notes." Even greater impact can be obtained when a verbal focusing statement is used in conjunction with a gesture—for example, a tap on the chalkboard in conjunction with a verbal statement such as "Remember these definitions!"

You can use any one of four basic interaction styles with your students: teacher-group, teacher-student, student-student, and student-group. The *teacher-group interaction* style should be used when you want to address the class as a whole—for example, when you are giving a lecture or when giving a demonstration. If, on the other hand, you want to address or question a specific student, the *teacher-student interaction* style is appropriate. When used wisely, this style enhances student interest in a lesson through involvement.

Sometimes you may want to redirect a student comment or question to another student for a response or for clarification. Such *student-student interaction* can be used when it is desirable to acknowledge a student's knowledge in the area being discussed or when it is desirable to direct an inattentive student's attention back to the lesson. At other times, you may want to withdraw from a discussion and direct a question or a request for clarification to a student, which would require that the student address the entire group. This *student-group interaction* should be used only with students who can assume a central role in a group discussion; avoid putting your students in uncomfortable situations.

Although most classroom communication is oral, you have four other communication channels: seeing, touching, tasting, and smelling. You can stimulate interest by shifting between these sensory channels. When you make such shifts, you prompt students to make a shift in reception modes, which in turn causes them to refocus their attention. The use of an overhead projector or PowerPoint, for instance, are typical examples of the effective use of refocusing, with students being required to shift their "primary" reception between aural and visual modes.

In most cases, you will be the most significant person in the classroom environment. Thus, any action on your part will draw students' attention. Consequently, you can refocus student attention during your lessons by incorporating simple movement in your teaching actions—for example,

1. Move to the left or to the right within the classroom.
2. Move to the back or to the front within the classroom.
3. Move among the students.

In general, you should avoid remaining stationary (or hiding) behind a podium or desk when you teach. You have probably been exposed to teachers who stood rigidly behind a podium and spoke in a low monotone voice; you probably had trouble maintaining attention and interest. Clearly, such experiences reveal the importance of developing skills in focusing student attention and interest on a lesson.

Finally, teacher enthusiasm should not be overlooked as a focusing technique. When you are enthusiastic, you keep students' attention as a result of your energy and excitement. Although focusing techniques are used for drawing students' attention and interest toward your lessons, they can refocus attention and interest *away* from the lesson if they are overused. That is, if you implement refocusing techniques too often, students may become more interested in the novelty of your presentation rather than in the lesson content. The continual use of "uh" or "okay," pacing, or the tapping of your foot, for example, can detract from your lesson. Indeed, even overly enthusiastic teachers can detract from their lessons when they exhibit excessive emotional behaviors.

Set Induction

Typically, you must get students' attention and interest at the outset of your lessons (see Chapter 4). That is, you must get the undivided attention of every student in your class and prepare them to listen (establish a cognitive set).

Many factors influence student attention and interest at the onset of a lesson— the weather, holidays, school sports, and so on. Therefore, you must develop a repertoire of techniques that will gain student attention and interest. For example, as pointed out in Chapter 4, the act of facing the class in silence is often all that is needed for gaining the attention and interest of your class. This technique is especially effective when you have a small group within the class that is inattentive. Silence and an intense stare in the group's direction will soon get their undivided attention. Silence and pauses are effective tools for gaining student attention.

Another often-used method that can be used in fostering student attention and interest is by beginning your class with a topic that is of vital interest to the class. Indeed, the topic itself need not even be closely related to the lesson of the day. For example, interest in cars can lead into a study of motion or friction. A discussion of the beach can lead into a discussion of the solar system. This technique needs to be developed; it is an art.

Such techniques as the use of gestures, teacher movement, suspense, models, and pictures can be quite effective attention getters. An interesting demonstration, a discrepant event, or a picture will usually attract students' attention. Even better, let your students conduct the introductory demonstration, lead in the discrepant event, or show the pictures. You should experiment with various attention-getting techniques when determining which ones will be the most effective with your students. Classes differ, based on such factors as course content, socioeconomic level, background, motivation, grade level, and class size.

Motivational Methods

Many of the teaching strategies described in Chapters 8 and 9 heighten student motivation through the direct involvement of students in their own learning. In addition, many of the strategies are motivational in that they can influence students' cognitive needs. The need for belonging, for example, can be met through cooperative learning—that is, through a classroom structure in which groups of students work together toward a common goal, with individual group members contributing for the benefit of the individual and the group. The interaction and sharing of responsibility in cooperative learning represents a form of social motivation in that they greatly enhance the sense of belonging. This sense of belonging can be accomplished through many of the instructional strategies that involve experiences that satisfy the need for affiliation and acceptance from others.

Vary your teaching methods. Variety reawakens students' involvement in the subject and their motivation. Break the routine by incorporating a variety of teaching activities and methods in your subject: role playing, brainstorming, discussions, demonstrations, case studies, audiovisual presentations, guest speakers, or small group work.

When students use their own initiative in exploring concepts and they meet with success, a sense of competence (an intrinsic need to cope with the environment) often results and the level of aspiration often rises. Therefore, the use of strategies that maximize student involvement in learning may well stimulate a sense of competence along with a sense of accomplishment. Moreover, if students can help select and plan their own activities, they will find them even more interesting. Consequently, some forms of self-directed learning represent effective motivational strategies.

Make students active participants in the learning process. Students learn by doing, making, writing, designing, creating, solving. Passivity dampens students' motivation and curiosity. Pose questions. Don't tell students something when you can ask them. Encourage students to suggest approaches to a problem or to guess the results of an experiment. Use small group work.

Students desire variety, action, excitement, and novelty. Indeed, they would much rather read a story with many subplots or a lot of action than read a slow-moving, single-plot story. Furthermore, they prefer stimuli that are new or represent new experiences to stimuli that are routine or familiar. In other words, you should try to add life to your lessons by keeping your lessons lively, by introducing interesting, stimulating materials and teaching techniques, and by using approaches ranging from pauses to humor. Humor, for example, will give your students a change of pace. The pauses will give students time to think, ponder, and reflect.

Teacher Expectations

Hold high, but realistic expectations for your students. Research has shown that a teacher's expectations have a powerful effect on students' performance. If you act as

"I'm not an overachiever. You're an overexpecter."

though you expect your students to be motivated, hardworking, and interested in your class, they are more likely to be so. Researchers have found that students who feel they have supportive, caring teachers are more strongly motivated to engage in academic work than students with unsupportive, uncaring teachers (McCombs, 2001; Newman, 2002).

Set realistic expectations for students when you make assignments, give presentations, conduct discussions, and grade examinations. "Realistic" in this context means that your standards are high enough to motivate students to do their best work but not so high that students will inevitably be frustrated in trying to meet those expectations. To develop the drive to achieve, students need to believe that achievement is possible—which means that you need to provide early opportunities for success.

Students tend to perform better and feel more personally adequate when you set high expectations and hold them to these expectations (Good & Brophy, 1987). This self-fulfilling prophecy holds important ramifications for teachers; namely, students behave and achieve in accordance with your expectations.

Help your students set achievable goals for themselves. Failure to attain unrealistic goals can disappoint and frustrate students. Encourage students to focus on their continued improvement, not just on their grade on any one test or assignment. Help students evaluate their progress by encouraging them to critique their own work, analyze their strengths, and work on their weaknesses. For example, consider asking students to submit self-evaluation forms with one or two assignments.

Classroom interaction studies suggest that teachers tend to favor students they perceive as high achievers. Indeed, high achievers often receive more time to answer questions and more positive feedback, and have more and higher-quality interaction with their teachers. In fact, Cooper and Good (1983, p. 10) offer several common ways that teachers respond differently to high-achieving students ("highs") than to low-achieving students ("lows").

1. Seating lows far from the teacher
2. Paying less attention to lows in academic situations (using less eye contact, nods, winks, and smiles)
3. Calling on lows less often to answer classroom questions
4. Waiting less time for lows to answer questions
5. Criticizing lows more frequently than highs for incorrect classroom responses
6. Praising lows less frequently than highs after successful classroom responses
7. Praising lows more frequently than highs for marginal or inadequate classroom responses
8. Providing lows with less accurate and less detailed feedback than highs
9. Demanding less work and effort from lows than from highs
10. Interrupting performance of lows more frequently than highs

These findings suggest that teachers tend to give more support to the students they view as more capable. As a result, the interactions between the more capable students and their teachers tend to be more positive.

Students' motivation, aspiration, and self-concept can be affected to a considerable extent by your viewpoints and actions. When you expect students to do poorly, you may unconsciously give them less encouragement, less time to answer questions, and less attention. As this pattern continues over the year, students move closer and closer to your expectations. Be aware, then, that students are using your actions as a mirror of themselves, so challenge your students and communicate a belief in their abilities—and mean it. Complete Expansion Activity: Classroom Design, which will let you design your own motivationally rich classroom.

EXPANSION ACTIVITY

Classroom Design

Design a motivationally rich classroom. What would it include? What types of activities would go on? How would you teach? Share your classroom with your classmates.

This concludes the discussion of the stimulation approach to motivation. Table 12.2 reviews the major concepts covered. Review the table and complete

Review, Extension, and Reflective Exercise 12.2, which will check your understanding of the concepts presented in this section.

TABLE 12.2 **Stimulation Approach to Motivation**	
Factor	**Description**
Classroom Atmosphere	The climate of the classroom, which generally is related to leadership style, environmental arrangement, and communication
Stimulation	Engaging and interesting factors that attract and involve students
Modeling	The demonstration of desired values and behaviors by a person admired by students
Set Induction	Gaining students' attention and interest at the outset of a lesson
Teacher Expectation	Perception of how well students will do, which often becomes self-fulfilling prophecy

Review, Extension, and Reflective Exercise 12.2

Discuss the key factors in the stimulation view of motivation.

Connection to INTASC Standards:
- Standard 5: Learning Environment. The teacher must be able to use an understanding of individual and group motivation and behavior to create a learning environment that encourages positive social interaction, active engagement in learning, and self-motivation.

Connection to the NBPTS:
- Proposition 1: Teachers are committed to students and their learning.

Review
- Define motivation from the stimulation perspective and describe its key components.
- How would you summarize the stimulation view of motivation?

Reflection
- Recall a school situation in which you were highly motivated to accomplish something. How would you describe your motivation in terms of the stimulation view of motivation?
- Think about several of your own past schoolmates who showed low motivation in school. Why do you think they behaved the way they did? What teaching strategies might have helped them?

The Reinforcement Approach to Motivation

Reinforcement, or the rewarding of desired actions, is a long-recognized motivational technique. This technique is based on the principle that actions that induce pleasure tend to be repeated. Essentially, we tend to behave in ways that result in a valued payoff, or reward. Thus, if a student will work at obtaining something, the something (event, object, action, etc.) acts as a reinforcer for that student and will be a motivator. A reinforcer, however, may serve as a motivator for one student, but not for a second. In other words, the reinforcement is proven to be a motivator only if the desired behaviors are increased or enhanced. Grades, for example, are not motivators to all students. Any repeated student actions, appropriate or inappropriate, are being reinforced in some way with a payoff; that is, the student is being motivated by a reward to behave as he or she does. Reinforcement, then, can be an effective motivator when used appropriately. Let's now take a close look at teacher reinforcement and its function as a motivator.

Positive Versus Negative Reinforcement

Reinforcement can be positive or negative. **Positive reinforcement** occurs when something valued by the student is presented as a result of some student action. Possible positive reinforcers are grades, praise, and stickers.

APPLY AND REFLECT: You should use a mix of reinforcers, tangible rewards, social rewards, feedback, and teacher actions in your classroom. Make a list of appropriate reinforcers for the grade level you expect to teach.

Negative reinforcement, on the other hand, involves the removal of an aversive stimulus, such as a test or the threat of detention. In effect, students are placed in an undesirable situation from which they are motivated to escape by means of appropriate actions. Note that the student is in control with negative reinforcement; that is, the negative situation can be escaped with appropriate actions.

Reinforcement Techniques

What types of reinforcement typically are best for motivating students? Unfortunately, this is not an easy question to answer. The most effective technique in any given situation depends on such variables as the grade level, the student, the learning activity, and you as the teacher. Four reinforcement sources, however, have proven to be effective at motivating students: teacher approval, observation of other students, knowledge of results, and reward mechanisms.

Teacher approval can take one of two forms: verbal or nonverbal. **Verbal reinforcement** occurs when you follow a student action or response with a positive comment. Typical examples often include one-word "Good!" or brief-phrase comments such as "That's right!" and "Great idea!" You should take care not to overuse such brief-phrase reinforcers, for they can lose their effectiveness if you use a single one exclusively. Therefore, be a wise verbal reinforcer: Choose a variety of comments, and make sure you use them only for appropriate actions or responses.

Most often, reinforcers that are used in schools are things given to students. Reward your students' successes. Both positive and negative comments influence motivation, but research consistently indicates that students are more affected by positive feedback and success. Praise builds students' self-confidence, competence, and self-esteem. Recognize sincere efforts even if the product is less than stellar. If a student's performance is weak, let the student know that you believe he or she can improve and succeed over time. Also, don't overlook how student ideas may be used as reinforcers: you should apply, compare, and build on contributions made by students. Consequently, when you show that what students say is important, they are motivated to participate even more.

APPLY AND REFLECT: Having students keep charts of their daily and weekly grades, and encouraging them to show improvement is a good reinforcer. Could this be used effectively at the grade level you expect to teach?

Not all reinforcers have the same effect on every child. You should find out what reinforcers work best with which children—that is, individualize the use of particular reinforcers. For one student it might be praise, for another it might be getting to spend more time participating in a favorite activity, for another it might involve being a hall monitor for a week, and for yet another it could be getting to surf the Internet. Natural reinforcers like praise and privileges are generally recommended over material rewards like candy, stars, and money.

Give students feedback as quickly as possible. Return tests and papers promptly, and reward success publicly and immediately. Give students some indication of how well they have done and how to improve. Rewards can be as simple as saying a student's response was good, with an indication of why it was good, or mentioning the names of contributors: "Robert's point about pollution really synthesized the ideas we had been discussing."

When a physical action is used for sending a message of approval for a student action or response, it is referred to as **nonverbal reinforcement**. A nod of approval, a smile, eye contact, movement toward a student, or any other positive gesture, for example, shows students they are correct or on the right track. Nonverbal reinforcement is a powerful motivator—perhaps even more powerful than verbal reinforcement.

When student actions are only partially acceptable, you want to motivate the student so that he or she will continue to attempt the desired action. For example, you might want to reinforce an attempt at solving a geometry proof or the fact that the procedure used in investigating a problem was correct. In effect, you want to differentially reinforce the acceptable parts of a student action or the attempt itself. In such situations, you are using the technique of **qualified reinforcement**. Qualified reinforcement can be an effective technique for getting your shy and less able students more involved in class activities.

Vicarious Motivation

Seeing other students being reinforced for their actions can motivate students. That is, if a student sees another student reinforced for certain behaviors, he or she tends to act in the same way if the reinforcement is desirable. For example, if a student is given exemption from the unit test for doing well on the chapter tests, that reinforcement may motivate other students to do well on chapter tests. The term applied to this type of motivation is **vicarious motivation**. In effect, the first student serves as a model for the desired behaviors.

Vicarious motivation usually is quite efficient in that desired actions are learned immediately; no teaching is required. Therefore, with properly chosen reinforcers and appropriate application, vicarious motivation can initiate desired new actions and behaviors.

One important principle of behavior is that we can promote less-desired (low-strength) activities by linking them to more-desired activities. In other words, access to something desirable is made contingent on doing something less desirable. For example, a teacher might say, "As soon as you finish your work, you may go outside" or "Clean up your art project, and then I will read you a story." These are examples of the Premack Principle (Premack, 1965). Teachers can use the Premack Principle by alternating more enjoyable activities with less enjoyable ones and making participation in the enjoyable activities depend on successful completion of the less enjoyable ones. For example, in elementary school it may be a good idea to schedule computer time, which most students consider an enjoyable activity, after completion of a difficult subject.

Consequences that weaken behavior are called punishers. Punishment can take two primary forms: presentation punishment and removal punishment. Presentation punishment is the use of unpleasant consequences, or aversive stimuli, as when a student is scolded. Removal punishment is the withdrawal of a pleasant consequence. Examples include loss of a privilege, having to stay in during recess, or having to stay after school. One frequently used form of removal punishment in classrooms is time-out, in which students who misbehave are required to sit in the corner or in the hall for several minutes.

Providing feedback on how well a student did on assigned work is often an effective motivator.

Feedback as Motivator

Three techniques can be used to provide feedback to students: praise, disclosure of results, and grades. If they are to be effective, these feedback techniques must be carefully and systematically applied. Simply "handing out" positive feedback will, in time, destroy any technique's effectiveness as a motivator. Appropriately used feedback, therefore, is contingent on the desired action, specifies clearly the action being reinforced, and is believable (O'Leary & O'Leary, 1977). In other words, positive feedback should be a sincere recognition of student work that has been well done.

Teachers have long acknowledged and recognized the power of praise as a compelling motivator. Brophy (1981), in a comprehensive analysis of praise, attests to the importance of teacher praise as a reinforcement technique. Indeed, Brophy suggests that praise is more powerful than general reinforcement, because it generally calls for teacher attention and energy beyond the use of the standard one-word or short-phrase response ("Good," "Fine answer," or "Okay"). Finally, praise can lay the foundation for lasting internal change because it works to improve students' self-esteem.

Providing students with the results of assigned tasks motivates some students because it communicates the correctness of responses. Results that indicate success lead to renewed vigor, whereas indications of needed corrective measures communicate what actions or efforts are needed for improving performance. If you are to ensure that students benefit from the motivational effects of work results, you must return papers and tests to students immediately—with more than a simple grade marked on them. Indeed, it is suggested that teachers can achieve maximum incentive from marking papers if each returned paper is personalized with comments about strengths and weaknesses. Simple comments written in the margins should be sufficient for offering students needed guidance.

Teachers have always considered tests and grades as highly motivational in nature. Unfortunately, the research does not support the conjecture that tests and grades motivate students to learn but, rather, that tests typically motivate students to cram—that is, learn for the test. Actually, tests and good grades seem to be motivational only to top students, while offering only limited incentive to low-ability students. Therefore, you would be wise not to make grades your primary source of motivation. Instead, you should appeal to students' intrinsic motives and rely more on cooperative and self-directed strategies. Such structures are more likely to be motivational for students.

Reward Mechanisms

As used here, a **reward mechanism** is a more formal system of reinforcement. It is an agreement whereby students earn specified rewards for displaying certain types of behaviors. In one such successful system, students earn tokens, points, stars, or checks—or anything else that seems appropriate—for performing desired academic and classroom behaviors. These tokens are then periodically exchanged for a desirable reward, such as free time, no homework, tangible objects, educational games, or anything desired by the students that is deemed appropriate.

You can also offer a menu of rewards in a reward-mechanism system. Students then purchase the rewards for different numbers of tokens—for instance, few tokens yield less desirable rewards, and many tokens yield more desirable rewards. For example, students might be excused from a homework assignment for a few tokens and be allowed to listen to music in class for several tokens.

APPLY AND REFLECT: Educational games are good reinforcers. What are some games that would be appropriate at the grade level you expect to teach?

An advantage to using the more formal reward mechanism is that students are not inadvertently overlooked from receiving reinforcement. It is, however, sometimes difficult to find adequate reinforcers for students. Two common ways of identifying such reinforcers are simply asking students directly or having them fill out a questionnaire about desired reinforcers. Moreover, simply observing students during their free time or after they finish their work can give you valuable clues as to what can be used for reinforcement. The best reinforcers frequently depend on the students, the subject, and the situation. Complete Expansion Activity: Motivators to identify classroom motivators and strategies for their use.

EXPANSION ACTIVITY

Motivators

Make a list of motivators as well as specific strategies that teachers can use to enhance individual and group motivation in their classrooms. Share your list and strategies with your classmates.

Contingency Contracts

Contingency contracts are formal, written agreements between a teacher and student that describe exactly what the student must do to earn a desired privilege or reward. These contracts can be written by the teacher and presented to the student for agreement, or the student can work out the contract and present it to the teacher. Contracts are usually best, however, when they are written by the teacher and student together in a negotiating process. Regardless of the contract-development process followed, the contract should specify exactly what the student will do to earn the privilege or reward. A sample contingency contract is shown in Figure 12.2.

Contracts should encourage students to make realistic expectations of their abilities. Accordingly, you can stipulate that the contract can be changed, but there should be a built-in penalty for any alterations.

Let us now apply the motivation concepts from this chapter. Complete Web Link: Motivation, which will let you develop some motivation ideas of your own.

WEB LINK   **Motivation**
Conduct a web search and locate several lesson plans in a subject area at the grade level you expect to teach. Analyze the lesson plans relative to their ability to motivate students. Write a summary of your findings. How would you change the lessons to make them more interesting and motivational?

No matter what your specific explanations for the sources of motivation, you should be aware that no one is completely unmotivated. Even doing nothing takes motivation. Table 12.3 gives a review of the major concepts in this section. Review the table and complete Review, Extension, and Reflective Exercise 12.3, which will check your understanding of this section.

Figure 12.2

A Sample Contract

Read through the listed items and check those you would like to do. Then decide for what grade you would like to contract. Grades will be given as follows:

> D - The starred items plus one more from each group
> C - The starred items plus two more from each group
> B - The starred items plus three more from each group
> A - The starred items plus four more from each group

Discuss your choice with your teacher, and sign your name in the proper place.

I, _____ , agree to complete the following work on the unit at a level of _____ or better.
> (Grade)

> * Read assigned text chapters
> * Complete in-class and out-of-class assignments
> * Complete unit test at or above contracted grade level

Group I

> * Do one library assignment

> 1. Prepare an outline of unit content
> 2. Write a one-page paper on a unit topic
> 3. Complete an optional writing assignment
> 4. Develop an annotated bibliography related to the unit
> 5. Review a textbook that addresses the unit topic and write a short report on its contents

Group II

> * Give one class demonstration

> 1. Conduct a short project related to the unit content
> 2. Lead a class discussion of a topic related to this unit
> 3. Locate and present to class unit-related newspaper articles
> 4. Draw some conclusions relative to the importance of the unit topic to your everyday life

_____

Date

_____

Student's Signature

_____

Teacher's Signature

TABLE 12.3 Reinforcement Approach to Motivation

Factor	Description
Positive Reinforcement	Presentation of a desired stimulus to strengthen the likelihood of a behavior or an event.
Negative Reinforcement	Removal of an unpleasant stimulus to strengthen the likelihood of a behavior or an event
Verbal Reinforcement	Presentation of positive comments as a consequence to strengthen student behavior or an event
Nonverbal Reinforcement	Use of a physical action as a positive consequence to strengthen behavior or an event
Vicarious Motivation	Strengthening of behavior because of a desire to receive consequences received by others who exhibit that behavior
Feedback	Disclosure of correctness of response
Reward Mechanism	Formal system of reinforcement
Contingency Contract	Formal, written agreement between student and teacher as to what students will do for receiving a reward

Review, Extension, and Reflective Exercise 12.3

Discuss the key factors in the reinforcement view of motivation.

Connection to INTASC Standards:
- Standard 5: Learning Environment. The teacher must be able to use an understanding of individual and group motivation and behavior to create a learning environment that encourages positive social interaction, active engagement in learning, and self-motivation.

Connection to the NBPTS:
- Proposition 1: Teachers are committed to students and their learning.

Review
- Describe the different reinforcement types.
- Define motivation from the reinforcement perspective and describe its key components.
- How would you summarize the reinforcement perspective to motivation?
- What is a contingency contract?

Reflection
- Explain how motivation has intensity and direction. How would you use rewards, praise, grades as incentives to enhance individual and group motivation to learn at the grade level you expect to teach? Would you use contingency contract at this grade level?
- Recall a school situation in which you were highly motivated to accomplish something. How would you describe your motivation in terms of the reinforcement view of motivation?

VIEW FROM THE CLASSROOM

What do teachers think about motivating students? Teacher survey results relative to topics presented in this chapter are expressed below. Review these results and discuss with classmates.

What is the most important quality for a teacher of teenage students?

A sense of humor	34%
Sensitivity to teenage issues	21%
Patience	16%
A passion for teaching	14%
Integrity	11%
Empathy	4%

SOURCE: Excerpted from *Teach-nology*, available at www.teach-nology.com/poll

Summary

- Motivation is largely influenced by internal factors, the teacher's action, and the physical environment.
- Motivation often comes from a person's active search for meaning and satisfaction in life.
- There is no surefire method of motivating students.
- Motivation techniques that work in one situation may be totally ineffective in another.

Intrinsic Versus Extrinsic Motivation

- Motivation can come from within (intrinsic motivation) or outside (extrinsic motivation) an individual.
- Intrinsic motivation is related to an individual's attitudes, needs, personality factors, and values.
- Extrinsic motivation comes from stimulation within the environment and from the application of desired incentives.

The Cognitive Approach to Motivation

- We are motivated by our perception of events.
- Our perceptions are related to such internal attributes as attitudes, needs, curiosity, interests, and sense of well-being.
- A student's desire to learn is related to the student's internal attribute structure.
- Central to the desire to attend to the learning process is classroom atmosphere.
- Teachers should establish a democratic classroom that is attractive and characterized by open communication.

The Stimulation Approach to Motivation

- Students seek stimulation.
- Teachers must use various stimulus variation techniques for gaining and maintaining student attention.
- Commonly used techniques for providing the needed changes in stimuli include using gestures, refocusing student attention, varying classroom interaction styles, shifting students' sensory channels, and using teacher movement.
- Teacher enthusiasm can also be an effective motivator. When you show excitement and interest in your lesson, that excitement is often communicated to students.
- Teacher enthusiasm is often contagious.
- A strong beginning for your lesson is crucial for motivating students' desire to learn.
- Begin each lesson with an attention-getting device that will stimulate interest in the coming lesson.
- The beginning of a lesson should be followed up with other stimulating devices that will keep students interested.
- Students are motivated by teacher expectations.

The Reinforcement Approach to Motivation

- Reinforcement is a long-recognized technique for motivating students.
- Teachers should select their reinforcers based on their knowledge of the students and subject.
- Don't rely on grades exclusively for providing feedback; offering praise and disclosing the results of assigned work can also motivate students.
- Reward mechanism and contingency contracts offer more formal motivational systems.

Discussion Questions and Activities

1. **Reinforcement menus.** Develop a list of incentives that could be used in the subject and at the grade level you expect to teach. Arrange them in ascending order of value.
2. **Contingency contracts.** Set up a sample contingency contract for a unit in a subject at the grade level you expect to teach.

Connection With the Field

1. **Interview.** Interview an elementary and a secondary teacher. Ask them to share the strategies they use to motivate their students. How do they compare?
2. **Classroom observation.** Complete several school observations. Plan your visits to collect viable observational data related to motivation:

    a. The use of stimulus variation
    b. The different types of stimulus variation utilized by the teachers
    c. Examples of teacher enthusiasm displayed
    d. The use of positive and negative reinforcement
    e. The different types of reinforcement utilized by the teachers
    f. The use of praise and encouragement

3. **Teaching.** Teach a 20-minute minilesson to a group of students or to peers. Try to use as much stimulus variation and as many reinforcement techniques as possible in your lesson. If possible, videotape the lesson.
4. **Teaching analysis.** Study the videotape you made in activity 3. Record your uses of stimulus variation and reinforcement. Draw some conclusions regarding your proficiency in the use of stimulus variation and reinforcement.

Praxis II Connection

The following test preparation exercises are intended to help you prepare for the Praxis II: Principles of Learning and Teaching. The Praxis II may be required by your teacher education preparatory program and for state certification or licensing. These exercises will give you direct access to pedagogical knowledge from Chapter 12 that may be expected of you on the Praxis II and other pedagogical exams that may be required at the end of your teacher education program.

Topic Connections

1. Cognitive View of Motivation
   (I. C1, C2, C3)

Describe the major features of the cognitive view of motivation and identify related strategies that will likely boost student motivation.

2. Stimulation View of Motivation
   (I. C1, C2, C3)

Describe the major features of the stimulation view of motivation and identify related strategies that will likely boost student motivation.

3. Reinforcement View of Motivation
   (I. C1, C2, C3)

Describe the major features of the reinforcement view of motivation and identify related strategies that will likely boost student motivation.

ON YOUR OWN

Log on to the web-based student study site at http://www.sagepub.com/eis for more information about the vignettes and materials presented in this chapter, suggestions for activities, study aids such as electronic flashcards and review quizzes, and research recommendations including journal article links and questions related to this chapter.

13
MANAGING THE CLASSROOM ENVIRONMENT

*Leadership means not having to be completely
in harmony with everyone else.*

WINSTON CHURCHILL

OVERVIEW

Conducting the business of the classroom for the achievement of learning intent is the function of a teacher, and one that requires skill at effective leadership and management. Management is often difficult in the classroom, which is a dynamic system of hundreds of interactions that must be monitored. In other words, classroom management is not an easy task. It takes planning.

All teachers have management problems. Therefore, you must deal effectively with misbehavior if you are to accomplish your instructional goals. How you deal with misbehavior depends on your management philosophy and the approach you tend to endorse. As such, this chapter will examine the principles of three current approaches to classroom management and some illustrative models.

Also, if classroom managers are to function effectively, they require an understanding of misbehavior. Therefore, I will address how to deal with misbehavior. I will examine such issues as ways to start the year off right, the establishment of rules, the effective monitoring of a classroom, and the appropriate use of punishment. Finally, teacher-tested ideas for conducting the business of the classroom will be presented.

OBJECTIVES

After completing your study of Chapter 13, you should be able to do the following:

1. Define *classroom management* and identify its various aspects.

2. Identify similarities and differences in classroom management at the elementary, middle, and secondary levels.

3. Identify and describe the self-discipline, instructional, and desist approaches to classroom management, as well as characteristics of the different

illustrative models of discipline associated with each approach.

4. Identify and discuss causes of classroom misbehavior.

5. Discuss organizational techniques that lead to effective classroom management.

6. Identify and discuss teacher-tested techniques for effectively preventing classroom management problems.

7. Identify and discuss punishment and its appropriate use in the classroom.

Effective teaching requires effective classroom leadership and management. Indeed, teachers, administrators, parents, and students report that misbehavior interferes a great deal with the ability of a teacher to teach and with the ability of students to learn (Charles, 2002; Evertson, Emmer, & Worsham, 2003; Gallup & Elam, 1988). Although such reports suggest that there are serious management and discipline problems in the public schools, it would be a mistake to assume that schools are out of control.

What is the role of classroom leadership and management? Before we can develop techniques for its improvement, we must know what their functions should be.

The Role of Classroom Leadership

What type of leader do you want to be? Do you want to be stimulating, warm, caring, fair, funny, and interesting? Or would you prefer to be commanding, dominating, sharp, critical, and harsh? Perhaps you choose to be lackadaisical and completely permissive? These characteristics determine your leadership style: authoritarian, democratic, or laissez-faire. The type of leader you become also depends on the policies of the school, your students, and your personality. Some teachers feel students lack the maturity and ability to be involved in decision making; therefore, they rely heavily on the authoritarian style of leadership.

The *authoritarian* style of leadership is characterized by power, domination, pressure, and criticism. The authoritarian teacher assumes the sole responsibility for making all decisions for the class and uses pressure, a sharp voice, and fear in forcing compliance. Accordingly, the authoritarian teacher uses criticism and "put-downs" for motivating students, which often results in an atmosphere of hostility and, for students, feelings of powerlessness, competitiveness, high dependency, and alienation from the subject matter (Schmuck & Schmuck, 1988). Students in this type of atmosphere often develop a fear of failure, low self-esteem, and a defeatist attitude. Consequently, students tend to give up when they encounter a new or difficult task.

Making instruction relevant and interesting keeps students on task and curbs potential undesirable behaviors.

The *democratic* teacher is kind, caring, and warm, but also firm. The democratic leader tries to provide stimulation from within through a sharing of responsibility and encouragement, rather than demands. Self-esteem is developed by a sharing of responsibility, and students are encouraged when they make mistakes. The democratic classroom atmosphere is one of openness, friendly communication, and independence, with a resultant high level of productivity and performance.

The laissez-faire leader is completely permissive. Anything goes, which generally leads to chaos. The classroom is often disorganized, which causes student frustration, a high level of stress, and a feeling of being totally overwhelmed and lost.

A change from the obsolete authoritarian approach of demanding submission to a more democratic approach based on freedom, choice, and responsibility would do much for helping students develop a positive feeling toward school and your subject. Students might learn to be truly responsible individuals.

The Role of Classroom Management

Classroom management is the process of organizing and conducting the business of the classroom relatively free of behavior problems. Classroom management is often perceived as related to the preservation of order and the maintenance of control. But this view is too simplistic; classroom management means much more. Indeed, it involves the establishment and maintenance of the classroom environment so that educational goals can be accomplished.

Managing the Classroom

1. Why is classroom management a major problem for many teachers?
2. Can teachers really treat all students equally?

I believe the selection of a classroom management strategy has to be based on the teacher's personality and the characteristics of the class being managed. To use a system that doesn't fit you will create unnecessary stress and you won't use it well. If it doesn't suit the students, it will not work either. So, I suggest that you study as many strategies as you can and evaluate them in terms of your personality.

My biggest suggestion is, whatever strategy you choose, do not attempt to teach until it is working. If you begin the year insisting on proper discipline and behavior, it will become a habit that will continue through the rest of the year. If you let things slide at the beginning, the students will expect it to last till the end. This doesn't mean that you have to be an ogre until Thanksgiving. It does mean that you must find a way to create the atmosphere you want before you do any serious amount of teaching.

As for respect, the students will respect you when you are consistent. Students, as a group, don't like surprises. There can be few, if any, exceptions to rules and procedures. If any exceptions should become necessary, you should explain to the students why an exception has been made. The other side of respect is to respect students in return. Whatever forms of respect you demand from your students you should extend to them as well.

—JOHN VOSE, *elementary school teacher*

SOURCE: Reprinted with permission from ProTeacher, a professional community for elementary school teachers (http://www.proteacher.net)

Central to effective management is the ability to provide a positive social and physical environment conducive to the learning process. Although not its sole component, another highly important aspect of classroom management is discipline, which, as noted earlier, perennially appears as the major concern of teachers, administrators, parents, and students. Discipline should not be viewed as being primarily concerned with punishment. **Punishment** involves the consequences of misbehavior, whereas discipline deals with the prevention of classroom misbehavior as well as the consequences of disruptive actions. This chapter will focus on discipline rather than punishment because your success as a classroom teacher will depend on your adequacy in making sound decisions in both of these areas.

Classroom management experts report changes in thinking about the best way to manage classrooms. The emphasis has been on creating and applying rules to control students' behavior. The newer focus, however, is more on students' needs for nurturing relationships and opportunities for self-regulation (Kennedy, Long, Kristine, Cox, Tang, & Thompson, 2001). The newer trend places more emphasis on guiding students to become more proficient at self-discipline and less dependent on external control. We will look at some of these models in the next section.

Elementary, middle, and secondary school classrooms involve many similar management issues. At all levels, good classroom managers design the classroom environment for optimal learning, establish and maintain rules, get students to cooperate, effectively deal with problems, and use good communication strategies. Middle and secondary students' problems, however, can be more long-standing and more deeply ingrained, and as such more difficult to modify, than those of younger children. Also, in secondary school, students sometimes are resistant to authority and discipline problems are frequently more severe and students potentially more unruly and even dangerous. At the same time, some adolescents resist authority and place greater importance on peer norms. Because most middle and secondary students have more advanced reasoning skills than younger students, they generally demand more elaborate and logical explanation of rules and discipline. Keep these differences between elementary, middle, and secondary schools in mind as we explore effective classroom management.

As a teacher, you must be aware of the principles and consequences of any classroom management decisions and strategies you may wish to implement. For an overview of the various strategies, let's take a look at three such management approaches: the self-discipline approach, the instructional approach, and the desist approach.

"I'd like to overwhelm them with instructional excellence, but I'm not above winning through intimidation."

Approaches to Classroom Management

The three approaches to classroom management form a continuum, from the self-discipline approach at one extreme, to the instructional approach, to the desist approach at the opposite extreme. The representative models to be discussed are depicted in Figure 13.1.

The Self-Discipline Approach

The **self-discipline approach** is built on the premise that students can be trusted to evaluate and change their actions, so their behaviors are beneficial and appropriate to self and to the class as a whole. The approach views classroom management as a function of the teacher's ability to build and establish working teacher-student relationships. In a word, advocates argue that teachers need to recognize the dignity of students and that they must exhibit the attitudinal qualities of realness, trust, acceptance, and empathy. This approach represents the most democratic view of classroom management. With these attitudinal qualities in mind, let's look at four of the more democratic classroom management models.

Reality Therapy

Developed by William Glasser (1965, 1977, 1986), **reality therapy** is a strategy that helps students take the responsibility for examining and solving their own problems. Glasser believes that students are rational beings and can control their behavior if they wish. For example, witness the usual good student behaviors found on the first day of school.

Furthermore, Glasser suggests that students often must be assisted in making good choices rather than bad choices. Indeed, he feels that students must be guided so that they become responsible individuals able to satisfy their needs in the real

Figure 13.1

The Continuum of Classroom Management Model

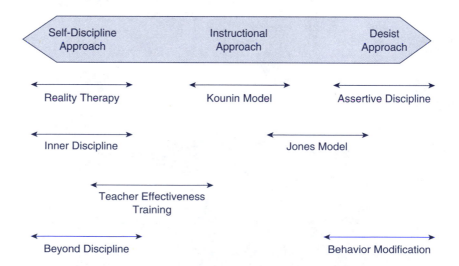

world. That is to say, they must be guided toward reality. It is the teacher's job to provide the needed guidance so that students make good choices. The teacher must help students examine their behaviors in light of their benefit to self and to the class. If a behavior is found inappropriate, the individual student must be assisted in devising a realistic, written plan for changing the inappropriate behavior. No excuses are acceptable for not carrying out the devised plan. The student has made a commitment and is held to it. If the original plan proves inadequate, it is essential that both the teacher and student be willing to reexamine the plan and to renew or change the commitment. If the student is unwilling to make the commitment, he or she should not be allowed to remain in the classroom.

Note that reality therapy places the responsibility on the student, not the teacher. The teacher does not punish. In fact, Glasser does not believe in punishment. He feels punishment hinders personal development and is ineffective. If a student disrupts the class, he or she simply is removed until a commitment for change has been worked out. Thus, the teacher's function is to assist students in becoming responsible, productive members of the classroom.

Rules that are enforced are essential according to Glasser. Indeed, background and poor upbringing do not make poor behavior acceptable. Student responsibility must be stressed continually. Students are forced to acknowledge their behavior, and they should make value judgments regarding that behavior. For example, when a disruption occurs, the teacher should never ask why a student is doing what he or she is doing; rather, the teacher should ask, "What are you doing?" The emphasis should be put on the *you* so that there is no misinterpretation as to who is responsible. This question should be followed up with queries such as "Is this behavior against the rules?" or "Is this behavior helping you or this class?" If the misbehavior persists, a (private) conference is needed for working out a commitment for change. If the disruptions continue or the commitment is not followed, the consequences should become progressively more severe: principal conference, followed by parent conference, followed by in-school suspension, followed by out-of-school suspension, and finally with permanent exclusion from school.

Classroom meetings are an essential element in addressing problems in the Glasser model. Students sit in a close circle and discuss classroom situations and problems. The teacher's role is to provide background information as needed by the group and to give opinions sparingly. Classroom rules, consequences, and procedures are developed at such meetings, and all students are expected to participate in their formation. All students are expected to observe the agreed-upon rules and consequences. The rules are flexible, however, and could be changed with another meeting as the situation changes.

APPLY AND REFLECT: You should always stress student responsibility. Emphasize that good behaviors result from good choices. How easy would this be at the grade level you expect to teach?

Teacher Effectiveness Training (TET)

Teacher Effectiveness Training (TET), conceived by Dr. Thomas Gordon (1974), stresses the establishment of positive working relationships between teachers and students. Gordon believes that teachers can reduce disruptive student behaviors by using clearer, less provocative communication. Furthermore, he recommends that nonverbal language and listening should be stressed as the teacher interacts with students in an atmosphere of openness and trust.

According to Gordon, the key to Teacher Effectiveness Training is to identify who owns the problem when one develops in the learning environment: teacher or student. If the teacher is blocked from reaching the instructional goals by the student's actions, then the teacher owns the problem. For example, if students continuously talk as the teacher tries to teach, the teacher owns the problem because he or she is kept from reaching the goal of teaching. On the other hand, if the teacher feels annoyed by a student's behavior or if the teacher wishes a student would change his or her behavior, the problem likely belongs to the student. The student who says he or she hates the teacher or hates the subject has a problem.

When the teacher owns the problem, an I-message should be sent. An **I-message** tells the student how you feel about a problem situation and invites the student to change, to correct that situation—for example, "I am angry with this continuous talking in class," "I am disappointed in your behavior at the assembly," or "I can't hear myself think with the noise in this classroom." If the process works, the student (or class) should see the harm being done and change his or her (or their) behavior. If an I-message does not correct the problem, however, the teacher and student (class) are in a conflict situation, which calls for finding a solution through problem solving. When this happens, Gordon recommends that a "no-lose" problem-resolution tactic be employed. The no-lose strategy is a six-step form of negotiation in which teacher and student (class) contribute relatively equally. First, the problem or conflict is clearly determined. Second, possible solutions are generated, with the teacher and student (class) presenting an equal number of ideas. These ideas are evaluated in the third step, and those unacceptable are rejected. During the fourth step, the remaining ideas are ranked and the best solution is selected. This is followed by the fifth step, a determination of how to implement the selected solution so that all parties are satisfied. The sixth and final step entails an assessment of how well the solution works. In general, punishment is not recognized as a viable option in the no-lose tactic, because the student (class) would be placed in a losing situation.

A student-owned problem calls for active listening (or empathetic listening) on the part of the teacher. That is, the teacher should listen carefully and become a counselor and supporter for the student who should be encouraged to express his or her views. As such, the teacher should reflect back only the student's point of view and help the student find his or her own problem solution. The teacher's function is not to give or impose solutions to students' problems.

Inner Discipline

Inner discipline, developed by Barbara Coloroso (2002), a former nun and now a teacher and author, rejects "quick fix" solutions to discipline problems. Instead, she suggests you focus on helping children develop their own self-discipline by owning up to their mistakes, thinking through solutions, and correcting their misdeeds while leaving their dignity intact.

Coloroso suggests that teachers treat kids with respect and help them develop inner discipline that will enable them to handle their own problems and to interact successfully with others. She believes that children can develop the ability to handle their own problems and can learn from their successes and mistakes. Coloroso suggests the teacher's role is to help students develop this ability by allowing them to make their own decisions and to grow from the results of those decisions, whatever they may be. It means giving students a sense of power in their own lives and offering them opportunities to make decisions, take responsibility for their actions, and learn from their successes and mistakes. Coloroso contends that students are worth all the effort teachers can expend on them and that school should be neither adult dominated nor student controlled. It should be a place where joint efforts are made to learn, relate, grow, and create community.

Teachers must, however, make sure that student decisions don't lead to situations that are life threatening, morally threatening, or unhealthy. This ability should be developed apart from typical systems of reward and punishment and will then serve individuals for the rest of their lives. Consequences, natural and reasonable, should be associated with rules, and should be allowed or invoked consistently when rules are violated. Students will then develop the inner discipline and self-confidence that will help them grow into responsible, resourceful, and resilient adults.

Coloroso suggests that teachers fall into three categories. "Brickwall teachers" are rigid, use power and coercion to control others, and teach what instead of how to think. They demand that students follow the rules without question. "Jellyfish teachers" provide little structure, consistency, or guidance, and rely on put-downs, threats, and bribery to control students. Punishment and rewards are often arbitrary and inconsistent. These teachers are lax in discipline, set few limits, and more or less let students do what they want. "Backbone teachers" provide the support and structure necessary for students to behave creatively, cooperatively, and responsibly, which leads to inner discipline. They use rules that are clear and simple, with consequences that are reasonable, simple, valuable, and purposeful. Students have freedom to pursue opportunities and solve problems within established limits.

Beyond Discipline

In his book, *Beyond Discipline: From Compliance to Community,* Alfie Kohn (1996) questions the assumption that classroom problems are always the fault of students who don't do as they are told. Most teachers work to control children's behavior either by punishment or reward, which is often ineffective. Instead of acknowledging the possible problems of a dull curriculum or poor teaching, teachers place complete blame on students for their negative behavior.

Kohn suggests that our present approaches that are based on reward and punishment are only short-term solutions to classroom problems. He contends that punishment only teaches students that they will suffer dire consequences when they are caught misbehaving and rewards teach them how to respond positively only in order to win a prize or praise. Therefore, both punishments and rewards do not cultivate long-lasting moral values in students.

Kohn would have teachers do away with classroom discipline and in its place have teachers work to develop a sense of democratic classroom community that recognizes the needs and interests of both teachers and students. A classroom community is a place where students are cared about and care about others, are valued and respected, and think in terms of *we* instead of *I*. Students are involved in the decision-making process and are continually brought into making judgments, expressing their opinions, and working cooperatively toward solutions that benefit the class, which will have a positive impact on students and eliminate behavioral problems. Kohn believes rules are of no practical value in the classroom; rules blind teachers to what students can achieve. When problems arise, the teacher should ask the student "What do you think we can do to solve this problem?" Class meetings should be used as the forum for addressing questions that affect the class, including problems of behavior.

APPLY AND REFLECT: Should you ask your students to make value judgments about their personal behavior? Should students be asked to make value judgments about each other's behavior?

The Instructional Approach

The premise that forms the basis for the **instructional approach** to classroom management is that well-planned and well-implemented instruction will prevent most classroom problems. Basically, the assumption is that students will not engage in disruptive behavior when lessons are geared to meet their interests, needs, and abilities. In other words, the instructional approach is predicated on the assumption that well-planned and well-implemented lessons that engage students in their own learning and afford them the opportunity to be successful learners will prevent and solve most management problems. Let's now look at two models of classroom management that focus on the principles of the instructional approach.

The Kounin Model

In a comprehensive comparison of effective and ineffective classroom managers, Jacob Kounin (1970) found that the teachers differed very little in the way they handled classroom problems once they arose. The primary difference was in the things the successful managers did that tended to prevent classroom problems. First, these teachers were environmentally aware. In other words, they knew everything that went on in their classrooms at all times. Second, the effective managers were skilled as group leaders and at keeping activities moving. That is, these teachers had students involved and doing something productive at all times. No one ever just sat and waited for work or watched others. The teachers had lessons that were well planned and conducted at a smooth, even, appropriate pace. Kounin concluded that some teachers are better classroom managers because of skill in four areas: "withitness," overlapping activities, group focusing, and movement management (Charles, 2002).

Withitness is the skill to know what is going on in all parts of the classroom at all times; nothing is missed. "Withit" teachers note and act quickly and accurately in curbing class disturbances. They prevent minor disruptions from becoming major, and know who the instigator is in a problem situation.

Effective classroom managers are also skilled at overlapping. **Overlapping** means handling two or more activities or groups at the same time. Essentially, it is the ability to monitor the whole class at all times. It involves keeping a small group on task, for example, while also helping other students with their seatwork.

Finally, Kounin notes that successful classroom management also depends on movement management and group focus—that is, the ability to make smooth lesson transitions, keep an appropriate pace, and involve all students in a lesson. Moreover, effective managers do not leave a lesson hanging while tending to something else or change back and forth from one subject or activity to another. They keep students alert by holding their attention, by holding them accountable, and by involving all students in the lesson.

The Jones Model

Frederick Jones (1979), in his more than 10 years of researching the problems teachers encounter in the classroom, found that most management problems result from massive time wasting by students. In other words, most classroom problems are a result of students being off task. In fact, Jones estimated that teachers lose 50 percent or more of their instructional time through student's time wasting (e.g., talking and walking around the room). Jones contends that this wasted instructional time can be reclaimed when teachers correctly implement four strategies: limit setting, good body language, incentive systems, and giving help efficiently.

Limit setting is the establishment of classroom boundaries for appropriate behavior. According to Jones, these **limits** should include the formation of rules of behavior, as well as descriptions of appropriate work behavior, procedures for getting supplies and materials, instruction on what to do when stuck on seatwork, and what to do when finished with assigned seatwork.

Ninety percent of discipline and keeping students on task, Jones contends, involved the skillful use of body language. **Body language** is a set of physical mannerisms that tend to get students back to work, the most effective of which are physical proximity to students, direct eye contact, body position (body orientation toward student), facial expressions, and tone of voice.

Jones contends that **incentive systems** also can be used effectively to keep students on task and to get them to complete their work. Indeed, he suggests that preferred activities, such as time on the computer, free time, use of educational games, and free reading, can serve as motivational rewards for desired behaviors. Furthermore, Jones adds, the use of peer pressure represents a quite effective motivator. For example, time can be deducted from the class preferred-activity time when an individual student misbehaves. The deduction of time can be recorded, as Jones suggests, with a large stopwatch placed at the front of the room, so the whole class can see. If a large stopwatch is not available, a standard amount of time (e.g., one minute) can be deducted for each instance of misbehavior.

Finally, Jones found that *giving help efficiently* is related to time on task. His research revealed that teachers on the average spend 4 minutes helping individual students who are having difficulty with seatwork. Jones recommends that this time be cut to no more than 20 seconds per student. Doing so allows more students to be helped and reduces the tendency for students to work only when the teacher is standing over them.

Setting limits, using of body language, implementing an incentive system, and giving help efficiently will not eliminate all behavior problems. When such problems do develop, Jones suggests, a back-up system, such as in-class isolation or removal from the room, is needed.

APPLY AND REFLECT: It is suggested that you use body language instead of words to show you mean business. How would you do this?

The Desist Approach

The **desist approach** to classroom management gives the teacher full responsibility for regulating the classroom. The teacher enforces a set of specific rules to control student behavior in the classroom. Because the desist approach models of classroom management give teachers power to deal forcefully and quickly with misbehavior, they can be viewed as power systems. The desist approach probably is the most widely used strategy in today's schools. Two common desist models of classroom management are *assertive discipline* and *behavior modification*.

Assertive Discipline

Lee and Marlene Canter (1976) contend that teachers have a basic right to require decent behavior in the classroom. To this end, the Canters advocate **assertive discipline**, which calls for assertive teachers. Assertive teachers clearly and firmly communicate needs and requirements to students, follow up their words with appropriate actions, and respond to students in ways that maximize compliance but in no way violate the best interest of the students (Canter & Canter, 1976, p. 9). Assertive teachers take charge in the classroom in a calm yet forceful way.

Assertive teachers do not tolerate improper behavior that interrupts learning. Commonly used excuses—peer pressure, home environment, and heredity, for example—are not accepted for misbehavior. The assertive teacher establishes rules and limits for behavior, along with consequences for proper behavior and improper behavior. Students who follow the established rules receive positive consequences, such as a material reward, free time, or special privileges, whereas students who break the rules receive negative consequences, such as detention, giving up part of their lunch period, staying after school, or going to the principal's office. The rules, limits, and consequences are communicated to students and parents in clear terms at the beginning of the year.

Assertive teachers insist on decent, responsible behavior from their students. After establishing expectations early in the year, assertive teachers consistently reinforce the established procedures and guidelines. In other words, the teachers make promises, not threats. They do not *threaten* to enforce the rules and guidelines and apply the consequences to misbehavior; they *promise* to do so. It is assumed that all students, if they want, are capable of behaving; it is a matter of choice.

APPLY AND REFLECT: Make promises, not threats. What does this mean to you?

Behavior Modification

Behavior Modification, based on the ideas and work of B. F. Skinner (1968, 1971), is an approach that evolves from the assumptions that students will change their behavior to receive definite rewards.

The basic premise of behavior modification is that student behavior can be changed by altering the consequences that follow their actions and behaviors. Technically, reinforcement principles are used systematically for changing some aspect of educational practice or student behavior. Students who follow established procedures, who follow the rules, or who perform well on required work are given reinforcers, or rewards. The reinforcers may be teacher praise, good grades, or even such tangible items as stickers or appropriate free movies. Students who do not follow the procedures, who misbehave, or who perform poorly are denied desired rewards or are punished in some way.

Basically, there are four general categories of consequences that can follow students' actions: positive reinforcement, negative reinforcement, punishment I, and punishment II. As noted in Chapter 12, positive and negative reinforcement are used for maintaining or increasing the occurrence of a desired student behavior. In the case of positive reinforcement, a reward (e.g., praise, grades, or free time) is presented for desired behavior, whereas negative reinforcement involves the removal of an undesired stimulus (e.g., weekend homework, no visiting, or a change in the seating arrangement).

Inappropriate student actions can be discouraged through the use of punishment. Like reinforcement, punishment comes in two categories, simply labeled I and II. Punishment I, the most commonly used form, involves the application of some undesirable stimulus. For example, undesirable student action can be followed by a private reprimand, isolation, or a trip to the principal's office. In contrast, punishment II involves the removal of a desired stimulus or the withholding of an anticipated positive stimulus. For example, inappropriate student behavior could be followed by a loss of free time, exclusion from a school film, or loss of computer time for a week. If used appropriately, both punishments I and II should result in the elimination of, or at least a decrease in, undesired student behaviors.

Reinforcement can also be a complex system. For example, one such program is the token reinforcement system, in which students earn tokens for both positive classroom behaviors and academic work. The tokens earned are then periodically exchanged for some desired activity or reward (see Chapter 12).

APPLY AND REFLECT: Accept no excuses for improper behavior. This is often not an easy task. Can you do so?

Management approaches can be studied and analyzed. But you must decide on your own modus operandi with regard to managerial style. These management approaches are summarized in Table 13.1. How you respond to management problems will depend on which approach or approaches along the continuum of management strategies best fits your educational philosophy. Moreover, how you respond to student misbehavior should also be related to the cause of the misbehavior. Complete Expansion Activity: Management Approaches to further address the different approaches to classroom management.

EXPANSION ACTIVITY

Management Approaches

Form groups of four or five. Discuss the virtues of the self-discipline, instructional, and desist approaches to classroom management. Which approach is most applicable to the elementary classroom? Middle school classroom? Secondary school classroom? Give a rationale for your conclusions.

Let's now look at some of the reasons students misbehave. But, first, review the approach summary and complete Review, Extension, and Reflective Exercise 13.1.

TABLE 13.1 **Management Approaches**

Approach	Description
Self-Discipline Approach	View that students can evaluate and change to appropriate behavior
Instructional Approach	View that well-planned and well-implemented instruction will prevent classroom problems
Desist Approach	View that the teacher should have full regulatory power in the classroom

Review, Extension, and Reflective Exercise 13.1

Describe the broad approaches to classroom management.

Connection to INTASC Standards:

- Standard 5: Learning Environment. The teacher must be able to use an understanding of individual and group motivation and behavior to create a learning environment that encourages positive social interaction, active engagement in learning, and self-motivation.

Connection to the NBPTS:

- Proposition 3: Teachers are responsible for managing and monitoring student learning.

Review

- Describe the goals and challenges of good classroom management.
- Is good classroom management related to school level (elementary, middle, high school)?
- Outline the major elements of the three broad approaches to classroom management.

Reflection

- What elements of the three broad approaches to classroom management would be effective at the grade level you expect to teach? What approaches have your past teachers used? Were they successful? If not, how would you change them?

Causes of Misbehavior

Classroom misbehavior can often be attributed to conditions that are not readily obvious. Therefore, if you are to deal successfully with misbehavior, you must try to identify the deeper problems that are causing the actions. That is, you must get to the root of the problems that are causing students to misbehave. A careful examination of students' classroom behaviors, desirable as well as undesirable, can reveal that they are influenced by forces and pressures inside and outside the classroom.

Home Environment

Relationships with parents and siblings often affect classroom behavior. Parents usually serve as models and communicate important attitudinal ideals and feelings to their children. If these parental influences are negative toward school or learning, a student might develop these same negative ideals and feelings.

Through daily interactions, parents establish the general acceptable conduct of behavior of their children and, therefore, directly influence students' classroom behavior. Consequently, when parents are extremely tolerant and do not teach respect for others, when they allow their children to talk back, or when swearing and fighting are tolerated in the home, these behaviors often carry over into the classroom. Conversely, students who come from homes with overly strict parents may be inclined to be followers who do not question authority, or they may resent anyone in authority—including the teacher. Therefore, you must try to determine the rules of conduct established in the home before you can deal effectively with misbehavior in the classroom.

Students from homes where there is constant family friction and a related lack of parental support sometimes develop discipline problems. Constant involvement in the home's emotional turmoil and a too-often associated feeling of rejection can also lead to problems in the classroom. You should be sensitive to abrupt behavioral changes that might be a result of a student's problems at home.

Lack of supervision in the home is a common problem in our society. Many students come from single-parent homes or from homes where both parents are too busy with their own lives to be concerned with the children. Therefore, you may have students who work, who stay out late at night, or who watch television late into the night. These students often fall asleep in class or are inattentive. Other students may live on junk food or come to school without breakfast. These students sometimes lack the energy to carry out assignments or even to pay attention. You need to counsel these students, and perhaps the parents, on the importance of rest and proper diet.

Parental attitudes toward schooling influence students' behavior in the classroom. Parents who put little value on education, for example, often instill these attitudes in their children. Furthermore, parents who communicate negative feelings toward educators (classroom teachers as well as administrators) often pass on such feelings to their children, who, in turn, will have little respect for educators.

Conversely, some parents value education so highly that they establish unreasonable expectations for their children—for example, parents who accept nothing but straight-A work. Similarly, problems may develop when parents have unrealistic goals for their children—for instance, parents who want their sons or daughters to be physicians and, so, insist that they enroll in advanced science courses. Problems often develop because of lack of interest or lack of academic ability. Both high expectations and unrealistic goals can result in poor motivation, low self-esteem, and behavior problems.

The Teacher

Teachers who do not plan have trouble with class control. Teachers who do not start class when the bell rings, who are sidetracked from their lessons into unrelated talk, or who are not sure where they are going next in their lessons communicate

Student busing often impacts what teachers can do in the classroom.

disorder to their students. Too often, such a message of disorder leads to disrespect toward the teacher and a dislike of the subject.

APPLY AND REFLECT: You should establish procedures for starting and ending

(dismissing) your classes. What will yours be?

Teachers must teach at the level of their students' ability. Lessons aimed too low bore and irritate bright students, whereas lessons geared too high frustrate low-ability students. But the teacher who focuses on the average students, as many teachers do, are still not challenging the bright students and are not giving low-ability students a reasonable opportunity to be successful. As a result, both groups can become mischievous, inattentive, and interruptive in class. In short, you must design lessons that offer challenge to your bright students but, at the same time, give low-ability students reasonable opportunities for success.

Teachers must show respect for students as individuals with rights, values, and feelings. They must exercise control and refrain from ridiculing them, both in front of their peers and in private. Ridicule and sarcasm back students into a defensive position to save face with peers, which can cause problems. Also, teachers should refrain from demanding an unreasonable degree of inactivity from students. Some talking, scuffling of feet, and paper shuffling is unavoidable. Remember that students need some outlets for their energy. In fact, students often find it difficult to be perfectly quiet, inactive, and attentive in the classroom for extended periods of time, as some teachers insist. In short, don't be oversensitive to noise in the classroom, but let common sense be your guide. Establish your limits, however, and don't tolerate all the desires of students in your classroom.

Personality and Health Problems

Some student classroom problems can be attributed to immaturity and/or problems related to health. Immaturity is especially a problem with elementary school students.

Older students often feel insecure about their appearance, lack of peer recognition, and lack of parental respect. Such feelings may stem from a lack of self-respect and self-control, which results in constant talking, no consideration for others, immature actions, and a lack of responsibility. These behaviors, although usually viewed as minor, when exhibited daily should be addressed at once so that their escalation into more serious problems can be averted.

More serious problems, such as cheating on tests and talking back to teachers, often can be traced back to the home environment or even to some deep, underlying causes, which may require expert assistance. Keep in mind, however, that some students go to such extreme measures to obtain attention from their parents, teachers, or classmates.

Some students present problems to the teacher because of health problems. Allergies, poor eyesight, respiratory ailments, and poor hearing can affect classroom behavior. It is difficult to concentrate when you have trouble breathing, or seeing, or hearing. Indeed, an illness may be so severe that students are not able to exert the energy needed for classroom activities or homework exercises. It is important that you be sensitive to the health problems of students and refer those with such problems to the school nurse, principal, and/or parents so they become aware of the problem.

Once a philosophy of classroom management has been formulated and the cause of misbehavior understood, your managerial style must be implemented in such a way that it prevents problems from developing and deals with the misbehavior that does take place. This requires that you organize for the prevention of problems, as well as deal with the ongoing management of the class.

Organizing for Effective Management

Effective classroom management takes organization. Indeed, much of what we have covered should prove useful in organizing your classroom for effective management. Such techniques as motivation and variety in instructional planning represent major factors in the prevention of management problems. Let's look, however, at some other key classroom problem-prevention areas.

Planning

Obviously, classroom order takes planning. Plans must be devised such that classroom problems are minimized and learning time is maximized. In other words, if you are to be effective, you should be well prepared: You should know exactly what and how you will teach and have all required materials ready for students. In fact,

Effective planning is often the key to a smooth-running classroom.

you should overestimate what can be accomplished in the allowed time. It can be extremely frustrating and embarrassing to find yourself with 15 to 20 minutes of class time and nothing to do. Needless to say, problems often develop. Therefore, overplan—with activities that are interesting, stimulating, and relevant—and keep your lessons moving at a brisk but appropriate pace. Finally, it is good practice to have alternative activities planned and available in case they are needed.

The school calendar should be consulted when planning, because certain days or weeks require special steps to avoid potential behavior problems. For instance, the day before a major holiday, the day of an afternoon assembly or pep rally, the day of a big football or basketball game, and the week before Christmas or spring break are apt to require special attention and preparation. At such times, it is essential that students be involved in highly motivating and interesting activities that will compete successfully with other, external events.

The Establishment of Routines

Many school and classroom activities are basically routine—for example, the taking and reporting of attendance, the issuing of passes for students to leave the room or building, and the distribution and collection of papers. Some of these routines are established by the school for all teachers, whereas others are established by individual teachers. Teachers often spend too much time on simple classroom routines. For example, some elementary teachers spend much time getting students ready for lunch, recess, and dismissal because they call students by name, one at a time. This time wasting is unnecessary. Many teachers establish routines early in the year that require an entire row or table to be quiet and ready to go before are students called to line up. Lining up then takes seconds, not minutes. Other such procedures should also become routine for students.

What are the standard school-operating procedures and routines? To find out, you should consult the school handbook and talk with your department head, other teachers, and the principal. In most schools, routines and procedures are established for (1) taking and keeping of attendance, (2) dealing with tardy students, (3) issuing passes to leave the classroom or building, (4) having students in after school, (5) recording and reporting grades, (6) using the school library, (7) dealing with ill students, (8) issuing failing notices, and (9) conducting parental conferences. Such school routines and procedures must be adhered to by all teachers, because if each teacher were to establish individual school routines and procedures, the results would more than likely be student uncertainty and discipline problems. Therefore, you should find out the established school routines and procedures *prior* to the reporting of students to class.

Routines and procedures must also be established for the classroom. Routines and procedures should be established for activities such as entering the classroom and starting class, checking attendance, passing out materials, and collecting and checking homework. You should, for instance, have a short activity ready when students enter the classroom (e.g., a problem or question on the overhead or a few pages to read) that they will complete as you take care of routine activities.

Attendance represents a problem area for many teachers in that they will spend as much as 10 minutes calling roll. Students usually use this wasted time at the beginning of the period for talking and other mischievous activities. Instead of calling roll, you should prepare a seating chart for each class (see Figure 13.2). A pocket-type seating chart works best, because you or your students will request

"Tommy's bad behavior wouldn't be so intolerable if it weren't for his perfect attendance."

Figure 13.2
A Seating Chart

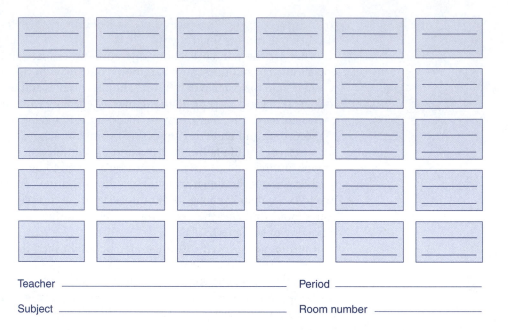

Teacher _____   Period _____

Subject _____   Room number _____

some changes in seating during the year. During the first class meeting, students should be given the opportunity to select a seat. Once the selection has been made, have students write their names—or you write their names—on slips, which are placed in the appropriate slots. You may have to change some seat assignments later, but in the beginning give them their choice.

The collection and distribution of papers should be streamlined as much as possible. Unnecessary amounts of time spent on such tasks often lead to student misbehavior. Collecting and passing out materials can be accomplished by passing to, or from, the front of the class seating rows. In other seating arrangements, a similar technique—for instance, assigning one student per group to collect or pass out materials—can be used.

Taking care of excused absences is another time-consuming administrative chore. In handling these, you must, of course, sign the admission slip, but you must also bring the student up-to-date as to missed classroom activities and assignments. When several students have been absent on a given day, the handling of missed work can often delay the start of class considerably. This delay usually will result in talking and general student misbehavior. A monthly calendar, such as that shown in Figure 13.3 can be helpful in dealing with absences. Students know what classroom activities were completed on a given day; they know what assignment was given. The calendar also gives your better students the opportunity to work ahead so they can work on other individual projects. Indeed, announcements, messages of recognition, and motivational messages (e.g., awards, birthdays, and accomplishments) can be shared with the class through the class calendar. Computer programs are available to make the construction of class calendars a relatively easy task.

Figure 13.3
Monthly Calendar

S	M	T	W	T	F	S
1 Welcome back to class, Jesse.	**2** Text pages 450–451. Do practice 1–10. Do pages 452–453: Apply section.	**3** Text pages 454–455. Do practice work 1–10. Persevere, you can do it!	**4** Text 456–457. Do all practice work.	**5** Text pages 458–459. Do all practice work. This one is a "piece of cake."	**6** Spelling test. All assignments must be in baskets today!	**7** Birthdays this month are: Kevin, Kendra, Thomas, Alison, Jennifer, and Hope!
8 Failing notices go out Friday. Don't be caught off balance. Turn in all work NOW.	**9** Spelling. Text pages 462–463. Do all practice work.	**10** Text pages 464–465. Do all practice work. Stretch your neck out and try Part C.**	**11** Text pages 468–469 do A&B.	**12** Text pages 470–471. Do all practice work.	**13** NO SCHOOL TODAY!	**14** ALCOHOL IS A DRUG.
15 Welcome back to class, Carlos.	**16** Tune into Spelling! 50 words this week for the spelling spin-off on Friday.	**17** Text pages 472–475. Do all practice work. Challenge** Try the Apply*	**18** Film today on preparing speeches!	**19** TIME FOR TALK. DISCUSS TOPIC FOR SPEECHES TODAY.	**20** SPELLING SPIN-OFF** Today!	**21** Character Comes from the Heart! Students Persevere** **************
22 "Write On" with Learning. Essay winners this month are Jay and Natalie****	**23** Library to begin research.	**24** Library work. Bibliography due end of class today. See page 339.	**25** Library work. Topic outlines due today!! See page 340 for help.	**26** Library work. Rough drafts due today. See page 343 for help.	**27** Library work. Final drafts due today. See pages 347–349 for help.	**28** Remember to say "NO" to drugs.
29 Don't forget to vote this month for the most improved student in your class.	**30** Text Pages 502–504. Do all practice work.					

You should never become a slave to routine; however, when routines will be of assistance in carrying out classroom business efficiently, they should be used. You should determine and use the routines and procedures that are appropriate for your particular classroom.

APPLY AND REFLECT: Set up a class routine or activity for the first 4 or 5 minutes of class. Share it.

Managing Space

Your classroom should be arranged to be an environment in which it is easy for you and students to work and so that it does not encourage misbehavior. The pencil sharpener, for example, should not be positioned in a place where students must pass close to other students when going to use it. Students often can't leave each other alone as they pass nearby. In addition, it is usually unwise to place the wastebasket at the front of the room; it is an inviting target for basketball practice.

Most classrooms today have moveable chairs. Therefore, don't get in the habit of seating students only in straight rows. You should try different seating arrangements (e.g., circles, semicircles, U-shapes, and squares). In fact, arrange your seating according to the activity to be completed by students. Experiment with various arrangements and see what works best with your students.

Constructive use of wall space makes a classroom more conducive to learning and evokes a more positive climate. For example, walls can display motivational statements, materials to spark interest in a topic, or classroom procedures. Moreover, before school begins, put up a bulletin board and be prepared to change it periodically. Make your bulletin boards attractive, interesting, and colorful so they help promote a positive attitude toward your room and subject. You might also want to devote one bulletin board to announcements, such as the bell schedule, the weekly lunch menu, news items of interest to the class, and classroom rules and consequences.

Establishing Usable Limits

Limits specify the expected and forbidden actions in the classroom. Students need and want limits (rules); that is, they want to know what is expected of them and why. Teachers who try to avoid setting limits and imposing necessary structure will often find that chaos results. But don't establish rules for the sake of having rules. Indeed, you should take care not to have too many rules, unenforceable rules, and unnecessary rules; only essential rules and limits should be set.

Clarity and consistency are vital in the establishment of rules. Your rules should always reinforce the basic idea that students are in school to study and learn. When no longer needed, a rule should be discarded or changed. But, as long as they are retained, rules must be enforced. You should always explain and discuss with students why certain rules are necessary. You may even want to spend time negotiating the establishment of certain rules with students at the beginning of the year.

It is often better to have five or six general rules that cover many specifics, rather than to list all the specifics. But if specific actions represent a problem area (e.g., chewing gum or using reference books), then a rule should cover the specific problem. Examples of appropriate general rules that might be established and discussed are these:

1. *Be prepared with books, paper, pencil, and so on when you come to class.* You should discuss exactly what is to be brought to class.
2. *Be in your seat and ready to work when the bell rings.* You may want students to begin working on a warm-up activity that is written on the overhead, you may require that they have homework ready to be checked, or you may ask that they have notebooks open and ready to take notes when the bell rings.

3. *Take care of your classroom and respect other people's property.* This means school, teacher, and fellow student property is to be left alone.
4. *Be polite and respectful.* This conduct covers verbal abuse, fighting, talking back, and general conduct.
5. *Obtain permission before speaking or leaving your seat.* Address exceptions to this rule—such as when to sharpen pencils, throw trash away, and go to the teacher's desk for assistance.

Again, your rules should always be discussed with and taught to students. In fact, some teachers require that students pass a test about classroom regulations at the beginning of the year. Specific behaviors that are included and excluded in each general rule should be explained and discussed at the beginning of the year. Indeed, you might be wise to have students record the rules for future reference. You should also consider sending parents a copy of your classroom rules.

APPLY AND REFLECT: Will you have rules in your class? If yes, why do you think you will need them? If not, why not?

As soon as you have established your rules, you must decide on the consequences for breaking a rule. It is often rather difficult to make this decision at the time the rule is broken. The appropriate response is often to have the student "do it right." For example, messes can be cleaned up, incomplete papers can be finished or redone, and broken property can be replaced.

When you have established the rules for your classroom and the consequences for breaking the rules, you have taken the first step in making students aware of what will and will not be tolerated in the classroom. You must now think about managing the classroom on a daily basis. Complete Expansion Activity: Misbehaving Students to explore some common classroom problems.

EXPANSION ACTIVITY

Misbehaving Students

Some students will misbehave or show off in class in an attempt to gain peer recognition and approval. Others will misbehave just for the sake of misbehaving. Some will deliberately not follow classroom procedures or break classroom rules in an attempt to challenge your authority or to find out how far they can push you. How would you go about getting the classroom cooperation of students without constant nagging and reminders? What about students who fail to get assignments turned in or turn in assignments late or poorly done? How would you address these problems?

Managing the Class

Effective classroom management is a daily and essential challenge to teachers. Managing a class basically involves getting off to a good start, then keeping the class moving smoothly toward established goals.

Sharing Control

Controlling the students is one of the biggest concerns of most teachers. They fear classroom chaos. They fear open defiance. Moreover, new teachers tend to be worried about basic classroom survival.

Some experts believe that the best way to avoid many of the classroom fears and concerns is through shared control. That is, the teacher should give students a voice in decision making. Students can be given the opportunity to provide input in establishing classroom rules and in curriculum decisions. This shared decision making gives students a stake in the educational process and a sense of ownership. You do not rely on "blind obedience" but, instead, "negotiate the learning space together."

Shared control does not mean students do whatever they want. Limits are established, but students participate in the setting of these limits. In so doing, they discuss appropriate and inappropriate classroom behaviors and ways to address classroom problems. The process gives students some ownership of the classroom environment. It places more of the burden on students for controlling their own behaviors, but the teacher still sets and guards the boundaries beyond which students may not transgress.

APPLY AND REFLECT: It is often suggested that you involve students as much as possible in the establishment of classroom rules and consequences. Do you think this is feasible in most classrooms? Why or why not?

Getting Started

Wong and Wong (1998) contend that the first days of school can make or break a teacher. They suggest that the first few days—or even the first few minutes—of school or a class will determine your success or failure for the rest of the school year. During these initial days, it is essential that you establish your credibility as a manager. In fact, student respect for you as a teacher will often be established during the first few days.

What do effective classroom managers do during those first critical days? Experienced teachers begin the first day of school or a class with an activity. Inexperienced teachers often want to begin that first day or class with a fun activity. This is not recommended. Effective managers begin with classroom management procedures. School should be viewed as a serious place to learn, not a place to go to have fun. You can make learning fun at times, but you can't make learning fun all the time.

Experienced teachers suggest the secret to successful management is organization. The focus during the first few days of school should be on the teaching of rules, the organizational system, classroom procedures, and expectations. Feedback on appropriateness of actions is essential in these early stages. In other words, you should create a positive classroom environment and establish rules and consequences. Planning is the key to management: Make sure your content is interesting and meaningful to students. Moreover, it is important that you clearly communicate standards for academic work and establish an atmosphere of free exchange. Indeed, involve students as much as possible in the learning process. Finally, monitor student behavior closely, and deal with misbehavior quickly and firmly.

Making full and meaningful use of time on the first day is especially critical. Therefore, it might be helpful to plan, using the following:

1. *Seating slips.* Pass out seating slips and have students sign them. Collect them in order, separating each row with a paper clip. It is often wise to count and inspect the slips as they are collected. If you don't, you may find slips signed by "Snow White" or not signed at all.
2. *Books.* Assign books to students keeping an accurate record of assigned book numbers. Books sometimes get lost or stolen. Remember, you or the student will replace any unreturned book. Have a short activity for students to do as you distribute books.
3. *Assignment sheet.* Distribute an assignment sheet with at least one week's work on it. Explain it to students. Make your first assignment short, interesting, involving, and not dependent on the textbook.
4. *Class discussion.* Discuss unique contributions of your subject that make it important and relevant to them.
5. *Homework.* Discuss assigned homework topic. Pose some provocative questions.
6. *Marking system.* Give a brief explanation of your grading system, of when you collect homework, of when tests are administered, and so on.

Completing all of these tasks will be difficult on the first day, but accomplishing a great deal the first day may serve you well. Students will be impressed with your organization and businesslike manner, and first impressions are important.

Finally, leave 2 or 3 minutes at the end of the period for closure. That is, save some time at the end of the period for needed cleanup and for giving assignments. When—and only when—you are ready, you should dismiss the class. Don't let the bell dismiss (or start) the class. This should be understood from the first day.

Getting to Know the Students

It is good practice to know as much as possible about your students. Of course, middle school and secondary teachers may have 25 to 30 students per class and up to 150 students total in all classes. Just learning names can be a chore. Learning names as soon as possible, however, shows definite interest. A seating chart is helpful in remembering names.

It is advisable to know more about students than just their names. An information card (Figure 13.4), completed during the first class period, can provide some of this information. If more information is needed, student files are usually available to teachers. Information on students often proves helpful in understanding why students act the way they do.

Enforcement of Rules

Lax enforcement of established rules makes them worthless. In fact, students like to know where they stand and will periodically test your enforcement of the rules.

Bored students often cause problems for teachers.

Figure 13.4
Information Card

Family Name: _____ First Name: _____

Address: _____ Telephone: _____

Homeroom Teacher: _____

Father's First Name: _____

Occupation: _____

Mother's First Name: _____

Occupation: _____

Number of Siblings: _____

Interests (hobbies, clubs, sports, other activities): _____

_____

_____

_____

When this happens, quick and firm application of the consequences should follow. If a student tries you—and one always will—you cannot ignore the breaking of the rules, because the behavior will ripple to other students, and they will also want to test you. Conversely, if you are firm when a student tests you, this action, too, will ripple out to other students, and they will be less likely to test you in the future.

The use of the **ripple effect** is especially effective with high-status students. Consequently, you should be firm with these students, and other students will give you fewer problems.

APPLY AND REFLECT: Effective managers use the "ripple effect" to their advantage.

How would you do so?

_____

Be consistent and fair in your enforcement of the rules. Treat all students the same, but be humane. Sometimes you must consider the reasons for misbehavior and make exceptions with regard to punishment. But make sure the class as a whole understands the reason for an exception.

Monitoring the Classroom

You should be aware of what is going on in the classroom at all times. Therefore, room arrangement is an important part of your ability to monitor the classroom: You must be able to monitor all areas of the classroom from your desk and from any other classroom area. When a potential problem is spotted, a simple pause in conjunction with eye contact (a stare) usually curbs the inappropriate activity.

Two aspects of room arrangement are critical to effective monitoring: your ability to see students at all times and the traffic patterns within the room. Your capacity for seeing students and moving quickly to be in proximity of a potential problem will often control the misbehavior. Therefore, apply careful thought to your room arrangement. Eliminate barriers that may keep you from seeing certain areas of the room.

Monitoring the classroom as you teach is not an easy task. You must be well prepared, know your content thoroughly, and maintain contact with all areas of the classroom at all times. If you are uncertain about what you are to teach or if there are dead spots in your lesson, students may recognize the insecurity and become inattentive.

Resolving Conflict

Modern society glamorizes violence. It portrays heroes as people who win through violence. In doing so, it teaches children to be violent. They are learning to inflict pain, to destroy, to kill one another with no apparent remorse. No school appears to be immune to the violence problem.

Violence, however, is preventable. Young people must realize that they have many choices for dealing with conflict other than passivity and aggression. They need to learn conflict-resolution skills. Conflict resolution encourages young people to openly discuss their conflicts. Young people must also learn the skills needed to make choices in light of their understanding and appreciation of their own and other cultures. A supportive atmosphere must be established to support these conflict-resolution skills.

Teachers, too, must learn and apply a new set of skills for heading off and resolving conflict. Teachers must learn to share their power with students, so that they can help deal with their own disputes. To this end, training in a peer mediation system can be indispensable (Johnson, Johnson, Stevahn, & Hodne, 1997). Peer mediation teaches young people how to engage in problem-solving negotiations and how to mediate schoolmates' conflicts.

Using Punishment

Sooner or later, no matter how well you plan to prevent problems, student misbehavior is going to demand that you administer punishment. Some student behavior will be so severe that some kind of adverse stimulus must be employed to decrease the occurrence of the behavior. You must be aware, however, that what is considered punishment by one individual might not be considered punishment by another—in fact, it may even be considered rewarding. Also, when applying adverse consequences for misbehavior, be sure that you communicate to students that they have chosen the consequence. They should understand that by choosing to misbehave, they have also chosen the consequences.

The most common consequence used for curbing disruptive behavior is probably the verbal reprimand. But, all too often, these reprimands become mere nagging. As a rule, older students are at an age when they react negatively to being treated other than as adults. Efforts to apply adverse stimulus such as criticism may provoke hostility. Indeed, the student may blow up and say something unintentional. Thus, criticizing, ridiculing, or embarrassing a student can result in a power struggle between the student and teacher, which does little for resolving the long-term behavior problem.

One way of avoiding a confrontation with offending students is to administer the reprimand privately rather than publicly. In this way, the student "saves face," and there is no need to engage in a power struggle. Moreover, a private talk gives you the opportunity to develop a closer personal relationship with the misbehaving student. If the private talk fails to solve the problem, more severe consequences must be administered. Other consequences often applied when severe misbehavior occurs are, in order of severity, loss of privileges, detention, in-school suspension, and out-of-school suspension.

Loss of privileges is a common and effective form of punishment. Examples are the loss of free time, the loss of time on the computer, the loss of a weekend free of homework, or the loss of any other preferred activities. Other options include requiring students to stay in the classroom when others attend an assembly or pep rally. Unfortunately, the problem with this form of punishment is the lack of privileges commonly available for use in most classrooms and, consequently, the shortage of privilege to be denied.

Detention is one of the most frequently used means of punishment, which generally comes in two forms. One type requires that all students serving detention report to a detention hall at a specified time (e.g., Monday after school or Saturday morning). The other kind requires that the students report back to the teacher's classroom after or before school. But because many students ride buses or work, many teachers have students return to the classroom during a break during the day (e.g., part of their lunch break). When using detention as a punishment option, the student should be required to complete a serious academic task. Moreover, you should avoid engaging in conversation with students serving detention. Conversation with the teacher may be perceived as enjoyable, and, hence, the misbehavior might be repeated for more of the "enjoyable" detention.

On occasion, misbehavior becomes so serious or persistent that you must solicit outside assistance. As a general rule, assistance comes from two sources: the school administration (e.g., the vice principal or principal) and parents. When a student is sent to the principal's office, you should phone or send a message to the office, reporting that a student is being sent and why. A call to parents about a behavior problem usually has positive results. Most parents are concerned about the behavior and progress of their children and are willing to work cooperatively in correcting any misbehavior. There are exceptions; some parents feel that taking care of school misbehavior is your job.

W E B   L I N K   **Classroom Discipline Techniques**

Access the following two Internet URL sites: www.teachnet.com/how-to/manage and www.theteacherscorner.net/resources/websites.htm. Review and analyze the techniques for better classroom discipline. Write a short paper on techniques that will and will not work with the age group of students you expect to teach. Share your findings with your class.

In-school suspension is becoming very common. This technique involves removing misbehaving students from a class and placing them in a special area, where they do their schoolwork. They generally are placed in a bare room, furnished with only a table and chair. They report to this room at the beginning of the school day and remain until the end of the day. Meals are sent in, and teachers send in the class work for the day. If the in-school suspension does not correct the misbehavior, out-of-school suspension usually follows. But, out-of-school suspension should be used with extreme cases and as a last resort.

Assigning extra work or deducting from academic grades for misbehavior should be avoided. Associating grades and subject work with punishment only creates a dislike for the subject. It is often good policy, however, to request that students redo sloppy or incorrect work. Indeed, accepting sloppy work or incorrect work only encourages more of the same.

Punishment of the whole class for the misbehavior of one or two students sometimes creates negative effects. Indeed, such an approach may curb the inappropriate behavior, but other students often feel the teacher is unfair and, as a result, will develop a negative attitude toward that teacher. On the other hand, if the teacher is well respected and viewed as fair, the use of peer pressure can be an effective approach to discipline.

To this point, I have not mentioned the use of corporal punishment as an option. First of all, it is illegal in most states for teachers to administer corporal punishment. Secondly, some students are too old for corporal punishment. Moreover, corporal punishment often fails to address the long-term problem.

In short, corporal punishment has proven to be ineffective. Also, other techniques can be more effective with older students. And corporal punishment can lay you open to accusations of brutality and legal difficulties.

APPLY AND REFLECT: The use of corporal punishment is not advised. Do you agree?

When used, punishment should be administered immediately after the misbehavior, and it should be fair—that is, the punishment should fit the crime. Certainly, the same punishment should not be administered for constant talking as for constant harm to other students. Of course, all misbehavior must be dealt with. Therefore, keep your emotions under control and deal with problems consistently, fairly, and professionally. In other words, when you do use punishment, make it swift, sure, and impressive.

When administered appropriately, punishment can be an effective deterrent to misbehavior. Punishment should only be used, however, when no other alternatives are available. If the misbehavior is not severe, a warning should first be issued. If a warning does not work, you should consider punishment.

This completes our study of classroom management. Complete Web Link: Classroom Discipline Techniques and Web Link: Discipline Problems, which will let you explore some of the problems you may encounter as a teacher.

W E B   L I N K   Discipline Problems

Access Internet URL site www.disciplinehelp.com. The site gives a list of 117 problem behaviors and suggestions for handling the problems. Select five of the problems that you think will cause you concern at the grade level you expect to teach. Analyze the website advice for the five problems and write a summary of your conclusions. Present your five problems and analysis to the class.

Table 13.2 summarizes the control aspect of classroom management. Review the summary and complete Review, Extension, and Reflective Exercise 13.2.

TABLE 13.2 Control Techniques

Element	Description
Routines	Classroom activities that are repetitive and follow a common procedure
Limits	The accepted and nonaccepted actions in the classroom
Monitoring	Being aware of what is taking place in the classroom
Punishment	The application of a negative stimulus or removal of a positive stimulus for inappropriate behavior

Review, Extension, and Reflective Exercise 13.2

Formulate techniques for effective classroom management.

Connection to INTASC Standards:

- Standard 5: Learning Environment. The teacher must be able to use an understanding of individual and group motivation and behavior to create a learning environment that encourages positive social interaction, active engagement in learning, and self-motivation.

Connection to the NBPTS:

- Proposition 3: Teachers are responsible for managing and monitoring student learning.

Review

- What elements contribute to an effective learning environment?

- What strategies are most likely to get the school year off to the right start for a teacher?
- Describe how you would prevent serious discipline problems.

Reflection

- How worried are you about problem behaviors among the students you plan to teach? In view of your own current skills, how prepared are you for dealing with these problem behaviors?
- Based on your personal experiences and classroom observations, which would probably be easier for you to manage—an elementary school classroom, a middle school classroom, or a high school classroom? Why? What standards of "good" behavior would be nonnegotiable? Would you be flexible about some things? Explain.

VIEW FROM THE CLASSROOM

What do teachers think about classroom management? Teacher survey results relative to topics presented in this chapter are expressed below. Review these results and discuss with classmates.

Where did you learn your most effective behavior management techniques?

On the job (in the trenches)	70%
From colleagues	15%
From a workshop	8%
From an excellent book	3%
College/university	4%

Are teachers getting the respect they deserve from students?

No	84%
Yes	16%

Do you feel you get the respect you deserve from your students' parents?

No	61%
Yes	39%

What do you consider to be the average size of a class where you work?

16–25 students	49%
26–35 students	40%
10–15 students	7%
5 students	3%
36–45 students	1%
46 + students	0.3%

SOURCE: Excerpted from *Teach-nology*, available at www.teach-nology.com/poll

Summary

- A classroom must be organized and orderly, and it must run smoothly for learning to take place.
- Handling management problems is an integral part of teaching.
- Positive management strategies are essential to effective teaching and learning.

The Role of Classroom Management

- There are many schools of thought on effective classroom management.
- Three common schools of thought on classroom management are the self-discipline approach, the instructional approach, and the desist approach.

Approaches to Classroom Management

- Principles of the self-discipline approach to classroom management are supported by the Glasser reality therapy model, Gordon teacher effectiveness training (TET) model, Coloroso inner discipline model, and Kohn beyond discipline model
- Principles of the instructional approach to classroom management are emphasized by the Kounin model and the Jones model.
- Principles of the desist approach to classroom management are integral components of assertive discipline and behavioral modification.

Causes of Misbehavior

- Misbehavior has many causes.

- Misbehavior sometimes can be attributed to influences outside the classroom, such as home environment or the community.
- Misbehavior can be caused by attributes associated with the teacher or with students themselves.

Organizing for Effective Management

- Effective classroom management requires organization as well as the ability to deal with an ongoing learning environment.
- Effective management calls for planning well, establishing routines, arranging your room to avoid problems, and formulating limits.
- Effective managers must try to foresee classroom problems and try to prevent their occurrence.

Managing a Class

- A class must be kept on task.
- Teachers must establish credibility at the beginning of the year—and then keep it.
- Teachers must be fair, firm, and consistent with students.
- Teachers must monitor their classrooms and apply the consequences to misbehavior.
- Teachers should use punishment only as a last resort.
- Teachers should establish a positive classroom atmosphere, where students have an opportunity to develop a sense of self-discipline.

Discussion Questions and Activities

1. **Discipline approaches.** Analyze the three approaches to classroom management. Which approach, if any, do you prefer? Can you put together parts of the different approaches and come up with an eclectic approach that you think would work for you? Can you identify some basic concepts that appear to be true of all three approaches?

2. **Causes of misbehavior.** Think back over the classes you have attended in which there have been disciplinary incidents. List the possible causes for any such misbehavior. How might knowledge of the causes of these incidents influence a teacher's actions? Some behavior problems are teacher-created and some are student-centered. Can you think of examples?

3. **Planning.** Plan a first day for a class you may teach. What activities would you try on the first day? The first few weeks? What rules and consequences would you plan to implement and discuss?

4. **Rules and consequences.** Prepare a list of rules for a classroom at the grade level you expect to teach. After you have established a set of rules, prepare a list of consequences for breaking the rules.

5. **Maintaining control.** What types of procedures would you use to maintain control throughout the year? What measures would you take for severe misbehavior problems?

Connection With the Field

1. **Behavior observation.** Complete several observations in various classrooms at different grade levels. How do the observed teachers control behavior? Observe the students as well, as you consider these questions:

   a. Do students seat themselves when the bell rings? Is there a warm-up activity?
   b. Do the students raise their hands before speaking?
   c. Do the students refrain from speaking during class?
   d. Do the students hand in papers in an orderly manner?

2. **Teacher interviews.** Interview several teachers at different grade levels. Do they have management problems? If so, how do they handle these problems? Do they support the self-discipline, instructional, or desist approach to classroom management? Make a list of ideas you can use when you become a teacher.

3. **Interview counselors.** Interview school counselors at elementary, middle, and high schools. Ask them to describe the discipline policies at their schools and how well they work. Could you support any or all of the policies?

4. **Student handbooks.** Examine and compare several student handbooks from different school districts. Discuss similarities and differences with your classmates.

Praxis II Connection

The following test preparation exercises are intended to help you prepare for the Praxis II: Principles of Learning and Teaching. The Praxis II may be required by your teacher education preparatory program and for state certification or licensing. These exercises will give you direct access to pedagogical knowledge from Chapter 13 that may be expected of you on the Praxis II and other pedagogical exams that may be required at the end of your teacher education program.

Case Histories Format

Now that you have completed your study of *Effective Instructional Strategies: From Theory to Practice,* once again access the Educational Testing Service (ETS) website below that corresponds to the grade levels you expect to teach. Review the site and again complete the site sample exercises. This will give you the opportunity to review the format and to reexamine your initial responses to the PLT assessment.

PLT: Early Childhood: ftp://ftp.ets.org/pub/tandl/0521.pdf

PLT: Grades K–6: ftp://ftp.ets.org/pub/tandl/0522.pdf

PLT: Grades 5–9: ftp://ftp.ets.org/pub/tandl/0523.pdf

PLT: Grades 7–12: ftp://ftp.ets.org/pub/tandl/0524.pdf

Topic Connections

1. Classroom management approaches (I. C4)

There are many approaches to classroom management. How you deal with classroom problems depends on your beliefs, personality, and goals. Describe the three broad classroom management approaches.

2. Rules (I. C4)

Rules are essential for the establishment of an effective learning environment. Describe how to establish and maintain classroom rules.

3. Behavior (I. C4)

All teachers encounter some behavior problems. Describe techniques and strategies for dealing with common behavior problems.

ON YOUR OWN

Log on to the web-based student study site at http://www.sagepub.com/eis for more information about the vignettes and materials presented in this chapter, suggestions for activities, study aids such as electronic flashcards and review quizzes, and research recommendations including journal article links and questions related to this chapter.

APPENDIX

Laboratory Experiences:
Microteaching and Reflective Teaching

The primary purpose of teacher education is to prepare novice teachers for the classroom. Because teaching is such a highly complex series of acts, however, becoming a skillful teacher takes practice. Further, teacher preparation cannot be accomplished through the application of a formula or recipe. In short, teacher effectiveness is best developed through application-type experiences. In general, there are two ways such practice can be provided: laboratory and field-based experiences.

Laboratory experiences usually take place on campuses, whereas field-based experiences generally take place in public or private school classrooms. Of course, field-based experiences would provide the most realistic experiences and, thus, would be more desirable. But because public or private school classrooms are not readily available to most methods classes for practice purposes, application-type experiences are most commonly achieved through laboratory practice. Laboratory experiences come in two forms: microteaching and reflective teaching.

Essentially, microteaching and reflective teaching differ only in the complexity of the experience. Whereas *microteaching* is concerned with the practice of a limited number of skills or behaviors, *reflective* teaching deals with the total teaching act.

Microteaching

Microteaching is a scaled-down sample of teaching in which a small group of four to six students are taught a 5- to 10-minute minilesson demonstrating one or more specific skills. In effect, microteaching provides a close simulation of public or private classroom teaching for the purpose of practicing designated skills and behaviors.

Microteaching is often an integral component of methods classes in teacher preparatory programs, whereby the various skills and behaviors addressed are practiced and demonstrated. Microteaching is a technique through which preservice teachers can home in on a particular aspect of teaching by placing it "under a microscope" for close examination. Each session focuses on a specific skill or behavior until a satisfactory level of mastery is demonstrated. Demonstration lessons usually are videotaped and critiqued by the teacher trainee and the instructor.

Microteaching simplifies the task of teaching by subdividing multifaceted teaching acts into simpler, less-complex components. Because the teacher trainee is teaching a shorter, less-complex lesson, he or she can better manage the lesson and focus it on a few major skills in the planning process. In addition, microteaching

435

provides an opportunity for self-analysis and allows for constructive feedback from both the students being taught and an instructor. Videotaping the microteaching lesson offers a further advantage because the tape can be replayed as many times as necessary, the viewer can focus on different aspects of a lesson with each viewing.

Microteaching does not just involve getting up in front of a small group and teaching. The experience must be carefully planned. First, the skills or behaviors that will and can be practiced in the short time span must be selected with care. For example, the teacher trainee may want to work on effective questioning techniques; the appropriate application of reinforcement; the effective use of stimulus variation; the implementation of a specific teaching method (discussion, lecture, inquiry, discovery, exposition with interaction, etc.); or some combination of these skills or behaviors.

Second, a topic must be selected that will be appropriate for demonstrating the selected skills or behaviors. Not every topic is automatically appropriate for being taught by any method. For example, time constraints dictate that the topic be somewhat narrow—a single concept or subconcept that can be taught in a 5- to 10-minute time span. Therefore, the topic concept must be analyzed carefully in relation to the proposed method and procedure to be used, as well as with regard to the allotted time.

Third, the teacher trainee should narrow the topic to a single concept or subconcept. Once the concept or subconcept has been determined, a limited number of objectives (perhaps only one) must be specified.

The Microteaching Preparation Form in this appendix can be used by the teacher trainee in developing a microteaching lesson. Remember to limit your teaching time to no more than 10 minutes.

Finally, a form must be developed that contains an appropriate set of criteria against which mastery of the desired skill(s) or behavior(s) will be judged. The Microteaching Evaluation Form and Microteaching Self-Analysis Form are examples of such evaluation forms and may be of some assistance in the design of similar evaluative instruments. The Microteaching Evaluation Form can be completed by the students taught and the instructor. The feedback obtained from the completed forms should be analyzed by the teacher trainee and the instructor with respect to mastery of stated skill(s) or behavior(s). The Microteaching Self-Analysis Form should be completed by the teacher trainee, and perhaps the instructor, as a videotape of the microteaching session is replayed for analysis. Such an analysis will help in identifying specific teaching skills that need improvement.

Reflective Teaching

Reflective teaching was developed by Cruickshank and associates (1987) as a result of a desire to provide on-campus laboratory and clinical teaching practice. Essentially, reflective teaching is a modified form of microteaching in that prospective teachers engage in the whole act of teaching; that is, they plan, teach, execute, and evaluate. Special emphasis is placed on a knowledge of whether the learners (peers) actually learned and how satisfied they were with the instruction. In effect, the potential teacher is called on to analyze and reflect on the teaching act itself.

Specifically, as conceived by Cruickshank and associates, reflective teaching has the following components and characteristics:

1. The total class is divided into groups of four to six students.
2. One student from each group is selected (designated) to teach the group.
3. Designated teachers teach toward *identical* instructional objectives, using their own choice of teaching methods.
4. Designated teachers teach at the same time, either in nearby classrooms or in different parts of the same classroom, and are required to finish within the same period of time (usually 15 to 20 minutes).
5. Designated teachers focus on two things: learner achievement and learner satisfaction.
6. Learners (peers) are asked to be themselves and not to play the role of school-age students.
7. There must be a measurable product (evaluation) resulting from the teaching experience, so that teaching and learning can be determined.
8. A learner satisfaction form is completed by the learners following the administration of the evaluation.
9. A large-group discussion follows the reflective teaching experience. That is, the total class reflects on and discusses the different teaching acts that took place.
10. The next teacher is selected (designated), and the cycle repeats.

The goal of reflective teaching is to teach and improve teaching skills through reflection on what was taught and how well it was taught. Each learner's achievement evaluation and lesson satisfaction is analyzed to elicit information relative to the effectiveness of the designated teacher. Reflection on this information is very instructive to the total class because the students can compare the different methodological approaches and become aware that the effectiveness of the approach depends on the objective(s) and the teacher.

Because practice of the total teaching act is the ultimate goal of reflective teaching, students should be responsible for the development and presentation of a complete lesson. Thus, when planning for a reflective teaching session, the instructor should provide the instructional objective and, in most cases, a common evaluative instrument. The designated teachers, however, should plan a total lesson using a form similar to the Lesson Plan Format in this appendix.

Feedback to the designated teachers is a major component in reflective teaching. It should be given as soon as possible after the teaching session, and it must be objective. If it is to be objective, the evaluation instrument used should be based on identified effective teaching skills. An example of such an instrument is shown in the Teaching Evaluation Form. Feedback can be provided by having the instructor and learners complete and share the evaluative information with the designated teachers. Moreover, if the lesson can be videotaped, the designated teachers can complete an evaluation of their own teaching. Learners also should be asked to complete a Learner Satisfaction Form like the one in this appendix. Feedback on lesson satisfaction can be used in addressing the areas that the learners found inappropriate in a lesson presentation.

Finally, grades are an important ingredient in any teacher-preparatory program. Thus, the Teaching Evaluation Form should be based on the program criteria for effective teaching. As such, the instructor's, learner's, and designated teacher's self-evaluation of a teaching session can provide input for grades.

MICROTEACHING PREPARATION FORM

Microteacher: _____ Date: _____

Course Title: _____

Use this form for preparation of your lesson. Prepare a copy for your instructor.

1. Concept to teach: _____

   _____

2. Skill(s) or behavior(s) to demonstrate: _____

   _____

3. Specific instructional objective(s): _____

   _____

   _____

4. Focusing activity: _____

   _____

   _____

5. Instructional procedure: _____

   _____

   _____

6. Closure: _____

   _____

   _____

7. Audiovisual materials and equipment needed: _____

   _____

   _____

8. Notes and comments: _____

   _____

   _____

MICROTEACHING EVALUATION FORM

Microteacher: _____   Date: _____

Subject: _____   Tape No.: _____

Rate the teacher trainee on each skill area. Code: 5 or 4, mastery of skill demonstrated; 3 or 2, some skill refinement needed; or 1 or 0, much skill refinement needed.

Organization of Lesson

5   4   3   2   1   0   Lesson preparation

5   4   3   2   1   0   Focusing activity

5   4   3   2   1   0   First skill/Behavior _____

5   4   3   2   1   0   Second skill/Behavior _____

5   4   3   2   1   0   Closure

5   4   3   2   1   0   Subject-matter knowledge

Comments: _____

_____

_____

_____

_____

_____

_____

MICROTEACHING SELF-ANALYSIS FORM

Microteacher: _____   Date: _____

Concept taught: _____   Tape No.: _____

Replay the tape of your microteaching session as needed to collect data for the following items. Analyze the collected data and draw conclusions with respect to the behavior addressed in each item.

1. **Teacher talk versus student talk. Set up a small chart as follows:**

    Teacher talk: _____

    Student talk: _____

    Silence or confusion: _____

As you view your microteaching tape, place a tally on the chart to represent who was talking approximately every three seconds. If no one was talking or if many people were talking simultaneously, then place a tally in the silence or confusion category. When you have finished, count the number of tallies in each category as well as the total number of tallies in the categories teacher talk and student talk combined. Use the following formulas to determine the percentage of teacher talk and student talk:

$$\text{Percentage of teacher talk} = \frac{\text{Tallies in teacher talk category}}{\text{Total tallies in teacher talk + student talk categories}} \times 100$$

$$\text{Percentage of student talk} = \frac{\text{Tallies in student talk category}}{\text{Total tallies in teacher talk + student talk categories}} \times 100$$

2. **Filler words.** Record the filler words or sounds ("okay," "you know," or "uh") and the number of times each was used:

    _____

    _____

    _____

    _____

    _____

3. **Questions**. Record the number of questions asked:

Convergent: _____

Divergent: _____

4. Student names. Record the number of times students are addressed by name:

_____

_____

_____

_____

_____

5. Pauses. Record the number of times pauses are used to give students time to think:

_____

_____

_____

_____

_____

6. Reinforcement. Record the number of times reinforcement is used:

Verbal Reinforcement: _____

Nonverbal Reinforcement: _____

7. Sensory channels. Record the number of times students are required to change sensory channel:

_____

_____

_____

_____

_____

LESSON PLAN FORMAT

Teacher: _____ Date: _____

Course Title: _____

Topic: _____

Instructional objective(s): _____

_____

_____

Focusing activity: _____

_____

_____

Content	Instructional Procedures
	a.
	b.
	c.
	d.
	e.
	f.

Closure: _____

_____

_____

Evaluation procedure: _____

_____

_____

Instructional materials: _____

_____

_____

Notes and comments: _____

_____

_____

TEACHING EVALUATION FORM

Teacher:_____ Date: _____

Subject: _____ Tape No.: _____

Rate the teacher trainee on each skill area. Code: 5 or 4, mastery of skill demonstrated; 3 or 2, some skill refinement needed; or 1 or 0, much skill refinement needed.

Organization of Lesson

5 4 3 2 1 0   Lesson preparation

5 4 3 2 1 0   Focusing activity

5 4 3 2 1 0   Closure

5 4 3 2 1 0   Subject-matter knowledge

Comments: _____

_____

_____

_____

_____

Lesson Presentation

5 4 3 2 1 0   Audience contact

5 4 3 2 1 0   Enthusiasm

5 4 3 2 1 0   Speech quality and delivery

5 4 3 2 1 0   Audience involvement

5 4 3 2 1 0   Verbal behaviors

5 4 3 2 1 0   Nonverbal behaviors

5 4 3 2 1 0   Use of questions and questioning techniques

5 4 3 2 1 0   Directions and pacing

5 4 3 2 1 0   Use of reinforcement

5 4 3 2 1 0   Use of aids and materials

Comments: _____

_____

_____

_____

_____

LEARNER SATISFACTION FORM

Teacher:_____   Date: _____

Subject: _____   Tape No.: _____

1. During the lesson, how satisfied were you as a learner (Rate your satisfaction by placing an X on the following scale)?

   Very satisfied   Satisfied   Very unsatisfied

   <----------------------·--------------------·--------------------·-------------------·-------------------·----------------->

2. What would have increased your satisfaction? _____

   _____

   _____

   _____

   _____

   _____

   _____

   _____

   _____

   _____

GLOSSARY

A

Absolute grading standard: Student grades given relative to performance against an established criterion—for example, 90 to 100%, A; 80 to 89%, B; 70 to 79%, C; and 60 to 69%, D.

Academic learning time: The time in class during which students are actively engaged in academic tasks that result in performance being at the 80 percent level or better.

Accountability: Holding schools and teachers responsible for what is taught and what students learn.

Accreditation: Procedure for verifying school programs and course quality and uniformity.

Active learning: Learning by doing with students engaged in reading, writing, discussing, and problem solving.

Advance organizer: An introductory statement, before instruction begins, which provides a structure for new information that is to be presented.

Affective domain: Learning domain in Benjamin Bloom's Taxonomy concerned with values, attitudes, feelings, and emotions.

Allocated time: Time appropriated for students to engage in school activities such as classes, lunch, announcements, and so on.

Assertive discipline: A classroom management approach developed by Lee and Marlene Canter that stresses the need for and rights of teachers to communicate classroom needs and requirements in clear, firm, nonhostile terms, and that stresses the rights of students to learn.

Assessment: Process of collecting a full range of information about students and classrooms for the purpose of making educational decisions.

Attitudes: Mind-sets toward a person, place, or thing.

B

Behavior modification: Shaping behavior by altering the consequences, outcomes, or rewards that follow the behavior.

Being needs: The three higher levels of Abraham Maslow's need hierarchy: intellectual achievement, aesthetic appreciation, and self-actualization.

Body language: Physical mannerisms that communicate and can be used to prompt students to stay attentive and on task—such as physical proximity, eye contact, body position, facial expressions, and tone of voice.

Brainstorming: Instructional technique in which small groups of students generate ideas, solutions, or comments relative to an assigned topic. All answers, no matter how wrong they may seem to the teacher or other students, are accepted as possibilities related to the assigned task.

Buzz group: Instructional technique in which a small work group is formed for a short duration to share opinions, viewpoints, or reactions.

C

Checklist: List of criteria or characteristics against which a performance or an end product is to be judged.

Classroom management: Process of organizing and conducting the business of the classroom to keep it relatively free of behavior problems.

Closure: Activity used for pulling a lesson together so concepts make sense and bringing it to a logical conclusion.

Cognitive domain: Learning domain in Benjamin Bloom's Taxonomy that focuses on information, thinking, and reasoning ability.

Cognitive set: Predisposition to act or behave in a certain way.

Communication: The process by which information and feelings are shared by people through an exchange of verbal and nonverbal messages.

Competitive evaluation: Evaluation that forces students to compete with each other.

Computer-based instruction (CBI): Use of computers for presenting instructional information, asking questions, and interacting with students. Individualized instruction administered by a computer.

Computers: Electronic devices that can store and manipulate information, as well as interact with users; commonplace in many classrooms and in everyday life.

Concept attainment: Strategy designed to teach concepts through the presentation of examples and nonexamples.

Constructivist approach: Approach to learning that emphasizes that individuals actively construct knowledge and understanding.

Contingency contract: Grading system in which a formal, written agreement between students and a teacher is drawn up as to what students will do to receive a specified reward.

Continuous diagnosis: Ongoing collection of information on students' needs after instruction begins.

Convergent questions: Questions that allow for only a few right responses.

Cooperative learning: Instructional technique in which students of mixed abilities work together as a team on an assigned task. Interdependence and support for all members of the group is stressed.

Course planning: Broadest and most general type of instruction planning, usually divided into a sequence of units of study.

Creative thinking: Process of assembling information to develop a whole new understanding of a concept or idea. Four stages generally associated with creative thought are preparation, incubation, illumination, and verification.

Creativity: Capacity for producing imaginative, original products, or ways of solving problems.

Criterion-referenced test: Testing in which interpretations are made by comparing a student's score against a predetermined standard.

Critical thinking: Analyzing complex situations critically, using standards of objectivity and consistency, and arriving at tentative conclusions.

Cumulative record: File that holds information collected on students over a period of school years.

Curriculum: Systematic plan of instruction for a school system. The learning, intended and unintended, that takes place under the sponsorship of the school.

Curriculum integration: Form of teaching and learning that draws upon the knowledge and skills of a variety of discipline areas as they become necessary in problem solving.

D

Daily lesson plan: A detailed outline used to structure instructional activities for a single day and to help with the flow of the instruction.

Decision making: Thinking that asks students to choose the best response from several options.

Deductive thinking: Thinking that asks students to consider given generalizations and provide supporting data.

Deficiency needs: The four lowest levels of Abraham Maslow's need hierarchy: survival, safety, belonging, and self-esteem.

Demonstration: Instructional method in which the teacher or some other designated individual stands before a class, shows something, and tells what is happening or what has happened, or asks students to discuss what has happened.

Desist approach: Method of classroom management that gives the teacher full responsibility for regulating the classroom.

Diagnostic evaluation: Evaluation administered prior to instruction to assess students' knowledge and abilities so that appropriate instruction can be provided.

Diagnostic pretest evaluation: See Diagnostic evaluation.

Differentiated instruction: A teaching theory based on the premise that instructional approaches should vary and be adapted in relation to individual and diverse students in the classroom.

Direct teaching: A structured, teacher-centered approach that is characterized by teacher direction and control, higher teacher expectations for students' progress, maximizing time students spend on academic tasks, and efforts by the teacher to keep negative affect to a minimum.

Disabled: Having an inability to do something.

Discipline: Dealing with the prevention of classroom misbehavior, as well as reacting to consequences of disruptive actions.

Discovery learning: Instructional method that focuses on intentional learning through supervised problem solving according to the scientific method. Students are encouraged to learn concepts and principles through their own exploration.

Discussion: Instructional method in which students exchange and share ideas relative to an assigned topic. Can take the form of either a small-group or whole-group activity.

Divergent questions: Questions that allow for many right responses.

Drill: Fixation of specific associations for automatic recall.

E

Educational games: See Simulations.

Empathic listening: Listening with feeling. An attempt to experience what a speaker is experiencing or feeling and responding to those feelings.

Empirical questions: Questions that require students to integrate or analyze remembered or given information and supply a single, correct predictable answer.

Engaged time: Actual time individual students are engaged in purposeful classroom learning.

Evaluation: Process of obtaining available information about students and using it to ascertain the degree of change in students' performance.

Evaluative questions: Questions that require that a judgment be made or a value be put on something.

Exposition teaching: Teaching method in which some authority—teacher, textbook, film, or microcomputer—presents information without overt interaction taking place between the authority and the students.

Exposition with interaction teaching: Authority-presented instruction followed by questioning that ascertains whether information has been comprehended.

Extrinsic motivation: Motivation created by events or rewards outside the individual.

F

Factual questions: Questions that require the recall of information through the mental processes of recognition and rote memory.

Focusing questions: Questions used to direct students' attention to a lesson or to the content of a lesson.

Formal curriculum: School learning experiences that are intentional.

Formative evaluation: Use of evaluation information for supplying feedback to students before or during the learning process and for promoting learning.

G

Gifted and talented (G/T) students: Learners with exceptional general intellect, specific academic ability, creative productive thinking, leadership ability, or visual and performing arts talents.

Goals: Broad statements of instructional intent that describe general purpose of instruction.

H

Halting time: Teacher's pause in talking, used for giving students time to think about presented materials and directions.

Handicapped: Possessing an impairment that limits one's activities.

Hearing: Transmission of eardrum vibration caused by sound impulses to the brain.

Heuristic approach: Active, reflective teaching methods that involve students in problem solving and comprise modes of discovery, inquiry (including Richard Suchman inquiry), and simulations and games.

Hidden curriculum: School learning experiences, both positive and negative, that produce changes in students' attitudes, beliefs, and values, but are not part of the intentionally planned curriculum.

I

I-messages: Teacher messages that tell students how the teacher feels about problem situations and implicitly ask for corrected behavior.

Incentive systems: Systems that offer preferred activities or items for motivational purposes or for keeping students on task.

Independent study: Instructional method in which students are involved in activities carried out with little or no guidance.

Individualized instruction: Instructional method in which instruction is tailored to interests, needs, and abilities of individual students.

Inductive thinking: Thinking that asks students to make generalizations based on knowledge of specific examples and details.

Informational objectives: Statements of instructional intent that are an abbreviation of instructional objectives with only the performance and product specified.

Infusion approach: Method of teaching thinking skills in which desired skill is used in conjunction with and incorporated into regular curriculum.

Inner discipline: Ability to control one's own behavior and make responsible decisions.

Inquiry: Instructional method that focuses on the flexible yet systematic process of problem solving.

Inquiry demonstration: Instructional method in which students are asked only to observe in silence.

Instructional approach: Method of classroom management based on the premise that well-planned and well-implemented instruction will prevent most classroom problems.

Instructional objective: Narrow four-component statement of learning intent. The components are: the performance, a product, the conditions, and the criterion.

Instructional strategy: The global plan for teaching a particular lesson consisting of the methodology to be used and the sequence of steps to be followed for implementing the lesson activities.

Instructional time: Amount of allocated time available for learning.

Internet: System established to let computers communicate with each other.

Intrinsic motivation: Stimulation of student learning that comes from activities that are rewarding in themselves.

L

Learning: Relatively permanent change in an individual's capacity for performance as a result of experience or practice.

Lecture: Teacher presents information with no overt interaction with students.

Lecture recitation: Instructional technique in which the teacher makes a clear presentation, followed by student responses centered on the ideas that were presented by the teacher.

Lesson procedure: Sequence of steps designed to lead students to the acquisition of the desired learning.

Limits: Accepted and nonaccepted actions in the classroom.

Listening: Active process of assigning meaning to what is heard, or the brain giving meaning to impulses transmitted from the eardrum to the brain. Larry L. Barker defines four components of listening as hearing, attending, understanding, and remembering. Listening styles can be one-way, two-way, or empathetic.

M

Mandated time: Total time available for all activities carried out in school.

Mastery curriculum: Learning considered essential for all students to know.

Mastery learning: Diagnostic-corrective-enrichment instructional model in which students work on objectives until mastery is achieved. It is based on the assumption that every student is capable of achieving most of the course objectives if given the time and appropriate experiences.

Measurement: Assignment of numerical values to objects, events, performances, or products to indicate the degree to which they possess the characteristics being measured.

Mental Operation system: Four-category question model composed of factual, empirical, productive, and evaluative questions.

Metacognition: Cognition about cognition, or "knowing about knowing."

Metaverbal component: Underlying, or hidden, message that cannot be directly attributed to the meaning of the words or how they are spoken.

Methodology: Planned patterned behaviors that are definite steps through which the teacher influences learning.

Microteaching: Technique of practicing teaching skills and processes in scaled-down and simulated situations.

Middle schools: Schools designed to meet unique needs of preadolescents, usually for grades 5 or 6 through 7 or 8.

Minimum competency tests: Exit tests designed to ascertain whether or not students have achieved basic levels of performance in basic skill areas—such as reading, writing, and computation—before they can graduate or continue to the next level.

Modeling: Person demonstrating or acting as one wants others to act and communicating examples of the values, ideas, and behaviors to be acquired by students.

Motivation: Influences of needs, desires, and drives on the intensity and direction of behaviors.

N

Natural motives: Individuals' internal desires. Many natural motives are believed to be innate.

Needs: Deficiencies or requirements in the individual or the absence of anything the person requires, or thinks he or she requires, for overall well-being.

Negative reinforcement: Strengthening the likelihood of a behavior or event by the removal of an unpleasant stimulus.

Noncompetitive evaluation: Evaluation that does not force students to compete with each other.

Nonverbal communication: Nonlingustic communication or the sending of messages without the use of words. Comprises facial language, body language (kinesics), use of the voice, and use of space, motion, and time.

Nonverbal reinforcement: Use of physical action as a positive consequence to strengthen behavior or event.

Normal curve: Bell-shaped distribution. Mathematical construct divided into equal segments that reflect the natural distribution of all sorts of things in nature.

Norm-referenced test: Test interpretation made by comparing a student's score with that of a norm group (a large representative sample) to obtain meaning.

O

Objective: Anticipated result or product of instruction. Unambiguous statement of instructional intent.

Overlapping: Engaging in or supervising several activities simultaneously.

P

Panels: Instructional technique in which five to eight students prepare and discuss a topic in front of a class. Also known as a *round table.*

Percentage grading system: Percentage correct is recorded for each assignment, and an average is calculated to determine a final grade.

Percentile score: Derived score on a distribution of scores below which a given percentage of raw scores fall.

Performance assessment: Assessment in which students demonstrate the behaviors to be measured.

PL 94-142: Federal law requiring provision of special education services to eligible students.

Point grading system: Student work is allocated points and grades are assigned according to an established grade range.

Portfolio: Systematic, organized collection of evidence (e.g., projects, written work, and video demonstrations of skills) that documents growth and development and that represents progress made toward reaching specified goals and objectives.

Positive reinforcement: Strengthening the likelihood of occurrence of a behavior or an event by presenting a desired stimulus.

Posttest evaluation: Evaluation completed after instruction to determine the extent of student learning.

Practice: Repeating of specified tasks or skills for the purpose of improvement.

Probing questions: Questions that follow a student response and require the student to think and respond more thoroughly than in the initial response.

Problem solving: Instructional technique that focuses on the intentional elimination of uncertainty or doubt through direct experiences and under supervision.

Procedure: Sequence of steps designed to lead students to the acquisition of the desired learning.

Productive questions: Broad, open-ended questions with many correct responses that require students to use their imagination, think creatively, and produce something unique.

Prompting questions: Questions that include the use of hints to aid students in answering or in correcting an initial response.

Psychomotor domain: Learning domain concerned with muscular abilities and skills on a continuum ranging from the simple to the complex.

Punishment: Application of a negative stimulus or removal of a positive stimulus as a result of inappropriate behavior.

Q

Qualified reinforcement: Differential reinforcement of acceptable parts of student actions or attempts.

Questionnaire: Lists of written statements regarding attitudes, feelings, and opinions to which the reader must respond.

R

Rating scale: Scale of values, arranged in order of quality, describing someone or something being evaluated.

Reality therapy: William Glasser's personality theory of therapy in which individuals are helped to become responsible and able to satisfy their needs in the real world.

Redirecting: Asking different individuals to respond to a question in light of, or to add new insight to, the previous responses.

Reflective teaching: Teacher as an informed and thoughtful decision maker, who analyzes past experiences in planning and teaching and in promoting thinking about the nature of teaching and learning.

Reinforcement: Theory that says the consequences of an action strengthen or weaken the likelihood of the behavior or event. Rewarding of desired actions.

Reinforcer: Anything found pleasurable by individuals.

Relative grading standard: Student's grades given relative to performance of other students. Grading on the curve.

Reliability: Extent to which individual responses are measured consistently. The coefficient of stability of scores.

Responsibility: State of being accountable or answerable for one's actions. Ability to meet obligations or to act without direct guidance.

Reward mechanism: A formal system of reinforcement.

Ripple effect: Spread of behaviors from one individual to others through imitation.

Role-playing: Instructional technique designed to let students assume the role(s) of individuals in a recreation of an event or situation.

Round table: See Panels.

S

Self-discipline approach: Method of classroom management built on the premise that students can be trusted to evaluate and change their actions so their behaviors are beneficial and appropriate to the self and to the class as a whole.

Self-fulfilling prophecy: Phenomenon in which believing that something will happen causes it to occur.

Separate approach: View suggested by Rueven Feuerstein that students need special, focused instruction on thinking skills.

Set induction: Something a teacher does at the outset of a lesson to get students' undivided attention, arouse their interest, and establish a conceptual framework.

Simulation: Instructional technique in which students are involved in models of artificial situations and/or events designed to provide no-risk experiences for students. Also referred to as *educational games.*

Socratic method: Instructional method in which a questioning-and-interaction sequence is used to draw information out of students.

Standard deviation: Extent to which scores are spread out around the mean.

Standardized test: Commercially developed test that samples behavior under uniform procedures.

Standard scores: Scores based on individuals' variance from the mean expressed in standard deviations.

Stimulus variation: Actions, behaviors, or behavior patterns designed to gain and maintain student attention during a lesson.

Strategy: Methodology and procedure of a lesson.

Student-centered curriculum: Activity curriculum that focuses on student needs and interests.

Subject-centered curriculum: School curriculum patterns wherein subjects are separated into distinct courses of study.

Suchman inquiry: Inquiry approach developed by Richard Suchman whereby students are presented and asked to explain discrepant events.

T

Task group: Instructional technique in which a group of four to eight students is formed to solve a problem or complete a project.

Teacher Effectiveness Training (TET): Self-discipline approach to classroom management conceived by Thomas Gordon that stresses establishment of positive working relationships between teachers and students. Key is based on who owns the problem when one develops—teacher or student.

Teacher-made tests: Evaluative instruments developed and scored by a teacher for classroom assessment.

Teacher-student planning: Participatory process that directly involves students in instructional planning.

Teacher testing: Requirement, usually legislatively mandated, that teachers pass a test prior to certification.

Teaching: Actions of someone who is trying to assist others to reach their fullest potential in all aspects of development.

Team planning: Coordination of teachers' instructional approaches among disciplines.

Technology literacy: Basic understanding of the general principles of technology and the application of technology.

Telelecture: Lecture transmitted from a central studio classroom to distant classrooms.

Test: Task or series of tasks used to obtain systematic observations regarding ability, skill, knowledge, or performance.

Textbook recitation: Instructional method in which students are assigned content to read and study in a textbook and are then questioned on what has been read and studied.

Thematic unit: Unit of instruction planned by a team of teachers that is organized for interdisciplinary/cross-curricular teaching over a block of time.

Thinking: Withholding judgment to use past knowledge and experience in finding new information, concepts, or conclusions.

Time on task: See Engaged time.

Transfer: Ability to use classroom-acquired information outside the classroom or in different subjects.

U

Unit plan: Plan that links goals and objectives, content, activities, resources and materials, and evaluation for a particular unit of study for a course.

Usability: Suitability of a measurement device to collect desired data.

V

Validity: Ability of a test to measure what it purports to measure.

Verbal communication: Communication through use of spoken words.

Verbal component: Actual words and meaning of a spoken message.

Verbal reinforcement: Presentation of positive comments to strengthen student behavior or event.

Vicarious motivation: Strengthening of behavior because of desire to receive consequences received by others who exhibit that behavior.

Vocal component: Meaning attached to a spoken message, resulting from such variables as voice firmness, modulation, tone, tempo, pitch, and loudness.

W

Wait-time: Time needed for students to consider their responses to questions. *Wait-time 1* is the initial time a teacher waits following a question before calling for the response. *Wait-time 2* is the total time a teacher waits for all students to respond to the same question or for students to respond to each other's responses to a question.

Weekly plan: Condensed version of a week's daily lesson plans, written on a short form provided by the school.

Weighted grading system: Assignments are given a letter grade, and all grades are weighted in determining the final grade.

Withitness: Ability of a teacher to be aware of what is going on in all parts of the classroom and the ability to communicate this awareness.

References and Suggested Readings

A

Airasian, P. W. (2001). *Classroom assessment: Concepts and applications* (4th ed.). New York: McGraw-Hill.

Alexander, G. A., Graham, S., & Harris, K. R. (1998). A perspective on strategy research: Progress and prospects. *Educational Psychology Review, 10*(2), 129–154.

Allen, D. W., Ryan, K. A., Bush, R. N., & Cooper, J. M. (1969a). *Creating student involvement.* Stanford, CA: General Learning Corporation.

Allen, D. W., Ryan, K. A., Bush, R. N., & Cooper, J. M. (1969b). *Questioning skills.* Stanford, CA: General Learning Corporation.

Alvermann, D. E., Moore, D. E., & Conley, M. W. (Eds.). (1987). *Research within reach, secondary school reading: A research guided response to concerns of reading educators.* Newark, DE: International Reading Association.

Anderson, J. R., Greeno, J. G., Reder, L. M., & Simon, H. A. (2000). Perspectives on learning, thinking, and activity. *Educational Researcher, 29*(4), 11–13.

Armstrong, D. G. (2002). *Curriculum today.* Englewood Cliffs, NJ: Prentice Hall.

Arons, A. B. (1988, April 9). What current research in teaching and learning says to the practicing teacher. Robert Karplus Lecture presented at the National Convention of the National Science Teacher Association, St. Louis, MO.

Ashton, P. (1988). *Teaching higher-order thinking and content: An essential ingredient in teacher preparation.* Gainesville, FL: University of Florida Press.

Association for Supervision and Curriculum Development. (1985). *Developing minds: A resource book for teaching thinking.* Alexandria, VA: Author.

Association for Supervision and Curriculum Development. (1988). *Content of the curriculum: ASCD yearbook.* Alexandria, VA: Author.

Association for Supervision and Curriculum Development. (1990). *Teaching thinking skills* [Video]. Alexandria, VA: Author.

Ausubel, D. P. (1963). *The psychology of meaningful verbal learning: An introduction to school learning.* New York: Grune and Stratton.

B

Banks, J. A. (2002). *An introduction to multicultural education* (3rd ed.). Boston: Allyn & Bacon.

Barker, L. L. (1971). *Listening behavior.* Englewood Cliffs, NJ: Prentice Hall.

Barron, D. D. (1994). Internet resources phase II and phase III. *School Library Media Activities Monthly, 10*(10), 46–48.

Beane, J. A. (1995). Curriculum integration and the disciplines of knowledge. *Phi Delta Kappan, 76*(8), 616–622.

Beane, J. A., Toepfer, C. F., Jr., & Alessi, S. J., Jr. (1986). *Curriculum planning and development.* Boston: Allyn & Bacon.

Beisser, S. R. (1998, March). Parent to parent: ABC's of parenting your gifted child. *Parenting for High Potential*, 25.

Beisser, S. R. (2000, September). Differentiating the curriculum for the high ability student. *Iowa Educational Leadership*, *111*(1), 8–13.

Berger, E. H. (1991). *Parents as partners in education* (3rd ed.). New York: Merrill.

Berliner, D. (1987). Simple views of effective teaching and simple theory of classroom instruction. In D. Berliner & B. Rosenshire (Eds.), *Talks to teachers* (pp. 93–110). New York: Random House.

Beyer, B. K. (1984). Improving thinking skills: Practical approaches. *Phi Delta Kappan*, *65*, 556–560.

Beyer, B. K. (1988). *Developing a thinking skills program*. Boston: Allyn & Bacon.

Bissell, J., & Newhoff, S. (1997). *Guide to the Internet in educational psychology* (2nd ed.). New York: McGraw-Hill.

Blenkin, G. M., & Kelly, A. V. (1981). *The primary curriculum*. New York: Harper & Row.

Block, J. H., Efthim, H. E., & Burns, R. B. (1989). *Building effective mastery learning schools*. New York: Longman.

Bloom, B. S., Engelhart, M. D., Furst, E. J., Hill, W. H., & Krathwohl, D. R. (Eds.). (1956). *Taxonomy of educational objectives: Handbook I. Cognitive domain*. New York: David McKay.

Boyer, E. L. (1983). *High school*. New York: Harper & Row.

Brandt, R. S. (Ed.). (1988). Teaching thinking throughout the curriculum. *Educational Leadership*, *45*(7), 3–85.

Brookfield, S. D. (1987). *Developing critical thinkers*. San Francisco: Jossey-Bass.

Brooks, J. G., & Brooks, M. G. (1999). *In search of understanding: The case for constructivist classrooms* (2nd ed.). Alexandria, VA: Association for Supervision and Curriculum Development.

Brophy, J. (1981). Teacher praise: A functional analysis. *Review of Educational Research, 51*, 5–32.

Bruner, J. S. (1977). *The process of education*. Cambridge, MA: Harvard University Press.

Butler, D. L., and Winne, P. H. (1995). Feedback and self-regulated learning: A theoretical synthesis. *Review of Educational Research, 65*, 245–282.

C

Campbell, D. (2000). *Choosing democracy* (2nd ed.). Upper Saddle River, NJ: Merrill/Prentice Hall.

Canter, L., & Canter, M. (1976). *Assertive discipline: A take-charge approach for today's educator*. Los Angeles: Canter and Associates.

Carnegie Task Force on Teaching as a Profession. (1986). *A nation prepared: Teachers for the twenty-first century*. New York: Carnegie Forum on Education and the Economy.

Charles, C. M. (2002). *Building classroom discipline* (6th ed.). New York: Longman.

Coloroso, B. (2002). *Kids are worth it! Giving your child the gift of inner discipline*. New York: HarperCollins.

Cooper, H., & Good, T. L. (1983). *Pygmalion grows up*. New York: Longman.

Countryman, L. L., & Schroeder, M. (1996). When students lead parent-teacher conferences. *Education Leadership, 53*(7), 64–68.

Cruickshank, D. R. (1987). *Reflection teaching*. Reston, VA: Association of Teacher Educators.

D

Danielson, C. (1996). *Enhancing professional practice: A framework for teaching*. Alexandria, VA: Association for Supervision and Curriculum Development.

Davidson, N., & O'Leary, P. W. (1990, February). How cooperative learning can enhance mastery teaching. *Educational Leadership, 47*(5), 30–33.

DeVito, J. A. (1985). *Communication.* New York: Harper & Row.

Dillion, J. (1987). *Classroom questions and discussions.* Norwood, NJ: Ablex.

Dillion, J. T. (1983). *Teaching and the art of questioning.* Bloomington, IN: Phi Delta Kappa Educational Foundation.

E

Ebel, R. L., & Frisbie, D. A. (1991). *Essentials of educational measurement* (5th ed.). Englewood Cliffs, NJ: Prentice Hall.

Eggen, P. D., & Kauchak, D. P. (1988). *Strategies for teachers: Teaching content and thinking skills* (2nd ed.). Englewood Cliffs, NJ: Prentice Hall.

Eisenberg, A. M., & Smith, R. R., Jr. (1971). *Nonverbal communications.* Indianapolis, IN: Bobbs-Merrill.

Eisner, E. W. (1985). *The educational imagination: On the design and evaluation of school programs* (2nd ed.). New York: Macmillan.

Ellis, A. K. (2001). Cooperative learning. In A. K. Ellis (Ed.), *Research on educational innovations.* Larchmont, NY: Eye on Education.

Evertson, C. M., Emmer, E. T., Clements, B. S., Sanford, J. P., & Worsham, M. E. (1994). *Classroom management for elementary teachers* (3rd ed.). Boston: Allyn & Bacon.

Evertson, C. M., Emmer, E. T., & Worsham, M. E. (2003). *Classroom management for elementary teachers* (6th ed.). Boston: Allyn & Bacon.

F

Fantini, M. D. (1986). *Regaining excellence in education.* Columbus, OH: Merrill.

Federman, A. N., and Edwards, S. (1997, May). Interactive, collaborative science via the net: Live from the Hubble Space Telescope. *The Internet in Education: A Supplement to T.H.E. Journal,* 20–22.

Friedman, P. G. (1986). *Listening processes: Attention, understanding, evaluation.* Washington, DC: National Education Association.

G

Gagne, N. L. (1985). *Hard gains in the soft sciences: The case of pedagogy.* Bloomington, IN: Center on Evaluation, Development, and Research.

Galloway, C. (1976). *Silent language in the classroom.* Bloomington, IN: Phi Delta Kappa Educational Foundation, Fastback 86.

Gallup, A. M., & Elam, S. M. (1988). The annual Gallup Poll of the public attitude toward the public schools. *Phi Delta Kappan, 70*(1), 33–46.

Gibran, K. (1989). *The prophet.* New York: Knopf.

Gilliland, H. (Ed.). (1988). *Teaching the Native American.* Dubuque, IA: Kendall/Hunt.

Gilstrap, R. L., & Martin, W. R. (1975). *Current strategies for teachers: A resource for personalizing education.* Pacific Palisades, CA: Goodyear.

Glasser, W. (1965). *Reality therapy: A new approach to psychiatry.* New York: Harper & Row.

Glasser, W. (1977). 10 steps to good discipline. *Today's Education, 66,* 61–63.

Glasser, W. (1986). *Control therapy in the classroom.* New York: Harper & Row.

Glatthorn, A. (1987). Cooperative professional development: Peer-centered options for teacher growth. *Educational Leadership, 44,* 31–35.

Goldman, L. (1984, September). Warning: The Socratic method can be dangerous. *Educational Leadership,* 57–62.

Good, T. L., & Brophy, J. E. (1987). *Looking in classrooms* (4th ed.). New York: Harper & Row.

Goodall, H. L., Jr. (1983). *Human communication.* Dubuque, IA: William C. Brown.

Goodlad, J. I. (1984). *A place called school: Prospects for the future.* New York: McGraw-Hill.

Gordon, T. (1974). *Teacher effectiveness training.* New York: David McKay.

Gronlund, N. E. (1999). *How to write and use instructional objectives* (6th ed.). Englewood Cliffs, NJ: Prentice Hall.

Guilford, J. P. (1956, July). The structure of intellect. *Psychological Bulletin, 53,* 267–293.

H

Hall, E. T. (1959). *The silent language.* Greenwich, CT: Fawcett.

Hallahan, D. P. (1991). *Exceptional children* (5th ed.). Englewood Cliffs, NJ: Prentice Hall.

Haller, E. P., Child, D. A., & Walberg, H. J. (1988). Can comprehension be taught? A quantitative synthesis of "metacognitve" studies. *Educational Researcher, 17*(9), 5–8.

Hannaford, C. (1995). *Smart moves.* Arlington, VA: Great Ocean.

Harrow, A. J. (1972). *Taxonomy of the psychomotor domain: A guide for developing behavior objectives.* New York: David Mckay.

Heiman, M., & Slomianko, J. (1987). *Thinking skills instruction: Concepts and techniques.* Washington, DC: National Education Association.

Hennessey, B. A., & Amabile, T. M. (1998). Reward, intrinsic motivation, and creativity. *American Psychologist, 53,* 674–675.

Hennings, D. G. (1975*). Mastering classroom communications—What interaction analysis tells the teacher.* Pacific Palisades, CA: Goodyear.

Hirsch, E. D., Jr. (1987). *Cultural literacy: What every American needs to know.* Boston: Houghton Mifflin.

Hunter, M. (1980). *Teach more—faster.* El Segundo, CA: TIP Publications.

Hunter, M. (1995). Mastery teaching. In J. H. Block, S. T. Everson, & T. R. Guskey (Eds.), *School improvement programs* (pp. 181–204). New York: Scholastic.

Hurt, H. T., Scott, M. D., & McCroskey, J. C. (1978). *Communications in the classroom.* Menlo Park, CA: Addison-Wesley.

I

Idol, L. (1997). Key questions related to building collaborative and inclusive schools. *Journal of Learning Disabilities, 30,* 384–394.

J

Jacobs, H. H. (Ed.). (1989). *Interdisciplinary curriculum: Design and implementation.* Alexandria, VA: Association for Supervision and Curriculum Development.

Jacobs, H. H. (1997). *Mapping the big picture: Integrating curriculum & assessment K–12.* Alexandria, VA: Association for Supervision and Curriculum Development.

Jacobson, D., Eggen, P., & Kauchak, D. (1989). *Methods for teaching: A skills approach* (3rd ed.). Columbus, OH: Merrill.

Jensen, E. (1998). *Teaching with the brain in mind.* Alexandria, VA: Association for Supervision and Curriculum Development.

Jewett, A. E., & Mullan, M. R. (1977). Movement process categories in physical education in teaching-learning. In *Curriculum design: Purposes and processes in physical education teaching-learning.* Washington, DC: American Alliance for Health, Physical Education and Recreation.

Johnson, D. W., & Johnson, R. T. (1985). The internal dynamics of cooperative learning groups. In R. Slavin, S. Sharan, S. Kagan, C. Webb, & R. Schmuck (Eds.), *Learning to cooperate, cooperating to learn* (pp. 103–124). New York: Plenum.

Johnson, D. W., & Johnson, R. T. (1999). *Learning together and along: Cooperation, competition, and individualization* (5th ed.). Boston: Allyn & Bacon.

Johnson, D. W., & Johnson, R. T. (2002). *Meaningful assessment: A meaningful and cooperative process.* Boston: Allyn & Bacon.

Johnson, D. W., Johnson, R. T., Stevahn, L., & Hodne, P. (1997). The three Cs of safe schools. *Educational Leadership, 55*(2), 8–13.

Jones, F. (1979, June). The gentle art of classroom discipline. *National Elementary Principal, 58,* 26–32.

K

Kagan, S. (1990). The structural approach to cooperative learning. *Educational Leadership, 47*(4), 12–15.

Karnes, F. A., & Bean, S. M. (Eds.). (2000). *Methods & materials for teaching the gifted.* Waco, TX: Pruftock.

Kaufman, R., Westland, C., and Engvall, R. (1997). The dichotomy between the concept of professionalism and the reality of sexism in teaching. *Journal of Teacher Education, 48*(2), 118–128.

Kennedy, C. H., Long, T., Kristine, J., Cox, M. J., Tang, J., & Thompson, T. (2001). Facilitating general education participation for students with behavior problems by linking positive behavior supports and person-centered planning. *Journal of Emotional and Behavioral Disorders, 9,* 146–160.

Kohn, A. (1996). *Beyond discipline: From compliance to community.* Alexandria, VA: Association for Supervision and Curriculum Development.

Kolesnik, W. B. (1978). *Motivation: Understanding and influencing human behavior.* Boston: Allyn & Bacon.

Kounin, J. S. (1970). *Discipline and group management in classrooms.* New York: Holt, Rinehart & Winston.

Krathwohl, D. R., Bloom, B. S., & Masia, B. B. (1964). *Taxonomy of educational objectives: Handbook II. Affective domain.* New York: David McKay.

Kulik, J. A., & Kulik, C. C. (1992). Meta-analytic findings on grouping programs. *Gifted Child Quarterly, 36*(2), 73–77.

L

Levin, J. A., and Thurston, C. (1996). Educational electronic networks. *Educational Leadership, 54*(3), 46–50.

Lillie, D. L, Hunnun, W. H., & Stuck, G. B. (1989). *Computers and effective instruction.* New York: Longman.

Lipman, M. (1988a, September). Critical thinking—What can it be? *Educational Leadership,* 38–43.

Lipman, M. (1988b). *Philosophy goes to school.* Philadelphia: Temple University Press.

Lyman, H. B. (1991). *Test scores & what they mean* (5th ed.). Englewood Cliffs, NJ: Prentice Hall.

M

Mager, R. F. (1984). *Preparing instructional objectives* (2nd ed.). Belmont, CA: David S. Lake.

Mager, R. F. (1997). *Preparing instructional objectives: A critical tool in the development of effective instruction.* Atlanta, GA: Center for Effective Performance.

Marklein, M. B. (1997, September 17). House blocks national school test plan. *USA Today,* p. 1.

Marzano, R. J., Brandt, R. S., Hughes, C. S., Jones, B. F., Presseisen, B. Z., Rankin, S. C., & Suhor, C. (1988). *Dimensions of thinking: A framework for curriculum instruction.* Alexandria, VA: Association of Supervision and Curriculum Development.

Maslow, A. H. (1970). *Motivation and personality* (2nd ed.). New York: Harper & Row.

McCall, A. L. (1995). Constructing conceptions of multicultural teaching: Preservice teachers' life experiences and teacher education. *Journal of Teacher Education, 46*(5), 340–350.

McCombs, B. L. (2001, April). *What do we know about learners and learning? The learner-centered framework.* Paper presented at the meeting of the American Educational Research Association, Seattle, WA.

McDaniel, T. R. (1984). Developing the skills of humanistic discipline. *Educational Leadership,* 41(8), 71–74.

Meyer, C. A. (1992). What's the difference between authentic and performance assessment? *Educational Leadership, 49*(8), 39–40.

Meyers, C. (1986). *Teaching students to think critically.* San Francisco: Jossey-Bass.

Miller, A. D., Barbetta, P. M., & Heron, T. E. (1994). START tutoring: Designing, training, implementing, adapting, and evaluating tutoring program for school and home settings. In R. Gardner, D. M. Sainatok, J. O. Cooper, T. E. Heron, W. L. Heward, J. Eshleman, & T. A. Grossi (Eds.), *Behavior analysis in education: Focus on measurably superior instruction* (pp. 265–282). Monterey, CA: Brooks/Cole.

Miller, P. W. (1986). *Nonverbal communications.* Washington, DC: National Educational Association.

Montagu, A. (1977). The skin, touch, and human development. *Somatics, 3,* 3–8.

Moore, K. D. (2001). *Classroom teaching skills* (5th ed.). New York: McGraw-Hill.

Murphy, K. R., & Davidshofer, C. O. (1991). *Psychological testing* (2nd ed.). Englewood Cliffs, NJ: Prentice Hall.

N

National Commission for Excellence in Education. (1983). *A nation at risk: The imperative for educational reform.* Washington, DC: Government Printing Office.

National Commission on Teaching & America's Future. (1996, September). *What matters most: Teaching for America's future.* New York: Author.

Newman, R. S. (2002). What do I need to succeed? . . . When I don't understand what I'm doing!?: Developmental influences on students' adaptive help seeking. In A. Wigfield & J. S. Eccles (Eds.), *Development of achievement motivation.* San Diego, CA: Academic.

Nichols, R. G., & Stevens, L. A. (1957). *Are you listening?* New York: McGraw-Hill.

Nickerson, R. (1985). Understanding understanding. *American Journal of Education, 93,* 201–239.

O

O'Donnell, A. M. (1996). Effects of explicit incentives on scripted and unscripted cooperation. *Journal of Educational Psychology, 88*(1), 74–86.

O'Leary, K. D., & O'Leary, S. (Eds.). (1977). *Classroom management: The successful use of behavior modification* (2nd ed.). Elmsford, NY: Pergamon.

Oliva, P. F. (2000). *Developing the curriculum* (5th ed.). Boston: Allyn & Bacon.

Orlich, D. C., Harder, R. J., Callahan, R. C., Kauchak, D. P., Pendergrass, R. A., Keough, A. J., & Gibson, H. (1990). *Teaching strategies* (3rd ed.). Lexington, MA: D.C. Heath.

Overturf, B. J. (1997). Reading portfolios reveal new dimensions of students. *Middle School Journal, 28*(3), 45–50.

P

Padron, Y. N. (1994). Teaching and learning risks associated with limited cognitive mastery in science and mathematics for limited English proficient students. *Proceedings of the Third National Research Symposium on Limited English Proficient Student Issues: Focus on Middle and High Schools: Vol. 2.* Washington, DC: U.S. Department of Education.

Palmer, S. E. (1983, April 13). The art of lecturing: A few simple ideas can help teachers improve their skills. *The Chronicle of Higher Education,* 19–20.

Paul, R. (1993). *Critical thinking: How to prepare students for a rapidly changing world.* Santa Rosa, CA: Foundation for Critical Thinking.

Perkins, D. N. (1986). Thinking frames. *Educational Leadership, 43,* 4–10.

Perkins, D. N., Lochhead, J., & Bishop, J. C. (Eds.). (1987). *Thinking: The second international conference.* Hillsdale, NJ: Lawrence Erlbaum.

Posner, G. J., & Rudnitsky, A. N. (2000) *Course design.* New York: Addison-Wesley.

Premack, D. (1965). Reinforcement theory. In D. Levine (Ed.), *Nebraska Symposium on Motivation: Vol. 13* (pp. 123–180). Lincoln: University of Nebraska Press.

R

Raths, L. E., Wassermann, S., Jonas, A., & Rothstein, A. M. (1986). *Teaching for thinking: Theory, strategies, and activities for the classroom.* New York: Teachers College Press.

Rea, P. J., McLaughlin, V. L., & Walther-Thomas, C. (2002). Outcomes of students with learning disabilities in inclusive and pullout programs. *Exceptional Children, 68,* 203–222.

Renzulli, J. S., Gentry, M., & Reis, S. M. (2003). *Enrichment clusters: A practical plan for real-world, student-driven learning.* Mansfield Center, CT: Creative Learning Press.

Renzulli, J. S., & Reis, S. M. (1997). *The schoolwide enrichment model: A how-to guide for educational excellence.* Mansfield Center, CT: Creative Learning Press.

Resnick, L. B. (1987). *Education and learning to think.* Washington, DC: National Academic Press.

Roberts, P., & Kellough, D. (2003). *A guide for developing interdisciplinary thematic units* (3rd ed.). Englewood Cliffs, NJ: Prentice Hall.

Rosenshine, B., & Stevens, R. (1986). Teaching functions. In M. Wittrock (Ed.), *Handbook of research on teaching* (3rd ed., pp. 376–391). New York: Macmillan.

Ross, A., & Olsen, K. (1993). *The way we were . . . the way we can be: A vision for the middle school through integrated thematic instruction* (2nd ed.). Kent, WA: Books for Educators. Available: ERIC Document Reproduction Service No. ED371906

Rowe, M. B. (1974a). Relation of wait time and rewards to the development of language, logic, and fate control: Part two. Rewards. *Journal of Research in Science Teaching, 11*(4), 291–308.

Rowe, M. B. (1974b). Wait time and rewards as instructional variables, their influence on language, logic, and fate control: Part one. Wait time. *Journal of Research in Science Teaching, 11*(2), 81–94.

Rowe, M. B. (1978). Wait, wait, wait. *School Science and Mathematics, 78,* 207–216.

S

Sadker, M., & Sadker, D. (1994). *Failing at fairness: How America's schools cheat girls.* New York: Scribner.

Sadler, W. A., & Whimbey, A. (1985). A holistic approach to improving thinking skills. *Phi Delta Kappan, 67*(3), 199–203.

Sanders, N. M. (1966). *Classroom questions: What kinds?* New York: Harper & Row.

Sathre, F. S., Olson, R. W., & Whitney, C. I. (1977). *Let's talk.* Glenview, IL: Scott, Foresman.

Sax, G. (1980). *Principles of educational and psychological measurement and evaluation* (2nd ed.). Belmont, CA: Wadsworth.

Schmuck, R. A., & Schmuck, P. A. (1988). *Group processes in the classroom* (5th ed.). Dubuque, IA: William C. Brown.

Schunk, D. H. (2000). *Learning theories: An educational perspective* (3rd ed.). Columbus, OH: Merrill/Prentice-Hall.

Schunk, D. H., & Ertmer, P. A. (2000). Self-regulation and academic learning: Self-efficacy enhancing intervention. In M. Boekarts, P. Pintrich, & M. Zeidner (Eds.), *Handbook of self-regulation.* San Diego, CA: Academic Press.

Schunk, D. H., & Zimmerman, B. J. (1997). Social origins of self-regulatory competence. *Educational Psychologist, 32*(4), 195–208.

Shulman, L. (1987). Knowledge and teaching: Foundations of the new reform. *Harvard Educational Review, 57,* 1–22.

Siegel, J., Good, K., & Moore, J. (1996). Integrating technology into educating preservice special education teachers. *Action in Teacher Education, 17*(4), 53–63.

Silverman, L. K. (1986). Parenting young gifted children. *Journal of Children in Contemporary Society, 18,* 73–87.

Silvernail, D. L. (1979). *Teaching styles as related to student achievement.* Washington, DC: National Education Association.

Sizer, T. R. (1984). *Horace's compromise: The dilemma of the American high school.* Boston: Houghton Mifflin.

Skinner, B. F. (1968). *The technology of teaching.* New York: Appleton-Century-Crofts.

Skinner, B. F. (1971). *Beyond freedom and dignity.* New York: Knopf.

Slavin, R. E. (1995). *Cooperative learning* (2nd ed.). Boston: Allyn & Bacon.

Snider, J., & Osgood, C. E. (Eds.). (1969). *Semantic differential technique: A sourcebook.* Chicago: Aldine.

Sokolove, S., Sadker, D., & Sadker, M. (1986). Interpersonal communication skills. In J. M. Cooper (Ed.), *Classroom teaching skills* (3rd ed.). Lexington, MA: D. C. Heath.

Solomon, G. (1992). The computer as electronic doorway: Technology and the promise of empowerment. *Phi Delta Kappan, 74*(4), 327–329.

Solomon, R. P. (1995). Beyond prescriptive pedagogy: Teacher inservice education for cultural diversity. *Journal of Teacher Education, 46*(4), 251–258.

Suchman, J. R. (1961). Inquiry training: Building skills for autonomous discovery. *Merrill-Palmer Quarterly of Behavior and Development, 7,* 147–169.

Suchman, J. R. (1966). *Inquiry development program in physical science.* Chicago: Science Research Associates.

T

Taba, H. (1962). *Curriculum development.* New York: Harcourt, Brace & World.

Tanner, D., & Tanner, L. N. (1980). *Curriculum development* (2nd ed.). New York: Macmillan.

TenBrink, T. D. (1986). Evaluation. In J. M. Cooper (Ed.), *Classroom teaching skills* (3rd ed.). Lexington, MA: D. C. Heath.

Tomlinson, C. A. (1995). *How to differentiate instruction in mixed-ability classrooms.* Alexandria, VA: Association for Supervision and Curriculum Development.

Tomlinson, C. A. (1999). *The differentiated classroom: Responding to the needs of all learners.* Alexandria, VA: Association for Supervision and Curriculum Development.

Torrance, E. P. (1983*). Creativity in the classroom.* Washington, DC: Library of Congress.

U

United States Congress. (1999). *Gifted and talented students education act of 1999.* 106th congress, 1st session; S. 505 in the Senate of the United States.

W

Walsh, D., & Paul, R. (1988). *The goal of critical thinking: From educational ideal to educational reality.* Washington, DC: American Federation of Teachers.

Waxman, H., Padron, Y., & Arnold, K. (2001). Effective instructional practices for students placed at risk of academic failure. In G. Borman, S. Stringfield, & R. Slavin (Eds.), *Title I: Compensatory education at the crossroads.* Mahwah, NJ: Erlbaum.

Wigfield, A., & Eccles, J. S. (2002). Students' motivation during the middle school years. In J. Aronson (Ed.), *Improving academic development: Impact of psychological factors in education.* New York: Academic Press.

Wiggins, G., & McTighe, J. (1998). *Understanding by design.* Alexandria, VA: Association for Supervision and Curriculum Development.

Wilen, W. W. (1982). *Questioning skills for teachers.* Washington, DC: National Education Association.

Winebrenner, S. (2002). *Teaching gifted kids in the regular classroom: Strategies and techniques every teacher can use to meet the academic needs of the gifted and talented.* Minneapolis, MN: Free Spirit.

Wittrock, M. (Ed.). (1986). *Handbook of research on teaching* (3rd ed.). New York: Macmillan.

Wlodkowski, R. J. (1982). *Motivation.* Washington, DC: National Education Association.

Wolvin, A. D., & Cookley, C. G. (1979). *Listening instruction.* Urbana, IL: ERIC Clearinghouse Reading and Communications Skills.

Woolfolk, A. (2004). *Educational psychology* (9th ed.). New York: Allyn & Bacon.

Wong, H. K., & Wong, R. T. (1998). *The first days of school.* Mountain View, CA: Harry K. Wong.

Worsham, A. M., and Stockton, A. J. (1986). *A model for teaching thinking skills: The inclusion process.* Bloomington, IN: Phi Delta Kappa Educational Foundation.

Wulf, K. M., & Schane, B. (1984). *Curriculum design.* Glenview, IL: Scott, Foresman.

Z

Zimmerman, B. J. (1998, April). *Achieving academic excellence: The role of perceived efficacy and self-regulatory skill.* Paper presented at the annual meeting of the American Educational Research Association, San Diego, CA.

Zimmerman, B. J., & Schunk, D. H. (Eds.). (2001). *Self-regulated learning and academic achievement: Theoretical perspectives* (2nd ed.). Mahwah, NJ: Lawrence Erlbaum.

INDEX

ABOUT THE AUTHOR

Kenneth D. Moore is Dean of Teachers College at Henderson State University. He received his Ed.D. degree in Curriculum and Instruction from the University of Houston. Dr. Moore has been involved in teacher education for more than 30 years at both the public school and higher education levels. During his tenure he has worked closely with school administrators, classroom teachers, student teachers, and teacher education candidates. He has traveled extensively, serving as accreditation consultant and conducting workshops. Dr. Moore has authored three books, numerous journal publications, an ERIC monograph, and has presented many papers at regional and national conventions. He has also served as director of the Southwest Regional Association of Teachers of Science, President of the Oklahoma Association of Teacher Educators, and President of the Oklahoma Association of Colleges for Teacher Education. He is presently involved in educational reform and authentic assessment and serves on the NCATE Board of Examiners (BOE). The texts he has authored include *Classroom Teaching Skills 5/e Clinical Supervision: a Practical Guide to Student Teacher Supervision* (co-authored), and *Middle and Secondary Instructional Methods.*